Scripta Series in Geography

Series Editors:

Other titles in the series:

Dando, W. A.: The Geography of Famine
Klee, G. A.: World Systems of Traditional Resource Management
Earney, F. C. F.:Petroleum and Hard Minerals from the Sea
Yeates, M.:North American Urban Patterns
Brunn, S. D./Wheeler, J. O.: The American Metropolitan System: Present and Future
Bourne, L. S.: The Geography of Housing
Jackson, R. H.:Land Use in America
Oliver, J. E.: Climatology: Selected Applications

China
The Geography of Development and Modernization

Clifton W. Pannell
University of Georgia

Laurence J. C. Ma
University of Akron

V. H. Winston & Sons

Edward Arnold

First published 1983 by
Edward Arnold (Publishers) Ltd.
41 Bedford Square, London WC1B 3DQ and distributed in the United States of America by
Halsted Press, a division of John Wiley & Sons Inc.

British Library Cataloguing in Publication Data

Pannell, Clifton W.
China: the geography of development and
modernization.—(Scripta Series in geography)
1. China—Social conditions
I. Title II. Ma, Lawrence J. C.
III. Series
951 HN733

ISBN 0-7131-6302-X

Halsted Press

ISBN Cloth 0-470-27376-3
ISBN Paper 0-470-27377-1

Typeset in the United States of America by
Marie Maddalena of V. H. Winston & Sons
Printed in Great Britain by
Richard Clay (The Chaucer Press) Ltd., Bungay, Suffolk.

Contents

For Our Parents

Acknowledgements

A number of associates and colleagues were good enough to assist in various ways. We appreciate very much the chapter review of James S. Fisher. Christopher L. Salter and Jack F. Williams read the entire manuscript and provided incisive and valuable critical evaluations and commentary for which we are most grateful. Anne Berryman of the University of Georgia read all chapters several times and was a skilled and thorough editorial reviewer and proofreader. Debbie Phillips and Margaret Geib of the University of Akron are responsible for most of the cartography, and they were most patient in handling and executing the numerous rough and crude maps they had to work with. Any remaining errors remain our responsibility.

Victor Winston initially encouraged the writing of this study, and we are grateful for his continued patience and support. Our families, especially Laurie and Amy, have been steadfast in encouraging us to take the time to complete this volume.

A Note on Romanization and Metrification

Romanization of Chinese names is something of a problem. We elected to employ the relatively new *pinyin* (spelling) system now in use in the People's Republic of China. In some cases this seemed awkward, so a few of the older but very commonly recognized spellings were also used. These include Peking (Beijing), Canton (Guangzhou), Nanking (Nanjing), Inner Mongolia (Nei Monggol), Tibet (Xizang), and Sinkiang (Xinjiang). In some instances we have attempted to include the Wade-Giles spelling for other place names the first time the name is used.

Another exception was made to the use of *pinyin*. In the chapter on Taiwan, spellings are rendered in both *pinyin* and Wade-Giles, because of continued local use of Wade-Giles. A Wade-Giles-*pinyin* conversion table is included as Appendix .1 to aid students unfamiliar with the system. Spellings on the maps, however, appear only in *pinyin*.

Metric units are employed throughout this study. A conversion table is provided for reference purposes:

1 *mou* = 0.0667 hectare (ha)
= 0.1647 acre
1 *jin* (catty) = 0.5 kilogram (kg)
= 1.1023 pounds
1 millimeter (mm) = 0.04 inch
1 meter (m) = 39.37 inches
1 kilometer (km) = 0.62 mile

15 *mou* = 1 hectare = 2.47 acres
100 hectares = 1 square kilometer (km^2)
1 *gongjin* = 1 kilogram = 2.2046 pounds
1000 *gongjin* = 1 metric ton = 2204.6 pounds

Preface

This volume is the result of extensive study and reflection as well as a number of visits to China to observe firsthand the geography of China's recent efforts to modernize. It represents the ideas and views of both authors, although sometimes in compromise over a varying interpretation or viewpoint.

The challenge of development in China is enormous. While China has substantial resources for economic development, problems and impediments are everywhere—the land, its vast size as well as its natural endowments; the climate, its extremes and variability of temperature and precipitation; the long history and conservative tradition; the huge number of people, many of whom are poorly trained and marginally employed. Yet some of these impediments are also resources, for they are really the bounty and talent of China as well.

How to marshal these resources and human forces to advance economic growth and national development requires detailed knowledge and skilled use of the land and water resources of the country. It also requires proper understanding and sensible approaches to the best spatial organization of human activities. Both of these topics in recent years have been the subject of extensive study and scientific investigation in China. They also serve as the basis for our inquiry and approach in attempting to provide Western students with details and insights drawn from China's geography as to how almost one-quarter of mankind is going about the crucial business of improving living conditions for the present and future.

CWP and *LJCM*

Chapter 1

Introduction

Everything about China is large–population, land area, landforms, resource base, economic production. No other facets of the geography of China are more striking or significant than its vast size, the enormous scale of the physical environment, and the large number and activities of humans who occupy, organize, and exploit this huge land. China's surface area is composed of 9,600,000 km^2 and the country is the world's third largest after the USSR and Canada (Fig. 1-1). China is slightly larger than the United States with its 9,363,000 km^2 (Fig. 1-2). An important consequence of this large land area is a large resource base. In fact, China ranks as one of the world's richest countries in terms of its fund of natural resources. Great quantities of coal, petroleum, iron ore, and many nonferrous metals are found in China, and the Chinese do not yet know the full extent of their rich and varied resource base. Clearly, the country has sufficient resources on which to build a powerful, modern industrial state.

The vastness and grand scale of China also may be appreciated by considering the size of its provinces. Most of China's 21 provinces and 5 autonomous regions are individually bigger than a number of the larger and most important countries of Europe (Table 1-1 and Figs. 1-1, 1-3).[1] For example, Guangdong in southeastern China and Jiangsu in east China each had as many or more people in 1978 than did the United Kingdom or France. Shandong and Henan each had more people than either West Germany or Italy. China's largest and most populous province, Sichuan, with 100 million people in 1978 and an area greater than 560,000 km^2, had more people than Nigeria, Pakistan, or Mexico. Sichuan alone would rank as the eighth largest country in the world, not far behind Japan in population and considerably larger than Japan in area (*Zhonghua renmin . . .*, 1974). China's

[1]For purposes of this text, Taiwan is considered a historical part of China. Statistics on Taiwan, however, are sometimes presented separately here because of the island's political status. Chapter 10 provides more details.

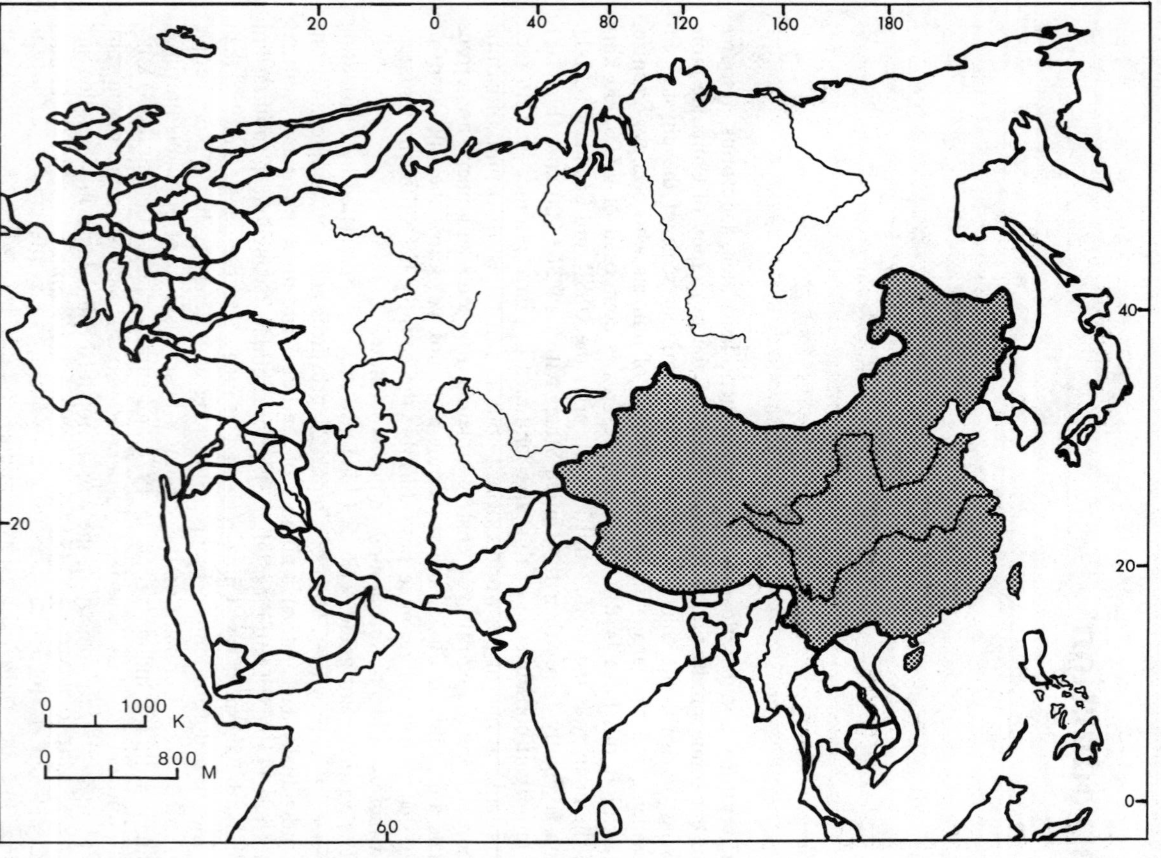

Fig. 1-1. Location map of China (shaded portion) in the setting of the Eurasian continental landmass.

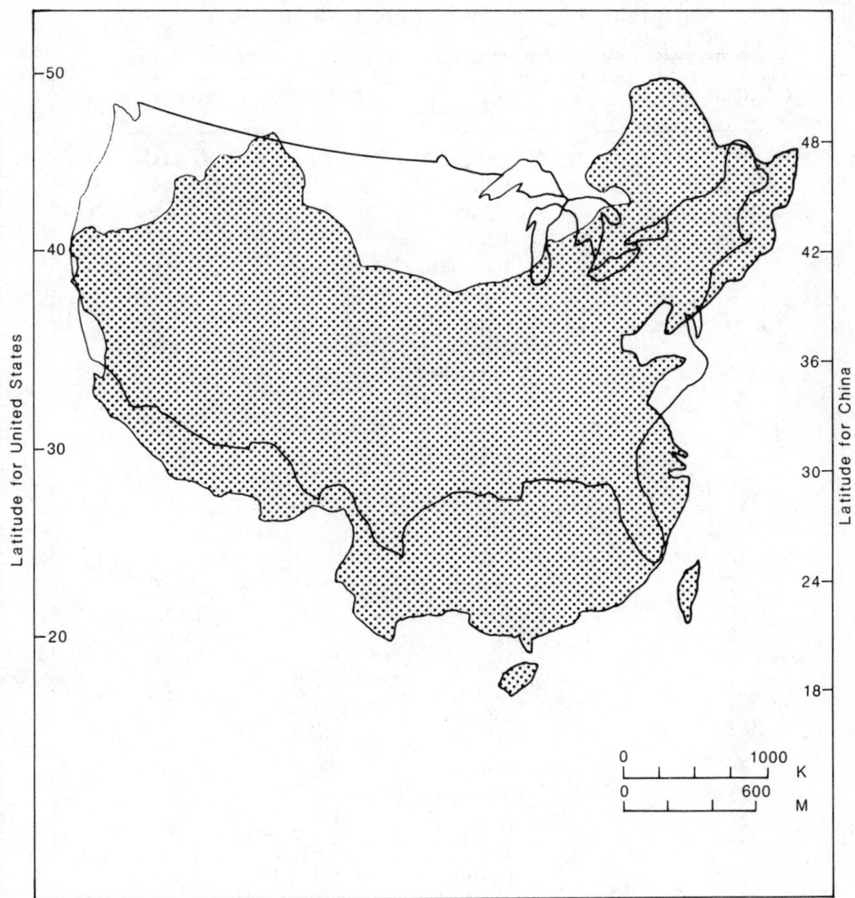

Fig. 1-2. Comparative size and latitudinal position of China (shaded portion) and the lower 48 United States.

population, moreover, continues to grow rapidly. This briefly illustrates the enormous scale of China today. These sheer numbers startle and remind us of the great importance of China as a member of the world community and as a large and vital segment of the total human experience in today's world.

Equally as significant as the size and resource base is the country's location. China, like the United States, is a middle latitude land where the eastern and southern peripheries open onto the Pacific Ocean and adjacent seas. The effect of this is to give the eastern half of the country a high index of accessibility to ocean shipping and international air transportation (Fig. 1-1). The middle latitude location and proximity to the ocean and seas help provide a source of moisture

Table 1-1. Population (mid-1978, millions)

Rank	Country province	Population
1	China	958[a]
2	India	638
3	USSR	261
4	US	219
5	Indonesia	145
6	Brazil	115
7	Japan	115
8	*Sichuan*	*100*
9	Bangladesh	85
10	Pakistan	77
11	Nigeria	72
12	*Shandong*	*72*
13	*Henan*	*70*
14	Mexico	67
15	FRG	61
16	Italy	57
17	*Jiangsu*	*56*
18	*Guangdong*	*56*
19	UK	56
20	France	53
21	*Hunan*	*51*
22	*Hebei*	*48*
23	Philippines	46
24	*Anhui*	*46*
25	Thailand	45
26	*Hubei*	*45*
27	Turkey	43
28	Egypt	40

Source: The China Business Review (1980).
[a]Does not include Taiwan.

and moderate temperatures. Summer onshore monsoon wind systems ameliorate what otherwise might be conditions of extreme continentality attributed to China's location on the eastern flank of the world's largest landmass. Both accessibility and middle latitude location are great advantages when compared with the relative isolation and extreme climatic conditions of China's northern neighbor, the Soviet Union. These advantages resemble, in part, similar conditions found in the United States. China, of course, has the disadvantage of having its west closed off by a high and extremely dry region of mountains and basins. China's west suffers from its inaccessibility and the rigors of a dry, cold climate. The west is sparsely peopled and poorly developed, partially a reflection of its location and environment.

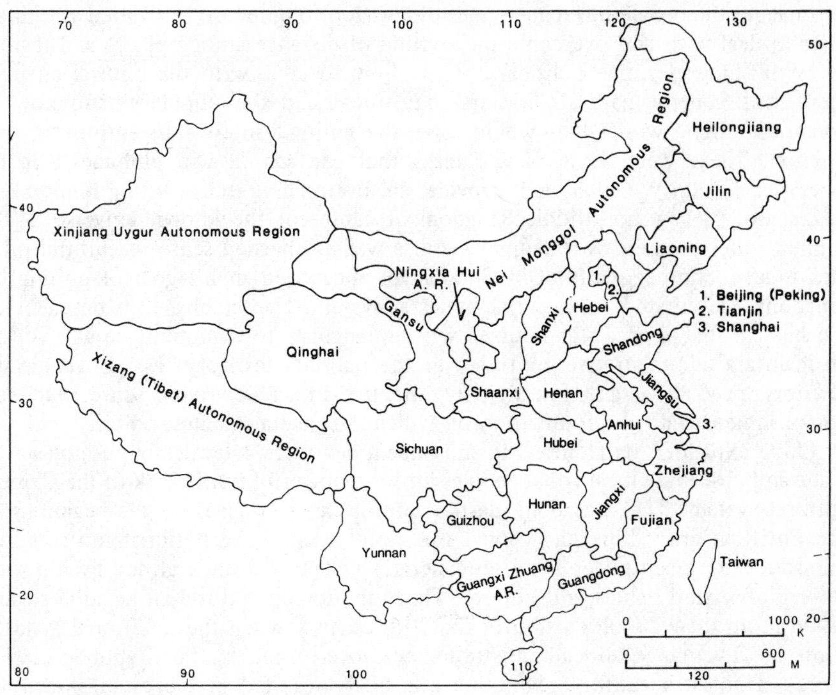

Fig. 1-3. Provinces, autonomous regions and municipalities of the People's Republic of China, 1981.

RECORD OF POLITICAL AND CULTURAL PERMANENCE

China's great size and large number of people have been cited as two of the outstanding features of the country and proof of the significance of the country in the panorama of contemporary world events. Another aspect of China that illuminates its importance in world history is the long record of political and cultural tenure. The Chinese people today occupy the original core area (as well as additional territory) that they have occupied since the beginning of Chinese recorded history in 1766 B.C. (the beginning of the Shang Dynasty). The Zhou (1122–255 B.C.) and Qin (255–206 B.C.) Dynasties followed and signaled an age of cultural development and unification in China. The first great imperial ruler of the Qin, Qin Shihuangdi, unified China, established a set of centralized rules for governing the country, and worked hard to standardize the laws, written language, weights and measures. He also sought to establish a Chinese imperium that would integrate the national territory of China, an awesome task in traditional times.

Imagine the problems facing a ruler of a nation so immense and varied as China—how to deal with and overcome the friction of distance among places and regions in establishing effective political control; how to cope with the natural environment and control natural disasters that threatened the populace; and how to construct public works that would serve the nation's interest by improving production. These were some of the tasks that confronted Qin Shihuangdi in his attempts to unify China and provide an overarching sense of nationhood to Zhongguo, (中国) the Middle Kingdom or center of the known universe as the Chinese refer to their own country, with a well-established sense of cultural pride and indeed ethnocentrism. Qin Shihuangdi succeeded in his goal of uniting his kingdom. He created an imperial dynastic system. He established a bureaucratic mechanism that used a standardized written language to communicate as it sought to maintain administrative control over the national territory. He also made the territory productive and functionally effective in an economic sense. Such accomplishments laid the foundation on which the ensuing Chinese empire was built.

China expanded its frontiers in subsequent centuries, relentlessly pushing southward and absorbing local tribal peoples into the powerful framework of the Chinese cultural system. This was done despite conflict and struggle. By the beginning of the Christian era, China had carved for itself a distinctive national territory, administered by a central political/bureaucratic system and undergirded by a powerful set of shared values and culture. That functioning cultural and spatial system lasted more than 2000 years, until the 20th century when the traditional dynastic form of governance and administration was overturned by the Republic (1911-1949). This 20th century revolution eventually resulted in the establishment of a Communist system of government and national management in 1949. Despite the fundamental change in political systems from dynastic to Republican to Communist, the national territory and the goals of the central administrations have largely remained the same. These goals have always been to integrate the large territory of the country and to manage that territory and widely dispersed population in such a manner that production rises and the national wealth and strength are increased.

The best way to explain to Western students the nature of the Chinese dynastic system and its remarkable accomplishments is to draw an analogy to the Roman Empire. Imagine the Roman Empire perpetuating itself from the time of Julius Caesar, at or near its zenith of power and vigor, to the 20th century. Had the Roman Empire continued to occupy most of southern, western, and central Europe and then been replaced by a new political system, but one which was derived from the old and which maintained the integrity of the national territory, such longevity could be likened to the actual accomplished unity of China. Europe, of course, fragmented and broke up politically into many small and competing units. China did not. Why? How, moreover, did China manage to remain intact as a functioning space economy and polity despite strong centrifugal forces, both natural and human, which constantly threatened to split the Chinese empire?

Natural forces would include rugged terrain and large rivers with highly variable discharge rates. These natural features, for example, made transportation slow, dangerous, and expensive in much of China except the Yangzi (Yangtze) River

Valley. Human forces would include, most importantly, the buildup of regional and sectional loyalties and rivalries, the same kind of forces which split the United States in the middle 19th century and were a major contributing factor to the Civil War. China, as a great empire that stretched over a large area and incorporated many people, was not immune to such forces. Various political undercurrents ran beneath the visage of unity, but the unity was never broken. Somehow China managed to succeed in controlling these forces longer than any other country, and in that way China insured the permanency of its political system and culture.

Answers to the why and how of China's political and cultural stability and permanence are historically interesting and are valuable for the insights they can provide into contemporary methods of environmental management and spatial organization. These questions are geographic because environment and space (territory), two of the key aspects of the subject matter of geography, are heavily involved. It is for this reason that we have selected these two topics (human use of the environment and spatial organization) to follow as basic themes in unfolding and helping to explain the geography of modernization and development in China.

The main theme of this text is developmental change and modernization within the context of China's geography. Beyond that, specific approaches described below will be used. China's large population and area, coupled with its middle latitude location and monsoon climate condition in the eastern third of the country, are fundamental geographical realities. These realities have dictated the approaches employed in this study. For example, the large territory and varied natural environments in China require considerable attention to achieve a real understanding of the manner in which the contemporary Chinese are setting about their goals of modernization. For it is the challenge of coming to terms with and exploiting this environment that occupies the activities and energies of a large portion of the Chinese population, including many geographers (Buchanan, 1970; Pannell, 1980). Thus, the interaction of man and environment is fundamental to comprehending contemporary China and its path to modernization and development.

THE IMPACT OF COMMUNIST IDEOLOGY ON THE GEOGRAPHY AND ENVIRONMENT OF CHINA

Environmental challenges and problems are many and diverse, and the Chinese over time have developed their own style and methods for confronting and dealing with the natural environment. In recent years, a number of changes have been introduced, for Marxism brings its own ideology relevant for confronting nature (Matley, 1966). A distinctly Chinese brand of landscape manipulation and environmental change has emerged, a blending of the idiosyncracies of China's way of doing things within the context of the Marxist/Maoist ideology and the natural reality of China's environment (Salter, 1972).

Contemporary China can no more be comprehended without reference to its ideologically-based, Marxist-derived Communist system than it can be understood with no reference to its history. Any student of this ancient and complex country must remind himself of the significance of ideology on the present reality, for ideology will shape policy and planning and these in turn will shape the economic and social pattern of the country. At the bottom, one goal of a Marxist society is equity among its citizens—equity of opportunity, income, and living conditions. Such a goal implicitly will have a strong spatial component to it, for equity means that greater investments must be made in poor regions of the country and in lagging sectors. Another example would be the impact of equity on the spatial structure of cities. By definition, social stratification by location in cities cannot occur in Communist cities, and land prices in such a nonfree market system will have no effect in determining land uses (Fisher, 1962). The type of socioeconomic urban land use structure common in North American and West European cities will not be found in China, a consequence of the different systems for organizing and controlling the country (Harvey, 1973).

An equally important aspect of the Marxist system is its approach to the environment. The environment should serve humans and be tamed by them. Value is created by human labor, and the environment is there to be used and exploited to serve humans. Man is supreme, although in recent years it has been recognized that man can abuse nature and the environment. The Chinese Communists believe strongly in science and scientific solutions to natural problems. Traditionally, the Marxist position on population has been that more people mean more labor value. In recent years, this notion has been modified as approaches have been adopted to reduce China's rapid population growth. The point is that a guiding philosophy or ideology lies behind specific actions and policies. Recent events after the death of Mao Zedong (Mao Tse-tung) in 1976 have led to policies that stress economic progress with less emphasis on Marxist ideology. It is wise, nevertheless, to keep the reality of the prevailing ideology of the country's leaders in mind in evaluating and explaining events and patterns in China. Policies change. Leaders come and go. Ideology, however, remains, although interpretations of it vary from time to time. Murphey (1980) has analyzed the changing role of ideology and its impact on China's development. Reminding ourselves of its presence and role will serve to keep the day-to-day policies and patterns in suitable perspective.

Ideology was prominent during the 1950s when China received some aid and guidance from the Soviet Union. Patterns of scientific analysis and development closely followed models developed earlier in the USSR. In the late 1960s, ideology and politics took command in the Cultural Revolution, but the effects were mostly negative. In the late 1970s, doctrinaire ideology and politics were played down, as the leaders have adopted more pragmatic policies that stress economic growth. Most recently China has looked to Japan, Europe, and North America for help in modernizing and in coping with the environment. This new direction has also reintroduced, at least to a limited extent, market approaches to environmental management and development to China.

All of this suggests that an approach to the study of the human use of the environment is certainly most appropriate. Western students should feel especially comfortable with such an approach, inasmuch as this is a well-established and basic theme in American and British geography, and one that has become increasingly popular in recent years. Despite the dissimilarities of culture, Americans who study China find many similarities and analogies in the natural setting and environment with the United States.

Equally significant and most pertinent for a geography of China is the study of the attempts of Chinese academic and research geographers, for example, in their studies of agricultural land use and surveys of natural resources, to devise ways for humans to improve their dominion and control over natural phenomena and processes (Ma and Noble, 1978; Williams, 1978). Thus, it seems especially appropriate to take a directional bearing from the Chinese geographers' compass and follow a basic organizing and conceptual approach in learning the geography of China. It is a coincidence that such an approach is compatible with conceptual traditions of American geography as well.

ORGANIZATION OF SPACE IN CHINA

The study of human-environment relations is the first of two main thematic approaches employed here. The second approach, like the first, is commonly used in geographical studies in the English-speaking world and has been especially prominent during the last two decades. This approach is usually called the spatial or spatial organization approach. China confronts us with a very large land area requiring some understanding of how it functions as a unified spatial system or set of different sized (or scaled) systems. For our purposes, a spatial system may be thought of as a clearly expressed unit of space (or area) made up of specific locations at which occur specific activities that are linked together by flows of people, goods, information, and money. To understand and make use of the spatial organization approach, it is necessary to examine, describe, analyze, and explain the structure and functioning of the national space and various regions within it. Another useful aspect of the spatial organization approach is to study the linkages among many different types of systems and subsystems seen in various aspects of the economic, political, and social patterns of the country today.

This spatial organization approach is less frequently used in China, but there is some evidence that human geographers in China are beginning to employ this approach to their recent studies of economic geography (Shen et al., 1978). Moreover, certain aspects of the economic and cultural geography of this large country and its people are better understood in the context of spatial organization. The history of China and its culture may be studied from the point of view of spatial organization. This approach can be especially valuable today in analyzing the manner in which China is developing its industries, agricultural production units, and settlement systems. The study of transportation, the linkage mechanism or bonding for the spatial system, also provides a basic means for analyzing how goods, people, knowledge, and money flow between functional units of organization in the system. As Morill (1970) reminded us, spatial (i.e., geographic) analysis provides a most basic and useful tool to work toward an understanding of the manner in which a society and economy are organized and operate. Spatial analysis also provides a good tool to gauge the degree of success that society and government have achieved in providing equity of opportunity to the citizenry.

The combination of these two approaches–human-environment and spatial organization–both familiar in the lexicon of contemporary geography and both employed to a greater or lesser degree in Chinese geographic study, should provide a workable and valuable means for achieving a high level of understanding of China. We begin our study with a detailed explanation of the natural environment and proceed from there to examine how the Chinese people have used their environment and organized their activities spatially to exploit best the environmental opportunities, resources, locational setting, and alternatives nature has provided.

THE MODERNIZATION OF CHINA–CONTRIBUTIONS FROM GEOGRAPHERS

Most of the topics and issues involved in China's modernization that we will discuss are related to the geography of the country. Of special relevance are the land and water resources of the country and their utilization for economic development. Here the efforts of geographers have been valuable in estimating the optimum use. Regional specialization of agricultural production has been studied intensively by Chinese geographers and related agricultural and environmental specialists.

Although there are only approximately 6,000 professional geographers in China (about the same number as in the United States), geography is a branch of the Academia Sinica and consequently is part of China's scientific establishment (admittedly, a small part). The national and regional institutes of geography employ several thousand researchers and technicians in areas ranging from historical and economic geography to hydrology, climatology, soil chemistry, photogrammetry, and environmental analysis. Most of the work is in physical geography and relates more or less to environmental analysis and agriculture. More recently, interest and work in geography have increased in studies of industrial location, transportation geography, and technique areas such as cartography and remote sensing (Ma and Noble, 1979; Pannell, 1980).

A review of the issues and tasks facing China as it sets about modernizing all sectors of its economy indicates much of what is needed can benefit from the efforts of geographers. Working both as investigators on the physical and agricultural environments or as spatial analysts investigating problems that face the organization and linkage of the space economy, geographers can contribute much of value to the development of this large country. In areas such as agricultural planning and the investigation of China's land resources, Chinese geographers have made significant contributions. Good geographical analysis can provide the basis for better planning and policy in China and can contribute significantly to more rapid modernization of the country.

LITERATURE CITED

Buchanan, Keith, 1970, *The Transformation of the Chinese Earth.* London: G. Bell and Sons.

The China Business Review, 1980, Jan.–Feb., pp. 20–21.

Fisher, Jack, 1962, "Planning the City of Socialist Man." *Journal of the American Institute of Planners*, Vol. 28, No. 4, pp. 251–265.

Harvey, David, 1973, *Social Justice and the City*. Baltimore: Johns Hopkins University Press.

Ma, Laurence J. C. and Noble, Allen, 1979, "Recent Developments in Chinese Geographic Research." *Geographical Review*, Vol. 69, No. 1, pp. 63–78.

Matley, Ian, 1965, "The Marxist Approach to the Geographical Environment." *Annals of the Association of American Geographers*, Vol. 56, No. 1, pp. 97–111.

Morill, Richard L., 1970, *The Spatial Organization of Society*. Belmont, Calif.: Wadsworth Publishing Co.

Murphey, Rhoads, 1980, *The Fading of the Maoist Vision, City and Country in China's Development*. New York: Metheun.

Pannell, Clifton W., 1980, "Geography." In Leo Orleans, editor, *Science in Contemporary China.* Stanford: Stanford University Press, pp. 567–586.

Salter, Christopher L., 1972, "The Litany of Tachai and the Foolish Old Man: Agricultural Landscape Modification in Mainland China." *The Professional Geographer*, Vol. 24, pp. 113–117.

Shen, Yuchang et al., 1978, "Woguo dili xue de fangxiang yu renwu ruogan wenti de shangtan" (The orientation and task of geography in China–a discussion of some problems). *Dili Xuebao (Acta Geographica Sinica)*, Vol. 35, No. 2, pp. 103–115.

Williams, Jack F., 1978, "Two Observations on the State of Geography in the People's Republic of China." *China Geographer*, No. 9, pp. 17–31.

Zhonghua renmin gongheguo fensheng dituji (Provincial Atlas of the People's Republic of China), 1974. Beijing: Ditu Chubanshe.

Chapter 2

China's Natural Environments: The Challenge to Development

TERRITORY AND LOCATION

China is a vast land (Fig. 1-1 and 1-2). Its area, as noted in the introductory chapter, spans approximately 9,600,000 km², an area slightly larger than the 9,363,000 km² of the United States (Fig. 1-2) and exceeded by only two countries —the Soviet Union and Canada. China is exceptional in that it must support and provide for more than one billion people (approximately 22% of the world's population) on this land area. Owing to its size and location, China exhibits a number of similarities to the United States. For example, both countries lie in the middle latitudes and both have extensive coastlines fronting on middle latitude oceans and seas. However, China occupies the southeastern flank of the world's largest landmass, Eurasia. Although it has approximately 18,000 km of coastline and is thus easily accessible for marine transportation in the east and south, its north and west are enclosed and to a large extent isolated.

Western China generally is high and mountainous (Fig. 2-1). Because of its interior location, the western area tends to be very dry. The advantages of easy accessibility and amelioration of climate, due to the proximity to an ocean, are not present, and the western region is sparsely populated. Spatial isolation, coupled with aridity and harsh winters that make agricultural development difficult, have given this region a different developmental and cultural history from the rest of the country. These differences have created problems of national integration, and traditionally western China has been viewed as a remote frontier region.

A country with a large area characteristically has a large resource base. China is no exception. Although precise identification and measurement of China's

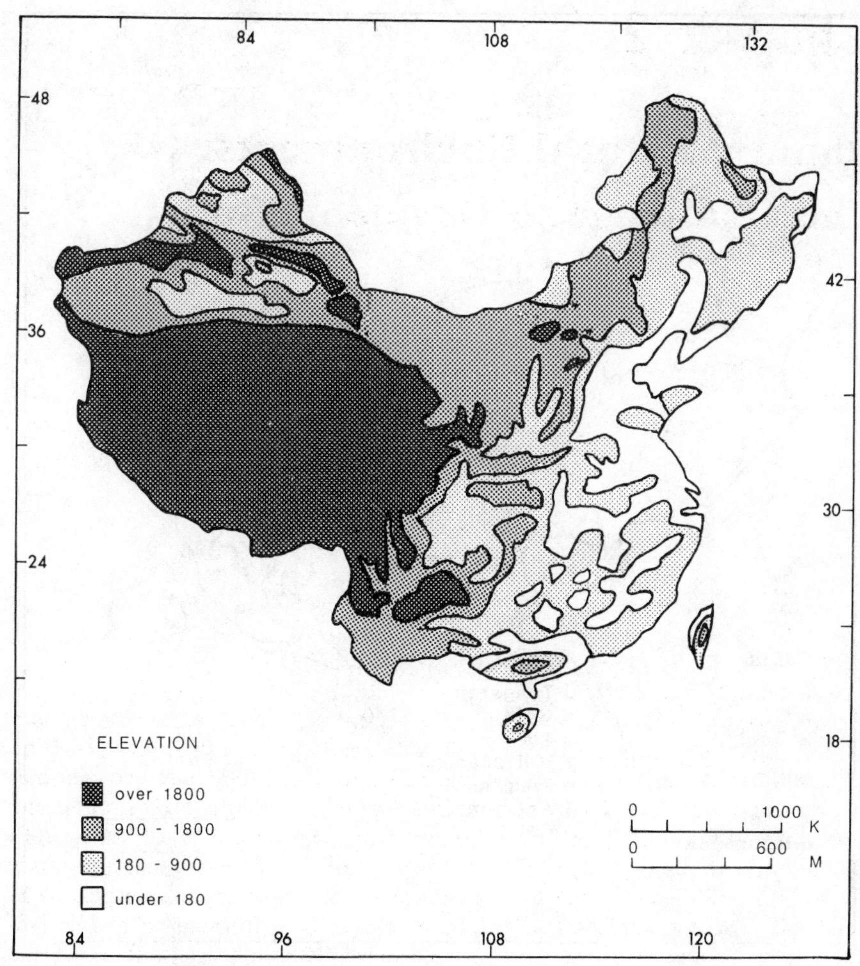

Fig. 2-1. China, elevation in meters.
Source: Zhonghua renmin gongheguo fensheng dituji (1974).

fund of mineral resources are incomplete, enough is known to indicate China has vast reserves of major minerals. Among these are leading reserves of tungsten, coal, antimony, tin, mercury, salt, fluorspar, and magnesite, and substantial reserves of iron and manganese ores, aluminum, limestone, and petroleum including natural gas (Fig. 2-2). In all the above, China may be considered to have front rank reserves at a world scale comparable to major reserves found in such countries as the United States, the Soviet Union, Canada, Brazil, Iran, and others. China's reserves of tungsten and antimony are believed to be the world's largest. Only in

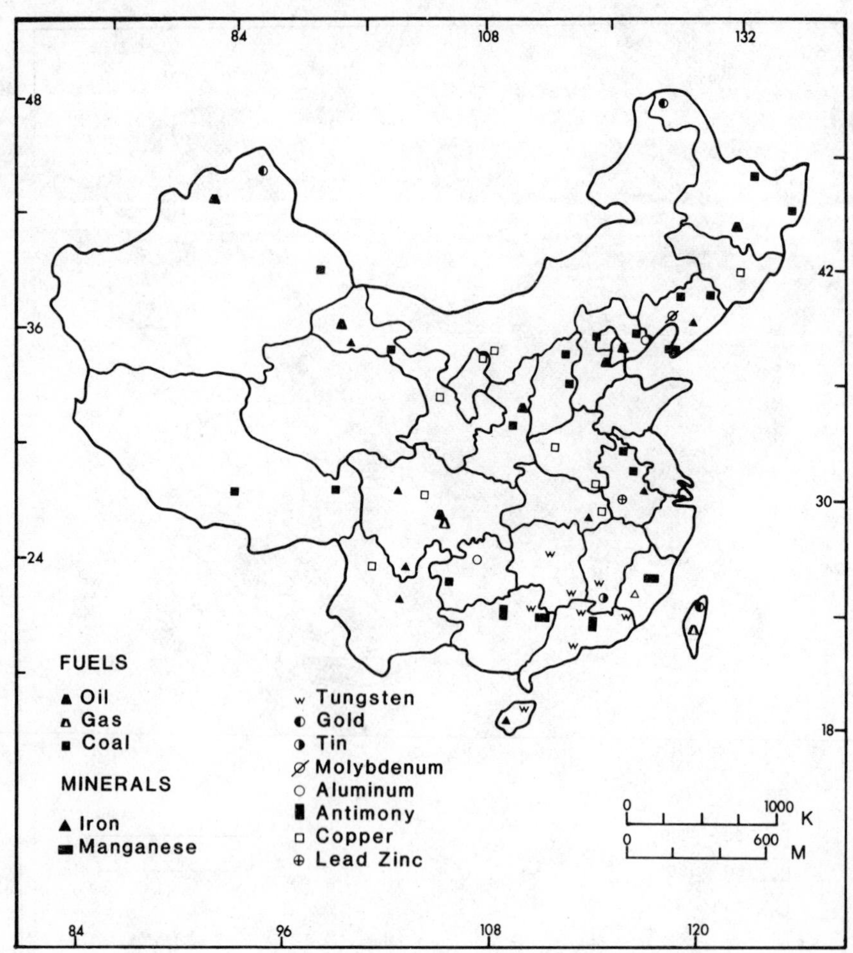

Fig. 2-2. China, distribution of major minerals.
Source: Compiled from various sources.

nickel, aluminum, and copper, among the commonly used and required minerals for modern industrialization, is China seriously deficient (Wang, 1977).

Another consequence of China's size and location is diversity of its regional and local environments. Continentality of climate in parts of the country was noted above. The northern and western regions are cold and dry. Central and south China, by contrast, are temperate to tropical in climate and typically receive 1,000 mm or more of rainfall (Fig. 2-3). Monsoon influences are found throughout eastern China, although north China receives much less precipitation than does the south. A major environmental distinction may be identified between humid,

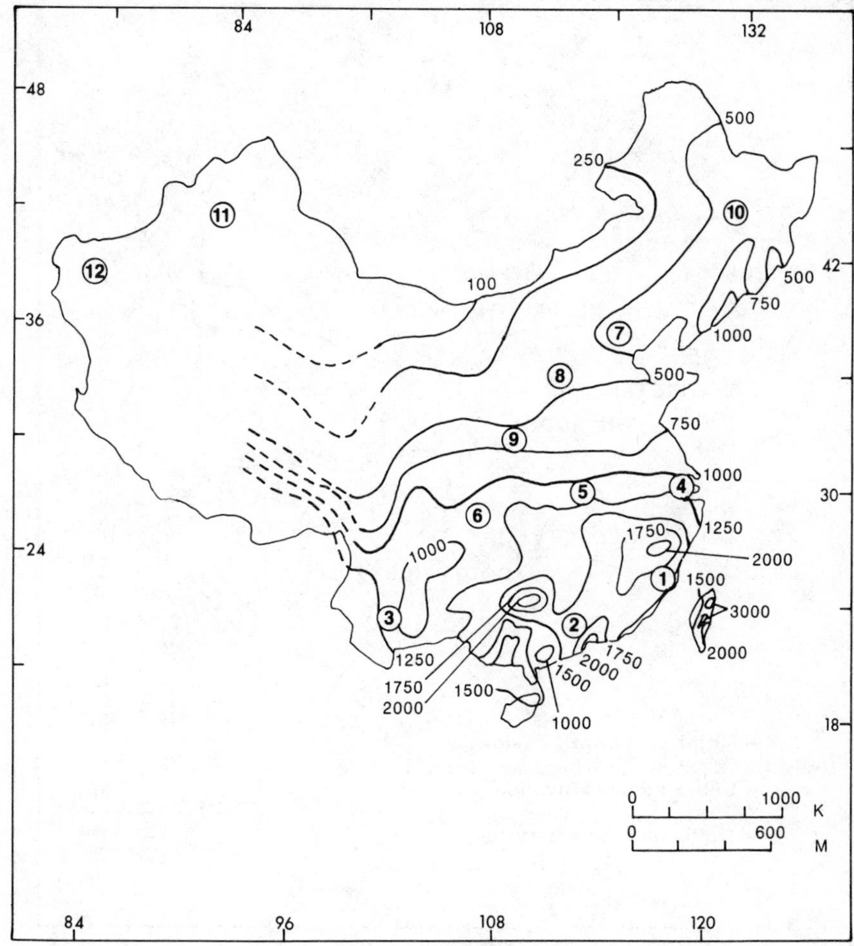

Fig. 2-3. China, average annual precipitation. Location of stations: (1) Fuzhou, (2) Canton, (3) Kunming, (4) Shanghai, (5) Wuhan, (6) Chongqing, (7) Beijing, (8) Taiyüan, (9) Xi'an, (10) Harbin, (11) Ürümqi, and (12) Kashgar as noted in Table 2-1.

Sources: Hsieh (1973); Central Meteorological Bureau (1960).

subtropical central and southern China and dryer, more continental west and north China (Fig. 2-4). In part, this division follows the east-west trend of the Qinling Shan (Chin-ling Mountains) extended eastward to the East China Sea along the course of the Huai He (Hwai River) (Fig. 2-5). Another environmental divide which parallels the physiography described above would be the division between regions

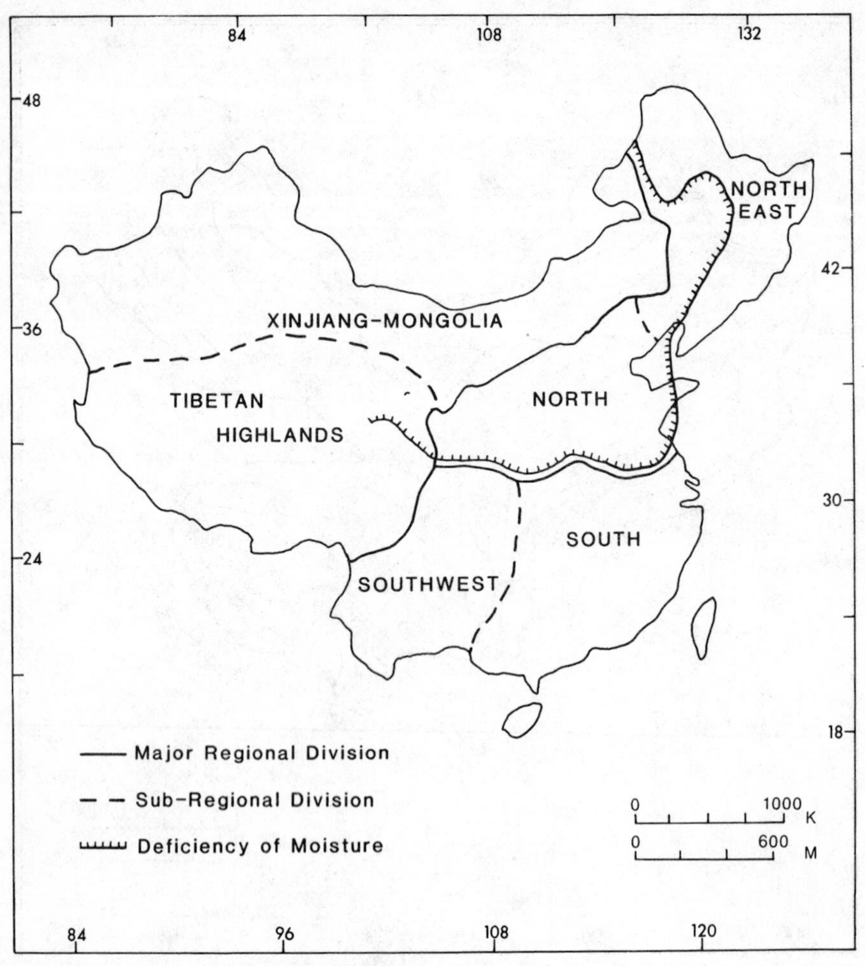

Fig. 2-4. China, major environmental regions.
Source: Whitney (1979).

of water surplus and deficiency (Fig. 2-4). Such a division identifies southern China as a water surplus area along with the southern part of the North China Plain and the southern part of the Northeastern or Song-Liao Plain in central northeastern China (Fig. 2-5).

As this study unfolds and we begin to see how the Chinese have spatially organized their economic activities and population, the environmental advantages or constraints of a given region will begin to take on a greater significance. It is at that point that two major themes developed in this text–human-environment

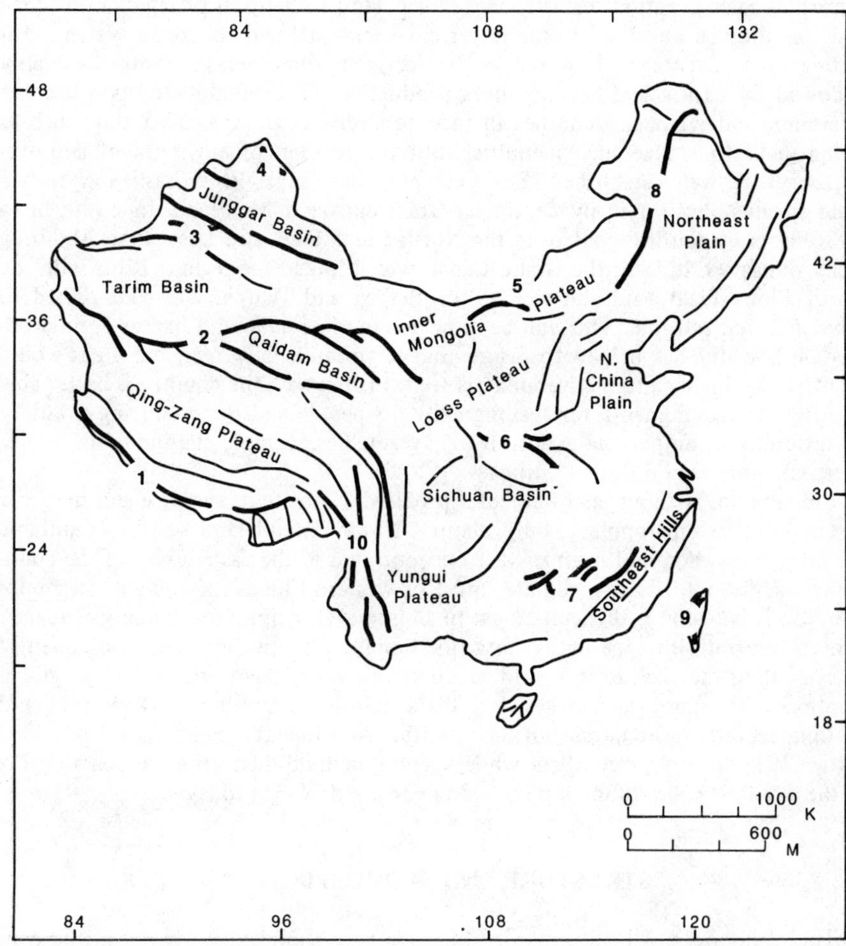

Fig. 2-5. China, major physical features and landforms. Name of major mountains: (1) Himalaya, (2) Kunlun, (3) Tian Shan, (4) Altay, (5) Yin, (6) Qinling, (7) Nanling, (8) Da Hinggan, (9) Taiwan, (10) Hengduan.
Source: Modified from *Jianming Zhongguo Dili* (1974).

relations and spatial organization–converge in a geographic explanation of the nature of modernization, development, and change in contemporary China.

An advantage of environmental diversity is that it provides a broader range of agricultural environments, and thus agricultural and other natural products. At the same time it may reduce the need for importation of goods desired or required by the local economy. Such environmental diversity also offers some insurance against natural catastrophes which tend to be local or regional in scope and can thus be absorbed in the larger environmental and economic system. Offsetting such advantages, however, is the fact that some areas are more favorably endowed by nature and become more productive. Their inhabitants soon become wealthier, and regional inequities in income levels occur. A socialist state such as China seeks to reduce such inequities, but the realities of environment and productivity are well established. For example, the Yangzi River Basin has been a grain surplus area for many centuries. Grain cargoes have been shipped north to the centers of political control in the North China Plain and Loess Plateau during many dynasties. Indeed, the Grand Canal, which linked the Yangzi River with the North China Plain, and the vicinity of Beijing and Tianjin, was constructed to serve just that purpose. This will be discussed in more detail in Chapter 3. Environmental diversity has helped to insure that environmentally marginal areas would be offset by highly productive areas as well. In this way, the country is better able to meet its requirements for feeding all of its people and for producing a variety of different commodities–grains, fruits, vegetables, commercial/industrial crops, livestock–for many different purposes.

China is not without environmental problems. Despite its vast size and the great diversity of its environment, only about 11% of China's land surface is suitable for crop cultivation and most of it is concentrated in the eastern part of the country. In additon to its dry climate, most of western China is also high and mountainous. This region is difficult to use in an intensive manner for human occupancy and to integrate into the nation in a functionally effective manner. Consequently in evaluating the size, extent, and location of China, the territory and its global location offer many advantages, but there are also a number of drawbacks and limiting factors. More details on the specific environmental elements are provided below. It is well to review them while keeping in mind their utility in contributing to the dynamic phase of modernization under way in China today.

STRUCTURE AND GEOMORPHOLOGY

The structure and landforms of China are very complex. If viewed in the context of continental crustal movements, the tectonic structure of China has resulted from the eastward and possibly southward movement of the gigantic Eurasian continental plate coming into contact with a westward moving Pacific plate. It has also been speculated that southwestern China came into contact with an Indian Ocean plate moving northward in what is today South Asia. The movement of these gigantic crustal plates in the locational context of today's China, or what has come to be called the geotectonic structural platform of China, helps to explain the major structural surface features of China visible today (Fig. 2-5).

These features are composed of a number of alternating plains, mountains, and basins, some of which are almost at right angles to one another. Associated with the gross outline of these features is the progressive decrease in elevation from west to east, for example, from 5,000 m on the eastern face of the Tibetan Plateau to sea level on the coast of the Yellow Sea. The Tibetan Plateau, a huge and high massif, is rimmed on the north and east by the landmass of China. The descent to this landmass is nowhere smooth and even but is more like what the Chinese geologist Lee (1939) has likened to descending the steps of a gigantic staircase. In proceeding from west to east, one descends several ranges and plateaux and discovers mountains and elevated basins beyond.

The country may be divided for physiographic discussion between east and west. In both parts, the structure is composed of several giant geosynclines, the result apparently of the tectonic movement described above. Synclinal structure is made up of alternating ridges and plains. In the east, the strike of these is generally northeast-southwest, and a number of related landform features are included. From east to west, most conspicuous are the Changbai (Ch'ang-pai) Mountains of northeastern China, the Northeast and North China Plains, the Hinggan, Taihang, and Wu Mountains, the Loess Plateau, Sichuan Basin, and Yunnan-Guizhou Plateau (Fig. 2-5).

Cutting across these features almost at right angles and on an east-west strike are, from north to south, the Yin, Qinling, Dabieh, and Nanling Mountains. It is this crisscross arrangement of major structural features that the geographer Spencer (1954) has labeled "the Chinese Checkerboard." Farther west, the strike of most of the major landscape features is east-west. Here are the truly great mountains and basins of China. Indeed these are some of the greatest physical features on earth–the Great Himalaya Mountains, the Tibetan Plateau, the Kunlun Mountains, the Tarim and Qaidam Basins, the Tian Shan (range), the Junggar (Dzungarian) Basin and the Altay Mountains (Fig. 2-5) (Ren et al., 1979).

Geologically, much of today's China was formerly under the sea, although three ancient granitic massifs or shields (one in southeast China, one in today's Tibet, and one in today's Mongolia) formed huge stable islands of ancient Precambrian rock. It is the combination of crustal movements against these massifs that gave rise to the various series of parallel ridges and plains described above. In addition, submergence of the troughs and basins during the Paleozoic Era hundreds of millions of years ago resulted in the formation of great quantities of carboniferous material, which created the basis for China's fossil fuel resources today. A large quantity of other materials has been associated with the old age and variety of China's rock structure and the past activity of tectonic processes in further altering igneous and sedimentary materials. In brief, China's area is large and its rock structure diverse and complex, the result of a great variety of past geologic environments and tectonic processes. The combination of these factors and forces has resulted in the presence today of a great variety of landscapes and a large and diversified stock of mineral resources.

CLIMATOLOGICAL PATTERNS AND RESOURCES[2]

Patterns of climate are as much a part of the resource base as are the patterns of landforms, and they are equally varied. Generally China may be divided into

[2]Detailed quantitative data on China's climate patterns may be reviewed and obtained for a number of stations (Central Meteorological Bureau, 1960).

Table 2-1. Mean Monthly Average Temperature (in °C) and Mean Monthly Precipitation (in mm)

Station	Elevation (in m)	Jan.	Feb.	March	Apr.	May	June	July	Aug.	Sept.	Oct.	Nov.	Dec.	Total rainfall (mm)
Fuzhou (Temp.)	20	11.7	11.1	13.3	17.8	22.2	26.7	28.9	28.9	24.4	19.4	15.0	10.0	
(Precip.)		46	96	114	122	150	207	160	183	213	51	41	48	1431
Guangzhou	15	13.3	13.9	17.2	21.7	26.7	27.2	28.3	28.3	26.7	23.9	19.4	15.6	
(Canton)		23	48	107	173	269	269	205	219	165	86	31	23	1618
Kunming	1805	8.9	10.6	15.6	18.9	21.1	22.2	21.1	21.1	18.9	17.2	13.3	9.4	
		13	13	15	18	96	155	249	208	137	91	43	15	1053
Shanghai	10	3.3	3.9	7.8	13.3	18.3	22.8	26.7	26.7	22.8	17.2	11.1	5.6	
		51	57	86	94	91	188	150	145	119	79	51	33	1144
Wuhan	36	4.4	6.1	10.0	16.7	21.7	26.7	29.4	29.4	25.0	19.4	12.8	7.2	
		48	48	97	152	165	244	180	97	71	81	48	28	1259
Chongqing	230	8.3	10.0	14.4	19.4	23.3	26.1	27.8	28.9	24.4	19.4	15.0	10.0	
		15	20	36	102	140	180	142	129	147	117	51	23	1102
Beijing	39	−5.1	−1.7	5.0	13.9	20.0	24.4	26.1	24.4	20.0	12.2	3.3	−2.8	
(Peking)		3	5	5	15	36	76	239	160	66	15	8	2	630
Taiyuan	788	−8.4	−3.3	3.9	12.2	18.3	22.8	25.0	22.8	17.2	10.6	2.2	−5.7	
		8	0	10	8	15	43	125	86	41	15	0	3	354
Xi'an	334	0.6	3.9	10.0	17.2	23.9	27.8	30.0	27.8	22.2	17.2	6.7	1.7	
		10	8	15	43	51	71	84	127	41	41	8	10	509
Harbin	159	−19.4	−15.2	−4.5	5.6	13.3	18.9	22.2	20.6	10.6	4.4	−6.2	−16.4	
		5	5	10	23	43	104	147	107	56	31	10	5	546
Ürümqi	903	−15.2	−13.4	−7.3	8.9	16.7	20.0	22.8	21.1	15.6	4.4	−4.5	−11.1	
		5	3	5	10	13	15	5	8	10	15	5	5	99
Kashgar	1218	−5.7	0.0	8.3	17.8	19.4	20.4	27.8	25.6	19.4	12.2	3.9	−2.2	
		5	5	5	15	20	25	5	5	0	15	0	0	100

Source: Central Meteorological Bureau (1960).

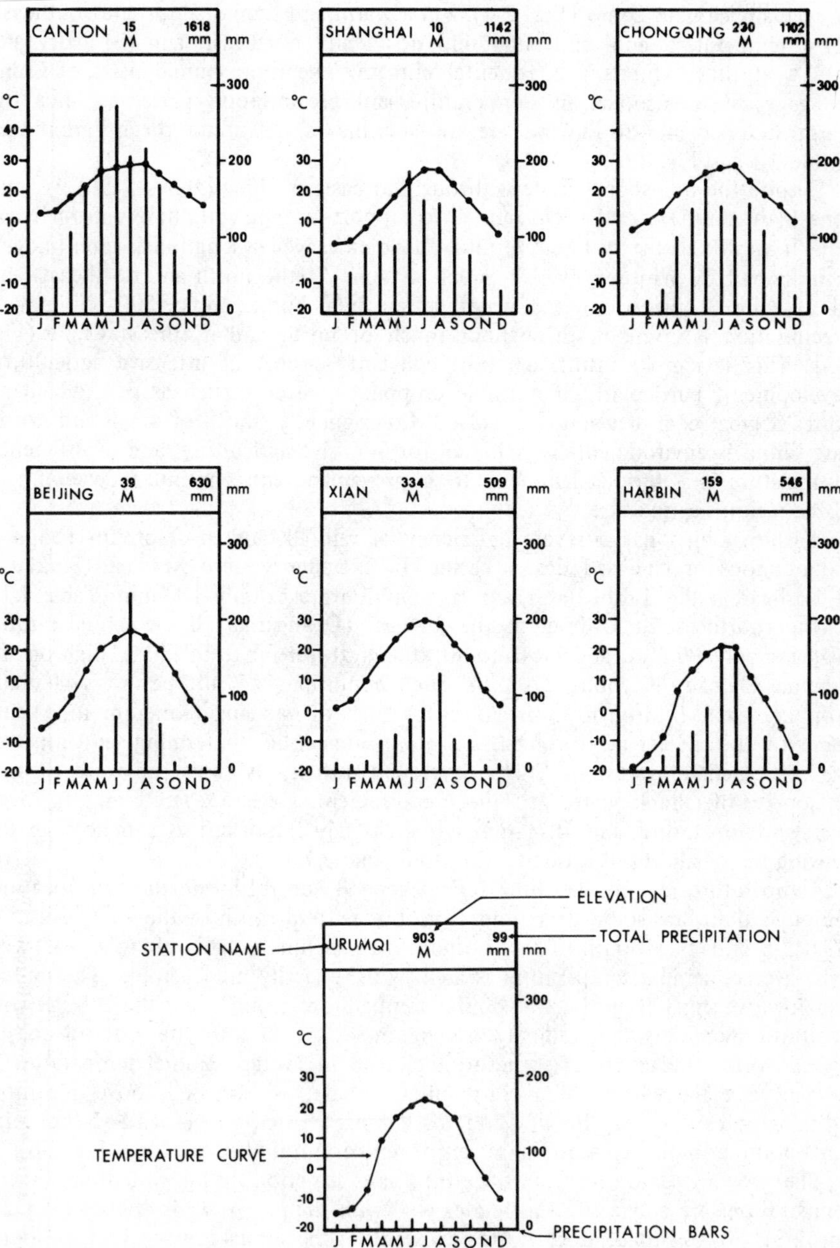

Fig. 2-6. Climagraphs of selected stations in China.
Source: Central Meteorological Bureau (1960).

three main climate zones (Fig. 2-4): (1) a warm and humid south and southeast; (2) a temperate-to-cool and subhumid north and northeast; and (3) a dry and cold west that exhibits a continental climate. The more humid parts of China are generally monsoonal in temperature and precipitation patterns. Thus the warm summer months always are the months of maximum precipitation (see (Table 2-1 and Fig. 2-6).

Despite the monsoonal pattern throughout eastern China (zones 1 and 2), only zone 1 (the south) has sufficient rainfall to support farming without relying on irrigation. If viewed in the systemic terms of a global as well as a national water budget, as described by Whitney (1979), much of zone 2 (the north and northeast) and all of zone 3 (the west) is a water deficit area. For example, 500–650 mm of precipitation is common throughout much of north and northeast China (Fig. 2-3). This is simply insufficient for constant support of intensive agricultural development, particularly if multiple cropping or a crop such as rice, which requires a great deal of water, is involved. Consequently, much of north and northeast China is environmentally marginal for intensive agriculture, and insufficiency of moisture is a serious handicap to improvement and continued development of the region's agriculture.

Western China has a severe deficiency of rainfall, and most of this region is mountainous or enclosed desert basins. In extreme western Xinjiang (Sinkiang) at Kashgar in the Tarim Basin, annual rainfall averages only 100 mm (Table 2-1). Farther northeast at Ürümqi in the Junggar (Dzungarian) Basin annual rainfall averages only 99 mm, and the amount at Jiangzi not far from Lhasa, high on the Tibetan Plateau, is about 270 mm. Such conditions do not permit systematic cropping even if drought resistant crops such as gaoliang (sorghum milo) and some of the millets are involved. Irrigation is essential to farming, and most of the settlements in western China developed initially as oases and were focused on sources of reliable water. In Tibet, requirements are less severe owing to lower average temperature, but irrigation is increasingly important as a means for improving the reliability of agricultural output (Fig. 2-7).

Temperature regimes in China reflect general control by north-south location, although there are some deviations from this pattern south of the 16°C isotherm (Fig. 2-6 and 2-7). South of this isotherm, which runs roughly along an east-west axis, average annual temperature is high, with generally mild winters. The middle and lower Yangzi Basin have a similar temperature regime, and the average temperatures increase only gradually as one moves south into the tropical coastal areas. North of the 16°C isotherm, the drop in average annual temperature is steeper, and the effects of a continental climate, as discussed above, are more prominent, as seen in climate data for Peking, Xi'an (Hsi-an), and Harbin with much more pronounced seasonal ranges of temperatures (Table 2-1 and Fig. 2-6).

The growing season for plants, defined as that period during which daily mean temperatures are above 6°C, correlates well with the pattern of isotherms (Fig. 2-7 and 2-8). For example, most of the area south of the annual average 18°C isotherm and some areas south of the 16°C isotherm have a year-round growing season. Light frosts may occur, but these are not severe enough to kill most plants. North of the Yangzi Basin, the average temperatures drop more sharply; a growing season

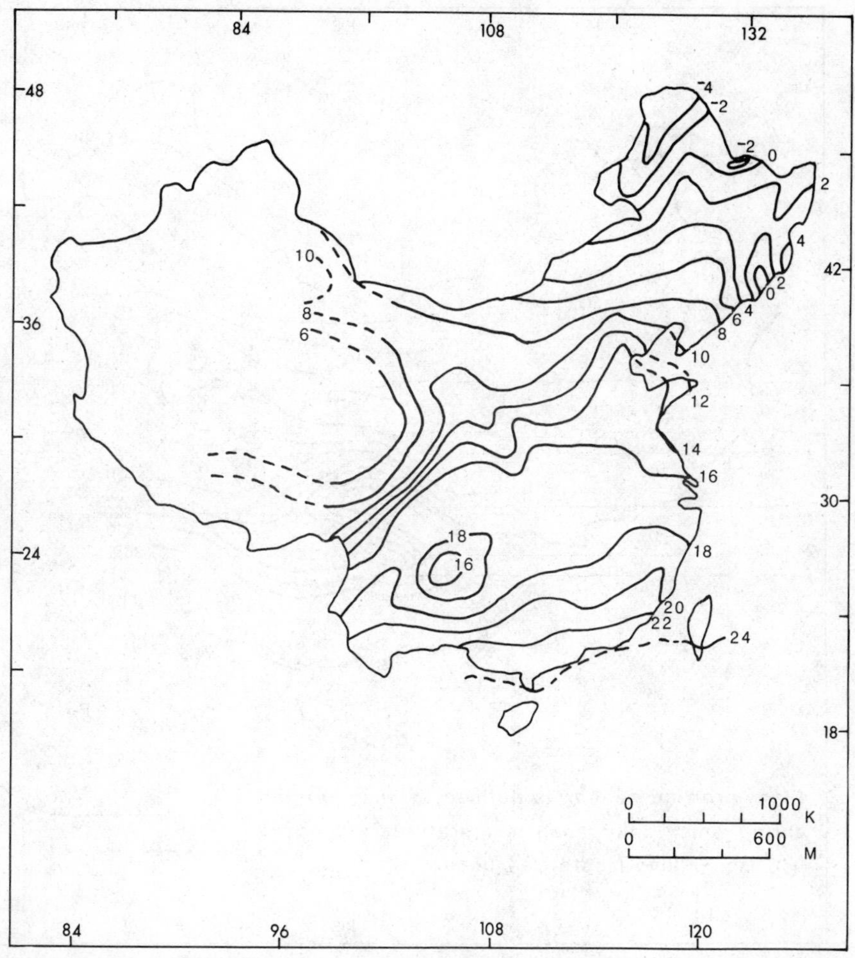

Fig. 2-7. China, average annual temperature in degrees Celsius.
Source: Hsieh (1973).

of fewer than 300 days reflects that drop. In the northern interior of Inner Mongolia, Heilongjiang, and Jilin (Chirin or Chi-lin), the growing season is less than 180 days (Fig. 2-8).

It is useful to compare the United States and China when discussing the environmental impact on development. It was noted that both countries are middle latitude lands, and both have great variety and diversity in their environments. The range of environmental diversity extends from humid subtropical regions found in the southeast parts of both countries to high and dry regions in the northwest.

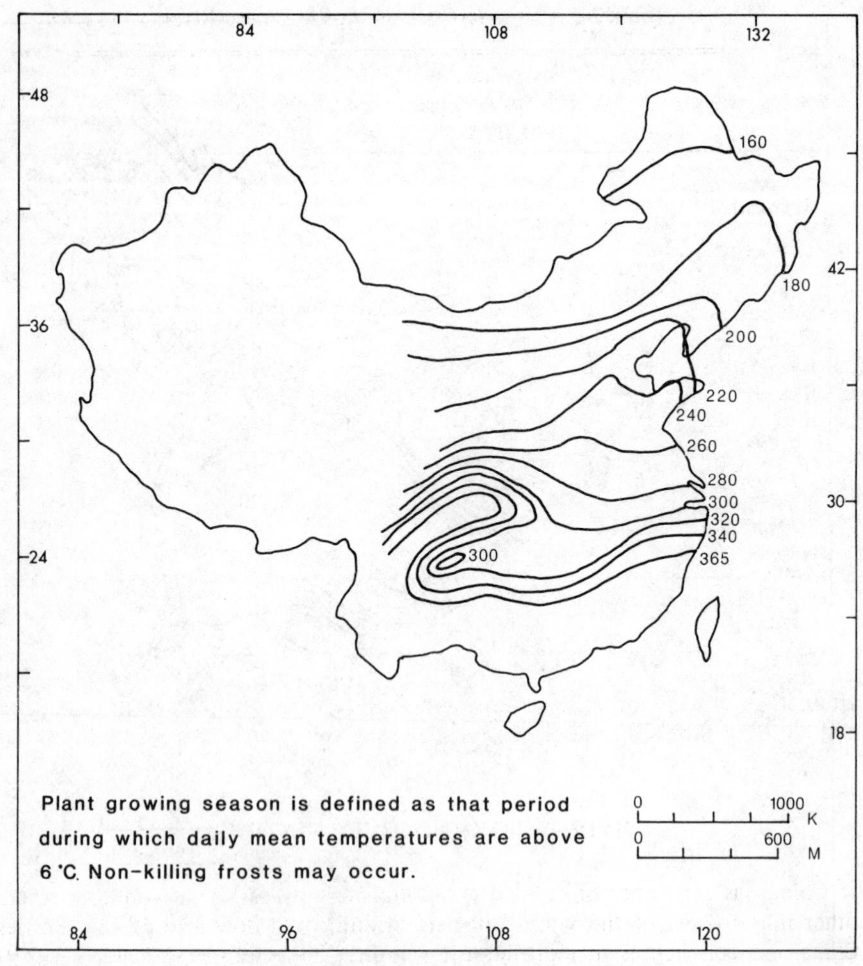

Fig. 2-8. China, maximum length of growing season.
Source: Central Intelligence Agency (1971).

China has greater extremes and fewer mild, well-watered regions. The United States has about one-third more arable land than China because of the greater availability of moisture in the U.S. midwest. The Chinese, it may be argued, have had more environmental challenges, and the Chinese have been particularly active in altering their landscapes. For example, about 45% of China's cropped land is irrigated today. In the United States, only approximately 14% of the cultivated land is irrigated. At the same time, China reflects, by the clustering of its people in the eastern part of the country and by their occupancy patterns, the particular

Table 2-2. Characteristics of Major Chinese Rivers

River	Average rate (m^3/sec) of discharge at mouth	Length (km)	Area (km^2) of drainage basin
Yangzi	32,190	5,980	1,827,000
Xi (West)	11,590	1,960	448,000
Amur (Heilong) (shared with USSR)	9,800	5,780	2,050,000
Songhua (Sungari)	2,000	1,860	524,000
Huang	1,530	4,840	771,000
Han	1,200	1,500	174,000
Huai	1,090	1,090	210,000
	North American Comparisons		
Mississippi	18,000	6,020	3,230,000
St. Lawrence	13,030	3,060	1,303,000
Potomac	314	620	38,000

Source: Showers (1979).

alternatives and opportunities these landscapes and regional climate regimes offer and the adjustments the people have made to these environmental alternatives.

HYDROLOGY AND RIVER SYSTEMS

China has a number of large rivers within its boundaries. In addition, several other major rivers of the world originate in China and flow into other countries. China also contributes major tributaries to these rivers (Table 2-2 and Fig. 2-9). Most of China's major rivers originate on or near the Qinghai (Ch'ing-hai)-Tibetan Plateau and flow south or east, emptying eventually into areas of the Indian or Pacific Ocean. The three major rivers that flow east and have virtually all of their drainage systems within the country are the Huang He (Yellow River) and Yangzi (Chang Jiang), and the Xi Jiang (Hsi River). Of these, the Yangzi is easily the largest in length, area of drainage basin, and in volume of discharge (Table 2-2). The Huang He is next in length and area of drainage basin, although its discharge is modest compared to the Yangzi and the Xi. The Amur or Heilong Jiang (Black Dragon River, as the Chinese call it) forms the boundary between China and the USSR for part of its course. It is a large (with a drainage area larger than the Yangzi) and very important stream, and much of its drainage comes from northeast China. However, it flows to the sea through Soviet territory, and is not examined in the same detail as the other three great streams of China.

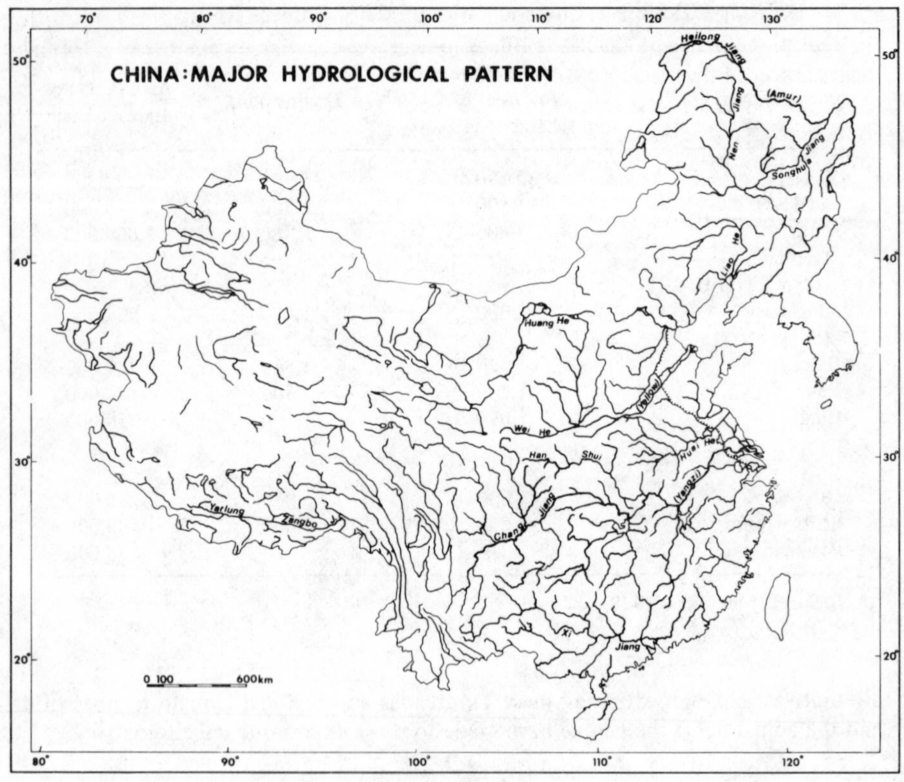

Fig. 2-9. China: major hydrological pattern.

The Huang He–China's Sorrow

The Huang He and some of its tributaries, such as the Wei, Fen, and Luo, are of special interest because of their role and location in the evolution of Chinese civilization. The middle part of the drainage system of the Huang cuts through the loessland, as do a number of important tributaries. Here the rivers pick up an enormous quantity of silt which is transported downstream. As the Huang He descends onto the North China Plain, its gradient is reduced sharply, resulting in its reduced ability to transport material in suspension. The result is deposition in the streambed and the accumulation over time of large quantities of silt and aggradation of the streambed.

Several factors contribute to exacerbating this situation. First, precipitation is concentrated seasonally in this region of China in the summer season. Xi'an, for example, located on the Wei He, approximately 120 km west of its confluence with the Huang, receives approximately 60% of its 550 mm of precipitation during the months of June, July, and August. By contrast, average precipitation in December, January, and February amounts to only 28 mm. This type of regime has resulted in great variation in the range of average stream discharge. Second, human beings have been particularly active for many millenia in this region known as the "Cradle of Chinese Civilization." One important consequence of human activity has been the removal of whatever natural forest and grass cover was present in late Pleistocene times and its replacement by a scrub vegetation cover much less resistant to the forces of erosion. Large areas of the Loess Plateau thus became rarely used badlands, supporting little flora or fauna of commercial value or consequence. Local inhabitants could do little to control or improve the environmental situation, and the degraded environment meant poverty and uncertainty for them.

As the Huang He continued to build up its bed downstream, flooding became increasingly common and serious. Inhabitants of the North China Plain responded by constructing levees to hold the river in its bed, but the levees were not high enough to contain large floods. A cycle of streambed aggradation coupled with levee building continued. Occasionally, gigantic floods would occur, the levees would be breached, and the river would inundate extensive areas of the neighboring plain. Eventually, a new channel and mouth hundreds of kilometers from the old one might be created, and the cyclical process would begin anew. Such catastrophes led to calling this river "China's Sorrow," and indeed it has been that for many centuries.

In 1947, the Huang was rechanneled to flow north of the Shandong Peninsula, and it has continued there ever since. The Chinese government has launched a major program to tame and use China's rivers and especially this one. Such projects as the large dam and reservoir at San Men Xia (Three Gates Gorge) near the Tongguan (T'ung-kuan) elbow of the river have been constructed, but the extremely high silt content has created technical problems beyond expectations. Overall the river has been contained, but the investment costs have been high. The multipurpose projects of hydroelectricity production, improved availability of irrigation waters, and better navigation have been achieved with only modest success (Greer, 1979).

The Yangzi–China's Mightiest River

China's largest river is the Yangzi (Chang Jiang) where the drainage basin is almost 2 million km^2. The Yangzi is also China's longest river (5,980 km) and has by far the largest annual average discharge of China's rivers. The average discharge of the Yangzi at its mouth near Shanghai is 32,190 m^3/sec. This compares with an average discharge of the Mississippi River near Vicksburg, Mississippi of 18,000 m^3/sec. One of the most significant features of the Yangzi when compared with the Huang is difference in both the rates of discharge and the silt burden or stream load. The Huang He average discharge rate near the mouth is 1,530 m^3/sec, about 20 times less than the Yangzi. The Huang, however, has a massive silt load, whereas the Yangzi has a more modest load (Stoddart, 1978). The Yangzi rises on the Tibetan Plateau and flows generally eastward. It drains the central part of China and provides water for irrigation. Also, it forms a major access corridor for maritime communication into the heart of central China. The Yangzi floods, but its floods are less serious than those of the Huang He. Moreover, the numerous large lakes in the middle part of its course act as giant flood reservoirs, expanding and contracting as the level of the river rises and falls. These gigantic holding lakes serve as natural regulators for flood waters and reduce the damage of any flood.

For many years, the Chinese have discussed diverting waters from the Yangzi and routing these waters north to the water deficient areas of the North China Plain. This project has been debated in China extensively, and project planning is now under way to develop a system to pump Yangzi River water north through the Grand Canal to provide irrigation water for north China. Other routes have also been proposed and more than one conduit may be developed and used (Kao, 1978) (Fig. 2-10). The scale of the project is immense, and it can have a great impact on continued growth of China's agricultural output. Of significance to American geographers is the knowledge that the Institute of Geography, Academia Sinica, in China apparently will be heavily involved in planning for the allocation of the Yangzi River water once it has been transported to the north, a valuable role for the country's professional geographers.

Some large gorges and a major change in the stream channel characteristics are located in the area where the Yangzi begins to emerge on the lower alluvial plains of southern Hubei Province. It is in this area, at Gezhouba, where China is constructing its largest hydro-project and is planning to begin construction on a second, even larger dam about 40 km upstream in the Three Gorges area. These two impoundments of the Yangzi are among China's largest investments and construction projects. Gezhouba is scheduled to be completed in 1986 after 16 years of work. The project will cost \$2.3 billion and will eventually produce 14 billion kwh/annum. As Ludlow (1980) pointed out, however, part of its significance is that it is a pilot project for the much larger Three Gorges (San Xia) Project. Three Gorges, as now planned, will be China's largest construction project; it will cost an estimated \$6.2 billion and will take 15 years to complete. The Three Gorges project has been in the planning stage for two decades and, if completed as planned, will have a yearly output of 110 billion kwh of electricity. The dam and turbine generator will be the largest in the world and will require approximately 30 million m^3 of concrete. About 44,000 ha of farmland will be inundated, and over one million people will have to move (Ludlow, 1980).

Both Three Gorges and Gezhouba, although primarily designed to produce power, are multipurpose projects and will provide improved flood control, navigation, recreation, and tourist attractions as well as power generation. Although

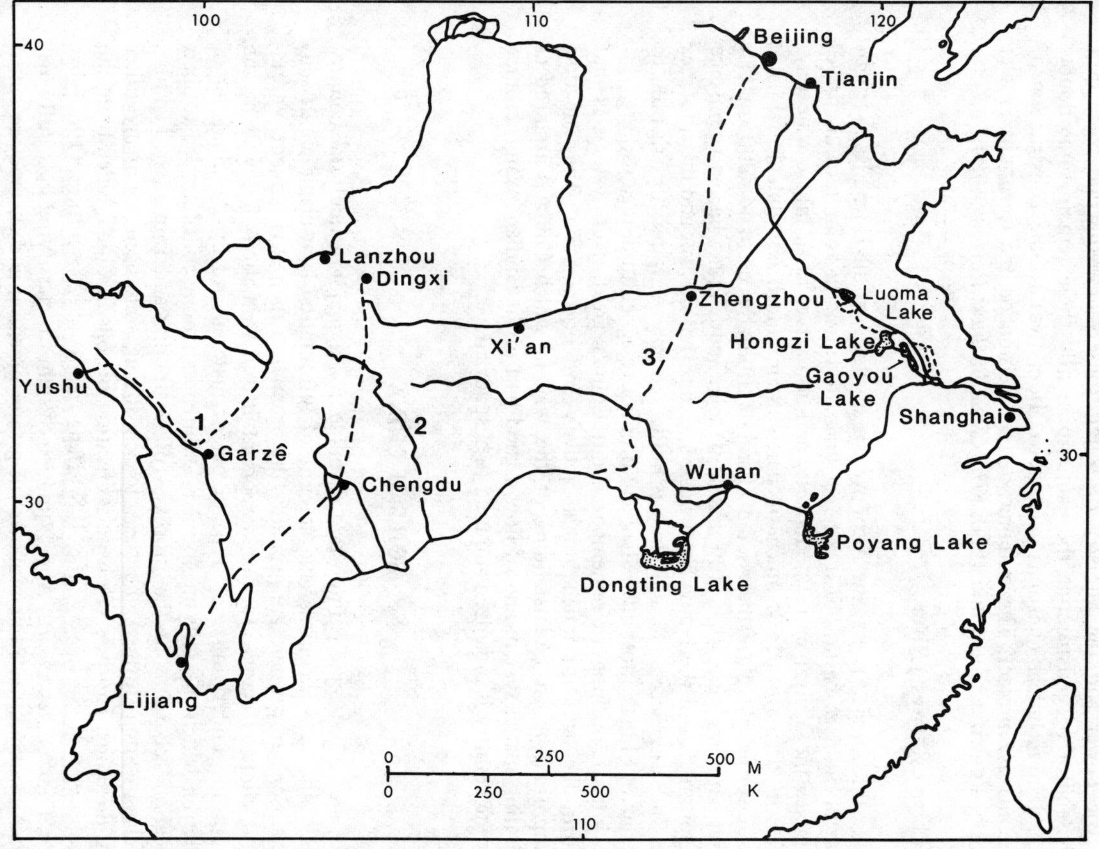

Fig. 2-10. Yangzi River water transfer projects. Possible routes of south-to-north water diversions: (1) Youji Route, (2) Wending Route, (3) Sanxia-Beijing Route, and (4) Hangqin Route.
Source: Greer (1979).

Gezhouba is nearing completion, the Three Gorges Project has spawned a major internal controversy between two of the Chinese ministries involved–the Ministry of Electric Power and the Ministry of Water Conservancy–that has raged over the advisability of constructing the dam. Apparently there remain some doubts about certain technical questions related to alternatives to the construction of this one massive project. The outcome of the decision on the Gezhouba Project may not be known until the mid 1980s (*The China Business Review*, 1980).

South China's Xi (West) River

Of the three major rivers, the Xi or West is smaller than the Huang He in length and size of drainage basin, but it is larger than the Huang in volume of discharge. It resembles the Yangzi more in character and also serves as an inland waterway. However, its drainage area is much smaller, contains much less agricultural land, and has fewer people. Nevertheless, the Xi and its tributaries drain 448,000 km^2, an area that supports more than 100 million people. South China has an abundance of precipitation, and the region has a water surplus. The Xi River and its tributaries provide an easily accessible and almost limitless supply of water for irrigation to supply one of China's most diversified and productive agricultural regions.

The important thing to remember about China's great river systems is that they form the axes for much human activity and organization. They are thus very important to an understanding of the way in which China is arranged as an operating spatial system and of how a good part of the land and water resource base of the country is organized and used to best advantage.

SOILS OF CHINA

Soils are an extremely important resource for a major agricultural country such as China, and a considerable amount of information is available about soils in China. Soils everywhere are primarily the product of their environment. Vegetation and climate factors are most important in soil formation, followed by the nature of the underlying rock type or parent material and by the character of the relief on which the soils are formed. Differences among soils have led to their classification according to the processes of weathering and formation. Marbut's 1935 classification formed the basis for classifying soils used for many other studies, including Thorpe's (1939) classification of soils in China. Since then, the Soil Conservation Service of the U.S. Department of Agriculture (1960) has adopted a comprehensive 7th Approximation System for classifying soils. Although the 7th Approximation System allows for greater precision and accuracy in classification, older terms drawn largely from Marbut and Thorpe are used in this discussion. The reason for this is that no careful, fully documented 7th Approximation study of China's soils is available. Where possible to relate the two, both Marbut (Thorpe) and 7th Approximation terms are used. Chinese scientists, it is understood, have developed their own classification of soils (Nanjing Institute of Pedology, 1978).

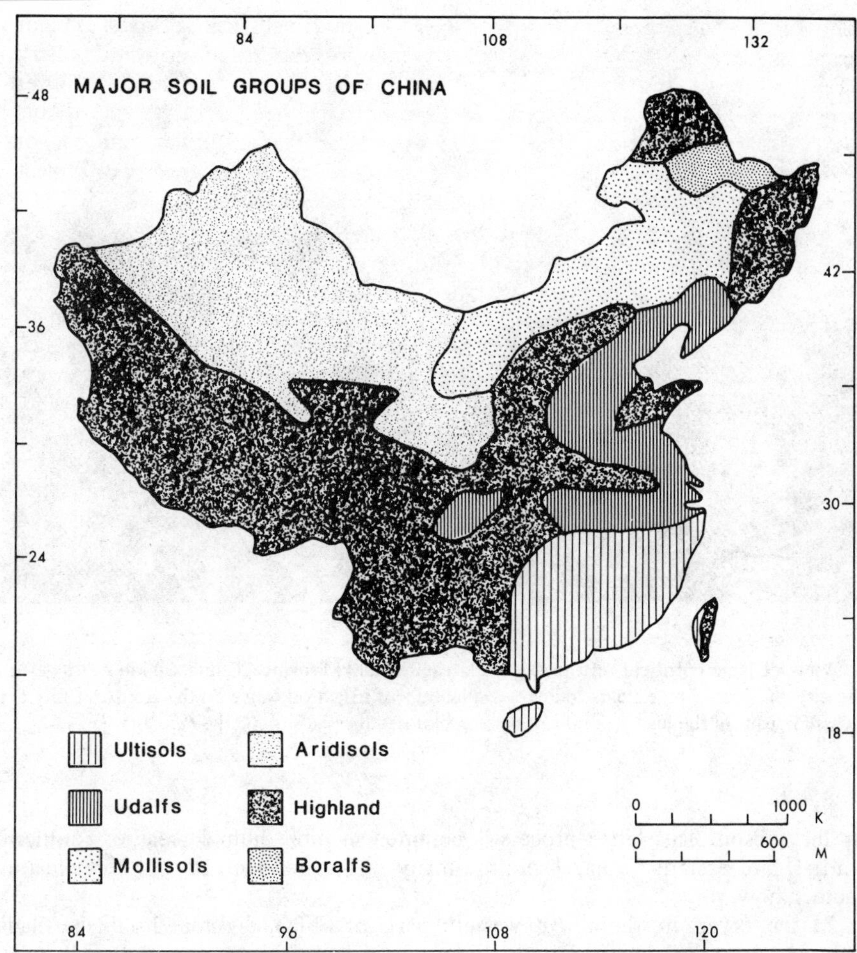

Fig. 2-11. Major soil groups of China.
Source: U.S. Department of Agriculture (1960) and Thorpe (1939).

China's soils can generally be differentiated in a manner related closely to the differentiation of climate and vegetation, i.e., between the high or dry western and northwestern regions and the humid central and southeast (Fig. 2-11). In general, this basic regionalization follows a fundamental division in soil science between processes of soil chemistry. One process concerns calcium and magnesium carbonate concentration (pedocal formation) in dryer areas. The other process involves leaching and eluviation of aluminum and iron oxides from the upper part of the soil and the deposition and concentration of these oxides (pedalfer formation)

View of large cornfield on the Loess Plateau, Shaanxi Province, China, 50 km northwest of the city of Xi'an. Large fields indicate availability of irrigation water on the comparatively dry Loess Plateau. In the background can be seen exposed loessial soil. (*C. W. Pannell*)

in the subsoil. This latter process is common in more humid areas of southern, central, and eastern China. There are many further refinements and complicating factors, however.

In the dryer, northern and western parts of China, division should be made between the very thin and poor mountain soils, found on the Tibetan Plateau, and the prairie, steppe, and desert soils, found in the regions of Xinjiang, Inner Mongolia, the Loess Plateau, and parts of northeast China (Manchuria). The thin and poor mountain soils of the Tibetan Plateau are the result of sparse vegetation, which is the result of the cold, dry climate. The prairie and steppe soils of north and northwest China developed under grasslands and are the result of the accumulation of humus and calcium carbonate in the soils. A variety of major soil types or orders are found that range from the rich black chernozems (mollisol types), as found in the northeast, to the thin and poorer brown steppe and grey-brown, near-desert soils (aridisol types), as found in Inner Mongolia. A complicating feature of soils in the dry northwest is the presence of an extensive loessial soil cover. Loess is a fine grained friable soil material of mechanical (windblown) origin and does not fit genetically into the classification schemes. In general, however, it fits with the dryer soils and has a high humus and calcium content.

Eastern China is humid, and its soils are generally podzols and are distinguished by the amount of moisture and the temperature regimes in which they develop. In the mountains of the northeast are the true podzols (cryic and udic types). The udic type extends into the central and southwestern region. The southeast is characterized by yellow and brown lateritic types (ultisols) very similar to soils found in the southeastern United States. The major complicating factor in humid eastern China is the presence in large areas of the northeast, North China Plain, and the lowlands of the middle and lower Yangzi Basin of alluvial soils (young soils with little or no profile deposited through the agency of water). These soils (aquent entisols in the 7th Approximation) are undeniably the most important agricultural soils in China. Generally they tend to be acidic in reaction. While not particularly fertile, they can be manipulated and worked easily. To these soils, Chinese peasants for many centuries have been adding a variety of organic manures, grasses, pond gucks, and other biodegradable materials. In a number of places, the soils have been remade into an artificial condition that is highly productive when replenished with organic nutrients on a regular, systematic basis. These are China's high yielding, intensively farmed soils which provide the basis for the great production of small grains and wet rice.

China is fortunate in having a large and diverse stock of soils which are suitable for intensive agricultural development. Equally significant is the long peasant tradition of manipulating and improving the available soils in order to increase agricultural output. The soils of China support almost one-quarter of the world's population. It is indeed remarkable that so much is produced on such a limited area. This accomplishment indicates the good quality and management of these soils. In the future, however, much more must be produced on these soils through better irrigation in the north and greater use of chemical and biological fertilizers in the south, if China is to provide more for its large and growing population.

FLORA

China, as befits a large country that stretches from 18° to 53°N latitude,[3] has a great range of vegetation. Included in this range are most of the vegetative types native to the northern hemisphere except for those varieties found in arctic regions. For example, in Hainan Island and along the southern coastal littoral of the country are found tropical rain forest and plant communities, which are familiar in the tropics. In the high mountains of western China and Tibet, alpine and subalpine plant communities may be seen. Throughout the rest of the country can be found vegetation communities common to desert, steppe, savanna, prairie meadow, coniferous evergreen, and deciduous forests. China has all of these and more (Fig. 2-12).

[3]Political/territorial claims of the People's Republic of China extend through most of the South China Sea almost to the equator. This claim is based on China's historical view of the South China Sea and certain small island groups within it. Inasmuch as these islands are insignificant physical features, their environmental characteristics are excluded from this discussion.

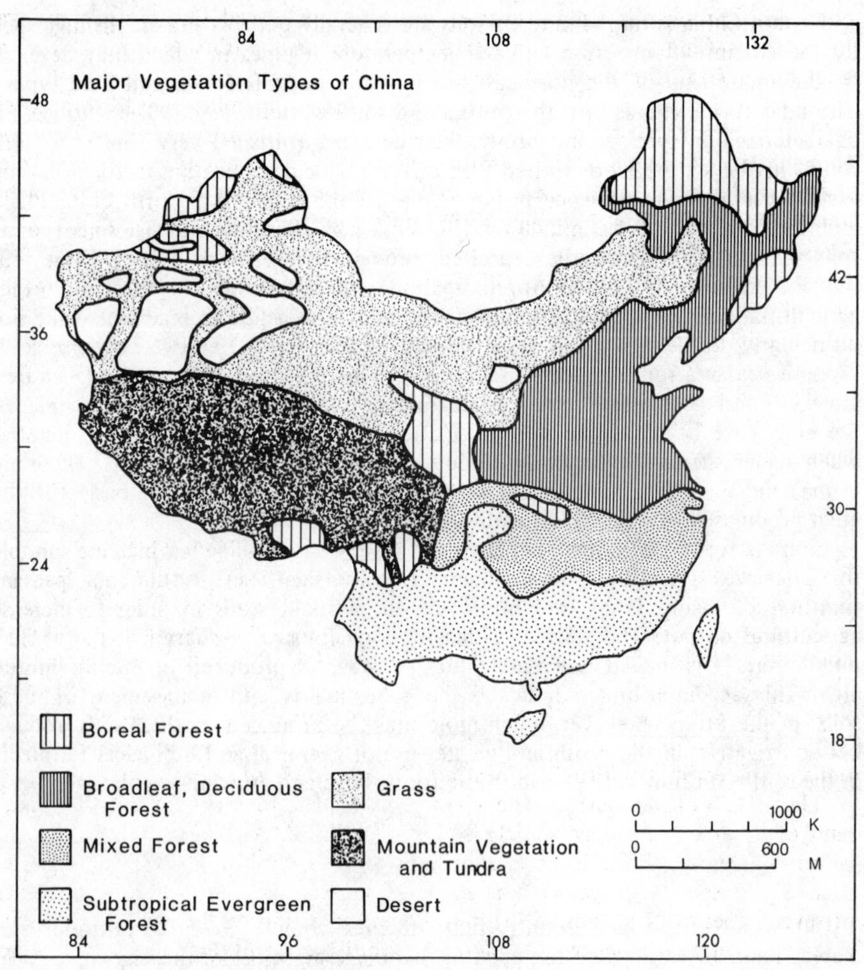

Fig. 2-12. Major vegetation types of China.
Source: Generalized from several sources.

Such a broad range of vegetation can be broken down into regional classes. Generally, the character of flora and vegetation in China can be divided between a humid east and a dry west, along a line that parallels roughly the line of rainfall surplus and deficiency identified previously. The eastern humid region of the country must be further subdivided into a tropical southern area which supports a tropical rainforest; a subtropical south and central area of broad-leaved evergreens, pines, and varieties of bamboo; and a humid but cooler north and northeast where evergreen conifers and other northern deciduous species are common. Throughout China, coarse grasses have replaced forests after removal. In southern China, much of this grass is of the tough, fibrous cogonal-type, an impediment to further economic use of the land.

In discussing vegetation in China, it is useful to remember that in the densely settled eastern part of the country, it is difficult to identify natural vegetation. Humans have been hard at work for several millenia cutting and burning trees, shrubs, and grasses and farming the cleared fields. Fuel for cooking and heat has long been scarce, especially in north China, and local peasants have devastated forests and grasslands in their search for fuel. Great pressure has been placed on forest resources, and the original vegetation has been much altered. The major commercial forests of the country are found in the northeast. Here large stands of conifers, birch, ash, and other northern species are found on the slopes of mountains that rim the Song-Liao Plain. The Communist government has placed great emphasis on reforestation in recent years, and a large quantity of trees has been planted throughout the country (see Chapter 6). The humid southern uplands would appear to be especially promising for the rapid growth of softwoods.

In eastern China, Chinese researchers have identified four main vegetational zones from south to north: (1) a zone of tropical forests and savanna; (2) a zone of subtropical evergreen forests extending north to the Yangzi River and west to the Qinghai-Tibet Plateau; (3) a zone of mainly deciduous forests extending from the Yangzi north to the Amur Basin; (4) a taiga zone in the Amur Basin.

In general, plant communities change with shifts in location from south to north as well as with increases in elevation. However, tropical plant communities are found as far north as 28°N in the river valleys of Yunnan Province and southeastern Tibet. Likewise the Sichuan Basin, characterized by a humid, mild climate with associated thermophilic plant species, does not exhibit vegetation associations indicated by its latitudinal location.

The dry, western part of the country is similar to much of Central Asia, a land of deserts and steppe mostly at great elevation. Although the area involved is very large, the flora is poor and, according to Grubov (1969), numbers less than 5,000 species. Vegetation is monotonous and is composed predominantly of several species of grasses and subshrubs. Composition of the flora and the character of vegetation along with ecological conditions permit dividing this vast region into three major vegetation zones: (1) Mongolia; (2) Dzungaria and the Tarim Basin; and (3) Tibet.

Within these three zones, flora vary according to natural, ecological conditions rather than by shifts in location north or south. Thus, trees will be found where precipitation is greatest and average temperatures permit their growth. For example, on the windward northern slopes of the Tian Shan, up to 3,000 m in height, may be found forests of spruce, birch, ash, and aspen. There is, however, great variation in the extent and types of tree cover owing to differences in geomorphology and climate. At higher elevations and in dryer steppe locations, a variety of grasses and sedges are common throughout western China. Ecologically, the most severe region in western China is the western part of the Tibetan upland, a high, cold desert above 4,500 m. Plant growth is limited, and the vegetation is sparse.

Despite China's vast area, its forest resources are modest, about 12% of the total land area. Too many centuries of cutting and burning have reduced its eastern forests to second growth, scrub, or recently planted stands. The western areas are generally not well suited environmentally to forest production and forest resources are not easy to exploit. Only in the northeast are large stands of timber-grade forests available. China's southeast has a climate that will permit rapid growth of trees. Recent intensified efforts to promote more rapid forest generation hold some promise.

REGIONAL CHALLENGES TO DEVELOPMENT AND MODERNIZATION

An interesting and significant feature of the Chinese landscape is that most of the people are concentrated in the eastern part of the country. This concentration relates partially to the availability of sufficient water for intensive agriculture, particularly in central and southern China. The agricultural environment in eastern China has also prospered from the extensive flat and low-lying plains in central, north, and northeast China, the Pearl River delta, and the large basin of the Sichuan region (Figs. 2-1 and 2-5). Alluvial soils found in most of these areas have further enhanced their attractiveness for agricultural development.

Large areas of China are not especially suitable for intensive settlement and development. Within these large areas, a number of distinctive regions for human occupancy are found (several are discussed below). Two of these are the Loess Plateau and the very extensive area of limestone found in southwestern China. Other places in the world possess similar natural environments, but nowhere is the extent of the conditions of loess and tower karst as great, nor the impact of man on these landscapes as long established, far-reaching and striking.

Loesslands

The Loess Plateau derives its name from the soil mantle of yellow earth or loess that covers most of Shaanxi and parts of western Shanxi, Honan, and Gansu Provinces of northwestern China. Loess is a fine grained, silt-like material with particle sizes that range between 0.01 and 0.04 mm (Stoddart, 1978). The soil, although lacking a distinctive profile, is well developed in vertical columns. The origins of loess are controversial, but generally it is agreed that sometime during the dry Pleistocene period strong winds picked up dirt particles in great quantities in desert areas to the north and west–in the Gobi, Alashan, and Ordos Deserts. These materials were blown southeast, and over long periods have accumulated over a large area. In many places, the loess may exceed 100 m in thickness and may reach 80 m over large areas within the Great Loop of the Huang He (Fig. 2-13). This accumulation has been going on for millenia, and the winter dust storms of that region indicate the process is continuing.

The loess here is frequently loose and unconsolidated. Consequently, it erodes easily, especially where trees and grass cover have been removed or are sparse. In those places, where slope is steep and there is concentrated precipitation in

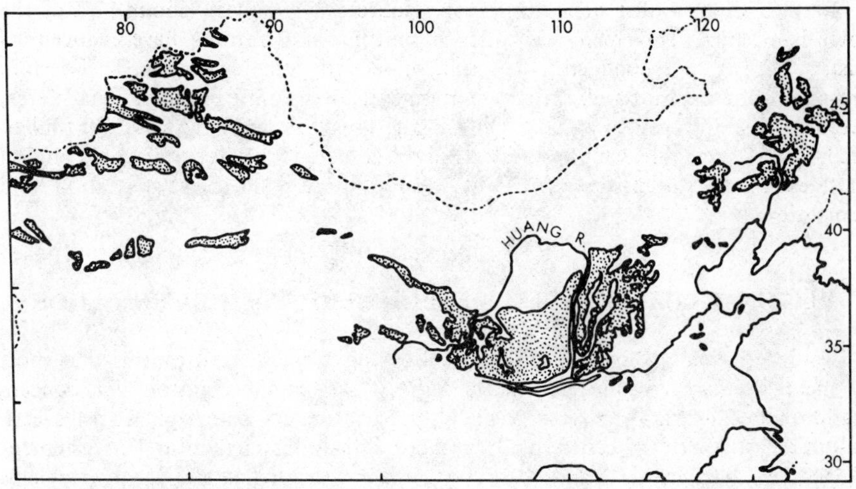

Fig. 2-13. Distribution of loess in China.
Source: Stoddart (1978).

summertime, erosion may be very serious. Traditionally, much of the Loess Plateau was carved and dissected into a landscape that resembled badlands. Obviously, such a condition created very serious problems for farming, and this region has been traditionally one of the more chronically impoverished areas of China. The Communist government has sought to improve things, and great effort has been expended in terracing the slope areas and in attempting to control runoff during rainstorms. The Dazhai (Ta-chai) Production Brigade on the eastern flank of the Loess Plateau (Taihang Mountains) pioneered this type of effort, and for more than a decade Dazhai was used as a model for agricultural development. Many improvements have taken place in the region, but the specific environmental conditions of loessial soil, slope, and precipitation will continue to be a major environmental challenge to Chinese planners in the years ahead, as the country seeks to improve the agricultural productivity of its land resources.

Chinese Karst

Another equally challenging environmental condition is found in the large limestone region of southwest China. Covering much of the area of three southern provinces, Guangxi, Guizhou, and Yunnan (Kuang-hsi, Kuei-chou, and Yun-nan), are massive beds of limestone which have been dissolved and eroded by the subtropical and tropical weathering elements of high annual average temperature and precipitation. The result has been some of the most beautiful and bizarre karst landscape found anywhere. Limestone towers and domes abound. Some rise 200 m above base level. These are the major terrain features. Other specialized karstic

Gully erosion of loess in Gansu Province. (*L. Ma*)

Much of southwestern China is underlain by limestone and some of it has been weathered into dramatic domes and towers such as these seen in Guangxi Chuang A. R. along the Li River. (*C. W. Pannell*)

Guilin, Guangxi Province, China. Building density is not too great in this small city in southwestern China. Tower karst can be seen in the distance. In the mid-ground are located high-rise housing for workers with a few small fields behind. (*C. W. Pannell*)

features, such as dolines (solution valleys), sinkholes, caves, and underground water courses, are also present. The scenery is spectacular, but the land is not easy to farm. Where the landscape is level or near level, it is difficult to keep water on the surface because of the solubility of the limestone. Otherwise the surface has been carved into unusual and strikingly magnificent landscapes that are renowned the world over for their beauty and splendor. Although much of the surface is too rugged for intensive agricultural use, enough level land within the karst region is available to support a modest level of agricultural development and population density.

Northeast China's Heilongjiang Province

Although Han Chinese have occupied and farmed most of northeast China for less than 100 years, agricultural and industrial development and population growth have been very rapid, especially in the two southern provinces of Liaoning and Jilin. Farming, for example, has developed extensively around grain crops. Wheat, corn, barley, millets, gaoliang, and soybeans are grown on chernozem and other

Low lying meadowland and marsh in Three Rivers Plain of Heilongjiang Province, northeast China. This area near the Soviet border is a major region of land reclamation in China. (*L. Ma*)

Chinese scientists inspecting virgin lands in the Three Rivers Plain region of Heilongjiang Province, northeast China. (*L. Ma*)

chestnut earth soils rich in calcium and humus. In the northern province of Heilongjiang, however, much of the arable land remains in grass or tree cover, and an active program of land reclamation has been under way under the Communist administration.

Environmental limitations to agricultural development are numerous. First, it is very cold in China's northernmost province, and the growing season is short. Second, precipitation is modest, approximately 500 mm in the Nen River Basin and a little more in the Songhua (Sungari) River Basin farther east. Flooding in spring is common in these basins, and much of the surrounding plain is composed of boggy grasslands, lakes, and saline marshes. These lands, which are being drained and cultivated, form the bulk of China's newly reclaimed agricultural lands. Between 1953 and 1975, it was reported that more than 900 state farms were set up in the Nen River Basin and along the lower marshes of the Songhua. About 470 reclamation areas had been established in Heilongjiang Province and the total newly reclaimed land was reported to exceed 13,000 km^2.

Farming in this region of China differs from most other parts of the country in that field size is generally large (20-800 ha) and machines are heavily used. In addition to state farms organized for land reclamation, communes have been formed, and fragmented land holdings have been consolidated into larger units. In recent years, all state farms and most of the communes were reported to be using machinery for plowing, seeding, and harvesting. Agricultural labor productivity is typically higher here than most other areas of China. Population densities are also much lower. According to a recent study employing remote sensing techniques and Landsat imagery, as much as 37,000 km^2 of wetland and grassland remain in the Nen River Basin for potential reclamation for agricultural development. One of the conclusions of that study pointed out that while this is a significant amount of potential new agricultural land, in the aggregated picture of China's large population and growing domestic needs, new lands in Heilongjiang hold only limited promise and should not be relied on as a solution to large increases in total agricultural output (Welch, Lo, and Pannell, 1979).

Western China: Xinjiang, Qinghai and Tibet

The western Chinese regions of Xinjiang, Qinghai, and the Tibetan Highlands account for about half of China's area. Western China is a land of extremes–very high mountains and plateaus, great basins, and extremely dry deserts. The physical features, however, offer extremely serious environmental problems for human occupancy and agricultural development. A large portion of this region–the Tarim, Junggar, and Qaidam Basins as well as much of northern and western Tibet–is an area of interior drainage, dotted with salt lakes and saline marshes. Despite the interior drainage, on the eastern and southern faces of the Tibetan Plateau originate the headwaters of several great rivers–the Huang He, Yangzi, Mekong, Salween, Brahmaputra, and Indus. This is a region of great water resource potential (Murzayev and Chou, 1959; Academy of Sciences, USSR, 1960).

Both climate and relief impose serious impediments to the development of western China. Coupled with the relative inaccessibility and isolation, it is not

"Gobi" type stony desert, Xinjiang A. R. (*L. Ma*)

Sand dune in desert in western Xinjiang. In background, note plantings to attempt to arrest the shifting sands of the arid regions. (*L. Ma*)

surprising that western China is sparsely populated. The major challenges to development have been the arid climate and the short growing season. These challenges are imposed by high elevation and the cold winters.

Xinjiang's most imposing physical feature is the Tarim Basin, one of the driest places on earth. Rimmed by tall mountains, most of the basin is uninhabited desert (Takla Makan) with very little vegetation. Only along the footslopes of the bordering mountains is there opportunity for human occupancy. This is due to the presence of mountain streams and easily worked alluvial soils.

North of the Tarim Basin rises the Tian Shan to elevations of 8,000 m. Beyond them is found the Junggar Basin partially open and facing Soviet Central Asia. Here rainfall may reach 300 mm/annum and is greater on the mountain slopes. Oasis agriculture is more extensive than in the Tarim, and land reclamation based on improved irrigation networks and mechanized farming has proceeded rapidly. Noteworthy among the growth centers has been Ürümqi (Urumchi), an administrative and industrial city of more than 800,000 surrounded by a thriving irrigated oasis farming system. Based on the improved control and management of streams that empty from the adjacent mountains, extensive land reclamation and cropping have proceeded throughout the southern and western margins of the Junggar Basin. Indeed, here and in Heilongjiang Province in the northeast are found the largest areas of land reclaimed since 1949.

The Tibetan Highlands (including Tibet Autonomous Region and Qinghai Province) include more than one-quarter of China's area. Three main physical divisions make up these highlands: (1) The large Qianzang (Chien-tsang) Region in the north and west is an area of mountain ranges, valleys, and plains. Owing to the great elevation, coldness, and aridity, most of this region has only sparse vegetation and is largely devoid of human habitation. (2) The alluvial river valleys of the south and southeast, generally with elevation below 4,000 m, contain most of the developed farmland and much of the Tibetan population. Here along the Yarlung Zangbo (Brahmaputra) River and its tributaries is the heartland of Tibet and the capital, Lhasa. (3) The older districts of Tibet that are now located outside the boundaries of the autonomous region include grasslands in Qinghai and rugged mountains in western Sichuan and northwestern Yunnan. Although much investment has been expended in building roads in the rugged southwestern mountains, the main efforts have been aimed at territorial integration through spatial linkages rather than through extensive agricultural development. The Tibetan Highlands are likely to remain marginally developed and sparsely populated. Isolation coupled with the rugged environment offer little incentive for heavy investment and developmental commitments.

LITERATURE CITED

Academy of Sciences, USSR, 1960, *Soviet-Chinese Study of the Geography of Sinkiang.* (Prirodnyye usloviya sintsyana,"Natural Conditions in Sinkiang.") Moscow: Publishing House of the USSR Academy of Sciences (JPRS 15084, Aug. 31, 1962).

Central Intelligence Agency, 1971, *Atlas of the People's Republic of China.* Washington, D.C.: U.S. Government Printing Office.

Central Meteorological Bureau, Office of Climatological Data Research, 1960, *An Atlas of Chinese Climatology* (Zhongguo Qihou Tu). Beijing: Map Publishing Society (JPRS 16321, Nov. 23, 1962).

The China Business Review, 1980, "The Three Gorges Controversy Rages On," Vo. 7, No. 3, May–June, p. 23.

Greer, Charles, 1979, *Water Management in the Yellow River Basin of China.* Austin, Texas: University of Texas Press.

Grubov, V. I., 1969, "Flora and Vegetation." In Institute of Geography, USSR Academy of Sciences, *The Physical Geography of China*, Vol. I. New York: Frederick A. Praeger, pp. 265–364.

Hsieh, Chiao-min, 1973, *Atlas of China.* New York: McGraw-Hill.

Jianming Zhongguo Dili (Concise Geography of China), 1974. Shanghai: Renmin Chubanshe.

Kao, Hsia, 1978, "Yangtze Waters Diverted to North China." *Peking Review*, No. 38, Sept. 22, pp. 6–9.

Lee, J. S., 1939, *The Geology of China.* London: Thomas Murby.

Ludlow, Nicholas, 1980, "Gezhouba on the Yangzi." *The China Business Review*, Vol. 7, No. 3, pp. 11–15.

Murzayev, E. A. and Chou, Li-san, 1959, *Natural Conditions in the Sinkiang Uighur Autonomous Region* (JPRS 18689, Apr. 15, 1963).

Nanjing Institute of Pedology, 1978, *Zhongguo Turang* (China's Soils). Beijing: Science Press.

Ren, Meie, Yang Renzhang, and Bao Haosheng, 1979, *Zhongguo Ziran Dili Gangyao* (An Outline of the Physical Geography of China). Beijing: Commercial Press.

Showers, Victor, 1979, *World Facts and Figures.* New York: John Wiley & Sons.

Spencer, J. E., 1954, *Asia, East by South: A Cultural Geography.* New York: John Wiley & Sons.

Stoddart, D. R., 1978, "Geomorphology of China." *Progress in Physical Geography*, Vol. 2, No. 2, pp. 187–236.

Thorpe, James, 1939, *Geography of the Soils of China.* Peking: National Geological Survey of China.

U.S. Department of Agriculture, Soil Conservation Service, Soil Survey Staff, 1960, *Soil Classification, A Comprehensive Seventh Approximation.* Washington, D.C.: U.S. Government Printing Office.

Wang, K. P., 1977, *Far East and South Asia.* In MP-1 Mineral Perspectives. Washington, D.C.: U.S. Department of the Interior, Bureau of Mines.

Welch, R. A., Lo, H. C., and Pannell, C. W., 1979, "Mapping China's New Agricultural Lands." *Photogrammetric Engineering and Remote Sensing*, Vol. 45, No. 9, pp. 1,211–1,228.

Whitney, J. B. R., 1979, "Temporal and Spatial Change in the Productivity of Chinese Farming Ecosystems." In Lee Ngok and Leung Chi-kung, *China: Development and Challenge*, Vol. II, Proceedings of the Fifth Leverhulme Conference, University of Hong Kong, Centre of Asian Studies, pp. 183–215.

Zhonghua renmin gongheguo fensheng dituji (Provincial atlas of the People's Republic of China), 1974. Beijing: Ditu Chubanshe.

Chapter 3

Historical Geography

ORIGINS OF CHINA

The origins of China and Chinese civilization are prehistoric. Although many questions remain, it is clear from archeological and related evidence in palynology (the study and analysis of pollen samples) that prehistoric humans lived and operated over extensive areas of what is today's China. A broad assemblage of plants and animals were associated with these early humans, and a tremendous diversity of natural environments was involved. An understanding of these natural environments and changes that took place in them during the Pleistocene Epoch (2,500,000-10,000 B.C.) is crucial to an understanding of early humans in China as they evolved and developed during this period—as K. C. Chang (1977) reminded us.

As in Europe and North America, the Pleistocene was a time of dramatic change in China's natural environment. Major natural changes involved were tectonic shifts, climatic cycles, several associated periods of extensive glaciation, and major cycles in fluvial activity during which distinct erosional and sedimentary periods were involved. Based on a variety of conclusions from evidence drawn from paleontology and geology, K. C. Chang (1977) observed that the Chinese Pleistocene was characterized by several periods of climate fluctuation accompanied by related changes in landforms, flora, and fauna. Four major cold-moist stages were involved, and these were likely correlated with the periods of glacial advance in highland areas. These periods of climate fluctuation and change provide a practical time scale that may be used to date the human fossils and evidence of paleolithic activities in the Pleistocene sediments (Chang, 1977, p. 29).

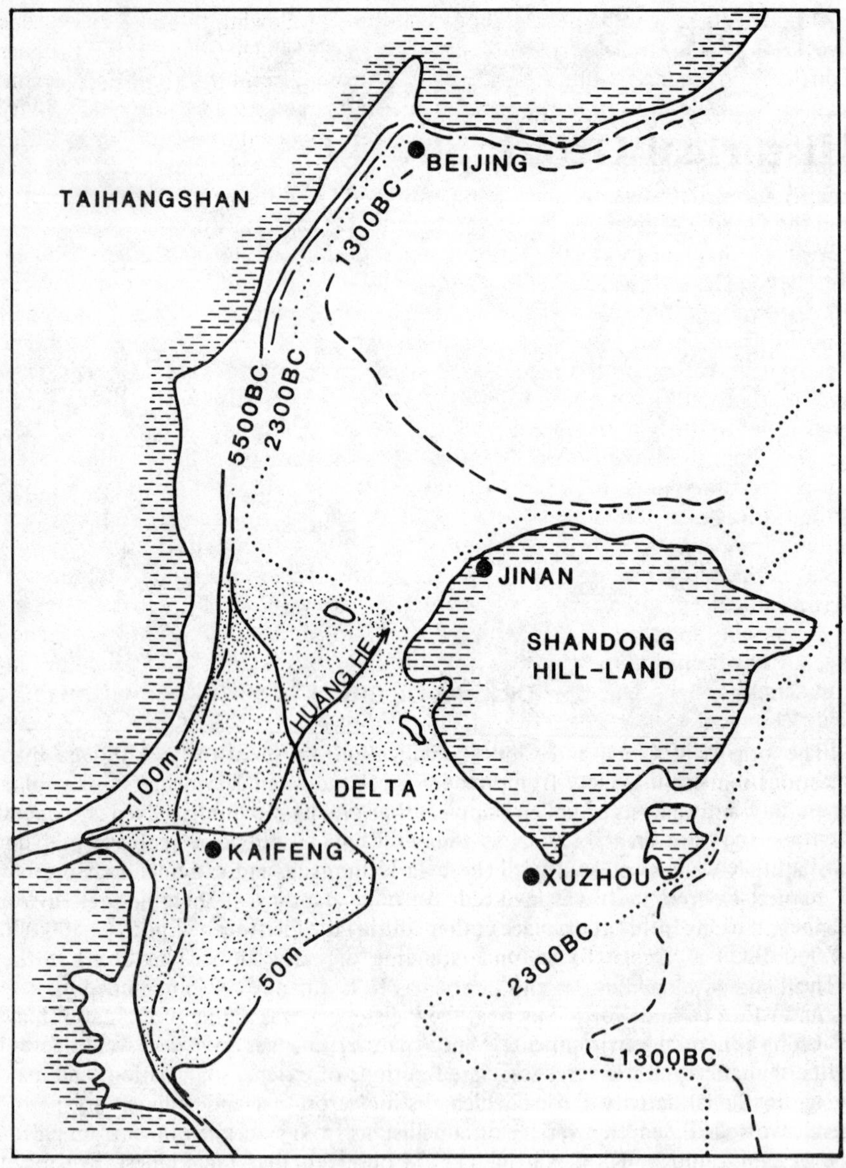

Fig. 3-1. Deposition and geological formation of the North China Plain. Note: Broken lines indicate approximate shoreline at different dates.
Source: Hsu (1981), as modified from Ting (1954).

Although there is some debate about conditions following the final Pleistocene stage (Ho, 1969), available palynological evidence, which Chang (1977) argues is difficult to counter, indicates a gradual warming trend with considerable increase in available moisture. The trend is further characterized by erosional activity with accompanying depositional action, and a sedimentary cycle. During this period, according to Hsu (1981), much of the North China Plain (Fig. 3-1) was a marsh and deltaic swamp, and the Shandong uplands formed an island separated from the Chinese mainland either by the sea or a series of marshes and lakes.

West of the marshy North China Plain, a low mountain range, the Taihang, rose. Beyond the Taihang Range stretched a large plateau, which was covered with loess during the late Pleistocene. The plateau composed much of that part of north China in the middle section of the Huang He Basin that was the home of early man. Although it is not possible to describe exactly what kind of natural conditions existed, it does seem that in the early postglacial period a thick vegetational cover existed in the high loesslands, and lowlands, and along watercourses. The area along watercourses in recent centuries has been denuded of much of its natural vegetation and to a large extent deforested. Some of this deforestation resulted from man and his activities in landscape transformation. Perhaps some resulted from an increasing cooling and drying of the climate in the very late stages of the postglacial period. There still remains some uncertainty about this. What seems clear is that the post-Pleistocene environment of the middle Huang He Basin and subjacent North China Plain offered early humans a broadened range of environments in which to develop their culture. And it is these new environmental options and associated culture changes that will begin our story of the development of Chinese civilization.

Before we get to Chinese civilization, however, we may review briefly the development of humans through prehistory. According to Chang (1977), Chinese culture as we know it was not evident in archeological records until after some sedentary (nonmigratory) or quasisedentary farming villages were found in the post-Pleistocene Mesolithic period (approximately 8000–4000 B.C.). The basis for such a farming culture was set much earlier, however, in Pleistocene times, and these earlier cultures are called conventionally Paleolithic.[4] Although a number of Paleolithic culture sites have been found in China, details remain sketchy.

The best known of the Paleolithic discoveries was located in the 1920s in a cave not far from Peking at the village of Zhoukoudian, where a large number of human fossils (*Homo erectus pekinensis* or Peking man) and stone implements were found (Teilhard de Chardin, 1941). The presence of charcoal and cut logs indicated the use of fire, and the nature of all the materials together suggests an assemblage of considerable sophistication (Movius, 1944). Unfortunately the remains of Peking Man were lost during World War II in the course of a mysterious set of events that occurred at the same time as the surprise attack on Pearl Harbor. These remains

[4]For our purposes, the Paleolithic may generally be dated from 500,000 to 8,000 years before the Christian era, and indicates the earliest period of human prehistory. It coincides with a good part of the Pleistocene ice age.

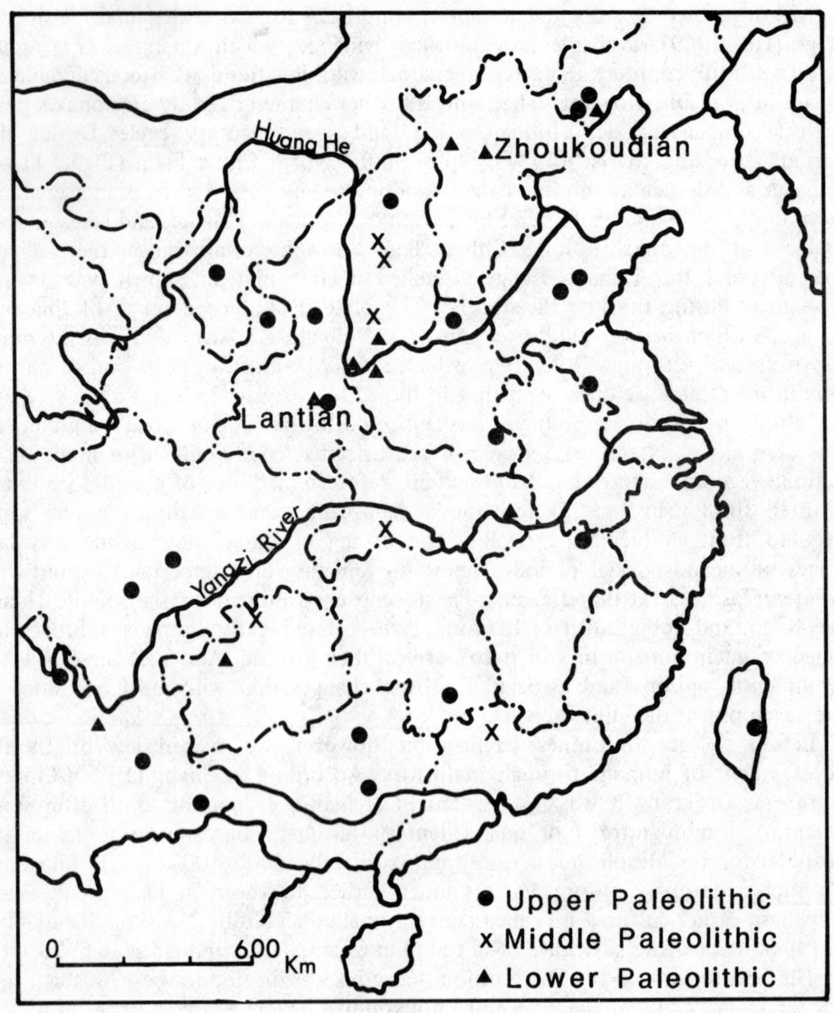

Fig. 3-2. Important Paleolithic sites in China.
Source: Chang (1977).

may have been lost in the sinking of a ship, but it is not certain. Whether or not they will ever be recovered remains to be determined.

Other important Paleolithic finds were discovered recently about 1,000 km southwest of Beijing in Shaanxi Province, not far from the city of Xi'an near the villages of Lantian and Kehe (Fig. 3-2). The Lantian remains indicated there existed individuals with somewhat smaller cranial capacity than at Zhoukoudian.

Stone implements and chopping tools were also found, but in general it appears that these groups were more primitive than the group at Zhoukoudian. According to Chang (1977), although evidence remains sketchy and significant differences are apparent, Zhoukoudian and Lantian hominid fossils may provide a significant link to Paleolithic remains discovered farther south, and may also indicate the possible existence of more extensive Paleolithic cultures than we know about at present.

Important distinctions have been noted among some of the Paleolithic sites, and two traditions have been identified as significant in differentiating the assemblages. One tradition is believed linked with groups associated with a primary hunting and fishing tradition only supplemented by gathering. This tradition, it has been posited, led toward the eventual domestication of animals as a culture stage and way of life. The other tradition was based more on food gathering supplemented by hunting and led logically toward cultivation and agriculture. Although such views are mainly speculative, as Chang (1977) pointed out, they suggested important possible aspects of regional diversity in the prehistoric landscapes of China, where an enormous range of ecological opportunity existed for varied adaptive living and behavioral patterns.

CHINA'S NEOLITHIC REVOLUTION

The human transition from gathering and hunting to the cultivation of plants and the domestication of animals has everywhere marked a turning point toward modernization (Childe, 1951). Domestication of plants and sedentary farming increased the reliability of a food supply and led to food surpluses which allowed the specialization of labor. Such specialization was crucial for human progress, and it permitted human groups to turn some of their energy and creativity into other activities. It was these activities which led to differentiation of social groups and the evolution of such artifacts as temples, engines of destruction and war, and cities.

The Neolithic age and the origins of agriculture in China are traced to a Chinese mythical figure and hero, Shen Nung, the putative inventor of agriculture (Chang, 1977). The importance of the legend appears to suggest that the Chinese in early historical times were aware of the developments of agriculture in prehistoric Neolithic times in China and to strengthen more the acceptance of the independent origins of Chinese agriculture.

Until the early 20th century, most scholars were convinced that China had not been the early site of an indigenous civilization based on the independent development of agriculture. It was believed that cultural diffusion from western Asia had brought agriculture comparatively late to north China. Since the 1940s, however, enough new archeological evidence has been assembled from north China to establish the independent origin of Chinese agrarian civilization in the region known as Zhongyuan (Central Plain) in the Central Huang He Basin of North China (Fig. 3-3). More recently, two other areas of China (southern coastal area of Taiwan, Fujian, Guangdong, and Guangxi and the Pacific coastal area

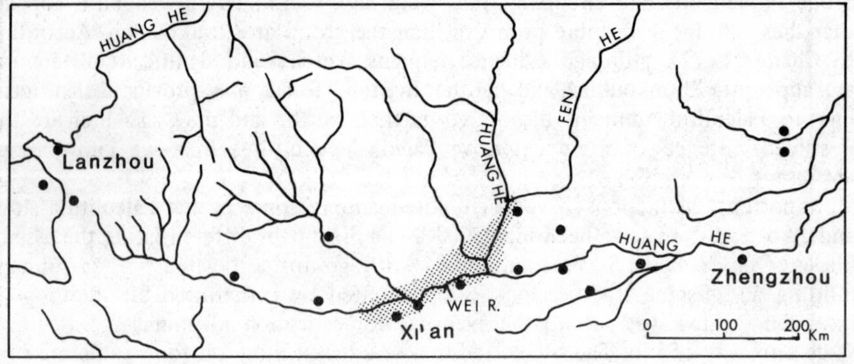

Fig. 3-3. Principal Yangshao and ancient Neolithic sites in the Middle Huang He Basin.
Source: Chang (1977).

stretching from Shandong south to Zhejiang) have been identified as the loci of the other early agrarian civilizations (Figs. 3-4 and 3-5). The prevailing view in Chinese archeology and prehistory is that the Neolithic farming revolution and culture developed in several regions of China roughly simultaneouly. What remains to be determined are the kinds of interrelationships and linkages which may have existed among the parallel groupings of Neolithic development in China (Chang, 1977).

Yangshao and Ancient Neolithic Culture

Of these three ancient Neolithic cultures in China, the best known is the Yangshao culture of the middle Huang He and Wei He Basins (the Zhongyuan regions). The Yangshao culture appeared, according to archeological records, by 5000 B.C., and may have existed considerably earlier (Fig. 3-3). The Yangshao culture of the Huang He sites has traditionally been regarded as the source of Chinese civilization. It was from this region that the first recorded dynasties sprang and grew, the apocryphal Xia (1994–1766 B.C.),[5] the Shang (1766–1122 B.C.), and the Zhou (1122–221 B.C.) (see Table 3-1). Thus it seems especially appropriate to discuss some of the details of the Yangshao culture.

[5]The apocryphal Xia Dynasty (ca. 1994–1766 B.C.) may have preceded the Shang Dynasty, but knowledge of the Xia is based primarily on ancient writings rather than archeological evidence.

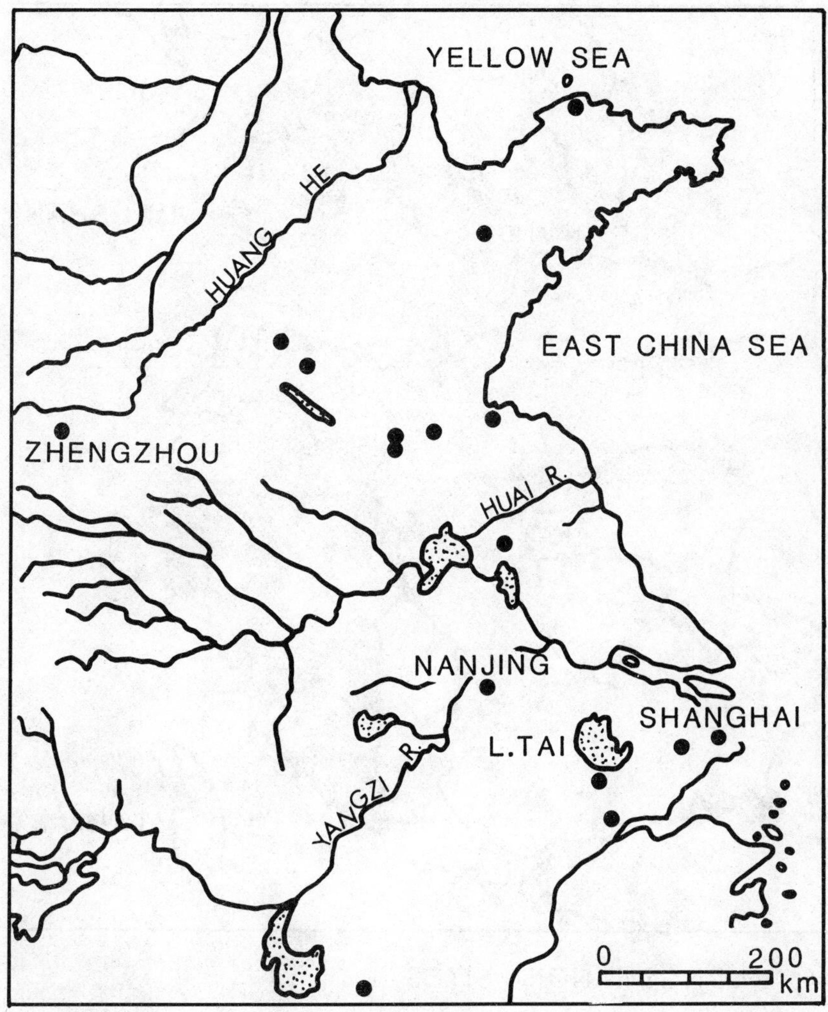

Fig. 3-4. Neolithic sites of the Pacific seaboard.
Source: Chang (1977).

First discovered by a local farmer near the village of Yangshao in northwestern Henan in 1920, the Neolithic implements symbolic of Yangshao culture were characterized by red pottery with black decoration (Andersson, 1934). Since then several hundred other sites have been discovered that extend from western Shandong along the Middle Huang He and its tributaries west of Gansu and Qinghai. The culture was characterized by sedentary farming and villages scattered along the

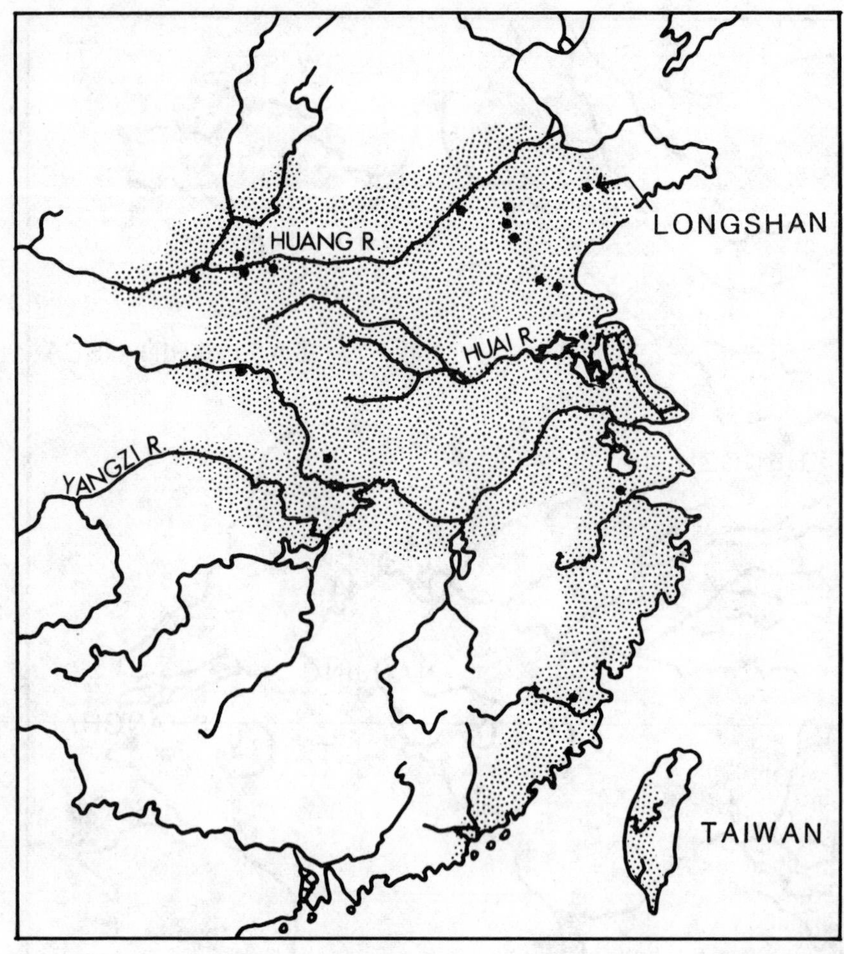

Fig. 3-5. Approximate distribution of Longshanoid cultures in early China. *Source:* Chang (1977).

loess terraces found in the river valleys of the drainage basin of the middle Huang He. The main crop of the Yangshao cultivators, according to Chang, was foxtail millet. Other millets have also been reported, but the evidence on them is scanty and not yet reliable.

A variety of stone tools and implements were employed, the most important of which were hoes, spades, digging sticks, and stone disks. Knives, axes, adzes,

Table 3-1. Chronologic Dynastic Table

Period or dynasty	Date
Yangshao Culture	ca. 5000 B.C.–3200 B.C. (?)
Longshanoid Culture	ca. 3200 B.C.–1850 B.C. (?)
Xia (mythological?)	ca. 1994–1766 B.C.
Shang	1766–1122 B.C.
Zhou	1122–221 B.C.
Qin	221–207 B.C.
Han	207 B.C.–220 A.D.
The Three Kingdoms	220 A.D.–280
The Southern Dynasties	280–589
The Northern Dynasties	386–581
Sui	581–618
Tang	618–907
The Five Dynasties	907–960
Liao (Khitan Tartars)	916–1125
Song	960–1279
Jin	1125–1234
Yuan (Mongols)	1279–1368
Ming	1368–1644
Qing (Manchus)	1644–1911
Republic	1912–1949 on the mainland; 1949–present on Taiwan
People's Republic	1949–

and chisels were also important as well as pottery jars of many different types and designs which were probably widely used for storing grain, a crucial function in times of agricultural surplus. The pottery was handmade. Domestic animals included the dog and pig, and there is clear evidence of silkworm cultivation and the crude development of the manufacture of fabrics.

Chang (1977) argued that the sedentary agriculture of Yangshao cultivators was supplemented by wild grain collecting, hunting, and fishing. There is substantial archeological evidence in support of his argument. More controversially, he claims that the Yangshao settlements were not permanent but were settled repetitively and discontinuously. He supports this idea by referring to a slash and burn style of cultivation reported by other scholars at the village of Banpo near modern Xi'an, Shaanxi Province. Chang adds that sequential layering of building structures on the same site indicates the repetitive occupancy. His views are not shared by some of his colleagues, however. The debate awaits additional new evidence.

Excavation of a few villages has yielded sufficient information to provide a brief sketch of village design. For example, the Banpo site was located on a terrace about 9 meters above the stream on a tributary of the Wei River. Oval shaped and enclosing approximately 50,000 m^2, the compound contained a cemetery, pottery kiln, a number of houses, animal pens, and storage pits. Houses were

Farm fields in the Wei River Basin of Zhongyuan (the Central Plain), the "Cradle of Chinese Civilization." These fields in the loessland of southern Shaanxi Province have been the scene of human activity for many thousands of years. In the background is the faint outline of the Qinling Shan. (*C. W. Pannell*)

generally small, subterranean, and made of mud and wattle construction. Longhouses were also constructed for communal living, but separate compartments were indicated.

The other important Neolithic sites discovered in China include the Pacific seaboard and Huai River Basin cultures, known respectively as the Qingliangang and the Dapenkeng cultures of central China (Fig. 3-4). At this point it is unknown as to what kind of ties existed among these three cultures, but it is clear that each had some independent origin generally traceable to the Paleolithic. The Chinese Neolithic is suggested by Chang to have extended from approximately 6000–3000 B.C., although the evolution would have varied from locale to locale. It was at the next stage of development, commencing at approximately 3200 B.C., that broadly common cultural types emerged. These types are termed conventionally Longshanoid and are the forerunners of true Chinese civilization.

Longshan and Longshanoid Cultures

The Neolithic archeology of China becomes increasingly complex as it approaches and blends into recorded Chinese historical civilization which began

Excavated Neolithic Longshanoid site at Banpo Village, Xi'an, Shaanxi Province. A dwelling unit with pottery remains is seen here at the excavation. (*C. W. Pannell*)

during the Shang Dynasty (1766–1122 B.C.). The painted pottery of Yangshao culture was replaced from about 3200 B.C. on by a black pottery assemblage (Longshanoid culture). Chang (1977) has noted the close linkages between the newer Longshan culture with features of the Shang period, specifically the symbolization on pottery, the oracle bones, and the construction techniques used in walled building. These assertions were based initially on archeological remains found near the town of Longshan in central Shandong in 1930 (Fig. 3-5). The discovery of these artifacts launched a debate over the chronology and the interrelationships between Yangshao and Longshan cultures, a debate which in fact continues as more and more archeological finds are uncovered and better data about these Neolithic cultures are made available.

First, a large number of Neolithic Longshan-type (termed Longshanoid) sites have subsequently been discovered over much of north and central China as well as southeastern China including Taiwan. The initial discoveries led scholars to speculate about the presence of two cultures, but additional studies of stratified sediments, as found for example in the Hougang sediments, indicated strongly that Longshan followed, indeed evolved out of Yangshao and itself was succeeded by Shang culture (Chang, 1977). Chang has worked out an evolutionary sequence to support his argument that the two cultures were successional (see Table 3-2). Chang's position has been supported in part by scholars in China. Although Chang

Table 3-2. Regional Grouping and Chronology of Selected Yangshao and Longshanoid Cultures

	Hubei	Shaanxi	Henan	Shandong N. Jiangsu	S. Jiangsu N. Zhejiang	Southeast coast
B.C.						
		Yangshao culture	Yangshao culture			Dapenkeng culture
4500						
	Yangshao culture			Qingliangang culture	Majiabang culture	
3200	Chujaling culture	Miaodiguo II culture	Miaodiguo II culture	Huating culture	Beiyinyangying culture	Fengbitou culture
2500						
	Longshan culture	Longshan culture	Longshan culture	Longshan culture	Liangchu culture	Tanshishan culture
1850						
	Shang Dynasty	W. Zhou Dynasty	Shang Dynasty	Shang Dynasty	Hushu culture	

Source: K. C. Chang (1977).

argued that Longshanoid culture was common throughout much of China, local scholars have accepted the evolutionary sequence only with reference to the Zhongyuan (Central Plain) area. Chang (1977) noted that many other scholars have not accepted his interpretation and schema.

Features of Longshanoid Cultures

Longshanoid culture assemblages have been located in Shandong, Shanxi, Shaanxi, and the lower reaches of the Huai and Yangzi Rivers as well as in several southeastern provinces (Fig. 3-5 and Table 3-2). Although these dates may vary generally, they share certain characteristics and features which have allowed labeling the typology of Longshanoid assemblages. Chang (1977) provided a good summary of these features, and a few of the most significant points shall be abstracted here.

First, all of these Longshanoid cultures were based on subsistence agriculture supplemented by varying degrees of hunting, fishing, and gathering. Evidence of rice cultivation has been found in areas of the central and southern regions, which are more suited environmentally to rice growing. This would seem to indicate that rice cultivation originated in southern China or perhaps farther south in Asia. Rice cultivation was not important in Yangshao culture sites; rather, Yangshao farming was based mainly on millet cultivation. Evidence of rice has

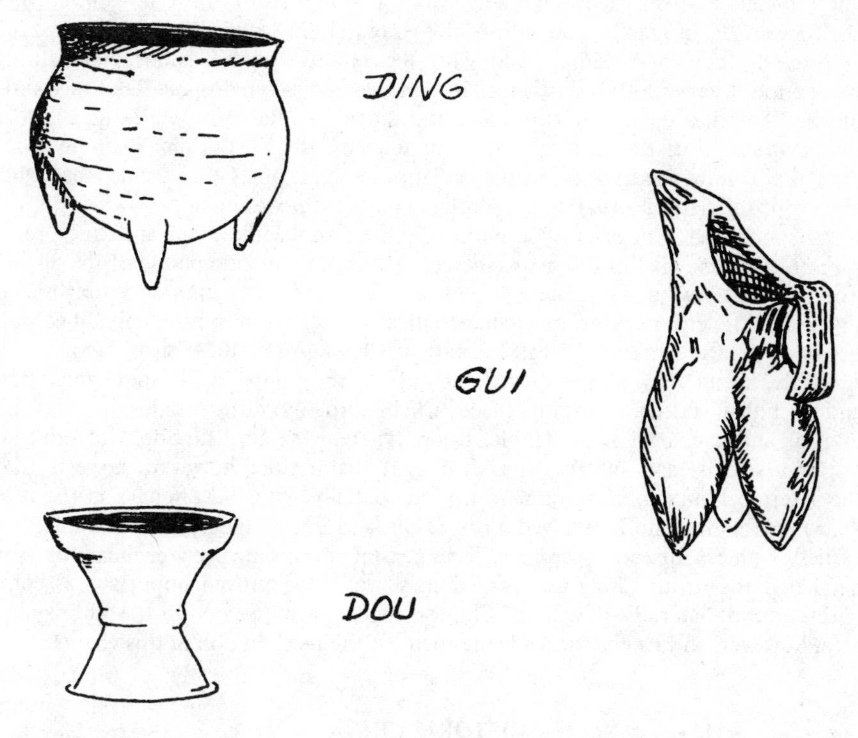

Fig. 3-6. Examples of Longshanoid pottery. (Drawings by *L. deB. Pannell.*)

been discovered in Yangshao sites, however, (Andersson, 1934; Ho, 1969, p. 61).

Second, all Longshanoid sites included distinctive types of stone implements useful for carpentry and advanced agricultural use. In addition, very distinctive pottery remains have been uncovered that included such forms as the *ding* or tripod vessel; the *dou*, a vessel with a distinctive ring foot design; and the *gui* or tripod jar with handles (Fig. 3-6). The potter's wheel, a device for fabricating pottery, is believed to have come into use in the latter phases of the earlier Longshanoid period.

Finally, Chang has asserted that the various Longshan-type cultures occupied distinctive and clear chronological niches that follow the Yangshao and blend into later Longshanoid assemblages. Thus the Longshan-type culture might have been more advanced at a specific time in one place or another, but a steady evolutionary chronology would have developed for each of the Longshanoid cultures. Added to this was Chang's belief that the cultures followed patterns, "determined by river valleys and seacoasts" (p. 171). Hsu (1981) has gone further and developed a graphic linear model to predict the advance of Longshan-type culture on the North China Plain with the buildup of the deltaic plain during the period after 5000 B.C. Hsu claims the ecological/environmental constraints of the estuarine environment limited the spread of the culture. He argues that the areal extent of the culture could proceed onto the North China Plain no faster than the Yellow River aggraded the estuarine delta, a point that seems reasonable in view of the natural situation and evolving physical environment.

In conclusion, Longshan-type cultures appear to be the main and true prototype for Chinese civilization as it emerged in the first historic period of the Shang. The occurrences of Longshanoid sites are frequent and common enough, and share a sufficient number of characteristics to indicate a substantial population occupied a large area of the eastern part of China. All of these signs suggest considerable interaction and exchange among these groups, with some migration and technical diffusion taking place. Chang broadly differentiates between an interior and a coastal Longshanoid group. There is some distinction in terms of pottery, vessels, and metals. The significant distinction, however, suggests that the interior Longshanoid group, identified spatially with the Zhongyuan (Central Plain), in all likelihood evolved into Shang and Zhou dynasty civilizations, the earliest Chinese historical periods. The coastal groups evolved civilizations that paralleled the north China groups and may well have proved important as competing groups later. The cradle of Chinese civilization appeared in the Zhongyuan area, however, and its emergence is the focus of the next section in this chapter.

HISTORIC CHINA

The transformation from a somewhat fragmented, partial farming existence to a formalized, clearly stratified social system with specialization of labor functions and an administratively dominant urban center, a capital city, apparently took place in China sometime between 3000 and 2000 B.C. The important mythical image, Shen Nung (lit., the Divine farmer), the founder of Chinese agriculture, has been mentioned. An even more significant figure in Chinese folklore is Huang Di, the fabled Xia Dynasty Yellow Emperor about whom the famous Chinese historian Sima Qian wrote in the *Shiji* (Records of History). Huang Di is claimed to have ascended to the throne in 2697 B.C. It is believed that he was the ultimate ancestor of all Chinese today. He is also credited with establishing codified rules of conduct and developing a military arm for enforcing his rule. Huang Di may be apocryphal, but the important thing here is that sometime during that era when he is believed to have ruled, ordered civilization based on socially stratified groups with specialization of labor activities and based in urban centers emerged out of the less formal late Neolithic culture assemblages. It is this transition that marked a great step forward in the cultural evolution of China. A legendary dynasty, the Xia (ca. 1994–1766 B.C.) has been discussed by historians, but no firm archeological evidence has been found to support its existence. Thus, until proper archeological evidence is discovered, the Xia must remain a legend. What is certain is the convergence of the legends and the archeology of prehistory that precede the first established Chinese dynasty, the Shang (Chang, 1977). At this point, evidentiary materials indicate that recorded Chinese history began ca 1800 B.C. with the appearance of divination records in the form of oracle bones.

Chang (1977) made an interesting point, however–that Shang-type civilization and the Shang dynasty are not exactly the same. The Shang dynasty (1766–1122 B.C.) (Table 3-1) was composed of an established set of rulers and their subjects occupying a definite territory (centered in Henan). This fact is supported by recognized written records. A civilization, with similar attributes to the Shang, occupied a much wider area of north China, and many sites with these attributes have been discovered. As Chang (1977) stated, "The Shang civilization definitely includes the civilization of the Shang dynasty but should not be restricted to it . . . The people sharing the Shang civilization are the Chinese people . . . " (p. 218).

Chinese civilization emerged in full from the Shang dynasty. Perhaps nowhere were the strength and beauty of the civilization and culture more obvious than in the urban capitals, the seats of authority, power, art, and economy. The great Shang capitals were not only loci of the most advanced activities; the cities, as Wheatley (1971) has well demonstrated, were physical artifacts, reflections of the vigor and progress in the society. The establishment and construction of cities are clear indications of cultural advancement and progress.

A number of Shang urban centers have been found, but three major sites stand out. Two are along the Yellow River in southern Henan, and the third, Anyang, is north of the Yellow River in northern Henan Province (Fig. 3-7). The oldest site is near Yanshi, which contains a palace foundation, and is believed to be the site of the first Shang capital. This is thought to be the oldest palace site known in China (Chang, 1977). A somewhat larger and more impressive walled city, rectangular in shape and enclosing an area of 3.2 km^2, has been found east of Ershi near the present city of Zhengzhou. Artifacts found indicated good quality bronze makings with numerous vessels, fine pottery, oracle bones with written records and solid construction based on *hangtu* (rammed or pounded earth) techniques, characteristic of the Shang period.

The most important Shang capital, and the site of what is believed the last three centuries of Shang rulers, was along the banks of a river near the present city of Anyang. Discoveries in the vicinity have provided the written evidence that corroborated the existence of Shang and indeed provided a record of its tenure. Thus, the importance of Anyang in Chinese history and archeology is unmatched. Palaces, burial grounds, bronze metallurgy founderies, pottery kilns, and bone carving chips, all attest the high degree of specialized activities and functions going on at the Anyang site. The nature of construction techniques also suggested a far more impressive kind of settlement than the characteristic subterranean structures. Large storage areas for grain and evidence of human sacrificial activity suggest the presence of an important ceremonial center associated with an administrative/religious capital.

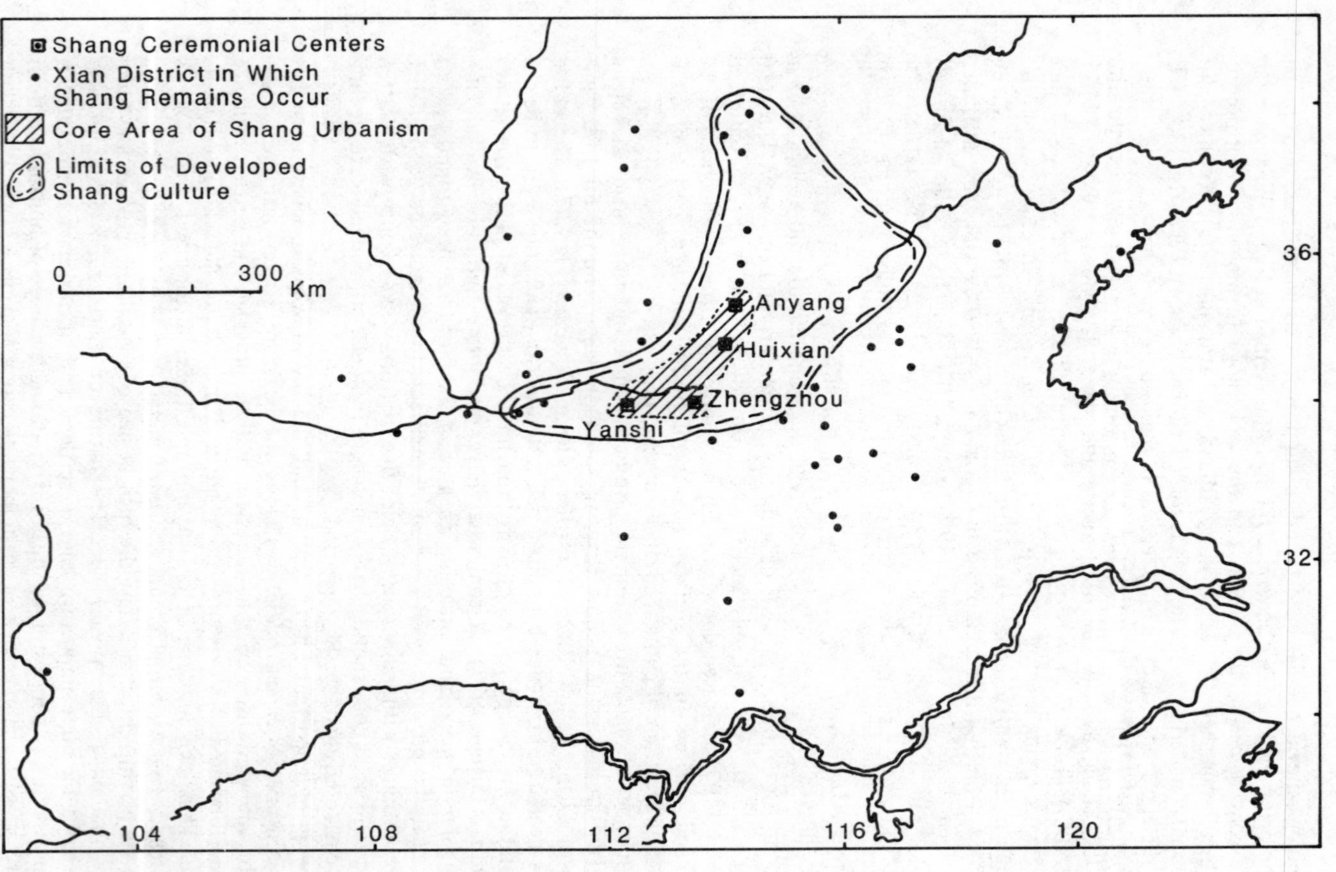

Fig. 3-7. Centers of Shang civilization.
Source: Wheatley (1971); Chang (1977).

ORIGIN OF CHINESE CITIES

One of the most interesting aspects of Shang civilization is the appearance of clusters of people or settlements that functioned as cities. Wheatley (1971) and others have argued that in China, as in the ancient Middle East, in the Indus River Basin and in the Meso America, was the site of an early and independently developed urban civilization. The evidence from the Shang civilization would support this contention strongly. The nature of Shang urban capitals was focused around a series of closely related settlements with each providing some special service or activity (Chang, 1977). For example, the center of such a set of villages was typically occupied by the imperial family and nobles. Around this center would be clustered industrial villages and housing craftsmen to serve the needs of the aristocracy and farm villages. Goods and people apparently circulated easily among these settlements with the administrative center overseeing the assembly and distribution of goods. Chang (1977) noted that although the Shang capitals were considerably smaller and had fewer people than the great ancient capitals, such as Ur in the Middle East, Mohenjo-Daro in the Indus Valley, and Teotihuacan in Mexico, all of the essential urban functions and the basic attributes of urban civilization as a culture stage were present.

The Shang states eventually fought among themselves and were weakened to

Zhou Dynasty guardian lion seen at museum in Xi'an, exemplary of the high development of the arts during China's classical period. (*C. W. Pannell*)

the point that a rival group established hegemony over the Shang dominion and areas farther south. This new power, the Zhou, had its capital located at the present city of Xi'an along the Wei River, an important tributary of the middle Huang He. Although the central authority of the Zhou began to break down and become diffused, in its middle and later periods, this was a classical age for Chinese literature, thought, and the arts.

Many of China's greatest classical thinkers and philosophers, such as Confucius, Mencius, and Laozi (Lao-tze), lived during this age. In addition to progress in the arts and literature, this period also witnessed great advances in technology; advances in the manufacture of iron tools, implements and weapons; and the further consolidation of institutions and traditions that came to be distinctively Chinese. Agriculture became sedentary and more intensive after 700 B.C. and the semisedentary and migratory farming of late Neolithic and Shang times ceased in the settled areas (Elvin, 1973). Manuring, fallowing, and careful attention to land management as part of farming came into common use.

THE CHINESE LANGUAGE[6]

Indispensable to an understanding of China's recorded history and development is a knowledge of the nature and working of the Chinese language. The Chinese language differs from European languages in several significant ways. First, the Chinese language does not employ an alphabet, but relies on the use of Chinese characters or ideographs (picture symbols) that have been developed over a very long period to depict objects, actions, and ideas. Each character is unique and is composed of pen or brush strokes. Some of the characters have a large number of strokes and are very complex.

Spoken Chinese is composed of many dialects, the largest of which is Mandarin or standard northern Chinese. The spoken language in some ways is simple in that verbs have no conjugations and nouns no declensions. Sentence structure is uncomplicated, and tense is usually determined by context or the use of simple suffixes. Written Chinese has been in use for at least 3,500 years, and this makes it the oldest written language continuously in use up to the present. As we shall explain later, the use of written Chinese has been very important in maintaining a spatially homogenous culture in the Middle Kingdom.

Origin and Development of Written Chinese

Although the exact origins of Chinese writing remain uncertain, the oldest use of Chinese character writing has been found on ancient cattle bones and tortoise shells. These ancient inscriptions concerned mainly political and ceremonial events or natural conditions, and they are called oracle bones. First discovered

[6]This discussion on the Chinese language, although it covers material that is general knowledge, is based in part on Wang (1973).

in traditional Chinese herb stores in the 19th century, more than 100,000 pieces of oracle bones have been discovered (Fig. 3-8), and 2,000–3,000 different characters have been identified, about half of which have been translated and relate to characters still in use.

Chinese characters can be examined in terms of their structure. Most basic is the stroke, of which there are about 20 types. Each character is composed of one or more strokes that are determined by the pen leaving the paper in writing the character. Each character always has a radical, that part or all of the character which usually holds the key to the meaning of the character. Traditionally there have been 214 radicals, and Chinese dictionaries typically are arranged according to radicals and the number of pen strokes in the character.

Some radicals are characters as well; for example 日 (ri) is the character for sun and day, and 山 (shan) is the character for mountain; both are also radicals and are frequently used in combinations with other characters to form new characters with a meaning related to the radical. For example, 星 (pronounced "xing") means star, whereas 峡 (pronounced "xia") refers to a ravine or gorge. Sometimes the other part of the character may contain the key to the pronunciation of the character and is then called the phonetic; but this is not always the case, and there are no rules to know when the phonetic is indicated and when it is not.

New characters have been added to the language ever since the language came into use, and today there are many tens of thousands of characters. In order to increase the ease of learning how to read and write, in 1956 the Chinese government simplified the writing of a number of characters in common usage. It is much easier to learn these, and literacy has increased rapidly. Another innovation aimed at simplifying the language has been the introduction of a standardized spelling system (*pinyin*) based on the Latin alphabet. This system, also introduced in the 1950s, is designed as an aid in the pronunciation of the Chinese character and is especially useful where the phonetics in the characters are inappropriate. *Pinyin* has been widely adopted as a means of romanizing Chinese outside China, and is employed as the romanization system in this text.

Spoken Chinese

China has many different dialects, and all sound to the Western ear somewhat melodic or "singsong." The reason for this is that China's languages are tonal in nature, and words with the same sound but rendered in different tones have different meanings. The numerous and various dialects, moreover, are generally unintelligible to each other. The dialect known in the West as Mandarin is spoken by the largest number of people. This dialect, also known as *putonghua* (common speech), is the language of north China and is found in its standard, pristine form in and around the city of Peking. Mandarin and several closely associated southern Mandarins are spoken throughout most of north and central China. Other major dialectical groups are found in the east and south (see Fig. 3-9). Among these dialects, Cantonese and southern Min are especially significant for overseas Chinese. It was from these areas in southern China that most of the Chinese have emigrated

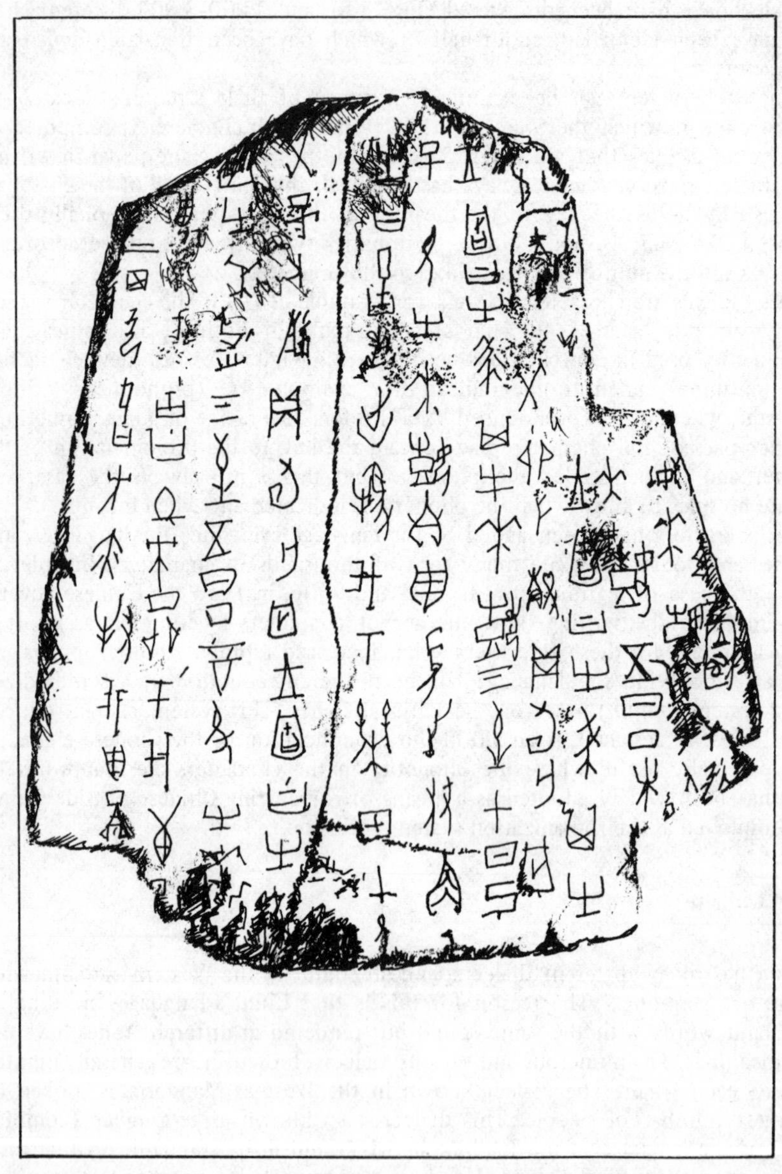

Fig. 3-8. Sketch of ancient inscription on oracle bone, the early writing of Chinese civilization. (Drawing by *L. deB. Pannell.*)

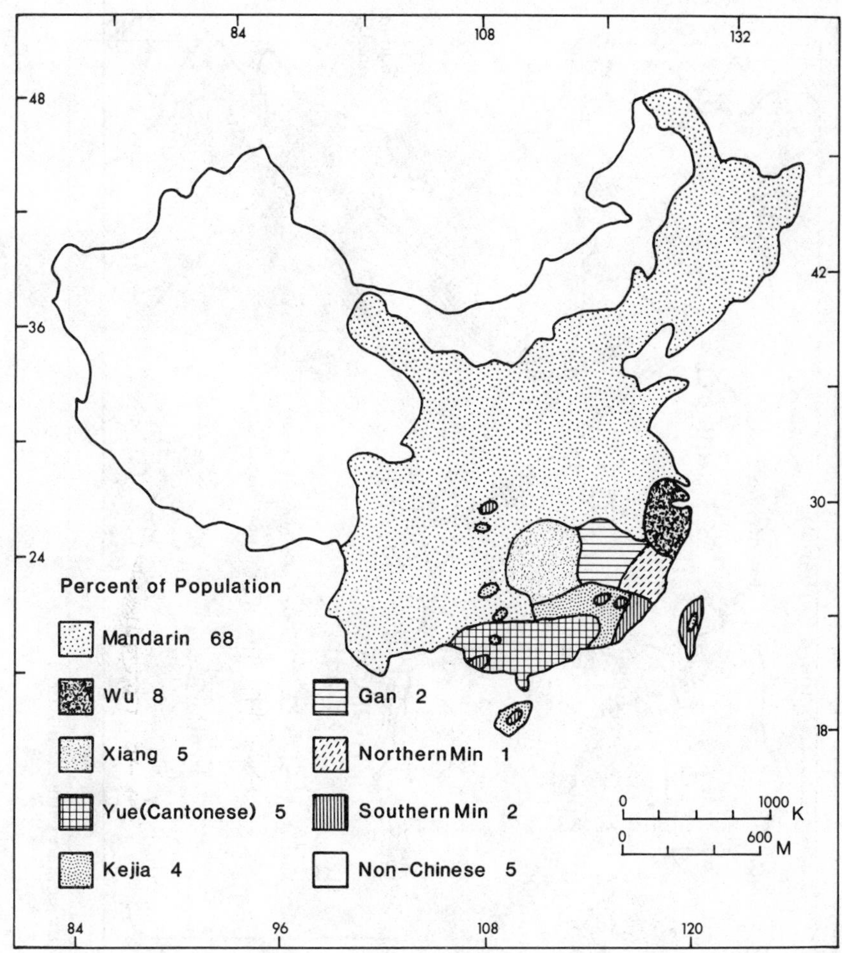

Fig. 3-9. Major dialects of the Chinese language.
Source: Wang (1973).

since the 19th century. Today all Chinese are required to learn Mandarin, and it has become the official spoken language for all the people of China.

The written language of China, based on character symbols, has served for 3,500 years as a powerful ingredient in the Chinese cultural system. The written language has enabled the Chinese to communicate among themselves despite strong dialectical differences. Many of the complex characters have been simplified, and the simplification has facilitated mass literacy and ease of communication among all Chinese. The written language has always played an important, perhaps a key role in integrating the Chinese people.

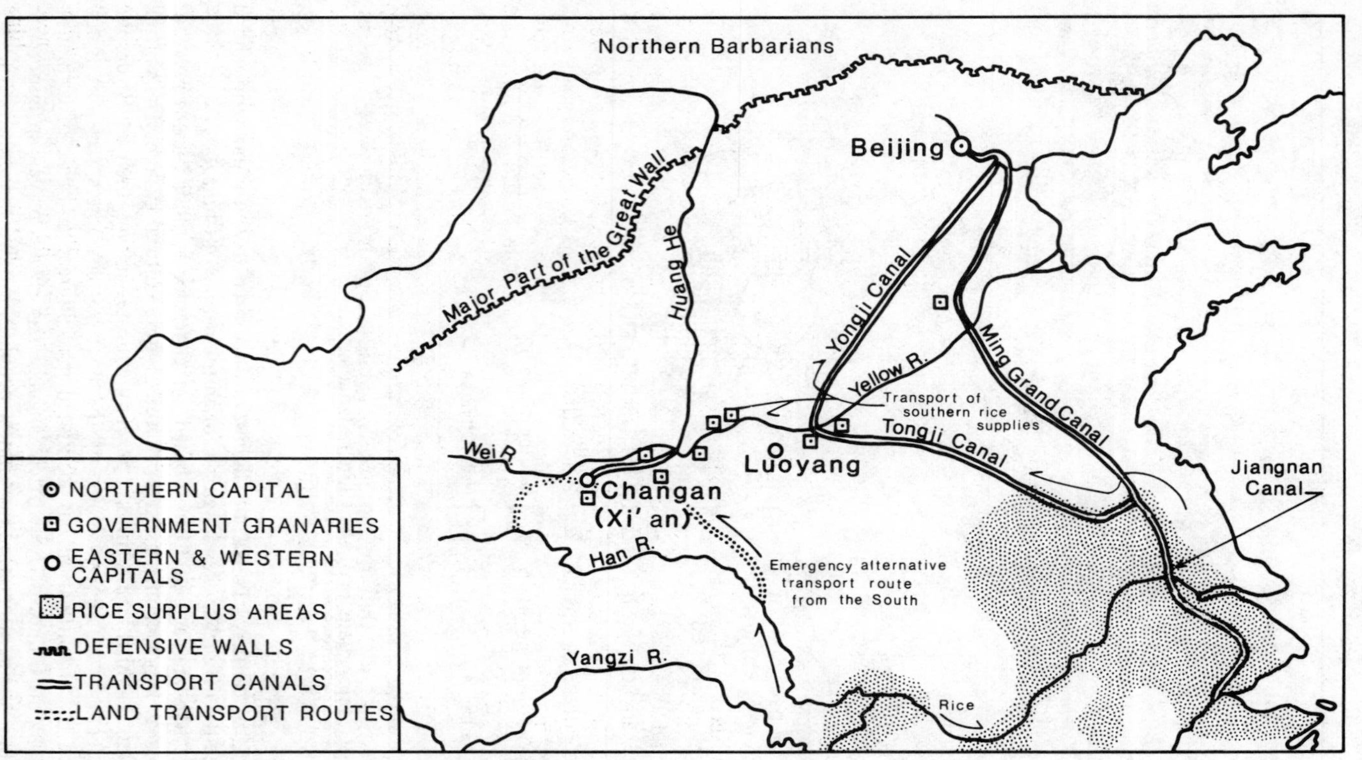

Fig. 3-10. Some major construction projects in Chinese history.
Source: Elvin (1973).

IMPERIAL CHINA

The divisions among competing states in the 3rd century B.C. eventually led to the dissolution of the power of remaining Zhou rulers and the emergence of a new and powerful state, Qin, which through superior military effort was able to consolidate power over the competing dominions and unite the country in 221 B.C. The ruler of this new state, Qin Shihuangdi (literally, the First Emperor of the Qin), after subduing his foes, established China as a great empire. The imperial dynastic-based system that he established lasted without basic changes until 1911, when a republican form of government was established. The system, begun by Qin Shihuangdi more than two millenia ago, provides an astonishing and unmatched record of political tenure.

Qin Shihuangdi introduced all kinds of rules for governing China which included a civil administration and the division of the country into a number of spatial units of administration (Hsiao, 1960). Weights and measures and axle lengths of carts were standardized. Chinese writing was likewise made uniform, and a great effort was expanded to unify the country and to promote administrative integration and centralization. A number of major projects were initiated, among the most significant of which was to connect the various segments of China's wall that had been built by various states during the Zhou period.

Ecological Accomplishments of Qin Shihuangdi

The Great Wall, as Lattimore (1937) and others have noted, was an attempt to stabilize an ecological boundary between a zone of sedentary agriculturists, the Chinese, and a zone of pastoral herders, the Xiongnu located north and west. The wall created a sharp and clear buffer that separated the Chinese farmers from the pastoral nomads. The wall was also a symbolic boundary between the "civilized" Middle Kingdom in the more humid south and the "barbaric" regions in the arid and semiarid north and west. Tregear (1980) indicates the 375 mm isohyet (line of equal rainfall) was the dividing line for the wall to follow, but that is an approximation only. Such a rainfall line is likely to be an extrapolated average, for its location may migrate dramatically from year to year. Moreover, the areas on both sides of the wall are ecologically unstable. Sedentary farmers might attempt to extend the range of their farming in good, moist years, especially if the population were growing and additional pressure were exerted on their space. Conversely, the horse nomads might have ranged farther south in especially dry years as they sought new grazing areas for their herds, which might have been threatened by dry and poor weather (Fig. 3-10).

Canal building was another aspect of the reign of Qin Shihuangdi, and more than one region was involved. In south China, a short canal was constructed in Guangxi. The canal linked the drainage system of the Yangzi and central China with tributaries of the Xi River in south China. In this way central and south China were integrated better for both administrative and economic purposes, and the southern territories were cemented further into the polity of the Chinese imperium. Other canals and drainage systems had been constructed in north China

Carved stele or frieze depicting scenes from early Chinese agriculture. Han period frieze. (*C. W. Pannell*)

and in Sichuan for irrigation purposes, and these canals and waterworks have become famous for their efficacy in promoting more reliable crop outputs, as well as in helping to regulate the flow and usage of water. In that way, the canals contributed to better water management and flood control.

Qin Shihuangdi died in 210 B.C., and the collapse of his authoritarian regime followed soon thereafter, but the tradition of imperial dynasties was sufficiently well established and effective to continue. The next dynasty, the Han (207 B.C.-220 A.D.) was established after a period of instability and fighting. The Han emperor reestablished some aspects of the feudal land ownership system. But the growing power of landed nobles led to a forced policy of subdividing land among all surviving sons. The policy created division of land into ever increasing smaller holdings, with consequences that continued right up to the 20th century. These consequences shall be discussed later in the chapter on agriculture.

The dynastic and imperial systems initiated by Qin Shihuangdi and consolidated during the expansive period of the Han dynasty continued for 20 centuries. Much of the administrative apparatus set up originally continued, although modifications were designed to promote better control and insure appropriate center management and direction of the peripheral areas.

Growth and Change in the Context of the Dynastic System

The political and administrative traditions of China, established early, were sufficiently vigorous and effective to achieve permanency for two millenia. At this point, we shall shift our discussion to more recent events that chronicle the rapid change that led to the breakdown of the *ancien regime* (the old system) and its replacement and the beginnings of the modernization of China. This should not be interpreted to mean that no change occurred in China for 2,000 years. Indeed it is clear that there were periods of rather decisive change and progress. For example, the period 581–907 A.D. (the Sui and Tang periods) was a time during which government sought to equalize income by equalizing land holdings through confiscation and redistribution. More successfully, the government oversaw the construction of a major integrated canal that ran from the lower Yangzi delta region and Hangzhou, north across the Yellow River to the Huai River, to the Tang capital of Changan (today's Xi'an), and to the vicinity of today's Tianjin, the center of political power (Fig. 3-10). This canal had two critical functions. It illustrated the power of the central government in the north to command grain shipments from the productive, rice surplus areas of central China, and it served a commercial function in fostering the exchange of commodities and monies between the two most important regions of China.

Another important example of progress and change in dynastic China occurred during the Song Period (960–1279), for it was in this period that farming and commercial life intensified and became more productive. In China, and especially south China, farm output increased greatly. Several factors accounted for this, but probably most important were the widespread use of the early-ripening rice at the beginning of the 11th century and the improvements in the cultivation and irrigation of wet rice. Leveling and smoothing land for paddy fields; constructing dams, bunds, canals, sluiceways; and developing pumping devices to control the application of water to the fields were examples of improvements. These things required enormous expenditures of human labor, but the result was a significant increase in output and a greater dependability for steady output year in and year out. China had the human labor, and it now began to systematize the processes of cultivation and knowledge about agriculture. Books and treatises on farming, better marketing and distribution systems available through the extensive canal network, and improvements in agricultural technology and water transportation meant that farmers had a greater opportunity to make money on grain sales and an enhanced incentive to produce more.

Elvin (1973) argued that the far-reaching changes in farming, which occurred between the 8th and 12th centuries in China, resulted from four causes:

(1) Better preparation of soil as a result of new knowledge; better tools; more extensive use of manure including nightsoil, mud, and lime; and better cultivation practices.
(2) Introduction of improved seed strains to provide higher yields and withstand drought, and the spread of double cropping as a common agricultural practice in China.
(3) New and improved techniques of water management and irrigation techniques.
(4) Increased commercial activity of the period led to greater opportunities for specialization in crops other than food grains, and thus a more efficient exploitation of the differences in resource endowments.

The consequence of all of these changes was, according to Elvin (1973), to give China the most sophisticated agricultural system in the world by the 13th century. Perhaps most importantly, a revolution in agriculture of this dimension with its potential for a vast increase in output laid the foundation for a great increase in population. Although population in the 13th and 14th centuries may have declined, for specific reasons such as political events and epidemic disease, population growth was set in motion. The large population in China today is in good part based on the agricultural innovations and developments that took place initially in China between the 8th and 12th centuries.

Interpretive Views on the Growth and Development of China

The history, and by extension the historical geography of China, have traditionally and frequently been interpreted as a series of cycles focused around the rise and decline of dynasties. The key idea in such an interpretation is that leadership was powerful and effective in the early stages of a dynasty, and thus conditions of fiscal, economic, and bureaucratic management were good. The irrigation systems were kept in good repair; flood control projects were well maintained; and canals and waterways kept clear to promote an effective and low cost transport system. Over time, the quality of leadership declined. Court living became luxurious and costs rose. Fiscal management was impaired and deficits mounted. Finally, necessary public works and water management projects deteriorated, and the entire economic system began to break down. Eventually, social and political conditions reflected the economic problems. Conflict erupted, leading to the overturn of the dynasty and its replacement by a powerful and effective leader who established a new dynasty.

Such a conventional interpretation is appealing in its simplicity and common theme, and no doubt it was useful as a superficial means of analyzing and explaining the changing political leadership throughout China's long history. Yet, as Fairbank, Reischauer, and Craig (1973) reminded us, there is validity to the Chinese concept of dynastic cycles, but such a view is far from complete and obscures a series of significant changes underway from Shang times all the way through the dynastic period of Chinese history. Concerning the concept of the dynastic cycles, they assert the "development of Chinese civilization has been all but hidden behind this apparent circular motion in human affairs . . . " (Fairbank et al., 1973, p. 71). Despite the common threads of dynastic succession at more or less regular intervals throughout Chinese history, important economic, social, and technologic changes were occurring, such as the aforementioned improvements in agriculture.

Other views of social and economic change in China have been advanced. At least one of them is based on the economic geography of traditional China and the necessity for controlling politically the changing "key economic areas" as a means for the successful governance of the country (Chi, 1936). According to Chi's thesis, beginning with the Qin dynasty, "China entered a long period characterized by territorial expansion and a shifting of the economic focus, together with alterations of political control, but practically without change in either the character of society or its political superstructure." (Chi, 1936, p. 3). According to Chi's interpretation, this pattern continued to the middle of the 19th century. Thus the critical element in the growth and development of Chinese civilization, as it expanded southward from the Huang He Basin to the Yangzi, was the relative strength and degree to which the new territories were integrated economically and administratively into the entire system. The question of regional political and economic control was primarily a spatial or geographic issue. According to Chi (1936), the regional shifts in the political and economic center of gravity of the country and the lack of concomitant structural changes in society or economy provide an important key to the study of Chinese economic history.

The idea in such an analysis is to establish for any given period the locus and extent of the key economic regions (defined on the basis of their productivity and effective transport systems) and the administrative space involved in their control. An administration, which could control such key economic areas and could organize and command shipments of grain from such economic areas to political centers (such as the national capital) through an efficient and effective transportation system, could thus control the country (Fig. 3-10). The problem of central control at all levels of the administrative hierarchy was a problem of geography. It was imperative to establish an operating spatial economy and polity that could be organized effectively as it changed over time and could be directed from some central location. Chi has argued that such a pattern existed throughout traditional Chinese history. Indeed, the construction of the Grand Canal in Sui times was one very effective means of the central government, headquartered in northern China, to transfer surplus grain from the acquired territory of south China to the political control centers in the north. The local officials were charged in good part with seeing that such transfers were carried out. There were periods of history when definite quotas were established and levied on various areas. The extent to which these could be enforced was a good indication of the vigor and administrative capacity of the central regime, which in turn was a reflection of the stability of the times.

Although Chi presents his analytical framework as a schema for historical explanation of Chinese history to the beginning of the modern period (1842), it might be extended as a form of contemporary analysis as well. Skinner (1977) used a similar framework for discussing and analyzing China's "great macro regions." The issue of regions of greater and lesser economic productivity in China, moreover, continues, and the contemporary government in China is faced with some of the same issues of regional inequality as well as some new ones. For example, production quotas continue to be set at levels of administrative and spatial control (province, prefecture, county, commune, brigade, and team). The central government is in a strong position to promote regional transfers of wealth and capital, if it so chooses. Equally pressing are the aims to make living standards and economic opportunity equitable, goals to which China's government appears to have been committed ever since 1950. Such issues will be examined in succeeding chapters, but it is well to put them in the context of China's history and historical geography, and to illustrate just how vital and crucial such matters have been in the development of Chinese civilization.

Chinese History and Historical Geography from a Marxist Perspective

A final interpretation of China's history would be to depict the country from a Marxist perspective, and to see it as a series of shifts in society and political control over time and space. Simply stated, Marxist historians see the evolution of human history in a predictable and necessary sequence, beginning with primitive communism and followed by slavery, feudalism, capitalism, socialism, and, finally, communism. China's Marxist historians have placed the Chinese slavery period in pre-Han times, but have not reached any agreement as to when the stage of feudalism ended and capitalism began. There are indications that mercantilism and capitalism began to bud and grow in China, perhaps as early as the 11th century and certainly by the 16th or 17th centuries. With the onset of urban based, western style industrialization in the late 19th century, capitalism became a powerful force. Modernization and political insurrection became significant features in 19th century China and had become consuming forces by the 20th century. Success of the revolutionary ideal culminated in the 1949 Communist victory and liberation from the old social order. The specific chronological periods and dates outlined above may not be accepted by all scholars, including some Marxists, for there is disagreement among these scholars over the beginning of the stages of economic and social evolution in China. That such phases existed in the rough chronology outlined, however, seems to be acceptable to Marxist doctrine and is useful in extending the discussion into the next section, the modern period of Chinese development.

MODERN CHINA

The period of modern China began with the Treaty of Nanking which was concluded in 1842 to end the Opium War between China and Britain. Although it failed to regulate the trade in opium, it was the first of the so-called "unequal treaties." These treaties served to open up China to commercial exploitation by Western powers and resulted in significant geographic and economic consequences.

The treaties provided extraterritorial privileges to foreigners, thereby making the foreigners immune to local Chinese law and custom. The significance of these actions was so great that the date of the signing of the Treaty of Nanking has been commonly used as a benchmark for signaling the beginning of China's modern period.

Signs of internal weakness were already evident before the Opium War. The domestic uprisings of the 18th and early 19th century, such as the White Lotus Rebellion (1795-1804) and the Taiping Rebellion (1850-1864), attested the seriousness of problems. Perhaps the major impact of the Opium War and its denouement was to set in motion a series of events that were cataclysmic and led to an overturn of the whole political, social, and economic system. The old system was replaced first by a republic in 1911, and subsequently a Communist revolution succeeded to power in 1949. The Communist revolution has meant a new system of development and growth in the context of China's traditional territory, economy, and society. The new system is the subject of most of the remainder of this volume. This revolution did not simply spring up overnight, but required a century or more of breakdown, change, gestation, and sporadic eruption before it finally succeeded.

The new forces unleashed by the Treaty of Nanking upon China after 1842 were social and political on the one hand, a basic challenge to the old order, and economic and technologic on the other hand, a high aspiration for industrialization and modernization. These latter economic and technologic forces had important ecologic and spatial ramifications as well. In the 19th century, it was becoming obvious that the combination of the increasing population and the prevailing systems of farming and industrial development were unable to provide a good life and livelihood for all of the people. It had also become obvious that China, with its vast territory, suffered from inadequate surface transportation, and by the mid-19th century was a poorly integrated spatial system. Consequently, problems of administrative control of the national territory and economic growth were seriously hampered.

Treaty Ports and Western Intrusions in China

One of the significant spatial consequences of Western intrusions in China was the emergence of treaty ports. Westerners came to China through treaty ports, newly opened commercial enclaves along China's coasts and major rivers. The ports gave the foreigners special privileges and permitted them to trade and promote commerce. Initially, five ports were opened by the Treaty of Nanking in 1842. Eventually there were more than 100 such treaty ports. A whole new stratum of commercial and industrial centers had been added to the preexisting urban system of traditional and largely interior administrative and marketing central places (Murphey, 1974). New technologies for manufacturing and developing tools, instruments and weapons; new techniques for assembling, storing, processing, and distributing goods; and modern means of doing business and managing accounts and commercial affairs were among the many innovations introduced to China through the newly opened and rapidly growing treaty ports. No concensus

Masoleum and monument to Sun Yatsen, patriot and father of the Chinese revolution. The site is outside the city of Nanking, Jiangsu Province. (*C. W. Pannell*)

has been reached by modern scholars on the impact of these treaty ports on the indigenous economy. It seems clear that the ports had a profound psychological and cultural effect, for a group of compradores–a new class of Chinese entrepreneurs and middlemen–was created, and a whole new set of ideas and values entered China. These values would shake China to its very foundations before a new and revolutionary order gained control of the Middle Kingdom (Murphey, 1974).

One of the most significant consequences of the establishment of the treaty ports was the spatial reordering of centers of economic growth. Development spread in the eastern coastal periphery of China, where the treaty port cities attracted large numbers of industrial and service workers in addition to those who sought to improve their own position in the new economic system. The transport system of China began to reorient itself toward these new commercial centers, especially after the beginning of rail construction in the late 19th century. New regional and local foci of growth emerged, and the economic and political control mechanisms of the country gradually began to shift to incorporate these new forces and realities.

Social and political instability continued throughout the 19th century. The Taiping Rebellion (1850-1864) was one of China's greatest domestic upheavals. It signaled clearly the seriousness of China's internal problems and the challenge to the *ancien regime*. The last Qing dynasty rulers were unable to reform sufficiently to satisfy domestic forces, and other rebellions and movements followed. Finally, the last dynasty, the Qing, collapsed and a republic, based on the vaguely democratic principles of Dr. Sun Yat-sen, was declared. The Republic of China, established in 1911, was weak. A period of factionalism in which powerful regional warlords fought for territorial control, followed. Out of this confusion and instability two main currents emerged. In 1921, the Chinese Communist Party (CCP) was founded in Shanghai. During the early 1920s, the Nationalist Party or Guomindang, which had been founded earlier by Sun and his associates to guide the Republic, was reorganized with the help of Soviet advisers. The reorganization was along the authoritarian lines of the Soviet Communist Party. Shortly thereafter a new revolutionary army was created with Chiang Kai-shek as its head. He was also Commandant of the Whampoa Academy, the training center for military officers and political cadres. Sun died in early 1925, and Chiang Kai-shek took over the reins of power in the Nationalist Party and began to launch military campaigns to unite the country.

CHINA'S COMMUNIST REVOLUTION

The story of the rise and development of the CCP and its famous leaders has been told often, and the details need not be repeated here. It is sufficient to review briefly a few highlights and then to explore the significance and effect of China's Communist revolution, as an ideologically based movement, on the physical environment and spatial organization of the country. The CCP was initially an urban based movement that sought support from the urban proletariat. After a period of little success, some of its leaders sought to base power in rural areas and to focus attention on disenchanted peasant masses. The leading proponent of this rural based strategy was a Hunanese cadre with a peasant upbringing, Mao Zedong. Mao worked hard in his native Hunan province in central China to organize poor and middle-class peasants during the 1920s and early 1930s, and he achieved considerable success in establishing a sizable party membership. Indeed he and his cohorts became so successful at promoting a rural Communist base of support that power and control in the party shifted away from the urban cadres to him.

Eventually competition between the Nationalists and Communists erupted into open conflicts, and Chiang Kai-shek and his forces almost succeeded in eradicating the Communist forces in southern and central China. In 1934-35, Mao and his peasant forces managed to escape through a long and harrowing migration to an isolated area of northern Shaanxi Province, the epochal "Long March," where a remote base area was established with its headquarters in Yan'an and from which the Communist Party gradually expanded its support. The Sino-Japanese War and the Second World War provided the Communist Party with a new opportunity to grow, and these cataclysmic events were exploited very effectively by the Communists, who focused their efforts on the patriotic struggle against the Japanese invaders rather than dissipating their strength on their domestic antagonists, the Nationalists. Following the Second World War, the Communist Party and its military arm, the People's Liberation Army, had grown tremendously

Mao Zedong, late, founding member of the Chinese Communist Party and long-time party chairman and most important figure. The portrait was seen in Peking in 1977. (*C. W. Pannell*)

in north China. Efforts to mediate the political struggle between the Nationalist and Communist forces failed, and a civil war followed. The Communists, with their strength in the rural areas, were able to dominate that struggle and isolate the Nationalist forces easily and quickly in the north. Whole Nationalist armies surrendered with their supplies and equipment. By 1949, the Nationalists had fled the Mainland and set up a kind of exile, rump government in Taiwan.

In October 1, 1949, the People's Republic of China was established with Mao Zedong as its first chairman. This marked the end of a century of domestic turmoil, foreign intervention, and struggle. More than 2,000 years of the imperial dynastic system had been replaced by a truly revolutionary system, which was committed to changing China fundamentally and modernizing its society, economy, and politics. A strong, new central government with a firm and definite ideological foundation and position, supported by a powerful army and civil administrative apparatus, had taken over China. A new age had arrived. It would mean a fundamental transformation of the way in which people organized their activities and contributed to the well-being of the entire country.

What kind of changes have resulted from the establishment of a Communist system in China? What has Communism meant at the various levels of human organization, right down to the level of the individual peasant or worker? These are important questions. One of the goals of this geographic study of China is to seek at least partial answers to some of these questions concerning spatial organization and the way the Chinese deal with their environment as they do. For example, rural social and economic organizations have been profoundly affected by the formation of people's communes, production brigades, and production teams. These are basic units of functional as well as spatial organization that affect the very livelihood and way of life of individual peasants. These rural organizations have brought about a basic change in China. The new political system provides a mechanism whereby the authority and control of the central government affects the individual. This authority and control exert a profound influence on the way in which the individual behaves. The government influences interactions the individual has with authorities and organizations beyond the purely local institutions of family, village, and clan. Under Communism, the people have been more closely integrated into the political, social, and economic systems of the state than during any other period in Chinese history. This kind of much advanced social, economic, and political integration, expressed both functionally and spatially, may represent the most far-reaching change that Communism has brought to China. Such change at the level of the individual peasant suggests that the basic fabric of China's social and economic order has been affected and that Communism has been truly revolutionary in China.

LITERATURE CITED

Andersson, J. G., 1934, *Children of the Yellow Earth.* London: Kegan Paul, Trench, Trubner.

Chang, K. C., 1977, *The Archeology of Ancient China.* New Haven and London: Yale University Press (3rd ed.).

Chi, Chao-ting, 1936, *Key Economic Areas in Chinese History.* London: George Allen & Unwin.

Childe, V. Gordon, 1951, *Man Makes Himself.* New York: Mentor Books.

Elvin, Mark, 1973, *The Pattern of the Chinese Past.* Stanford: Stanford University Press.

Fairbank, John K., Reischauer, Edwin O., and Craig, Albert M., 1973, *East Asia: Tradition and Transformation.* Boston: Houghton Miflin & Co.

Ho, Ping-ti, 1969, "The Loess and the Origin of Chinese Agriculture." *American Historical Review,* Vol. 75, No. 1, pp. 1–36.

Ho, Ping-ti, 1975, *The Cradle of the East, An Inquiry into the Indigenous Origins of Techniques and Ideas of Neolithic and Early Historic China, 5000–1000 B.C.* Hong Kong: The Chinese University of Hong Kong Press.

Hsiao, Kung-chan, 1960, *Rural China, Imperial Control in the Nineteenth Century.* Seattle: University of Washington Press.

Hsu, Shin-yi, 1981, "The Ecology of Chinese Neolithic Cultural Expansion." *The China Geographer,* No. 11, pp. 1–26.

Lattimore, Owen, 1937, "Origins of the Great Wall of China: A Frontier Concept in Theory and Practice." *Geographical Review,* Vol. 27, No. 4.

Movius, Hallam L., 1944, *Early Man and Pleistocene Stratigraphy in Southern and Eastern Asia.* Papers of the Peabody Museum, No. 19, Harvard University.

Murphey, Rhoads, 1974, "The Treaty Ports and China's Modernization." In Mark Elvin and G. William Skinner, *The Chinese City Between Two Worlds.* Stanford: Stanford University Press, pp. 7–72.

Skinner, G. William, 1977, "Regional Urbanization in Nineteenth-Century China." In G. William Skinner (ed.), *The City in Late Imperial China.* Stanford: Stanford University Press, pp. 211–249.

Teilhard de Chardin, Pierre, 1941, *Early Man in China.* Beijing: Institut De Geo-Bilogie.

Ting, W. S., 1954, *Zhongguo dixing xue* (The Geomorphology of China), Vols. 1 and 2, Taibei.

Tregear, T. R., 1980, *China, A Geographical Survey.* New York: John Wiley & Sons.

Wang, William S. Y., 1973, "The Chinese Language." *The Scientific American*, Vol. 228, No. 2, pp. 50–60.

Wheatley, Paul, 1971, *The Pivot of the Four Quarters, A Preliminary Enquiry into the Origins and Character of the Ancient Chinese City.* Chicago: Aldine.

Chapter 4

Political Geography

One of the basic requirements of any political system is the organization of its territory for the most effective and efficient operation of governance. The functions of government and the control and support of the population must be managed effectively if the state is to rule as a credible and legitimate institution. The state must incorporate the territory of the country in a manner which allows that territory to contribute to the national well-being in an economic and political manner (Whitney, 1970).

In China, traditionally, the main goal of the imperial authority was to establish central control, for the task of organizing the large population and territory was gargantuan indeed. As Hsiao (1960) noted:

> the solution as it was worked out in China during the successive dynasties from Ch'in [Qin] to Ch'ing [Qing] consisted essentially in the development of an administrative apparatus which helped the emperors to assure obedience and forestall rebellion, partly by ministering to the basic material needs of the subjects so that few of them would be driven by unbearable hardships "to tread the dangerous path," partly by inculcating in their minds carefully chosen precepts (mostly from doctrines of the Confucian tradition) that tended to make them accept or acquiesce in the existing order, and partly by keeping constant surveillance over them so that "bad people" might be detected and dealt with in time (p. 3).

This type of administrative apparatus, supported by the army, permitted a dynasty to maintain control for long periods of time. Indeed, as we noted earlier, the basic system of control and governance lasted more than 2,000 years. The goal of this chapter is not to recount the historical method of administrative control, but rather to begin our discussion with a recognition of a significant change in that administrative system after 1949. Our specific goals are to describe the new administrative system and especially its territorial aspects; to explain and evaluate some of the functions of that system; and finally, to examine the nature of the system's organization of that territory not regarded as traditionally Chinese, e.g., the outlying associated territory peopled by China's ethnic minorities.

GEOGRAPHY OF ADMINISTRATION

Administrative Changes

The administrative framework of the People's Republic of China has undergone significant changes since 1949. Under the Nationalist rule, China consisted of 35 provinces (including Taiwan); 1 autonomous region (Nei Monggol, or Inner Mongolia); 1 territory (Xizang, or Tibet); 1 special district (Hainan Island); and 12 centrally governed municipalities. After 1949, major changes were effected.

First, the numbers of provinces and province-level cities decreased. In 1951, China reduced the number of provinces in the northeast (Manchuria) from nine to six, and again, in 1954, from six to three, the remaining provinces being Liaoning, Jilin, and Heilongjiang. During 1954–55, the provinces of Rehe, Suiyuan, and Chahaer were eliminated, with most of their territories transferred to Nei Monggol (Inner Mongolia) Autonomous Region. In the 1950s, too, the number of centrally governed cities was reduced from 12 to 3 (Fig. 4-1).

Second, autonomous geographic units in border areas inhabited by minority nationality groups were established. In addition to Nei Monggol Autonomous Region, established in 1947, four new province-level autonomous regions were created in the decade 1955–65. Xinjiang (Sinkiang) Province became Xinjiang Uygur Autonomous Region in 1955. In 1958, Guangxi Province was redesignated as Guangxi Zhuang Autonomous Region, and Ningxia (Ninghsia) Hui Autonomous Region was created. Finally, in 1965, Xizang Territory (Tibet) was changed to Xizang Autonomous Region (Fig. 4-1). Meanwhile, lower-order minority districts such as autonomous prefectures (*diqu*), counties (*xian*), leagues (*meng*),[7] and banners (*qi*)[8] were established as second- and third-order geographic areas. Minority peoples and area will be discussed in detail in the last section of this chapter.

Third, huge regional administrative units above the provincial level were created and then abolished. During the period from 1949 to 1954, when much of China's administrative power was decentralized, the country was divided into six Great

[7]The term *meng* or "league" refers to second-order administrative units in areas with Mongol populations. These are located in Inner Mongolia and northeast China.

[8]The term *qi* or "banner" refers to third-order administrative units in the same Mongol-populated areas.

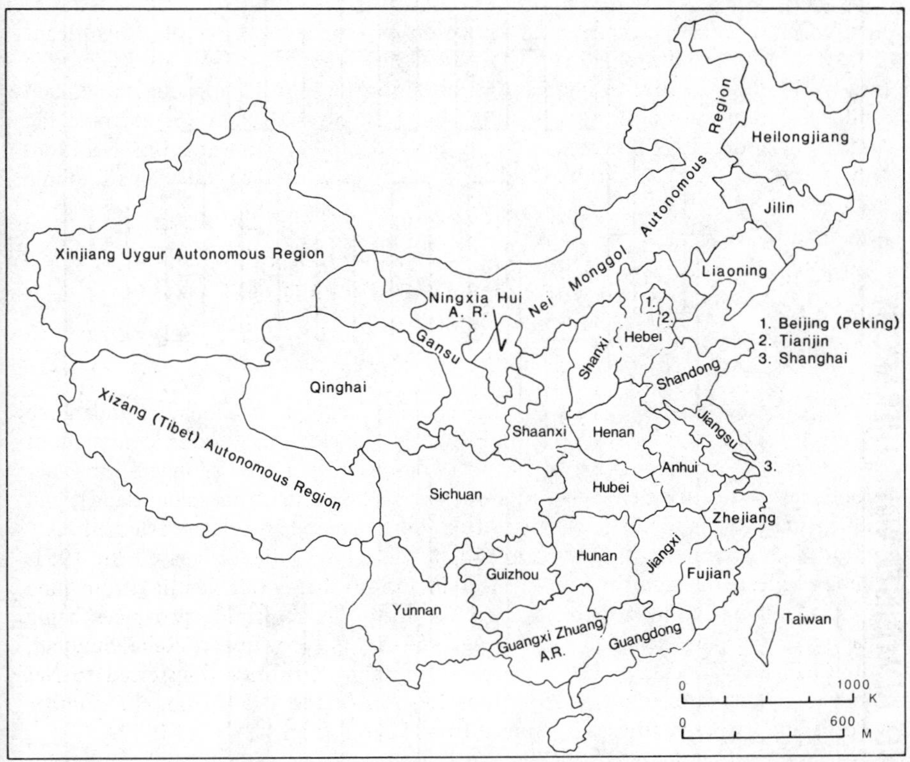

Fig. 4-1. First-order (provinces, autonomous regions, and municipalities) administrative units of China, 1981.

Administrative Areas, plus Nei Monggol Autonomous Region. Each area (except for Manchuria and north China) featured a Military and Administrative Committee, which served as the highest organ of political control in charge of several provinces. These regional authorities initially had considerable power and enjoyed a significant degree of autonomy. But, gradually, as the political power of the new regime was consolidated, Chinese leaders, perhaps motivated by the fear that the regional governments could become too powerful for the central government to control, began to increase the power of the central government. In November, 1952, the regional governments were stripped of most of their power. Two years later the entire structure above the provincial level was abolished.

Fourth, basic level administrative units have been established. The most revolutionary changes in China's administrative structure have occurred at the grass-roots levels. Prior to the revolution, the central government and the basic level administrative units below the county level were poorly integrated. Although there were administrative systems developed below the county level, such as the *baojia* and *lijia*

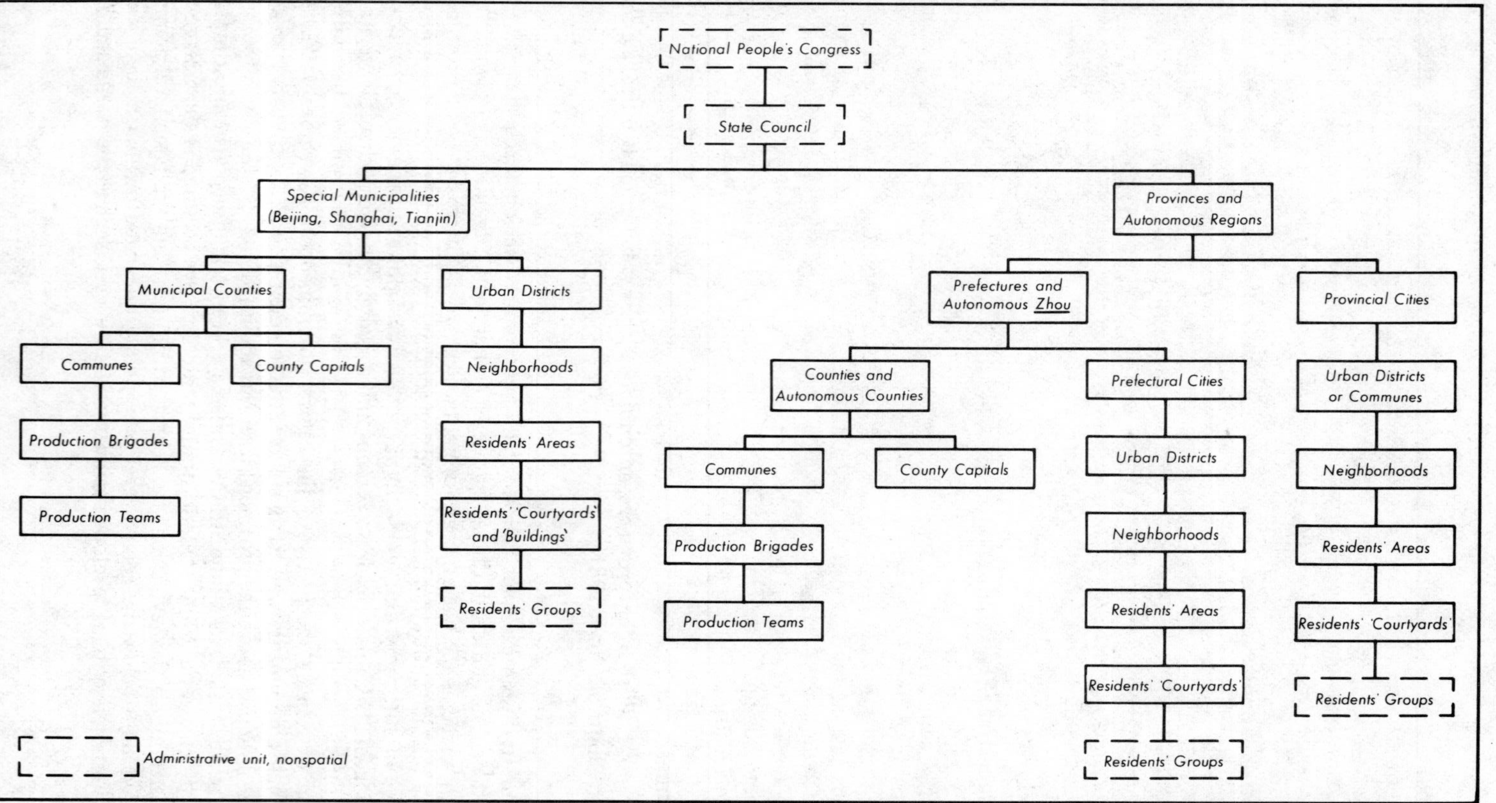

Fig. 4-2. China's spatial and administrative hierarchy, 1981.

systems, they were concerned chiefly with taxation, internal security, and corvée functions. Very little of the state's resources for economic development were allocated to villages, where most people lived, and there was virtually no systematic socioeconomic planning by the state for the masses at the village and urban neighborhood levels. Direct participation by the masses in the political and economic affairs of the state was hampered by a large administrative gap separating the central government from the villages. Members of the rural gentry class almost invariably dominated the affairs of the villages, often at the expense of peasant interests. All these fundamentally changed after the Communist revolution, and new basic level administrative units were designed which proved to be highly effective (Fig. 4-2). The entire administrative hierarchy is now tightly integrated. As a consequence, mass participation in, and state control of, political, social, and economic affairs of the country at the grass-roots levels have been much more efficient than before.

Administrative Hierarchy and its Spatial Expression

The administrative geography of China today continues to be organized along hierarchical lines (Figs. 4-1 and 4-2). Three main levels in the hierarchy account for the major organizational units in the system: Level 1–the provinces, autonomous regions, and special municipalities; Level 2–the prefectures, autonomous prefectures, and provincial cities; and Level 3–the counties, autonomous counties, and prefectural cities. The numbers of units at the various levels shift over time due to administrative changes; in 1973 there were 30 first-order units (if Taiwan is included), 389 second-order units, and 2,135 third-order units. Below this level are found smaller units of urban organization, such as county capitals, urban districts, neighborhoods, and residents' areas. The rural areas are further subdivided into communes, production brigades, and production teams. More details on all of these units in the hierarchy will be provided below.

The first-order units are all administered directly by the central government (Figs 4-1 and 4-2). The three municipalities are the capital city of Peking, Shanghai, and Tianjin (Tientsin). Greater Shanghai consists of 10 primarily rural counties plus the city proper, and in 1981 had a total population of about 12 million, of which 7.0 million lived in the city proper. The municipality of Peking contains nine counties. Peking in 1981 had a total population of 8.8 million, while Tianjin in 1980 had 7.4 million. The area under the jurisdiction of Tianjin doubled in 1973 when five rural counties were transferred from Hebei Province to the city. The expansion was undoubtedly a result of the increasingly important role played by the city as the largest commercial and industrial port in north China. As a consequence, Tianjin Municipality is now contiguous to Peking Municipality (Fig. 4-1).

Under the provinces and autonomous regions in 1973, there were 174 intermediate or second-order level units called prefectures (diqu); 178 provincial and prefectural cities, including all of the capital cities of the provinces and autonomous regions; 29 autonomous prefectures for various minority nationalities; 7 leagues for the Mongolian population in Inner Mongolia and the northeastern provinces;

and the administrative district of Hainan Island under Guangdong Province. Known as "Special Districts" before 1970, the prefectures are an intermediate-level administrative/spatial division between province and county. The prefectures are designed to coordinate the administration of several counties. It appears that the prefectures have become a permanent administrative/spatial unit.

Under the prefectures and the largest cities are counties, of which the total number had remained remarkably stable at approximately 2,000 for several centuries. Parallel to the 2,012 counties are 66 autonomous counties, 53 banners, and 3 autonomous banners in areas inhabited by the Mongols. The only county-level town (zhen) is Wanting in Yunnan Province. The town's unique status is perhaps related to its strategic location on the Burma border. It monitors and controls the traffic on the Burma Road.

Rural Administration

In rural areas, the commune was created in 1958 largely on the basis of the traditional *xiang* (an administrative village consisting of a number of natural villages). The commune is an important administrative, spatial, and economic unit. Currently there are roughly 50,000 communes in China, about 25,000 less than in the early 1960s. The average commune has about 3,300 households, 15,000 persons, and 2,000 hectares (close to 5,000 acres) of farmland. The commune is further divided into production brigades and production teams. In general, the brigade corresponds to a natural village and is the lowest administrative level where the CCP maintains an office. The average commune has about 15 brigades and 100 teams. On the average, a brigade has approximately 7 teams, 220 households, 980 persons, and cultivates 136 hectares (336 acres) of arable land. The production team is the basic rural accounting unit in China's planned economy. The average team has about 33 households, 145 persons, and cultivates 20 hectares (49 acres) of arable land. The sizes of the communes vary greatly in China. The communes tend to have a larger population, but not necessarily a larger area, in economically more advanced regions. Many suburban communes near large cities have twice as many people as rural communes. More details on the functions and operations of these rural administrative units are provided in Chapter 6 on Chinese agriculture. Important changes have occurred since 1978.

Before 1949, the basic service centers below the county level in the administrative hierarchy of the countryside were the *zhen* (towns), which almost invariably were centers of trade for the rural population rather than seats of administration. There were roughly 50,000 towns in 1953. It appears that during the period of communization after 1958, many towns were incorporated into communes, serving in many cases as commune headquarters as well as centers of collection and distribution of goods and services in rural areas.

Urban Administration

The built-up areas of most of the large and medium-sized cities are divided into urban districts, although some cities, such as Guilin, are spatially demarcated into urban communes. The urban district, governed by a district people's government, is divided into urban neighborhoods, created in 1954. A neighborhood is governed by a neighborhood office which directs the work of residents' committees that are immediately below the neighborhood. The neighborhood office is the basic organ of political power and the lowest level of government administration in the city.

The urban neighborhood is by no means a small spatial unit. Several tens of thousands of people usually reside in such a unit. The city of Peking has 85 neighborhoods, each with more than 50,000 residents (Luo, 1980). The Fengsheng Neighborhood in the Xicheng District of Peking, for example, has 14,136 families and 52,978 persons. Many neighborhoods are organized around workers' housing estates. For example, in Shanghai, which has 110 neighborhoods, the Caoyang Workers' Estate located in Putuo District is an urban neighborhood with a population of 72,000.

A neighborhood office has a director, a deputy director, and a number of office workers, all appointed by the People's Committee of the district above the office. The functions of the neighborhood office are to direct the work of residents' committees, implement Party policies, reflect the requests and opinions of the people to higher authorities, distribute ration coupons, organize study groups, mobilize the residents for housing and social work, and run neighborhood shops, restaurants, factories, schools, nurseries, clinics, and recreation facilities.

Although the neighborhood is the most basic official urban administrative unit, it is further subdivided into at least three levels of "mass organizations" in the large cities. Inasmuch as they affect deeply the daily life of the urban population but are little understood outside of China, their functions, structure, and activities are explained below in some detail.

The first such mass and partially autonomous organization under the neighborhood is the residents' committee, which was first established in 1954. According to the decree, the functions of the residents' committee are as follows (*Beijing ribao*, 1980):

1. Undertake public welfare for residents;
2. Reflect the views and demands of the residents to higher authorities;
3. Mobilize the residents to respond to the calls of the government, and to encourage the residents to obey laws;
4. Direct the work of public security that belongs to the people; and
5. Mediate disputes among residents.

In addition, the residents' committee has been involved in directing public health campaigns to improve the urban environment, in organizing social work, in actively promoting family planning and distributing contraceptives, and in making recommendations to housing authorities on housing allocation, especially for newlywed couples, and housing adjustments.

A neighborhood may contain a dozen or more "residents' areas," each governed by a residents' committee. The area of jurisdiction of a residents' committee is demarcated on the basis of the actual conditions of the place, with additional consideration given to the existing area of the public security office located there. Normally a residents' committee covers between 100 to 600 households, but in large cities some of them may have as many as 800 households. In Fengsheng Neighborhood, for example, each of the 25 residential areas takes in from 1 to 8 lanes with 400 to 800 households, and the neighborhood's Minkang Residents' Committee has jurisdiction over 466 households and 1,658 persons.

According to the 1954 decree, a residents' committee should have 7 to 17 members, each elected from a residents' group to serve a 1-year term. Members are subject to the approval of higher authorities. The committee may establish up to five permanent subcommittees to be responsible for such duties as, "social welfare, security, culture/education/health, medication, and women's work." Ad hoc committees may also be formed when needed. The operating budget of the committee, including the living expenses of committee members, is allocated mainly by the state. Expenses to be incurred for public welfare programs, however, may be collected from residents on a voluntary basis subject to the approval of higher offices. No other funds may be raised from the residents.

Under the residents' committee are second-order mass organizations known variously as "residents' courtyard," "sun-facing courtyard," "residents' building," and "sun-facing building," each having from one to several dozens of households. The first two names are commonly found in areas with one- or two-story houses, whereas the latter two are associated with multi-story buildings. In Peking at least, certain "courtyards" are run by a "courtyard management committee." For example, in the "courtyard" at No. 21, Nanxiao Street, Beixinqiao Neighborhood where 35 families and 145 persons reside, there is a management committee consisting of 4 industrial workers, 1 student, and 2 other representatives.

These mass organizations at the grass-roots levels appear to have been established mainly to organize and serve housewives, children, the retired, and students after school hours and during school vacation periods. They do not directly affect the working residents, who are generally organized in some way at their places of employment. A number of functions are performed at "courtyard" levels. Study and political sessions may be structured for adults to learn newly released government documents, to study recent political developments, and to criticize the "enemies of the people" as defined by the Party leadership. Evening shows may be put together by and for the residents. Efforts are made to organize sports teams and study groups for students, and to arrange reading, music, dancing, and story hours for small children. Because of their intimate relationship with the urban residents, the "courtyards" and "buildings" may be viewed as basic "cells" of the urban neighborhoods.

Finally, urban residents belong to a variety of "small residents' groups" for different purposes. A small group usually has between 8 and 15 members, chiefly a political unit rather than a geographic unit. The small group keeps the people at the lowest level of society in close contact with the government. The group leader has the power to bar residents from participating in certain group meetings if they are considered by the Party as socially and politically undesirable.

It appears that structured urban activities are carried out mainly above the level of the residents' committee. At the neighborhood level, urban administration

Table 4-1. Minority Nationalities of China, 1965 and 1978

Nationality	1965 population	1978 population	Area of concentration
1. Zhuang	7,780,000	12,000,000	W. Guangxi, E. Yunnan, SW Guangdong
2. Hui	3,930,000	6,400,000	Ningxia, S. Gansu
3. Uygurs	3,900,000	5,400,000 5,000,000 + (1979)[a]	Xinjiang (Sinkiang)
4. Yi	3,260,000	4,800,000	Sichuan, Yunnan
5. Zang (Tibetans)	2,770,000	3,400,000	Xizang (Tibet), Qinghai, Sichuan
6. Miao	2,680,000 4,000,000 (1976)[b]	3,900,000	Guizhou, Guangxi, Hunan, S. Yunnan
7. Manzhou (Manchus)	2,430,000	2,600,000	Liaoning, Jilin, Heilongjiang
8. Monggol (Mongols)	1,640,000	2,600,000	Nei Monggol, Qinghai
9. Buyi	1,310,000	1,700,000	SW Guizhou
10. Korean	1,250,000	1,600,000	SE Jilin
11. Tong	820,000 1,300,000 (1976)[c]	1,100,000	Border region of Hunan, Guizhou and Guangxi
12. Yao	740,000	1,200,000	Guangxi, N. Guangdong, S. Hunan
13. Bai	650,000	1,000,000	Dali and Jianzhou Counties of Yunnan
14. Tujia	630,000	770,000 590,000 (1978)[d]	NW Hunan, Hubei
15. Hani	540,000 780,000 (1971)[e]	960,000	S. Yunnan
16. Kazak	530,000	800,000	Xinjiang, Qinqhai
17. Tai (Dai)	503,000	760,000	W. Yunnan
18. Li	390,000	680,000	S. Hainan Island, Guangdong
19. Lisu	310,000	470,000	W. Yunnan
20. Wa	280,000	260,000	SW Yunnan
21. She	220,000	330,000	N. Fujian, Zhejiang
22. Gaoshan	200,000	300,000	Central Taiwan

Table 4-1. (Continued)

Nationality	1965 population	1978 population	Area of concentration
23. Lahu	180,000	270,000	SW Yunnan
24. Shui	160,000	230,000	SE Guizhou
	200,000 (1976)[f]		
25. Dongxiang	150,000	190,000	Linxia Co., S. Gansu
26. Naxi	150,000	230,000	N. Yunnan
	200,000 (1977)[g]		
27. Jingpo	100,000	80,000	W. Yunnan
28. Kirgiz	68,000	90,000	W. Xinjiang
29. Tu	63,000	120,000	Qinghai, Gansu
30. Daur	50,000	70,000	Central Heilongjiang, Nei Monggol
31. Molao	44,000	70,000	N. Guangxi
32. Qiang	42,000	80,000	NW Sichuan
		82,000 (1979)[h]	
33. Bulang	41,000	50,000	S. Yunnan
34. Sala	31,000	50,000	E. Qinghai, Gansu
35. Moanan	24,000	30,000	N. Guangxi
36. Gelao	23,000	20,000	W. Guizhou
37. Xibo	21,000	40,000	W. Xinjiang
38. Pumi	15,000	20,000	NW Yunnan
39. Tajiks	15,000	20,000	W. Xinjiang
40. Nu	13,000	10,000	NW Yunnan
41. Uzbeks	11,000	7,000	W. Xinjiang
42. Achang	10,000	10,000	W. Yunnan
43. Jinuo	10,000	10,000 (1980)[i]	S. Yunnan
44. Russians	9,700	600	W. Xinjiang

45. Ewenki	7,200	10,000 10,000 (1979)[j]	W. Heilongjiang, Xinjiang
46. Benglong	6,300 8,000 (1977)[e]	10,000	W. Yunnan
47. Baoan	5,500	6,000	S. Gansu
48. Yugu	4,600	8,000	Border of Gansu and Qinghai
49. Jing	4,400	5,000	N. Guangdong
50. Tartars	4,300	2,000	W. Xinjiang
51. Menba	3,800	4,000	S. Xizang
52. Dulong	2,700	4,000	NW Yunnan
53. Oroqen	2,400	3,000	N. Heilongjiang, Nei Monggol
54. Hezhe	600	800	Heilongjiang
55. Loba	—	300	Tibetan Autonomous Region
Total	38,035,500 (1965)	55,116,400 (1978)	

Source: 1965: *1965 Renmin shouce* (*1965 People's Handbook*).
Beijing Review, 1980.

[a] Ma (1979).
[b] *Dili zhishi* (1976a).
[c] Ibid.
[d] *China Reconstructs* (1978a).
[e] *China Reconstructs* (1978b).
[f] *Dili zhishi* (1976b).
[g] *Dili zhishi* (1977).
[h] Zhang (1979).
[i] Zhi (1980).
[j] Qi Ya (1979).

since 1979 has been directed by the director of the neighborhood office, who in turn reports to the mayor. It goes without saying that urban administration at all levels is dictated by the CCP. Once a decision is made by the Party, it is put into effect almost immediately through the various levels of the urban administration/spatial network.

A Retrospective View of China's Administrative Geography Under Communism

As was noted previously, the 20th century brought a fundamental change in the nature of China's political system with the overturn of the long-lived dynastic order. The Communist administration, which took over in 1949, focused especially on territorial organization and greatly strengthened the administration of territory at the local level. Among the most significant accomplishments of the Communist administration have been the extended control and involvement of local people at both urban neighborhood and commune levels in the affairs of economy and politics.

At the local level, not only does government control the people, but it receives contributions from its citizenry. These contributions are economic and fiscal on the one hand (goods, services, and taxes) and political on the other (the feedback and viewpoint of those who live under the government system). This idea of contribution and involvement is positive, while the concept of control has a more negative association. Both are no doubt necessary to effective governance in China. Yet the factor of involvement and contribution implemented today in China at the local level promises to be a new and worthwhile achievement, if, in fact, it is implemented as successfully as the Chinese tell us it is.

MINORITY NATIONALITIES

China is a state of many nationalities. Approximately 94% of China's total population are Hanren, meaning the Han people, an ethnic term which the Chinese have used since the Han dynasty (207 B.C.–A.D. 220) to distinguish themselves from the non-Han minority nationalities.

A nationality is defined in China as a group of people of common origin living in a common area, with a common language, and having a sense of group identity in economic and social organization and behavior. In 1965 there were approximately 40 million people classified as minorities who belong to 50 minority nationalities (Table 4-1) (Dreyer, 1976). By 1978 this had increased to 55 million. Ten minorities have a population of more than 1 million each. Although China's minorities constitute only about 6% of the national total population, they inhabit about 60% of the nation's territory. Although none of them is economically more advanced than the Chinese majority, their significance is far greater than their numbers would indicate. They receive much attention from the Chinese government, which has pointed out on numerous occasions that the minorities are not only politically equal to the Han majority, but also deserve preferential treatment because of their small populations and less developed economic situations. Efforts have been made by the central government to ensure that the minorities are well represented at various national conferences. Certain national policies, such as family planning, which might hinder minorities' socioeconomic development are not enforced in minority areas (Schwarz, 1971).

Several reasons account for the special treatment given to the minority nationalities. First, most of the minority groups occupy China's border areas, which are strategically important. Several groups, including the Shan, Koreans, Mongols, Uygurs, Yao, and Kazaks, are also found in neighboring Thailand, Burma, Korea, Mongolia, and the Soviet Union. If hostile to the Chinese central government, these groups could significantly weaken border defense and increase the threat of attack by foreign countries.

Second, most minority regions are sparsely populated relative to the rest of the country but are richly endowed with natural resources. There are extensive oil reserves in Heilongjiang and Xinjiang; tin and copper in Yunnan and Guizhou; and uranium deposits along the Sino-Soviet border in Xinjiang. The majority of China's forestland is also found in border regions, especially in the northeastern and southwestern provinces. Large numbers of livestock are raised in the arid and semiarid northwestern areas, where more than 80% of China's wool and animal skins are produced. In addition, certain minority localities have virgin land that can be reclaimed for settlement to alleviate population pressure of the densely populated regions of China. Extensive virgin land in Heilongjiang, Xinjiang, and other places has been developed by Chinese settlers in the last 30 years for agriculture.

Third is the matter of the political image of socialism. A contented, cooperative, and prosperous minority population is living proof of the superiority of socialism and enhances the political image of the central government. On the other hand, minority problems not only tarnish the image of the government, but also generate domestic and international crises.

Han Expansion

Historically, the Han Chinese were never isolated from the peoples who inhabited the areas surrounding the Chinese cultural realm. Interactions between the Chinese and the non-Han groups were already extensive as early as the Zhou dynasty (ca. 1122–221 B.C.). Frequent invasions of the Chinese territories by the non-Han peoples along the northern borders necessitated the construction of defensive walls against the nomads by various states as early as the Zhou period. The walls were linked together to become the Great Wall during the Qin dynasty (221–207 B.C.). Although built primarily for defense agianst nomadic invasions from the north, the Great Wall was not always militarily effective. Its symbolic significance, however, never changed. For the Chinese, it symbolized a line of demarcation separating the steppe from the sown, nomadism from agriculture, and barbarism from civilization.

Chinese civilization primarily spread from the Huang He basin toward the south, which offered the Chinese a favorable agricultural environment. Before the establishment of the first empire of the Qin in 221 B.C., most of south China, including the middle Yangzi region, was inhabited by various Tai peoples, many of whom were displaced, absorbed, or acculturated in later centuries by Han colonizers.

The tempo of the southward spread by the Chinese varied considerably. During periods of nomadic invasions from the northern border regions, alien rules were established in north China and large numbers of Chinese were pushed to the Yangzi valley areas. There were, of course, gradual shifts of population to the productive Yangzi River basin, where the alluvial soil has always been fertile and the amount of precipitation normally adequate. Further southward expansion took place along the tributary river valleys of the Yangzi, notably along the Gan, Xiang, and Yuan Rivers. The highly fertile farming region of the Guangzhou (Canton) delta began to grow rapidly after the 8th century (Wiens, 1967).

With the exception of the Mongols during the Yuan dynasty (1279–1368), virtually all of the non-Han peoples who had established alien states on the Chinese soil, including the Xianbei, the Jurchen, the Khitans, the Tanguts, and Manchus, were in the end assimilated by the culturally more advanced and numerically greater Chinese. Over the centuries, intermarriage between the Han and other groups has made the population of China genetically heterogeneous. Genetically, there is no such thing as "the Chinese race." Alien groups, once they had been Sinicized, were readily accepted by the Chinese.

The spread of Chinese culture was confined primarily to areas where agricultural cultivation based on lowland rice was possible, leaving the more hilly, arid, and nonproductive border regions largely to non-Han peoples. Although some of the border areas, such as Xinjiang and Xizang (Tibet), were nominally Chinese provinces, they existed largely as de facto kingdoms frequently challenging the Chinese overlordship until after the Communist revolution.

Autonomous Areas

The special status of the minorities in the People's Republic of China is manifested in the administrative system. Parallel to the Chinese provinces are five leading minority nationalities: Uygurs, Mongols, Hui (Chinese Moslems), Tibetans, and Zhuang (Fig. 4-3). In the autonomous regions where minority groups concentrate, as pointed out earlier, there are second-order administrative units known as autonomous prefectures (*zhou*) and "leagues" (*meng*), which are the equivalents of Chinese prefectures. Third-order minority units are autonomous counties and "banners" (*qi*) which parallel the counties in Han areas. An autonomous area usually carries the name of the largest minority group living there. For example, in Xinjiang Uygur Autonomous Region, the Uygurs are the largest minority group. Where no single group predominates, the area is named after the area's two or three leading minorities, such as Jiangzheng Hani–Yi Autonomous County in Yunnan and Haixi Monggol–Tibetan–Kazak Autonomous Zhou in Qinghai. Not all minority nationalities have their own autonomous areas, however, and no autonomous areas may be established for the Han even in places where they are a minority.

According to the Chinese government, the purpose of regional autonomy is to guarantee political equality for the national minorities and to give special

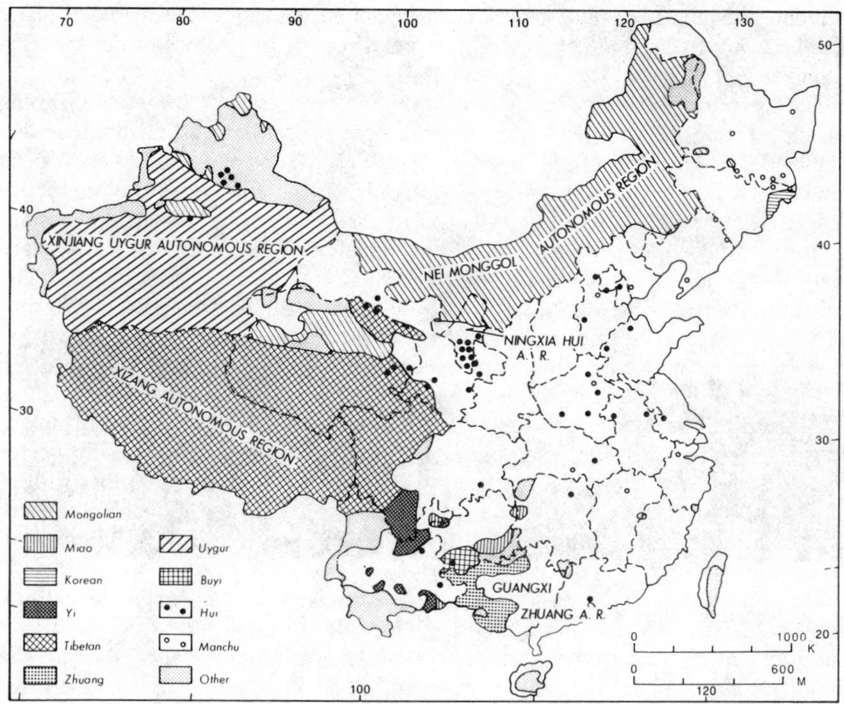

Fig. 4-3. Minority nationalities of China.
Source: China Reconstructs (1972).

consideration to the development of the minority areas. In these ways, the government indicates, the policies and principles of the CCP and government can be implemented more effectively. It would seem that minority nationalities are entitled to the right of self-government in their own areas. In reality, political administration in such areas is identical with that in Han regions, and the minority nationalities must conform to the rules established by the CCP. Although political autonomy exists in name only, there is a considerable degree of cultural autonomy. Comparatively greater freedom is given to the peoples who work to retain their ethnic customs and beliefs and to use their native language to conduct such official business as public meetings and legal proceedings. While the Chinese language is taught everywhere in China, serious efforts have been made by the government to create new scripts or to improve the written languages in minority areas. Of the 55 officially recognized nationalities, at least 25 now have their own written languages (Ma, 1962).

A Uygur farmer in Xinjiang A. R. (*L. Ma*).

Members of a Kazak family in the Tianshan Range, Xinjiang A. R. (*L. Ma*).

Xinjiang Uygur Autonomous Region

Xinjiang, meaning "New Territory" in Chinese, used to be known as Chinese Turkestan. With more than 1,600,000 square kilometers of territory, it is the largest among China's provinces and autonomous regions. Aside from Xizang (Tibet), Xinjiang is the only minority region where the Han Chinese are outnumbered by minorities. Thirteen nationalities are found in Xinjiang: Uygur, Han, Kazak, Mongol, Hui, Kirgiz, Russian, Uzbek, Xibo, Tajik, Tartar, Daur, and Manchu. In the mid-1960s, there were about 4 million Uygurs and half a million Kazaks. The total population of Xinjiang now exceeds 12 million.

The population of Xinjiang has been increasing steadily as a result of improved medical and health services. Smallpox has been eliminated and leprosy, malaria, typhoid, venereal disease, and other infectious diseases have been brought under control. Infant mortality rates and postnatal deaths are greatly reduced. Birth control is not enforced in minority regions because the population is generally much more sparse than in other parts of China, but family planning guidance and assistance are readily available for those who seek them. From 1949-74, the Uygur population in Xinjiang increased by 42% and the number of Kazaks grew from 50,000 to 160,000 (*Peking Review*, 1974).

Another factor of population growth in Xinjiang has been large-scale inmigration of Han Chinese. The majority of the migrants are demobilized troops; young people recently graduated from secondary schools; and "idle and undesirable" elements from large cities (*Renmin ribao*, 1957; Husayin, 1966). The rate of Han influx was particularly high during 1957-58. By the end of 1958, some 556,000 Han Chinese had been settled in Xinjiang (Lal, 1970).

The Production and Construction Corps of the People's Liberation Army forms the basis of Chinese colonization of Xinjiang. The size of the Corps has increased from 100,000 in the early 1950s to more than 500,000. The troops have reclaimed more than 700,000 hectares (more than 1.73 million acres) of virgin land in Xinjiang for cultivation, contributing to 35% of the 2 million hectares opened for agriculture in Xinjiang during the Chinese Communist rule (Heaton, 1971). In addition to land reclamation, the army also develops mines, builds railroads and factories, and operates more than 100 state farms. According to a journalistic account, the number of ethnic Chinese in Xinjiang is officially 3 million, which is 10 times larger than the number given in the 1953 census. More than 700,000 of them are concentrated in the Shihezi district at the northern foot of the Tian Shan.

For decades, Xinjiang has been a politically sensitive area because of its proximity to the Soviet Union. Several minorities, including the Uygurs, Kazaks, Hui, Uzbeks, Tajiks, and Kirgiz, inhabit both sides of the international border. Isolated rebellions by the Kazaks against the Chinese government took place in the late 1950s and the early 1960s, when China's relations with the Soviet Union became strained. Since then, no serious international problems related to the minorities have been reported either by China or by the USSR. However, since 1970, radio programs designed to further anti-Chinese political unrest have been broadcast from the Soviet Union in languages spoken by the nationalities in Xinjiang.

Xizang (Tibet)

Until the 1950s, Tibet was largely isolated from other parts of China without any significant Chinese influence. The Tibetans are culturally distinct from other nationalities of China. Prior to the entry of the Chinese Communists, Tibet was traditionally a theocracy of about 3 million people living in an area approximately twice the size of Texas. Tibetan politics were dominated by a small group of nobles and by the powerful Lamaist monasteries. The best agricultural land belonged to the monasteries, where members of the upper clergy were drawn from the noble class. Approximately one-third of the male Tibetans were monks. Political and religious powers were centralized in the hands of the Dalai Lama, traditionally the king, god, and high priest in one, who was believed to be a reincarnation of the Buddhist deity of Avalokitasvara. When a Dalai Lama died, his successor was sought from among the children who were born shortly after his death. The new leader was identified by a complicated religious ritual. The present Dalai Lama is the fourteenth in succession and is in exile in India.

Much publicity was given by the press in the West to the Tibetan resistance against Chinese control in the 1950s. The relationship between China and Tibet in historic times remains confusing. In the 18th and 19th centuries, Chinese officials in Lhasa were known as *Ambans*, or Residents, appointed by the Chinese government. Beijing (Peking) regarded the Residents as Chinese governors, a status the Tibetans never accepted. However, gestures of accepting the Chinese overlordship were made periodically, mainly for the sake of furthering independence. In the waning years of the Qing dynasty, Tibet almost completely broke away from China. Since the downfall of the Qing, regional autonomy existed for about four decades, while China proper was torn by Chinese warlords and Japanese invaders, and by the civil war between the Nationalists and the Communists. The Nationalists never had an opportunity to deal effectively with the Tibetan question.

It should be noted that Tibet has never been recognized by any country as an independent state. The Dalai Lama readily acknowledged in 1950 that there were times when Tibet sought, though rarely received, the protection of China. According to the Simla Convention of 1914, held between Tibet and British India and designed to reduce Chinese involvement in Tibet, China was to recognize Tibetan autonomy, to accept the so-called McMahon Line delimiting the border between Tibet and India, and to station no more than 500 troops in Tibet. The Tibetan authorities, on the other hand, agreed to a statement to the effect that Tibet was under Chinese suzerainty and that it was part of Chinese territory. In the following years, British India, when dealing with questions involving Tibet, made clear to the Chinese that Tibet was under Chinese suzerainty, although in reality India almost invariably dealt with Tibet as an independent state. China, however, has never accepted the Simla treaty, and some Tibetans have argued that they are not bound by it.

As far as the Chinese are concerned, Tibet is a Chinese territory. All of the maps, which were published in the last 100 years and which show China's administrative regions, invariably include Tibet, as do all school textbooks, published after the fall of the Qing. So when the Chinese Communists came to power and sent their armies to occupy Tibet in 1950, they did not feel they were invading any foreign country but were merely establishing political control of an area traditionally considered Chinese territory. In 1954, India and China signed a treaty, which accepted Chinese sovereignty in Tibet.

There were frequent reports in the late 1950s of Tibetans defying the Chinese rule. The rapid and forceful introduction of socialist systems in Tibet was accompanied by the simultaneous abolition of traditional Tibetan socioeconomic institutions such as monasticism, serfdom, slavery, and forced labor. These institutions had been deeply rooted for centuries. The nobles and monastic orders resisted the new measures by armed rebellions, which culminated in the well-known 1959 uprising. In March 1959, the rebels seized the Tibetan capital of Lhasa for several days, only to be driven out by the Chinese troops stationed there. The Dalai Lama and many of his followers fled southward into India, where he still resides. The Chinese happily dissolved his government and handed over the administration of Tibet to the Preparatory Committee for the Tibetan Autonomous Region, which had been established in 1956. However, the status of autonomy was not formally granted to Tibet until 1965. Although very little is known about conditions in Tibet after the uprising, an unusually lengthy period of time elapsed before the granting of autonomy. The status of autonomy reflects some degree of confidence in Chinese control in minority areas, but the lengthy time elapsing before the granting of autonomy suggests that establishing Chinese rule in Tibet was not an easy matter. The administration of the Chinese in Tibet in the last three decades has produced mixed results. While secular schools, health facilities, modern postal services, airlines, roads, industries, newspapers, radios, etc., have been introduced into the region where none existed and a railroad linking Tibet with Qinghai is now under construction, the standard of living of the Tibetan people has not improved.

Minorities in South and Southwest China

Of the 55 officially recognized minority nationalities, 25 are found in the provinces of Guangxi, Yunnan, and Guizhou. Approximately 50%, or about 19 million, of China's 1978 minority populations inhabit these three provinces. Two large nationalities, the Zhuang and the Yi, with a combined population of 11 million, are concentrated in Guangxi while about 4 million Miao, Buyi, and Shui live in Guizhou. At least 15 small minorities with a total population of more than 3 million are scattered in the hilly regions of Yunnan.

Because of the lack of historical data, it is extremely difficult to clarify the pattern of sequential occupance of China's southern and southwestern border regions by the diverse minority groups. Before the establishment of the first Chinese empire of the Qin dynasty in 221 B.C., most of south China, including the middle Yangzi valley, was inhabited by Tai groups (Moseley, 1973). Subsequently, the Tai moved southward as a result of Chinese expansion into the Yangzi valley, Gradually over the centuries, many Tai peoples migrated, primarily in small groups, into Yunnan and various parts of southeast Asia.

China's largest minority nationality, the Zhuang, is believed to be ethnically a mixture of the Yue people, who were indigenous to the southeast coast of China, and a Tai group. By Song times at least, the Zhuang had already settled in today's Guangdong and Guangxi areas, and the Tai had also established communities in southern and western Yunnan. The Mongol conquest of South China in the mid-13th century prompted a massive migration of the Tai farther south into the territory of the Khmer Empire of Angkor in southeast Asia. In the 14th century, the Tai founded the kingdoms of Siam and Laos in the valleys of the Chao Phraya and upper Mekong rivers. Today, there are more than half a million Tai in China who live mostly in the Xishuangbana Tai Autonomous *zhou* in southern Yunnan and in an autonomous *zhou* established for the Tai and the Jingpo peoples in western Yunnan.

Large-scale settlement by the Han in Yunnan and Guizhou did not begin until the Ming dynasty (1368–1644), when the Chinese government encouraged the people in the Yangzi valley to migrate southward. Displacement of the indigenous ethnic populations by the Chinese took place during the course of their southward migration, forcing many ethnic groups into remote hilly regions that were much less attractive to the Chinese, who preferred a natural environment suitable for wet rice paddy farming. In the lowlands, where rice cultivation was possible, the indigenous peoples, such as the Zhuang and the Yi, were largely assimilated rather than displaced by the Chinese.

The consolidation of the southern border provinces by the Communist Chinese in the early 1950s was largely a peaceful act. Since then, some industrial enterprises have been introduced, and the traditional slash-and-burn agriculture has become a special target for reform. Increasingly, the Chinese way of farming, characterized by intensive cultivation, multiple cropping, vegetable gardening, and systematic application of animal and human manures, is replacing traditional shifting agriculture. As a result, the productivity of the land in the Zhuang areas in Guangxi has greatly increased, contributing directly to a higher standard of living (Moseley, 1973).

Efforts at National Integration

China's minority nationalities have enjoyed considerable cultural freedom and experienced significant changes in their traditional ways of life. The ultimate goal of the Chinese ruling authorities appears to be the integration of the minorities into the national socioeconomic and political systems. Several methods of integration have been used by the government. One is the settlement of millions of Han Chinese in minority areas where they help develop the local resources and bring about a firmer Chinese control. Efforts at integration also include the recruitment of young minority people who are sent to centers of higher learning for education. After graduation, they are sent back to their homelands to assume leading positions.

The development of minorities' written languages based on the *pinyin* system may be taken as another method of integration. Since all languages used in China employ the same alphabet for spelling, communication among ethnic groups and with the Chinese has become much easier. The introduction of written languages to minority groups and the publication of books and other materials, of course, greatly facilitates the spread of official doctrines.

The lack of information does not permit one to say with confidence whether the minority nationalities have been successfully integrated into the Chinese socialist systems and whether the standards of living of the minorities today are better or worse than those prior to 1949. Few objective and in-depth studies, historical or contemporary, exist on these groups. The Chinese press invariably reports only on the positive accomplishments made in the minority areas. The few Western journalists who have recently visited such areas tend to be extremely critical of the Chinese performance there, especially when reporting on Tibet. One Western journalist reports that there is much mutual distrust between the Chinese and the Tibetans, that the Tibetans resent Chinese incursions into their religious life, that they long for the return of the Dalai Lama, and that there is poverty, starvation, and political imprisonment (Kulkarni, 1981). If the conditions in Tibet are indeed as miserable as the reports say they are, then the Chinese goal of integrating the Tibetans into the Chinese systems in the last 30 years has not been achieved.

While it appears that the Tibetans, historically a very independent people with a strong and unique religious tradition, have passively resisted the Chinese Communist rule since the 1959 uprising, one should not automatically infer that the Chinese are having similar difficulties in other minority areas, at least not to the same degree. Poverty is not a problem unique only to the minority nationalities; it is, by Western standards, almost ubiquitous in China. There are indications that many of the local problems are not always known to the central government in Peking, and no large-scale funds have been specially infused into the minority economies.

For example, it is clear that the Chinese government is unwilling to grant full political autonomy to the minorities; most of the top political positions have been held by the Chinese. Religious worship is now again permitted after it was violently denounced and severely prohibited during the Cultural Revolution (1966–69) and its aftermath in the early 1970s; nevertheless, active and structured religious propagation is still not acceptable anywhere in China. Such policies and restrictions have made the minorities unhappy. But with only about 5% of the nation's population inhabiting largely environmentally marginal areas that require more financial input than elsewhere to obtain the same developmental results, it is understandable why the central government has not been more concerned with the needs of the minorities. With the possible exception of the Tibetans, all of China's minority nationalities, including the Zhuang, the Hui, the Uygurs and the Yi, the largest minority groups in China, appear to have at least passively accepted the Communist rule. Whether or not full integration with the Chinese can be achieved in the future remains to be seen.

LITERATURE CITED

Beijing Review, 1980, Vol. 23, No. 9 (March 3), p. 17.
Beijing ribao, 1980, (Peking Daily), January 19, p. 4.

China Reconstructs, 1972, "About National Minorities in China," Vol. 21, No. 12, p. 8.

China Reconstructs, 1978, "The Tuchia-Miao Autonomous Prefecture," Vol. 27, No. 7, p. 35. (a)

China Reconstructs, 1978, "At the Hsishuangpanna Tai Autonomous Prefecture," Vol. 27, No. 12, p. 31. (b)

Dili zhishi, 1976, "Miaoling jubican" (Great Changes in the Miao Hills), No. 6, p. 1. (a)

Dili zhishi, 1976, "Meilide Sandu Shuizu zizhixian" (The Beautiful Sandu Shui Nationality Autonomous County), No. 12, p. 14. (b)

Dili zhishi, 1977, "Yulong xeushaxia de Naxizu" (The Naxi Nationality of the Snowy Yulong Mountains), No. 10, p. 10.

Dreyer, June T., 1976, *China's Forty Million*. Cambridge, Mass.: Harvard University Press.

Heaton, Bill, 1971, "Red Sun in Sinkiang." *Far Eastern Economic Review*, Vol. 71, No. 3 (Jan. 16), p. 46.

Hsiao, Kung-chuan, 1960, *Rural China, Imperial Control in the Nineteenth Century*. Seattle: University of Washington Press.

Husayin, Abayduila, 1966, "The New Sinkiang." *China Reconstructs*, Vol. 15, No. 1 (Jan.), p. 26.

Kulkarni, V. G., 1981, "Tibet" (4 article series, January 5–8). *The Christian Science Monitor*.

Lal, Amrit, 1970, "Signification of Ethnic Minorities in China." *Current Scene*, Vol. 9. No. 4 (Feb. 15), p. 16.

Luo, Fu, 1980, "City Dwellers and the Neighborhood Committee, *Beijing Review*, Vol. 23, No. 44 (November 3), pp. 19–25.

Ma, Hsueh-liang, 1962, "New Scripts for China's Minorities." *China Reconstructs* (Aug.), pp. 24–25.

Ma, Laurence J. C., 1979, Field notes, Ürümqi, Xinjiang Province (Aug. 16).

Moseley, George V. H., 1973, *The Consolidation of the South China Frontier*. Berkeley and Los Angeles: University of California Press, p. 16.

Peking Review, 1974, "Rapid Growth in China's Minority Population," No. 49 (Oct. 4), pp. 30–31, 40.

Qi, Ya, 1979, "Visiting the Ewenkis." *Beijing Review*, Vol. 22, No. 6, p. 25.

Renmin ribao, 1957, (People's Daily), April 30.

1965 Renmin shouce, 1965, (*1965 People's Handbook*). Beijing: Xinhua shudian.

Schwarz, Henry G., 1971, *Chinese Policies Towards Minorities*. Western Washington State University, Program in East Asian Studies, Occasional Paper #2.

Whitney, Joseph B. R., 1970, *China: Area Administration and Nation Building*. Chicago: University of Chicago, Department of Geography Research Papers, No. 123.

Wiens, Herold J., 1967, *Han Chinese Expansion in South China*. Hamden, Conn.: Shoe String Press.

Zhang, Delin, 1979, "People of the Qiang Nationality." *China Pictorial*, No. 5, p. 25.

Zhi, Exiang, 1980, "The Jinuos: China's Newest Nationality." *China Reconstructs*, Vol. 29, No. 2, p. 55.

Chapter 5

Population and the Dynamics of Growth

About 22% of the human race lives within the borders of the People's Republic of China. The State Statistical Bureau of the Chinese government officially reported on June 27, 1979 that China's population at the end of 1978 was 975.23 million, including Taiwan, and that its natural growth rate (the annual death rate subtracted from the annual birth rate) was 12 per thousand (*Beijing Review*, 1979). This announcement ended several years of conflicting per annum estimates by Western demographers, and some observers were surprised by the officially reported large size but small growth rate. The estimates of China's population among China scholars in the United States had ranged between 800 and 950 million in the latter part of the 1970s, and it was believed that the population was growing at an annual rate slightly under 20 per thousand (Orleans, 1977; Aird, 1978).

China's official population data, both historical and contemporary, should be used with caution because of incomplete coverage. Historically, population data were never collected for the sake of objective knowledge or national economic planning. Population registrations were carried out mainly for the purposes of taxation or conscription of the able-bodied males for military or corvée duties. To evade registration in order to avoid paying taxes or the draft was a common practice. Females and children, considered socially inferior and physically unfit for labor services, were largely unreported in dynastic times (Ho, 1959). In the 20th century, census counts have not been sophisticated enough for meaningful analysis of population changes. Data on such demographic variables as age-specific birth and death rates, migration rates, regional demographic characteristics, rural and urban differentials, sex and age compositions are largely lacking. Figures cited

Table 5-1. Official Population Data

Period	Year	Population
Western Han Dynasty	2 A.D.	59,594,978
Eastern Han	156	50,066,856
Three Kingdoms	220–280	7,672,881
Western Jin	280	16,163,863
Sui	606	46,019,956
Tang	742	48,909,809
Song	1110	46,734,784
Yuan	1290	58,834,711
Ming	1393	60,545,812
Qing	1661	21,068,609
Qing	1757	190,348,328
Qing	1901	426,447,325
The Republic of China	1928	474,787,386
The People's Republic of China	1949	548,770,000
The People's Republic of China	1953	583,600,000
The People's Republic of China	1957	656,630,000
The People's Republic of China	1978	975,230,000
The People's Republic of China	1980*	982,550,000

Source: Shou Jinghua (1979). The figures from 1949 on do not include the population of Taiwan.

*State Statistical Bureau, 1981.

in this book are meant to suggest rough orders of magnitude rather than precise demographic realities.

HISTORICAL GROWTH PATTERNS

Historically, China's population varied greatly (Table 5-1), and large discrepancies existed between official population data recorded in historical documents and the demographic truths. In addition to the reasons for the unreliability of data mentioned above, another important factor contributing to the varied historical figures was China's changing national boundaries in different dynastic periods following the rise and fall of the nation's political and military strength.

The earliest national population figures date back to the beginning of the Christian era. In the year A.D. 2, the Han dynasty reportedly had a population of about 60 million. For the next 16 centuries there were drastic population fluctuations both temporally and spatially. Population tended to increase steadily during the more peaceful years and to decline in times of war and natural disasters.

The most rapid growth of population took place during the period from 1757 to 1901 when the size jumped from approximately 190 to 426 million. This growth was particularly noticeable during the two centuries from 1650 to 1850 under the benevolent despotism of the early Qing (Manchu) rulers when stable political and favorable economic conditions generally prevailed (Ho, 1959). The national economy reached a new stage of development. The dissemination and widespread use of such newly introduced food crops as the early-ripening rice, Irish potatoes, maize, and sweet potatoes greatly enlarged the nation's capability to produce food. More and more new areas previously unsuitable for agriculture were now brought under cultivation. However, the trend of population growth was again checked during the last six decades of the Manchu rule when a series of rebellions—such as the White Lotus (1795-1804), the Taiping (1850-64), and the Nian (1853-68)—coupled with widespread floods, droughts, and famines, resulted in millions of deaths. Thus, when the Manchu empire ended in 1911, the population was probably no more than 400 million.

Prior to the establishment of the People's Republic of China in 1949, the Nationalist government made several attempts to come up with a realistic population count. Many government institutions, including the Post Office Department, the Ministry of Internal Affairs, the Bureau of the Budget, and the Maritime Customs Office, carried out enumerations. But political instability, caused by internal warlord politics and by the Japanese invasion, hindered a registration system from being satisfactorily implemented. There were conflicting reports regarding the actual size of the population. It was generally believed, however, that in the 1930s and the 1940s the population of China was in the neighborhood of 450 million.

POPULATION DISTRIBUTION

The present pattern of population distribution is a consequence of expansion and migration by the Chinese in historical times. Today the vast majority of the Chinese people are concentrated in a few areas where the environment offers the necessary conditions for the development of intensive agriculture. Four major regions have especially dense population: the North China Plain (primarily Hebei, Shandong, and Henan Provinces); the middle and lower Chang Jiang (Yangzi) River basin and the river delta; the Sichuan Basin; and the Xi (West) and Zhu (Pearl) Rivers delta (Figs. 5-1 and 5-2). In addition to relatively abundant precipitation and level topography, these areas have fertile alluvial soils produced by the river systems. In the south, the Chang Jiang and its several tributaries are navigable. The river has greatly facilitated the development of trade. Most of China's major cities are found in these four fertile regions.

Secondary population concentrations with lower density are found throughout the rugged uplands of much of South China; in the Songliao River Basin in the northeast (Manchuria), where colder climate and extensive marshlands have discouraged higher population concentration; along the Hexi Corridor in Gansu Province; and in the oases in Xinjiang Uygur Autonomous Region. Xizang (Tibet), Inner Mongolia, Qinghai, Xinjiang, and Heilongjiang, where minority nationalities reside, have very sparse population. Insufficient rainfall, extremes of temperature, and poor soils have limited agricultural development and production in western China. In such areas, pastoral nomadism predominates.

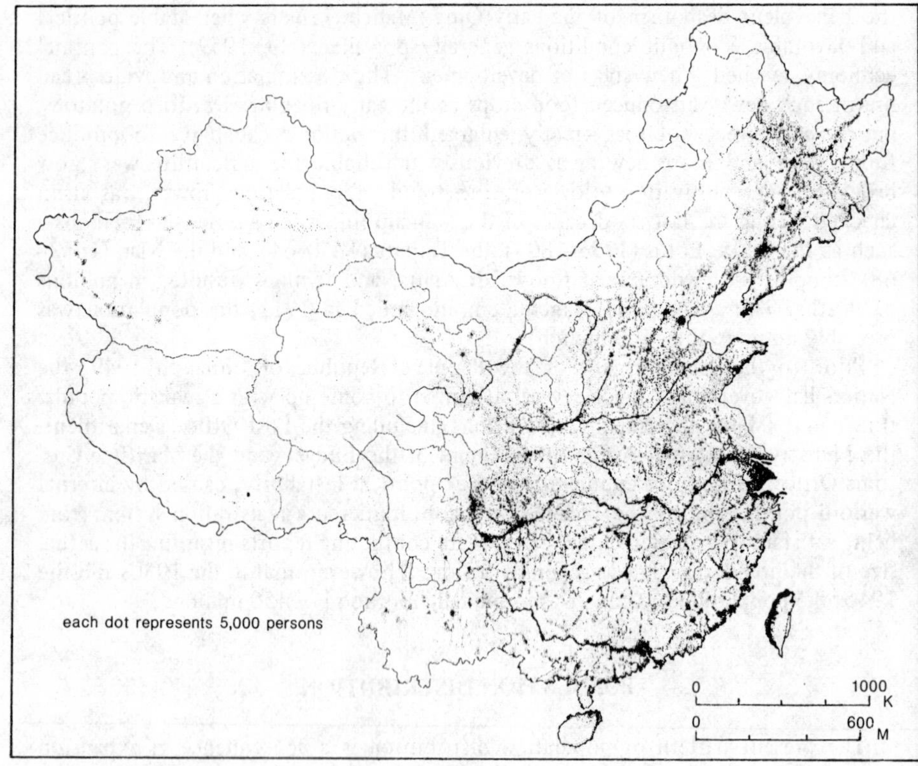

Fig. 5-1. Distribution of China's population.
Source: Courtesy of Sen-dou Chang.

POPULATION SIZE AND VITAL RATES

When the Chinese Communists came to power, they decided to conduct a national census to obtain information indispensable for the preparation of the First Five-Year Plan (1953–57). The information sought was quite simple: the address of the household; the names, ages, sex, ethnic status of all its members; and their relationship to the head of the household. According to the census results, China in mid-1953 had a total of 583.6 million people, plus 11.7 million overseas Chinese and 7.6 million on Taiwan. Since this census was the only official population count China made in the last three decades, it has been used widely as a basis for population estimates and projections of future growth by Western scholars (Tien, 1973).

There are indications that even the Chinese leadership was unclear about the actual size of the population. In the 1970s, top level Chinese leaders and other

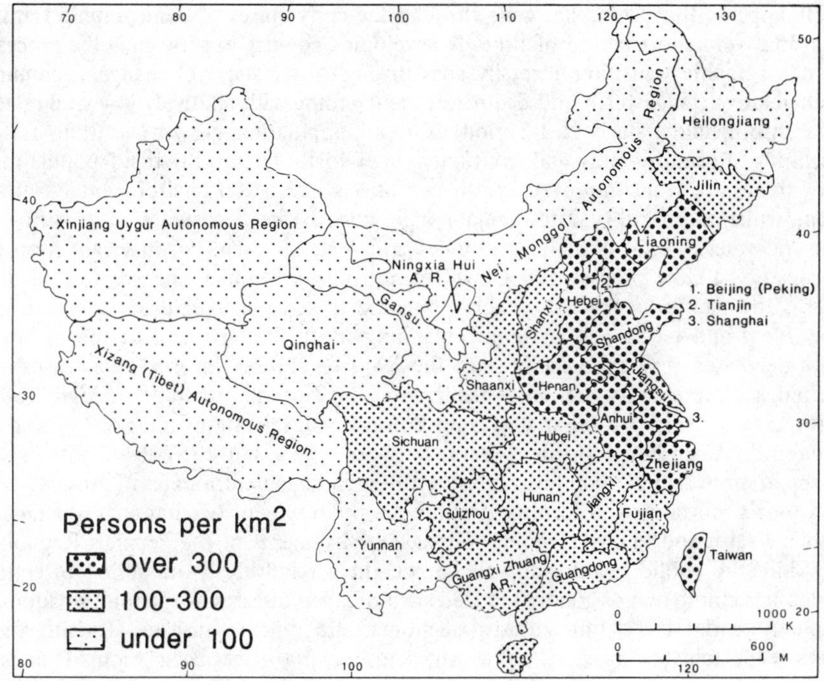

Fig. 5-2. China's population distribution by province, 1977.

informed sources used national figures that differed by as much as 100 million. In the 1970s, officials at the supply and grain departments believed that the size was 800 million, while the Ministry of Commerce stated that it was 830 million. In 1972, the head of the Chinese delegation to the United Nations Environment Conference held in Stockholm said that China had as many as 900 million people, a figure that was widely used in the Chinese press until mid-1979 when the figure of 975 million (1978 population) was released by the State Statistical Bureau. It is not clear how this new figure for the population of 1978 was calculated. No national census is known to have been taken in 1978.

Recent official information from China indicates that the rate of population growth in the 1950s and the 1960s averaged 20 per thousand. Since the early 1970s, stringent policies of family planning have been enforced with impressive results. Vice-Premier Chen Muhua disclosed in late 1979 that the rate of China's natural population growth had gone down from 23.4 per thousand in 1971 to 12.05 per thousand in 1978. Such a drastic reduction of the natural growth rate in a few years is extremely rare in the history of the world's population evolution. The present Chinese government has called for a further reduction to about 5 per thousand in 1985 and to zero growth by the year 2000.

It appears that China has gone through the early stages of demographic transition in a very short period of time. A developing country experiencing the process of demographic transition normally goes through three stages of change, beginning with relatively high birth and death rates and ending with relatively low vital rates. The intermediate stage is a period of rapid population growth resulting from declining mortality rates and continued high birth rates. This rapid population growth results from improved health conditions and better environmental sanitation, while the fertility rates remain high due to the persistence of traditional cultural values in favor of large families and male children. Fertility reduction is necessarily a slow process, for it involves not only attitudinal changes toward the role of the family in the social fabric, but also the awareness and the adoption of new ideas and techniques of family planning. Both the birth and the death rates have decreased very appreciably since the 1949 revolution. In 1953, the census reported an impressively low crude death rate of 17 per thousand and a high crude birth rate of 37 per thousand, leaving a crude natural rate of increase of 20 per thousand. According to official data, between 1954 and 1957 death rates also dropped more rapidly than birth rates, resulting in large natural rates of growth.

China's mortality and fertility declines are the results of two national programs: public health and family planning. The accomplishments of the People's Republic of China in public health are well known. In a relatively short period of time, China has eliminated or greatly reduced such dreaded diseases as typhoid, smallpox, cholera, scarlet fever, tuberculosis, trachoma, and venereal diseases. Parisitic diseases–e.g., schistosomiasis, hookworm, and malaria–have been brought under control and pose no serious threat to the population. These accomplishments were achieved through massive inoculation drives, pest-eradication programs, environmental cleanup campaigns, and preventive medicine. Public health programs are carried out in every province, city, and county.

At the average rate of natural growth of 20 per thousand, China in the last 30 years had a net gain in population of 426 million (Table 5-1). Such a large increase in a relatively short period of time is unprecedented in China's history. People under 21 years of age now constitute one-half of the population total, and virtually all of them will get married before the end of the century (Fig. 5-3). About 10 million couples will reach childbearing age each year. If the current rate of population growth of 12 per thousand should continue without reduction, China would have 1,300 million people by the year 2000 (Shou, 1979).

Population growth in the last 30 years was not matched by any increase in the amount of the nation's cultivated land. Shortly after the 1949 revolution, China had a total of 106 million ha of cultivated land and approximately .20 ha of cultivated land per capita. As a result of urban, industrial, transportation, and water conservancy projects which encroached on farmland, the total amount of cultivated land in 1979 was reduced to less than 100 million ha, while the per capita figure had decreased to .10 ha (*Renmin ribao*, 1979). Since the nation's economy is and will be based on agriculture for many years to come and most of the reclaimable land has long been developed, the declining man-land ratio is perhaps the most fundamental problem of national development facing China today. More details on this will be discussed in Chapter Six.

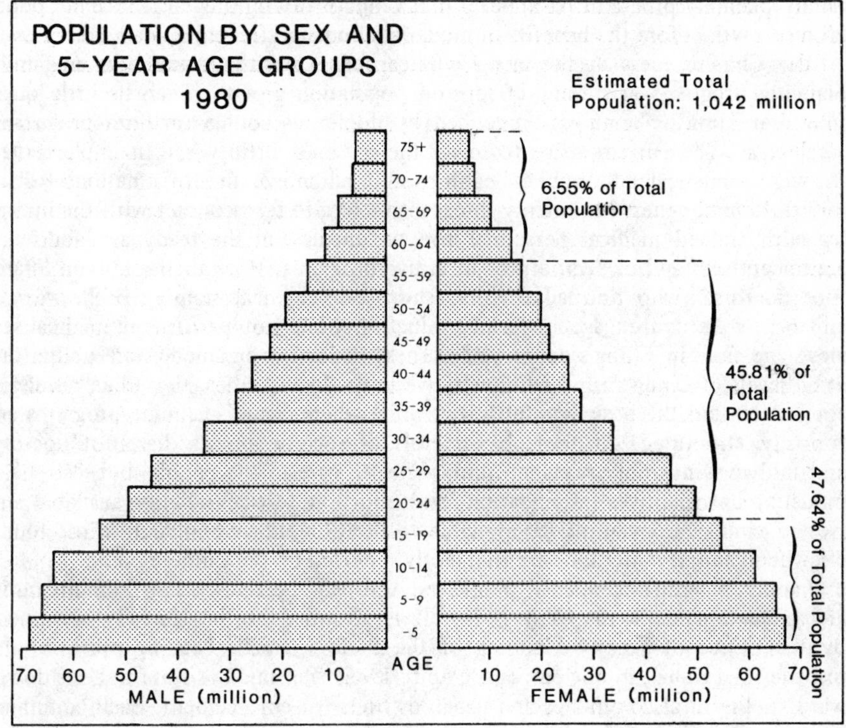

Fig. 5-3. China: Population pyramid based on high estimate of 1980 population. *Source:* Aird (1978).

FAMILY PLANNING

Failure to take effective actions before the early 1970s to stabilize the rapidly growing population was perhaps the most serious mistake committed by Mao Zedong, who used to think that a large population would bring more producers. The Chinese leadership only recently recognized the fact that an excessively large population is detrimental to the growth and development of the nation's economy, and serious efforts have been made to reduce the birth rate. China hopes to reach zero population growth by the year 2000. This hope, of course, is highly ambitious, especially considering the fact that the nation has not experienced industrialization and modernization, which have proved to be essential to curb population growth. In a country where tradition has placed a high value on male children, the target is even more difficult to reach. The Chinese government, however, is firmly committed to limiting the growth of population and has provided effective leadership. The new social structure of the nation is such that it greatly facilitates family planning programs. It appears that China is attempting to reduce her population growth before the benefits of modernization are affected.

The Chinese press in the late 1970s carried extensive information on family planning programs and their effects on population growth. There is little question that family planning is practiced by numerous couples in both urban and rural areas. The current drive to lower the nation's fertility rate is implemented through a medical and public health system unknown in other nations (Chen, 1976). Its uniqueness lies mainly in extensive face-to-face contact with the masses by both trained medical personnel and paramedics; in the ready availability of contraceptives; and in a variety of incentive programs. More than a million "barefoot doctors," who normally receive short-term medical training of between 3 and 6 months and engage in farm production while not performing medical services, are now in China's countryside. These dedicated paramedics are ubiquitous at all levels of China's rural administrative units. In the cities, the urban residents' committees are the basic administrative units where family planning programs are formally structured. At these basic levels of society, nurses, barefoot doctors, and midwives not only provide ordinary health care to the people, but also make modern contraceptives, sterilization, and abortion services readily available and free of charge. Contraceptives available to the Chinese are similar to those found elsewhere, and new methods are frequently reported by the Chinese press.

Family planning is openly publicized through the tightly knit administrative and educational systems (Yu, 1979). It is governed at the central government by the Office of Family Planning of the State Council. Leading cadres at the provincial, regional, municipal, and county levels transmit the state policies downward to the rural communes and urban districts for enforcement. Each commune has a family planning committee which coordinates and supervises family planning work. Family planning subcommittees are responsible for such details of birth control as disseminating family planning information and contraceptives; organizing and leading study groups; persuading nonparticipants to adopt family planning; and checking the results of these programs. In the cities, similar activities are found in offices and factories as well as in residents' committees. At these lowest levels of family planning, detailed records are kept on the number of population, the number of women in childbearing age, the methods of male and female contraceptives used, and the projected number of births each year. Women who fail to practice birth control, who have too many children, or who have the right number of children (no more than two) at the wrong time may encounter unpleasant social pressure from their colleagues and neighbors for conformity.

Three key words characterize the present goals of China's family planning education: late, thin, and few–meaning late marriage, spacing births at intervals of no less than 4 or 5 years, and fewer children per couple. Late marriage is encouraged everywhere. In the countryside, the youngest age for marriage is generally 23 for women and 25 for men. In the cities, the minimum ages are slightly higher; in Shanghai, they are 25 for women and 27 for men.

Since the late 1970s, families have been encouraged to have only one child. Many places have issued honor certificates to families which have decided to have no more than one child. The certificate allows the qualified families to receive monthly subsidies and other incentives. For example, in many urban places one-child families receive a monthly "health maintenance fee" of five *yuan*, or about 10% of an average worker's monthly income, until the children have reached 14 years of age (16 in Shanghai). In the countryside, one-child families are awarded additional work points equivalent to five *yuan* every month. Priorities of admitting children to nurseries and kindergartens are granted to these families, often free of charge. In the cities of Shanghai, Kunming, and Jinan, such families enjoy priorities of housing allocation and receive the same amount of living space as families with two or more children. In Shanghai, a retiree with only one child will get an additional amount of pension to be calculated on the basis of 5% of his wage at retirement. In Sichuan, single children receive the same amount of grain as that of an adult and are counted as 1.5 grown-ups in the allocation of private plots. These incentives, however, are canceled if a second child is born. In Shanghai (and perhaps elsewhere too), such families must return the acquired benefits to the state in installments.

Education is assigned a high priority in China's family planning. The masses are taught that there is no need to adhere to the old saying that "grain is stored against famine and sons are brought up to ensure security for one's old age." Under the Communist system, they are told, everyone is guaranteed a certain amount of basic daily necessities (such as grains, cooking oil, and cloth), and there is no need to have several sons and a large family. It is also argued that improved medical care and public health services have greatly increased the probability of infant survival, and there is no need to produce many sons to ensure the survival of a few. The masses are told that successful family planning would help improve the health of both the mother and the child and bring about a higher standard of living for the family. Since the late 1970s, population planning has been justified on the basis that the nation's large population has hindered the development of the national economy; created serious problems of food supply, housing, education, and employment; and reduced per capita income and the already small man-land ratio (Yu, 1979).

Through the mass media, study classes, and small group discussions, reasons for family planning are persistently explained to the masses. Furthermore, health workers make frequent home visits, during which pressure to adopt family planning measures is privately exerted. There are indications that the younger generation is more receptive to family planning than the older generation and that the urban population is more actively involved in family planning than the rural people. Local cadres must work closely with the childbearing women to determine who shall have a child and when. Such intensive family planning programs, of course, affect personal freedom of action and frequently generate dissatisfaction. In the long run, however, a smaller population will benefit the entire nation. The central government of China has drafted a "Law of Family Planning" which is being discussed by various government organizations. Among the family planning incentives included in the draft are a health maintenance fee for one-child families in the cities and extra work points for those in the countryside; additional retirement compensations; better housing and employment opportunities; and preferential treatment of rural one-child families in the allocation of private plots and

Table 5-2. Population Growth Rates in Selected Areas, 1978

Location	Natural growth rate (per thou.)/annum
Guangdong Province	14.75
Tianjin City	less than 10.00
Sichuan Province	6.06
Chongqing City	3.56
Shanghai City	5.07

Source: Guangming ribao (1979).

land for housing construction. Also being discussed is the possibility of imposing a "multiple-children fee" on those parents who insist on having many children after they have been taught the necessity of practicing family planning.

Since the early 1970s, many Western visitors to China have reported on the vital rates of selected localities which they have visited. These places are almost without exception relatively wealthy and located in or near the major cities. The reported vital rates are invariably extremely low. Serious scholars have warned that the reported rates should not be taken as a reflection of the national picture. Since the late 1970s, however, the Chinese press has been publishing vital rates for selected provinces and cities, some of which are very large, where family planning has been successful. This development is an indication that the intensive family planning program has produced concrete results beyond a small number of model localities (Table 5-2).

In the late 1970s, population growth rate was less than 1% in the cities of Peking, Shanghai, Tianjin, and in the provinces of Sichuan, Hebei, Jiangsu, Shandong, and Hubei (*Beijing Review*, 1978). This report is significant because these cities are the largest in China and the provinces are among the most densely populated regions of the country (Table 5-3). Their natural rates of growth, however, are uneven, as Table 5-2 indicates.

Among the large, first-order administrative divisions, Sichuan, China's most populous province with approximately 100 million people, seems to have done most to curb its population growth, whereas Guangdong has been far less successful (Table 5-4). In Guangdong, the rates of growth have risen again since 1977. In 1978, Guangdong was ranked 21st in terms of natural growth rate among China's 29 provinces, autonomous regions, and province-level municipalities. For the nation as a whole, the natural growth rate of 12 per thousand is quite low in relation to those in other nations. Yet China adds about 12 million people each year to its population, and it is safe to say that the population in 1982 exceeded one billion. Only through more stringent family planning policies and practice can China be expected to reach the goal of zero population growth by the year 2000.

Table 5-3. Distribution of Population by Province-level Unit, Estimated as of December 31, 1978

Region* and province-level unit	Population (in millions)	Area (in square kilometers)	Density (people per square kilometers)
Northeast			
Heilongjiang	33.76	710,000	48
Jilin	24.74	290,000	85
Liaoning	37.43	230,000	163
North			
Beijing	8.50	17,800	478
Hebei	50.57	218,400	232
Nei Monggol	8.90	450,000	7
Shanxi	24.24	157,100	154
Tianjin	7.21	11,000	655
East			
Anhui	47.13	139,900	337
Fujian	more than 24.50	123,100	199
Jiangsu	58.34	108,000	540
Shanghai	10.98	6,185	1,775
Shandong	71.60	153,300	467
Zhejiang	37.51	101,800	368
Central			
Henan	70.66	167,000	423
Hunan	51.66	210,500	245
Hubei	45.75	187,500	244
South			
Jiangxi	31.83	164,800	193
Guangdong	55.93	214,600	261
Guangxi	34.02	237,200	143
Southwest			
Guizhou	26.86	174,000	154
Sichuan	97.07	567,600	171
Yunnan	30.92	436,200	71
Xizang	1.79	1,223,000	1
Northwest			
Gansu	18.73	530,000	35
Ningxi	3.66	77,000	48
Qinghai	3.65	720,996	5
Shaanxi	27.79	195,800	142
Xinjiang	12.33	1,662,600	7

*Regional divisions are for descriptive purposes only and have no official administrative significance.

Source: Bunge and Shinn (1981).

Table 5-4. Rates of Population Growth, Sichuan and Guangdong Provinces, 1965–78 (per thousand)

	Sichuan	Guangdong
1965	–	29.40
1970	31.21	–
1975	–	14.97
1977	8.67	12.60
1978	6.06	14.75
1979 (projected)	–	(16.00)

Sources: Renmin ribao (1979); *Nanfang ribao* (1979).

EDUCATIONAL OPPORTUNITIES

China is a poor nation with severe problems of economic development. The nation's large and growing population poses an extremely serious threat to the hope of lifting itself out of the vicious cycle of underdevelopment. One cause as well as symptom of underdevelopment is that advanced educational opportunities are available to only a very small number of people, and this affects directly the quality of the population. China's current program of "Four Modernizations" (agriculture, industry, defense, and science and technology) can hardly be achieved without the necessary technical manpower.

The financial resources of the Chinese government are strained to such an extent that the nation can barely take care of its most essential needs. Investment in education in 1980 was one of the lowest among the nations of the world. Although 90% of Chinese children enroll in primary schools, only 60% finish the 5-year primary schooling. Only a small percentage of the primary school graduates enroll in middle schools (5 years), and even fewer can enter college. There are only about 600 colleges and universities in China which can accommodate only 2% of the nation's college-age students, compared with 2,600 institutions of higher education in the United States which can take 40% of the college-age students. Only the best students can be expected to pass the stiff nationwide college entrance examination. In 1979, 6 million college aspirants competed for 300,000 places in the colleges and universities.

One serious consequence of overpopulation and underdevelopment is unemployment. While no firm statistics are available, unemployment among the young people is known to be widespread, especially in the cities where factory jobs are not enough to meet the demand, and the service sector has not been fully developed to absorb more unemployed. As in other countries, lack of jobs has led many to roam around and get into problems with the law. Unemployment in the countryside seems to be less serious because jobs on the farm are always available. In fact, some parents in the villages see little use in sending their children to middle schools which can neither guarantee them jobs nor a college education.

LITERATURE CITED

Aird, John S., 1978, "Populaton Growth in the People's Republic of China." In *Chinese Economy Post-Mao*, Vol. 1, *Policy and Performance.* Papers submitted to the Joint Economic Committee, 95th Congress, 2nd Session. Washington, D.C.: Government Printing Office, 439–475.

Beijing Review, 1978, "Meeting on Family Planning," Vol. 21, No. 29, p. 4.

Beijing Review, 1979, "Communique on Fulfilment of China's 1978 National Economic Plan," Vol. 22, No. 27 (July 6, 1979), p. 41.

Bunge, Frederica M. and Shinn, Rinn-Sup (eds.), *China, A Country Study* (Area Handbook Series) (DA pam; 550-60). Washington, D.C.: Department of the Army, 1981.

Chen, Pi-chao, 1976, *Population and Health Policy in the People's Republic of China.* Interdisciplinary Communications Program, Smithsonian Institute, Washington, D.C.

Guangming ribao, 1979, Aug. 14, p. 2.

Ho, Ping-ti, 1959, *Studies on the Population of China, 1368–1953.* Cambridge, Mass.: Harvard University Press.

Nanfang ribao, 1979, July 4, p. 1.

Orleans, Leo A., 1977, *China's Birth Rate, Death Rate, and Population Growth: Another Perspective.* A report prepared for the Committee on International Relations, U.S. House of Representatives, 95th Congress, 1st Session. Washington, D.C.: Government Printing Office.

Renmin ribao, 1979, August 11, p. 2.

Shou Jinghua, 1979, "Interview with a Specialist on Population." *Beijing Review*, Vol. 22, No. 46 (Nov. 16), pp. 20–21.

State Statistical Bureau (1981), as reported in "Communique of fulfillment of China's 1980 National Economic Plan." *Beijing Review*, Vol. 24, No. 19 (May 11, 1981), p. 20.

Tien, H. Yuan, 1973, *China's Population Struggle, Demographic Decision of the People's Republic, 1949–1969.* Columbus: Ohio State University Press.

Yu, Y. C., 1979, "The Population Policy of China." *Population Studies*, Vol. 33, No. 1 (March), pp. 125–142.

Chapter 6

Chinese Agriculture and Primary Production

China's agricultural production is globally significant because of the size of China's population and economy and the potential political and security ramifications associated with China's economic growth and stability. The data assembled and analyzed below suggest several challenging points and conclusions.

First, China is a large country with an area of approximately 9.60 million km^2. Despite its vast size and substantial land resource base, China's potential for agricultural development has been constrained by the relatively modest supply of land suitable for agriculture in relation to the country's large and rapidly growing population.

Second, China's modernization depends on the ability of the country to increase rapidly total and per capita agricultural production and to accumulate surplus capital to invest in other sectors of the economy (Ding, 1980).

Third, Chinese agriculture is becoming more productive in terms of yields, and the total yields have increased rapidly in recent years. Substantial investments in irrigation systems and the use of chemical fertilizers as well as improved quality of seeds and plants account for this. These dramatic gains, however, have been offset, in large part, by the continued growth of China's population. Also, only a modest increase in per capita grain production has occurred (see Fig. 6-1). Chinese agriculture will no doubt continue to expand production, but there are limits to how rapidly these increases will continue and at what point diminishing returns on agricultural investments will be reached.

Fourth, approximately four-fifth's of China's population is involved directly or indirectly in agriculture. Thus the performance and productivity of agri-

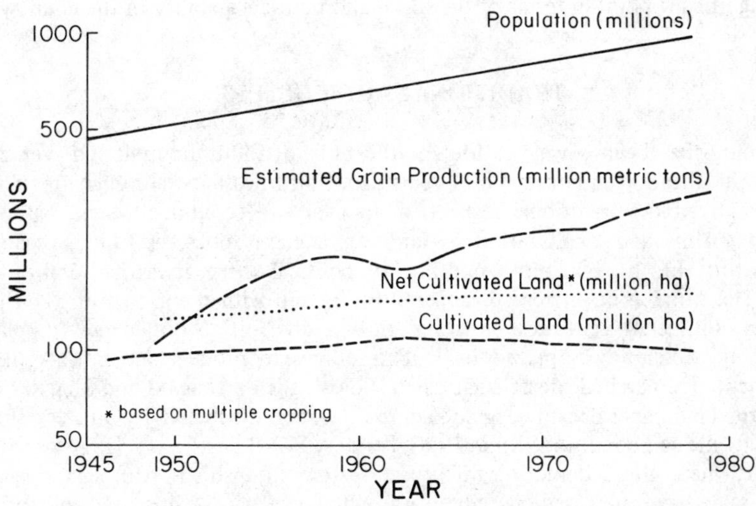

Fig. 6-1. China, recent changes in population, grain production, and cultivated land. *Source:* "China's Shrinking Cropland" (C. W. Pannell, 1981).

Plowing on a state farm in Xinjiang near the city of Ürümqi. All farming in this area is based on irrigation waters. (*L. Ma*)

culture has an immediate effect on the well-being of most of China's people, a most significant point in terms of the social and political stability of the country.

TRADITIONAL AGRICULTURE

Farming has been a way of life for the bulk of China's population ever since Chinese civilization emerged 4,000 years ago. Farm peasants, although frequently poor, enjoyed the traditional respect of a social and economic system based on the ownership and exploitation of land. In ancient times, as China expanded its territory and brought more land into its political scope, its agricultural output grew. The population increased, apparently, in step with the growth in food production. In recent centuries, however, it was difficult to obtain new cropland. Increasing pressure was placed on land resources to produce more food. In environmentally marginal areas, such as the loesslands of Shaanxi and Shanxi Provinces, the landscapes became degraded, a result of too much activity on steep slopes with a fragile soil condition (King, 1926; Perkins, 1969).

Everywhere the sedentary agricultural system intensified. Although per unit yields may have increased, population growth kept pace. Thus, the bulk of the population remained in an endless cycle of near poverty. The social system exacerbated this development by requiring equal division of property among surviving sons. Over time, most peasant families came to have smaller amounts of land on which to support themselves. More labor could be applied, but incremental output did not match population growth. Poverty became more serious for more people. Many eventually lost their land and became indentured, and there seemed little hope for improvement without a fundamental change in the entire system of society and landholding. The revolution of 1911 overturned the existing dynastic order. The Chinese Communist Party (CCP), founded in 1921, initially followed an urban based strategy and enjoyed only modest success. Mao Zedong early took the lead in organizing peasants in his native province of Hunan. Organizing the peasants into an effective social and military force proved to be a successful strategy. Under Mao's leadership, the CCP ascended to power in 1949. An important aspect of Chinese Communism has involved agricultural transformation, for the demands of feeding a rapidly growing population and providing a surplus for capital accumulation to support investments in economic development became ever more pressing.

Writing in the middle 1950s, a geographer, Herold Wiens, noted that more than 80% of China's population lived in farm villages and small market towns, and three-fourths of China's workers were employed either directly or indirectly in agriculture. Despite considerable economic growth, progress, and modernization, it is unlikely that these percentage figures have changed very much since Wiens's statement. Although China's economy has shifted increasingly toward the industrial/commercial sector in recent years, agriculture continues to be overwhelmingly important in terms of the people employed and involved. The number of people employed in agriculture has grown in step with the rapid growth in China's huge population. To that extent, Chinese agriculture remains critically

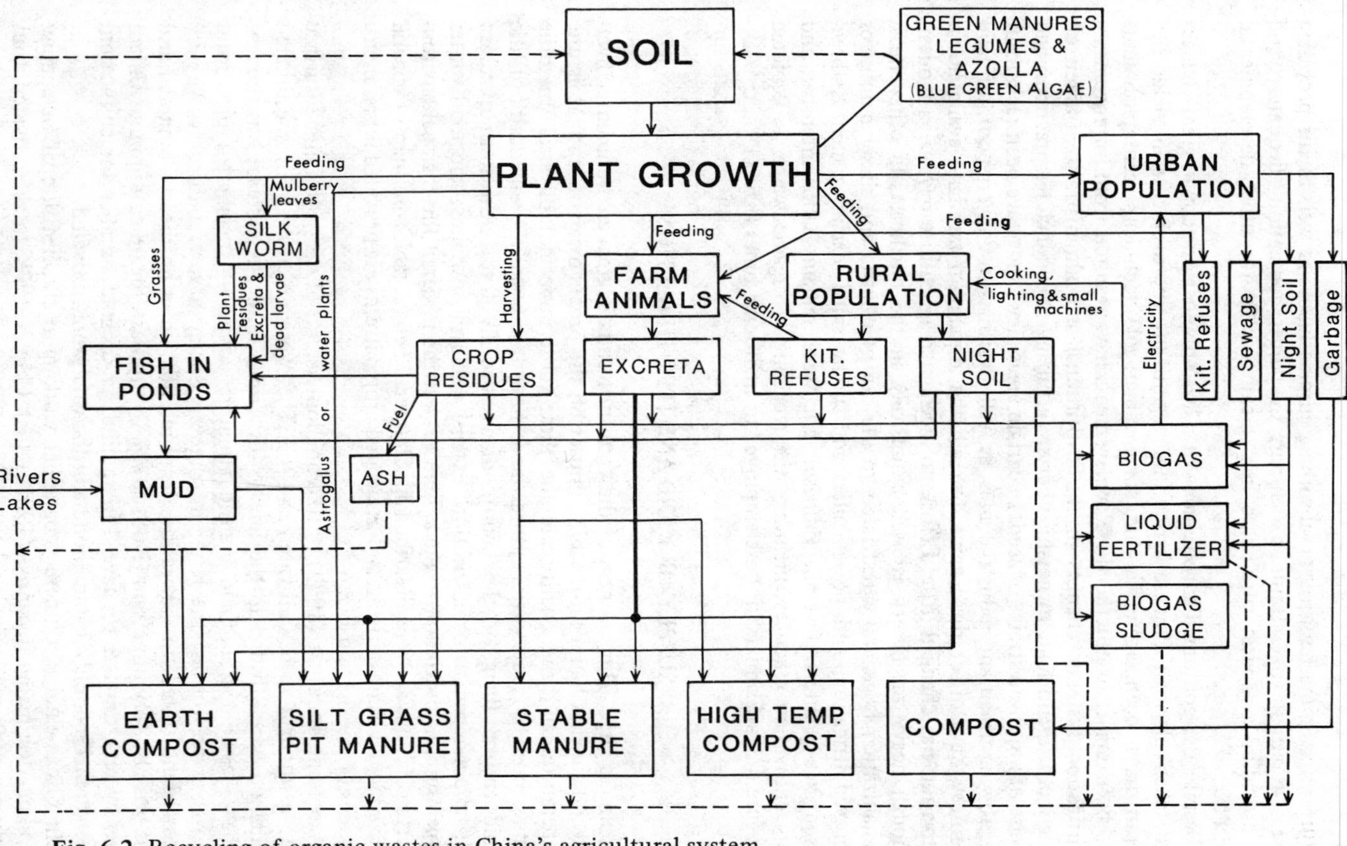

Fig. 6-2. Recycling of organic wastes in China's agricultural system.
Source: FAO/UNDP (1977).

important as a mechanism for absorbing surplus labor, as well as for providing increased output to continue to support the larger population adequately, and for providing a modest surplus to help create capital for other developmental projects.

Despite the continued involvement of a large number of people, great changes have taken place in Chinese agriculture. Significant improvements in yields and output have been achieved, and some remarkable technical accomplishments have been made. In general, these achievements have resulted from improvements in irrigation systems; changes in the institutional and administrative framework of agriculture and land ownership; better fertilizing and mulching practices; and the use of improved strains of seed. In certain areas, new lands have been reclaimed, but growing urban and industrial sites, as well as efforts to convert poor farmland to forest, have offset these gains. Overall, the amount of farmland available for cultivation has changed little. Efforts to mechanize agriculture have been modest, although heavy machinery is used extensively in the northeast. In other areas, mechanization is generally restricted to the use of electric and diesel pumps for improved irrigation, and power tillers and similar small machines such as three-person rice planters. Overall, Chinese agriculture remains labor intensive, and many cultivation practices, including the recycling of organic wastes as depicted in Figure 6-2, are similar to those employed in traditional times (Kuo, 1972).

SUPPLY OF LAND AND ITS UTILIZATION

China is large. This vastness of the country results in great environmental diversity, and this has had a far-reaching impact on the productivity of land. Moisture, temperature, and soil quality are the three most important physical variables. China's most productive agricultural lands have traditionally been located in the humid eastern flank of the country and especially the southeastern quadrant with its abundance of precipitation, extensive alluvial lowlands, and mild winter temperatures. No attempt is made here to describe in detail the regional environments of China, as were described in Chapter 2, but a table and map of general environmental characteristics and associated crop patterns are provided for reference purposes (Table 6-1 and Fig. 6-3).

According to Chao (1972), 110.6 million ha, or 11.45%, of China's surface area was thought to be cultivated in 1963. That was an increase from an estimated 94 million ha cultivated in the late 1940s (Table 6-2). The increase was thought to have resulted from field consolidation, reduction of fragmented plots, and removal of grave sites; the latter in some areas may have amounted to 2 to 3% of total land suited for cultivation. Land reclamation in northeast China and arid areas was also very important (Kuo, 1972). By contrast, the 48 coterminous United States were estimated to have 156 million ha of land suitable for cultivation, although in 1964, only 116 million ha of the total were cultivated.

Wu Chuan-chun, a Chinese geographer working at the Institute of Geography in Peking, estimated recently (1981a) that China's 1978 total cultivated land supply was 100 million ha, or 10.4% of the total land stock. Based on the various

Table 6-1. Major Environmental and Agricultural Regions of China

Region	Annual mean precipitation (mm.)	Growing season with daily mean temp. $>2^{\circ}$C (days)	Main agricultural soil	Chief natural hazard	Main summer crops	Main winter crops
Nei Monggol-Xinjiang	25– 500	25–175	Desert lithosols	Aridity, strong winds	Wheat, oats, millet	None
The Northeast	400–1200	75–200	Chernozem and chestnut	Spring low temperature, early frost	Maize, gaoliang, soybeans	None
North China Plain	400– 800	150–225	Chestnut and brown podzols, calcareous alluvium	Spring drought, alkalization	Wheat, maize, gaoliang, rice	Wheat, barley, peas
The Loess Plateau	300– 600	75–200	Loess and calcareous soils	Soil erosion, spring drought	Millet, maize, gaoliang, cotton	Wheat, barley
Middle-Lower Chang Jiang	800–2000	225–300	Red and purple lateritic types, some alluvium	Flood, waterlogging, autumn drought	Rice, cotton, tea	Wheat, barley, rapeseed, peas
South China	1000–2500	300–365	Alluvium and lateritic types	Typhoon, spring cold wave	Rice, peanuts, sweet potatoes	Wheat, rapeseed, barley, peas
The Southwest	600–1800	175–325	Red and yellow lateritic types	Low solar radiation	Rice, maize	Wheat, rapeseed
Qinghai-Tibet Plateau	100–1000	0–150	Desert and alpine types	Severe coldness, aridity	Wheat, barley	None

Source: Derived from Kung (1975) and Wu (1981b).

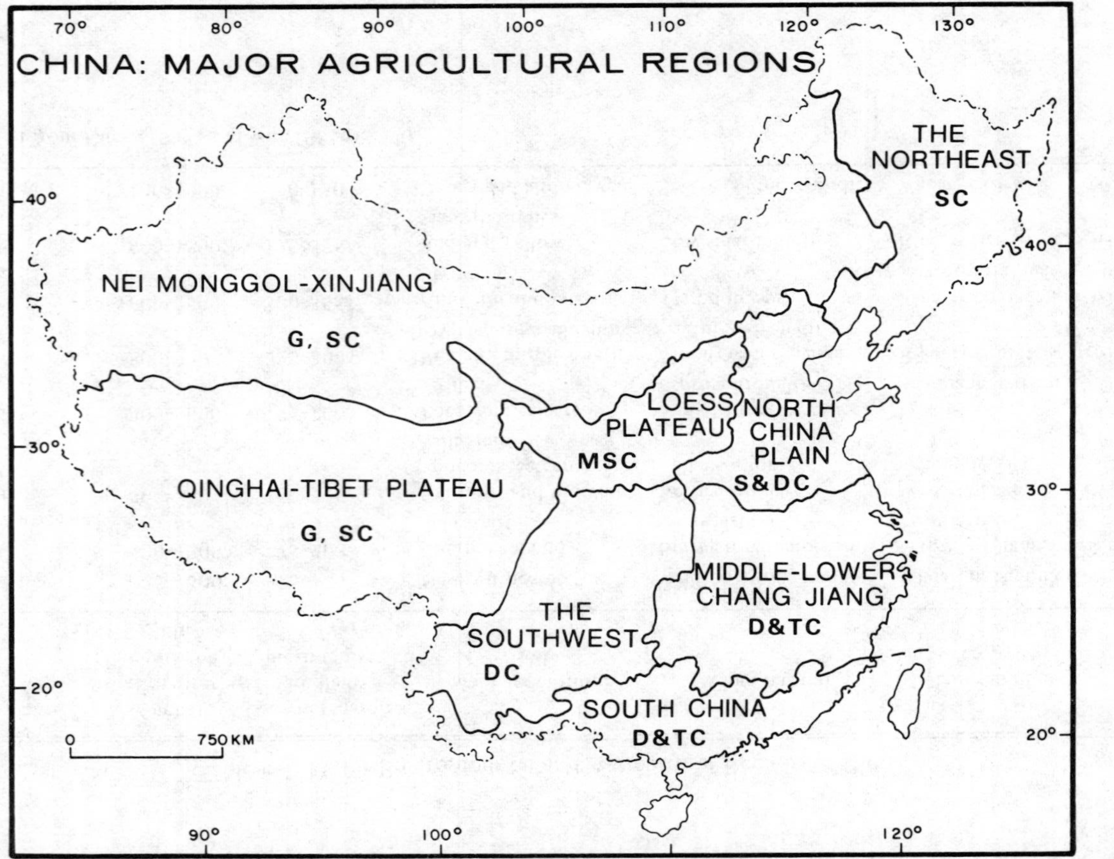

Fig. 6-3. China: Major agricultural and environmental regions. G—grazing, SC—single crop, MSC—mostly single crop, DC—double crop, TC—triple crop.

Source: Kung (1975); Wu (1981b).

estimates in recent years, the supply of cultivated land in China has declined by close to 10%. Much of the decline is accounted for by the recent afforestation of poor and marginal farmland. Although there may have been a modest increase after the end of World War II, there appears to have been a significant decrease in recent years despite an active and vigorous land reclamation program. Land reclamation has been greatest in the northeast (especially Heilongjiang Province) and in arid lands of western China. This land reclamation, however, has been offset by loss of farmland in China's growing cities, along transport lines, to water conservancy and afforestation projects and industrial areas. Wu (1981a) has claimed that approximately 20 million ha have been lost to such conversions, a tremendous amount. Any major increase in agricultural output, it appears, must come from increased yields, for the amount of cultivated land is not likely to increase much in the years ahead.

Other land uses provide an indication of the value and potential development of China's land stock. For example, in 1963, approximately 8% of China's land area was estimated to be in forests. Wu (1981a) indicated that 12.7% of China's land area in 1978 was composed of forestland. Chao (1970) noted that 30 million ha were suitable for reforestation. Some of this latter amount is former cropland degraded through intensive erosional processes as found, for example, in the loess-land of Shaanxi Province. Grasslands accounted for approximately 28% of the total while deserts, high mountains, and wasteland totaled approximately 18% (Table 6-2). China's land stock is a vast and rich resource, but it has not always been managed wisely and well. Without question, one of the most pressing issues facing the present leadership and government is how best to use and manage their large but qualitatively variable land resources to support China's enormous population.

Agricultural Land Use and Multiple Cropping

Traditionally, the agricultural system of China had intensified internally through increased use of a given unit of land. This was achieved by heavy labor input and maintenance of soil nutrients through the addition of a variety of organic manures (King, 1926; American Plant Studies Delegation, 1975; Whitney, 1973). This system of traditional farming has been continued, and indeed, refined, through more scientific approaches to green manuring and composting of human excreta (night soil), swine and poultry manures, and organic garbage from urban areas. Equally important has been the long-established practice of multiple cropping, more common in the south where environmental conditions favor such an approach (Evans, 1980).

Multiple cropping involves growing more than one crop per year on a given unit of land. In China the practice is very old, and many different types of tillage, cropping practices, and crop rotations are involved. These practices depend both on physical constraints, such as length of growing season, quality of soil, and availability of water, as well as on cultural habits related to local practices, specific needs, and administrative policies. Despite the enormous variations throughout the country, some general patterns may be identified. For example, in central China, a common pattern is to grow one summer rice crop, followed by wheat

Table 6-2. Supply and Utilization of Land in China (millions of hectare)

Year	Cultivated Area	Uncultivated	Forest	Land suitable for reforestation	Grassland	Deserts, high mts., other	Total** area
1946[a]	94.0						973
1957[b]	111.8						
1963[c]	110.6	36.8	76.4	30.2	268		964.8
1970[d]	107*					171.5	973
1978[e]	100		122		356	303	960

[a]T. H. Shen (1951).
[b]Official Chinese estimate from the State Statistical Bureau (*Ten Great Years*, 1960).
[c]Chao Shih-ying (1972).
[d]USDA (1976).
[e]Wu (1981b).
*Includes land used for crops and for soil improvement crops and fallow land. Pastureland is excluded (American Plant Studies Delegation, 1975).
**Reported total area of the country and not the total of the land categories enumerated here.

or an industrial (cash) crop such as rapeseed in winter. In the tropical south, two warm season rice crops and a short winter crop are common. In the north, winter wheat is the main crop, and it may be followed by summer grain or an industrial crop (Chang, 1971; Kung, 1975).

Wortman (1975) estimated that China's net cultivated area increased from 107 million ha to 150 million ha through the technique of multiple cropping. Wu (1981b) indicated that two large areas of China–the lower Chang Jiang (Yangzi) Basin and South China (Fig. 6-3)–have regional multiple cropping indexes of more than 200 (when 100 equals one crop per year on a given unit of land). The multiple cropping index for the entire country, according to Wu (1981b), has increased from 130 in 1949 to 150 in 1977. Such high indexes are a good indicator of the extreme intensity of the farming systems in these regions and the great efforts that are being made to increase crop production in these areas.

The important point to keep in mind about China's land resource is that one of the major factor endowments–cropland–is limited and has declined slightly in recent years. China can expand its agricultural land supply only with great cost and difficulty. Land conversions indicate good agricultural land near large cities is being lost, while land is being reclaimed in areas such as the arid west and cold northeast, where environments are more marginal for agricultural purposes. Thus, it is clear that future increases in agricultural production must come primarily from increased yields on the current land stock. The near term solutions for more agricultural production appear to be more investments in agriculture (irrigation systems, fertilizers, and seed improvement), which lead to continued increases in yield. At the same time, population growth must be reduced continually to permit increased per-capita output and and a better life for all of China's citizens. Recent evidence suggests both solutions are being followed at this time.

INSTITUTIONAL CHANGE–THE REORGANIZATION OF CHINESE AGRICULTURE

China's Communist Revolution, which succeeded in 1949, was a rural-based, agrarian revolution. Land reform and agricultural reorganization were important tenets of the revolutionary movement. As the Communist armies and cadres (political and administrative functionaries who are Communist Party members) extended their control over various areas of China in the late 1940s, one of the first policies to be established was confiscation of land from landlords and redistribution to poor peasants. Since then, the land reform has proceeded through several stages and culminated in the formation of agricultural communes (*gongshe*) in 1958–59. It is these communes and their subunits, the production brigades (*shengchan dadui*) and production teams (*shengchandui*), that form the essential units of agricultural production and organization today.

Although initially the government indicated it would proceed cautiously with land reform, by 1955 several good years of crop production led to growing confidence and the rapid increase in the socialist transformation of agriculture. Several stages of this change may be identified:

(1) *Land reform and redistribution:* Landlords were eliminated in 1950, and 46 million ha of land were redistributed to approximately 300 million "poor" peasants in an effort to persuade this group to support the new government. In 1952, production increases were announced as levies, as the government sought to strengthen its control over the peasantry.

(2) *Mutual Aid Teams:* In 1952, Mutual Aid Teams were established to help organize peasants into labor teams to provide labor supply for periods of peak labor demand, for example, during sowing and harvest periods. This move built on the traditional mutual support function of the peasant family and clan, but it left intact the concept that land remained owned by the peasant producers.

(3) *Agricultural Producer Cooperatives:* In 1955, Agricultural Producer Cooperatives were introduced through combining neighboring Mutual Aid Teams. In this arrangement, land was pooled into larger areal units of administration and given to the cooperatives. The peasants received a return remuneration, based on their land contribution and labor. The peasants also were allowed to retain a small private plot for their personal use. A committee with cadres was employed to oversee the activities of the cooperative.

(4) *Collective Farms:* The pace of socialization picked up rapidly after 1955. By the end of 1956, most farm households were collectivized. At this point, it became clear that ownership of land had passed to the state, although each peasant family continued to be allowed to retain a small private plot. The collective farms grew larger as more and more of the small units of production were combined, and more complex levels of leadership were called on to manage the affairs of the collective.

(5) *The Commune:* Finally, in 1958, in an enthusiastic Maoist inspired mass movement known as the "Great Leap Forward," the collectives were merged into larger units called communes. At the time the communes were formed, the government sought to galvanize the peasant masses into greater effort in order to achieve a purer form of communism. Thus, rewards were to be in part contingent on need rather than work. Private plots were abolished. Certain functions of village government were integrated with the administration of the commune. Production fell and economic problems followed. Some of the more radical aspects of the commune were abandoned, e.g., communal mess halls. Private plots have been restored, and today the commune remains a central unit of rural administration and land organization in China.

Communes account for 90% of the arable land. In 1973 there were approximately 50,000 communes in China. The number has decreased from 74,000 in 1964, but the decrease in number indicates an increase in the scale and size of the average unit (American Plant Studies Delegation, 1975). Communes range in area from 25–130 km^2 and average 15,000 members. Size varies between 8,000 and 80,000 people. Although it is difficult to generalize about their size, usually where agriculture is most intensive, communes have the largest and most densely clustered populations. Their areas may be smaller where environmental circumstances are especially propitious for farming, a reflection of the productivity and labor requirements of the individual communes.

Communes in contemporary China are conjointly the lowest level of central government administration and the highest level of rural organization and administration. For example, the central commune administration will typically be located in a market town and will include official personnel to perform such functions as banking, tax collecting, agricultural procurement, commerce, and public security. As the highest level of rural organization, communes typically will operate their own schools, hospitals, power stations, irrigation systems, industries, factories, and recreational facilities. Local personnel, who assume management positions, are usually trained in management techniques and are frequently Communist party members (Crook, 1975; Bennett, 1978).

Communes are organized into a three-tiered system, composed of production brigades, which can be subdivided into production teams. The production brigade is the second level of rural organization. Its main function is to assist the production teams in coordinating team plans and production with state economic plans. The production brigade exists to insure that state targets and plans are fulfilled. Brigade leaders spend half of their time as administrators and the remaining time working in the fields. In recent years, the brigade appears to have had a more important political than economic function in assisting production teams, although brigades will frequently take on an economic function that is too big to be managed at the team level. For example, brick making, repairing machinery, and providing electricity are frequently brigade functions. Conflict resolution among teams or hamlets is frequently handled by the brigade leader. Political exhortation, aimed at increasing production, may also be important at this level. Chen Yongui, the local peasant leader of the Dazhai Production Brigade in Shanxi Province, became a member of China's Politburo and a national symbol of peasant self-reliance during the late stages of the Cultural Revolution[9] (Salter, 1977). Although Chen and Dazhai are now in eclipse as examples used to galvanize the peasant masses to higher levels of production and activity, both Chen and Dazhai were enormously important political symbols for more than a decade throughout China (Salter, 1977).

The production team is the basic, essential unit of agricultural organization and production in China today. It is there that decisions about specific crops to be grown, techniques of cultivation, and farming inputs are made. Teams are generally composed of 80 to 160 people and are responsible for cultivating 8 to 38 ha of land (American Plant Studies Delegation, 1975). The team would correlate reasonably well with what in traditional times would have been a nucleated hamlet or village cluster, often based on one or more common surname clans or groups. Teams are further broken down into work groups which perform specific functions, such as pig raising, fertilizer management, or rice sowing.

Renumeration is based on an incentive system, which involves the individual's seniority, attitude, and skills, as determined by the team as well as the number of work days, i.e., the work points that an individual accumulates. The most

[9] The Cultural Revolution, which began in 1965 and continued through the early 1970s, was a radical Maoist-inspired, student-supported mass movement aimed at reducing the power of entrenched bureaucrats and party officials who were accused of being "capitalist roaders." Youthful "Red Guards" provided the manpower for this internal upheaval.

significant thing about the production teams, brigades, and communes is that for the first time in Chinese history, the authority of the central government extends down to the working level and daily lives of the individual peasant and his family. In the context of traditional China, where imperial governmental authority typically stopped at the level of the *xian* or county administration, this development is a remarkable achievement (Crook, 1975).

Team leaders are farmers first and leaders second, and their homes frequently serve as their headquarters. The team owns the land and all within it. It is the basic accounting and production unit. With the guidance and help of the brigade, the team decides on the type and quantity of crops to be grown and the type and quantity of manures and fertilizers to use. The team must take care of its own irrigation facilities, machines and equipment, as well as its own granary and draft animals (Bennett, 1978). One of the major problems is to obtain good leadership at the team level. The teams may or may not have Communist party members.

The families within the teams augment their income derived from labor contributions to the team by farming a small private plot, about 5% of a commune's farmland, and raising a few pigs and chickens. The family may sell homegrown commodities at "free markets" at unmonitored prices competitve with state-owned markets. Approximately 20% of the income of peasant families has been estimated to be derived from private activity. Production of individual teams and brigades may now be marketed at free markets, which form a vital adjunct to the state-controlled markets and food cooperatives. It appears that since 1976, marketing control of foodstuffs has been continually reduced. Control over food marketing was much less strict in 1980, and as a consequence, a large and varied selection of fresh produce is readily available in urban and rural areas alike.

Recently, there have been efforts to promote incentives and production by decentralizing authority and responsibility to family units. It is premature to know the extent and impact of this new unit production and responsibility system.

(6) *State Farms:* One additional unit of farm organization has also been developed–the state farm–which is a government owned and managed enterprise. These are estimated to occupy less than 4% of the total cultivated land area and generally are found in northeast China or in western China. State farms have been especially important in more sparsely populated agricultural areas, where a higher degree of mechanization exists and where active land reclamation programs are under way. Heilongjiang Province, for instance, is known to have a number of these farms (Welch, Lo, and Pannell, 1979).

AGRICULTURAL PRODUCTION

China is the world's largest producer of grains. Statistics on grain production since 1952 indicate generally steady increases from 161 million metric tons in 1952 to an estimated 318 million tons in 1980 (Table 6-3). Variability in rainfall, however, has led to good and bad years of production increases. China has invested heavily in irrigation facilities in an effort to reduce the dependency on annual rainfall and the vagaries of natural conditions. Offsetting the increases in grain

Table 6-3. Chinese Output of Selected Agricultural Commodities, 1949-1980 (millions of metric tons)

	1949	1952	1957	1965	1970	1977	1978*	1979*	1980***
Rice			86.8			129		141**	139
Wheat			23.6			41		61	54
Corn			21.4			48			
Soybeans			10.0			7			7.9
Other			49.3			67			
Total grain*	108	154	185	200	240	285	304.75	332**	318
Cotton			1.64			2.00			2.7
Sugarcane			10.39			17.70			
Sugar beets			1.50			2.48			
Tea			.11			.25			

Source: Wiens (1981).

*The Chinese define grain as staples that include rice, wheat, and other small grains; coarse grains such as corn, millet, gaoliang; beans and lentils (peas); and tubers (potatoes, yams, and cassava) are based on one-fourth of their field weight. Rice, small grains, and coarse grains are reported unmilled.

**USDA (1980).

****Beijing Review* (1981).

production, as noted, have been steady increases in population growth, which means only a very modest increase in the per capita grain produced in the country since 1952 (1952–282 kg/person; 1980–324 kg/person).

Rice accounts for the largest quantity of sown area in China and was estimated in 1976 to total 36 million ha (Groen and Kilpatrick, 1978). This total has increased modestly but steadily in recent years and has climbed from an estimated 32.2 million ha in 1957. Rice is also the leading grain produced in China, and the USDA estimated 141 million tons were produced in 1979 (Table 6-3), a considerable increase from the 86.8 million tons produced in 1957. In 1980, 139 million m tons were produced. Crop production figures, however, as well as land utilization data, are from Chinese official and unofficial reports, and one may encounter conflicting statements and statistics (Wiens, 1980). [Tables presented here indicate the sources of data and in some places different sources are employed.] Available evidence indicates there have been substantial improvements in rice farming in China, and several key aspects of the "Green Revolution" have had an impact. The American Plant Studies Delegation (1975) that visited China in 1974 observed and was told of extensive plantings of the International Rice Research Institute IR-8 *indica* dwarf varieties of rice throughout southern China. The delegation observed only dwarf, high yielding varieties of rice during its visit. Overall, the delegation credited China's success in increasing rice production to "the combination of extended irrigation, increased application of fertilizer, and the introduction of high yield varieties of rice" (Wortman, 1975).

Wheat continues to be China's second most important grain crop. Recent crop area was estimated to be 28.2 million ha with a 1979 large increase in crop production to 61 million metric tons (USDA, 1980). Wiens (1981) estimated wheat production in 1977 at 31 million tons, a significant increase from the 1966 total of 28 million tons, attributable to one of the same factors that influenced rice production, namely, the introduction of new high-yielding varieties of wheat. In addition, Wortman indicated the Chinese have extended the range of wheat, especially winter wheat, southward, where it is used as a winter crop in an annual rotation with rice. Wortman noted that its success as an intercrop depends on the use of quick maturing varieties as well as the increased use of chemical fertilizer. Wheat yields in the period 1967–71 averaged 1 metric ton per ha, but the yields have risen rapidly since then and averaged 1.6 ton/ha in 1979 (USDA, 1980).

Millets of two types, *Setaria italica* and *Panicum miliaceum*, are grown in China and were the first food grains domesticated in China. The *Setaria* type is the most common and is grown throughout China, although it is seen most in the north and is frequently interplanted with corn. Sorghum or *gaoliang*, as it is known locally, is an import from Africa that resembles some of the Chinese millet. Gaoliang is a very important crop and grown commonly in areas where precipitation and water supplies are modest. Consequently, it too is grown most widely in north China. The plant provides low quality food for humans and fodder for animal consumption, and is the base grain for the mash or brew used in the fermentation and distillation of grain alcohol for many Chinese distilled spirits. Varieties of the plant are tall, and the stalk is much valued for fencing and other purposes. It has often been used as a kind of insurance crop in areas where water deficiencies have occurred or are anticipated. The millets and gaoliang account for much of the remaining grain crop production which amounted in 1977 to 67 million tons (Wiens, 1981).

The soybean is a native of northern China and continues to be an important crop. Only in northern China is it grown as a major field crop, however, and its production has declined since 1957. Wiens estimated a 1977 total production of 7 million tons, and the USDA (1980) estimated production of 8.3 million m tons in 1979. The 1967–71 average production area was estimated at 8.1 million ha with a per unit yield (800 kg/ha) less than half that produced in the United States. By 1979, the estimated yield was 1137 kg/ha. The crop is very important in the Chinese diet, and a considerable amount of soybean breeding research is under way (Sprague, 1975).

Another crop which has apparently undergone a great increase in production is corn (maize), and the production has more than doubled between 1957 and 1977 to an estimated 48 million tons (Wiens, 1981). USDA (1980) reported an increase to 56 million tons in 1978. The crop is grown throughout the country, although it is most important in the north. Nearly 20 million ha were planted in corn in 1979, and extensive increases have taken place in north China and the northeast. Most of the corn grown in China is hybrid corn, being a cross of local lines with U.S. lines, and the results have been good. An extensive amount of plant breeding research on corn is under way (Sprague, 1975). In general, corn is grown as an irrigated crop, and most of the cultivation is done by hand. Increases in corn plantings in north China appear to have followed increases in the expansion of irrigation facilities. Corn stalks are a very important mulching material

Table 6-4. Estimated Livestock in People's Republic of China, 1949-1980 (1,000 head)

Animal	1949*	1957**	1972*	1977**	1978	1980***
Large animals[a]	59,775	83,500	95,042	96,000	93,750	95,246
Sheep and goats	42,347	98,600	148,215	160,000	161,360	187,311
Hogs	57,752	145,900	259,884	290,000	301,290	305,431

[a]Includes cattle, water buffalo, horses, donkeys, mules, and camels.
*USDA (1976).
**Wiens (1980).
****Beijing Review* (1981).

and are also needed for animal forage. Kernel corn is also used as a stock feed as well as for human consumption.

China produces an enormous range of agricultural commodities and products. Figures for some of these are provided in Tables 6-3 and 6-4. In addition to the large quantities of various grains, China is a major world producer of oilseeds, fruits, and vegetables. As with grains, China produces an astonishing variety of different oilseeds, fruits, melons, and vegetables, and this permits the country to provide its people with a wholesome, nutritious, and varied diet. A strategy of producing vegetables and fruits as well as basic grains to feed the local population has been developed and applied throughout China. Although there are obviously areas of higher and lower agricultural productivity, owing largely to environmental differences, the strategy of local production seems to work well and has made the various regions and metropolitan centers throughout China generally self-sufficient in foodstuffs (Skinner, 1978).

LIVESTOCK AND ANIMAL PRODUCTION

Although Chinese agriculture has not been renowned for the production of livestock, China is a major producer of farm animals (Table 6-4). Hogs are especially important, and China has the world's largest swine herd (305 million estimated in 1980; more than 5 times the number in 1949). In addition to swine, China in the same year had 187 million sheep and goats, mostly in the dry areas of western and northwestern China, and 95 million other large animals (horses, mules, buffalo, and cattle). Large animals are used mainly for draft purposes throughout the country.

Hogs are unquestionably the most important animals in China. They are found throughout the country. Most farm families own one or two hogs, and the animals are valuable both for their meat as well as the prodigious quantities of high quality manure they produce. Unlike pork production in the United States, where emphasis is placed on the rapid production of pork through high quality feeding,

Chinese pigs are scavengers and are fed scraps and grasses with little economic value. Swine fodder in China includes vegetable wastes, water plants, and the bran of rice, wheat, and millet. At this time in China, swine do not compete for food usable for humans, and the economic utility of the hogs is viewed differently from the fast weight gain approach employed in the United States. Hogs are highly valued in China and will no doubt continue to play a vital role in the production of organic manures as well as in providing an inexpensive, easily available source of animal protein throughout the country.

China produces a large quantity of poultry, mostly chickens and ducks. As with swine, the various fowl are treated to some extent as scavengers that can subsist off of materials not useful to humans. The Chinese see poultry as inexpensive to produce and as providing eggs, meat, and feathers, in addition to manure.

USE OF FERTILIZERS

One of the most remarkable things about Chinese agriculture, both in traditional times and even today, is the extent to which it depends on the recycling of organic materials and wastes for the maintenance of soil nutrients. In China all waste is precious, and the approach to using waste materials as an economic asset is followed conscientiously. The Chinese have been following this organic approach for many centuries and have built up an enormous range of experience in matching local soils with particular organic manures (King, 1926).

In recent years the use of chemical and mineral fertilizers has become increasingly popular. These new fertilizers are important, yet the traditional manurial resources continue to be the main source of nutrient materials. The FAO (1977) estimated that two-thirds of the total nutrient intake was derived from natural manures, and their contribution is, and will continue to be, crucial to the nutrient supply for Chinese farming. Among the many factors that promote the continued use of these manurial resources are their relatively low cost and local availability. Few capital costs are involved; the main costs are the labor and other costs involved in collecting, storing, and transporting the manures. Moreover, organic manures improve soil structure and do not create soil problems through long-term applications; and for these reasons, commune peasants prefer them.

Manurial resources include a number of different materials: animal wastes, especially swine and cattle manure and urine; human wastes (night soil, urine, sewage sludge from biogas digesters, and garbage); crop wastes (husks, stalks, straw, stubble, grasses, weeds, leaves, industrial crop wastes); green manures and water plants; atmospheric nitrogen fixing bio-fertilizers such as Azolla; silt and mud. Figure 6-2 depicts the recycling of organic wastes in a circular manner through soil and the growth of plants that supplies China's large human and animal population. It is clear from the flow diagram that little organic material associated with human beings escapes the recycling mechanism.

It is apparent that China has taken a long-used, efficacious and traditional agricultural technology based on locally available resources and adapted and improved it for contemporary use. The improvements include better methods of

Night soil being taken to field for application as a top dressing in the loess area of Taihang Mountains. (*C. W. Pannell*)

handling and processing animal and human wastes, as well as advanced technological methodologies involved in the development of bio-fertilizers, which fix atmospheric nitrogen and which are especially appropriate for fertilizing wet rice. Organic materials are applied through a number of techniques. In some cases, manures are mixed with straw, ground stalks, and/or mud and silt, and are applied as a dry mulch. In other cases, night soil may be applied in liquid or slurry form as a top dressing. An enormous amount of experience has been gained in the use of the traditional fertilizers at the local level. To this well-established fund of knowledge and experience, recent approaches have stressed scientific methods in evaluating nutrient content and utility of the various fertilizers and their value in application to specific soils.

China does not avoid the use of all mineral and chemical fertilizers. Indeed, China's recent plans for economic modernization have included industrial plants to produce such fertilizers. Moreover, small-scale fertilizer plants that produce ammonium bicarbonate have been developed at the commune level throughout China. Application of mineral fertilizers has increased but is modest by the quantities employed in Japan and Taiwan. The Chinese have preferred to use superphosphates and ammonia with organic fertilizers in the belief that a better balance of nutrients is maintained and better nutrient flow and soil quality results throughout the growing period of crops and afterwards. Such an approach is appropriate and well suited for China, given the present level of resources available as well as the amount of capital available for investment in agricultural chemicals and technology.

AGRICULTURAL MECHANIZATION

One of the significant components in China's agricultural development is mechanization, for it is through mechanization that labor productivity will rise and thus enhance the levels of living of the hundreds of millions of Chinese peasants. The difficulty with mechanization is the cost and the necessity for increasing production and land productivity, while shifting from hand labor to machine labor. The Chinese appear to be committed to raising both labor and land productivity in their efforts to mechanize agriculture.

The term "mechanization" has been used widely and sometimes loosely in China during recent years. The precise meaning and goals of mechanization have never been well defined and appear to have changed along with basic policy changes (Butler, 1978). Such changes have been especially prominent when related to the "Dazhai Production Brigade Model," as an example of self-reliance in agricultural development. Dazhai as a model, however, has been discredited since 1979 because of supposed falsification of records and other problems. Thus, it no longer seems appropriate to focus on the previously widely proclaimed but poorly defined goal of basic mechanization of Chinese agriculture by 1980. Generally, it seems that a flexible approach to mechanization has been followed since the late 1970s to comport with local and provincial conditions and goals. The components of this approach to mechanization, which appear not to have changed greatly, may be identified.

Mechanization since the late 1970s has emphasized the production of mechanized equipment for irrigation and water conservancy projects; the production of hand tractors useful for tillage and cartage operations; and the production of diesel and internal combustion engines to power this equipment. Overall, as Whitton (1976) noted, in following the mechanization of water conservancy projects, the emphasis in Chinese agriculture seems to be on (1) plowing, (2) processing, (3) threshing, and (4) rice transplanting. All of these are particularly onerous, labor intensive operations, and the major goal of agricultural mechanization appears to be to free farm labor from the post-harvest operations, in order to get the peasants back into field operations more rapidly. In this way, greater expansion of the area and practice of multiple cropping is promoted.

Another important aspect of this mechanization program is to decentralize the production of the tractors and engines to the county and even commune level. Local production insures the practice of mechanization diffuses rapidly throughout the country. Consequently the production of machinery was one of the key elements in the development of "five small industries"[10] associated with

[10]The "five small industries" refer to agricultural machinery, chemical fertilizers, cement, iron and steel, and coal mining and the small-scale production of these goods at the local level. More details are provided in Chapter 8.

rural industrialization in China. An important associated issue, however, is that factories producing such machines and equipment are expected to operate efficiently and produce a profit. Thus, they must be managed carefully within the organizational setup of whatever unit they belong to. This is not always an easy task.

Chinese farm machines are designed to be relatively simple and able to perform specific functions, such as plowing, threshing, or planting easily and efficiently. The hand tractors are now reported to have more than 30 implements to permit them to perform a variety of other functions, such as harrowing, leveling land, seeding and even spraying and producing electricity. But the idea remains. That is to produce simple equipment, which is easy to operate and effective for farm tasks. Different areas of China have different needs. For example, large, heavy equipment is required for the sparsely settled area in the northeast and northwest, where there are extremely large fields. By contrast, the smaller field size in the southeast requires more hand tractors and devices such as rice planters. Nevertheless, the priority for farm machinery throughout the country remains equipment, which is low cost, simple and easy to operate and repair, able to perform a variety of functions, and able to release human labor from the most difficult tasks.

At this point, it is difficult to know exactly how far mechanization of agriculture has proceeded in China and what its consequences are. Farm machines are produced all over China and are widely used and available. Machines have not replaced farm labor, however, and there has not been a great farm-to-factory-and-town migration. Given the enormous pressure to continue to increase crop production and land productivity, it does not appear that the mechanization currently being practiced or foreseen will release a large labor force. It does appear that farm mechanization will help raise levels of labor productivity, but at what point yields and land productivity begin to taper off as a result of less attention by human beings is difficult to know at this point.

IRRIGATION AND ITS USE

Although it remains difficult to get accurate figures on the irrigation of farmland in China, it is clear that one of the most significant achievements of the Communist period has been investment, improvement in, and expansion of the irrigated farmland of the country. There has been a steady investment of both fixed and labor resources in the construction of reservoirs, ponds, ditches, canals, irrigation networks, power and pumping stations, and related earthworks for three decades. Since the early 1970s, the Chinese have claimed that more than 40% of their total cropland (44 million ha at the end of 1977) was irrigated; 46.7 million ha were believed to be a reasonable estimate for irrigated land in 1979 (USDA, 1980) (Tables 6-5a and 6-5b).

Extent of irrigated land, although known only to be estimates, reveals rather sharp regional differences (Tables 6-5a and 6-5b). Substantial gains in irrigated acreage since 1949 have been reported throughout the country, but the largest increases have been made in two major regions—North China (including the North

Table 6-5a. Total Area Irrigated, People's Republic of China, 1949, 1957, and 1973-76 (thous. ha)

Administrative unit	1949	1957	1973	1974	1975	1976
PRC total	15,995	34,320–35,527			min = 37,489 max = 44,660	min = 40,895 max = 47,119
Heilongjiang	54	320–300	783–833	933	1,130–1,600	1,310–1,780
Jilin	86	280–324	NA	600	680–714	788–814
Liaoning	60	460–486	NA	1,333	NA	NA
Total Northeastern	200	1,060–1,110			3,143–3,647	3,423–3,927
Henan	480	2,810–2,860	NA	3,000–3,200	3,300–3,530	3,500–3,730
Hebei	820	1,760–1,800	NA	3,300	3,560–3,690	3,733–3,863
Peking			257	300	338	347–364
Shanxi	245	750–753	688	931	NA	NA
Shandong	235	1,990–2,460	2,907–3,207	3,200–3,530	2,600–3,300	3,530
Tianjin			35	NA	64	NA
Total Northern	1,780	7,310–7,870			9,831–11,151	12,105–12,482
Anhui	1,130	2,280–2,260	3,000	530	NA	796
Zhejiang	1,300	1,590–1,600	1,440	1,060	1,325	1,514
Jiangsu	1,820	2,560–2,553	NA	3,300	2,666	3,400
Shanghai			331–356	331–356	331–356	NA
Total Eastern	4,250	6,430–6,410			4,852–8,096	6,041–8,270
Hunan	NA	2,660–2,778	2,310	1,236	1,260	NA
Hubei	NA	1,930–1,860	2,400	NA	NA	2,600
Jiangxi	1,114	1,720–1,930	1,460	NA	NA	NA
Total Central	(4,680)	6,310–6,570			5,120–6,170	5,320–6,370

Fujian	570	990–986	1,080	NA	975–1,125	999–1,149
Guangxi	472	1,330–1,664	1,300	1,056–1,064	1,130	1,185
Guangdong	860	2,600–1,393	2,900	2,530	2,578	1,800–3,088
Total Southeastern	1,900	4,920–4,040			4,683–5,325	3,984–5,537
Guizhou	190	610–529	800	NA	NA	NA
Sichuan	730	2,560–3,690	3,600	NA	NA	NA
Tibet	NA	NA	141–152	161–172	167–178	177–188
Yunnan	295	770–820	860	NA	NA	NA
Total Southwestern	1,220	3,940–5,040			5,427–5,438	5,437–5,448
Nei Monggol	285	800–804	151	191	283	328
Gansu	320	1,060–1,200	400	NA	NA	167
Ningxia			230	60	60	NA
Shaanxi	235	650–648	1,300	1,093	1,130	1,203
Xinjiang	1,075	1,710–1,718	NA	666	2,400	2,667
Chinghai	50	130–111	137	147	160	NA
Total Northwestern	1,965	4,350–4,480			4,433–4,773	4,585–5,085

Source: USDA (1977).

Table 6-5b. Estimated Irrigated Area, People's Republic of China (thous. ha)

1949	1957	1977	1979
15,995	34,924	44,007	46,670

Based on averages of U.S. Department of Agriculture estimates (1980).

Irrigation canal in the Turpan Basin of Xinjiang. (*L. Ma*)

China Plain and Loess Plateau regions) and the northeast, especially Heilongjiang Province. One of the more serious challenges in the future, and especially for North China, will be not only the supply of capital and labor to construct expanded irrigation facilities, but perhaps more importantly, the source of the irrigation waters. The Yellow River and its tributaries do not have sufficient supplies to meet the irrigation demands of North China. It is here that the importance of diverting and pumping Yangzi River water north may become critical, as discussed in Chapter 2.

The significance of irrigation to agricultural development in China cannot be overstated. Tremendous efforts to expand and improve irrigation facilities and networks have been made, and they help account for the gains in crop production. Much of the investment and productivity gained in association with agricultural mechanization in China are, in fact, investments and improvements in irrigation systems. A great deal more can be done, but much of the easier and less expensive work has already been accomplished. The Chinese must now concern themselves with availability and transfer of water over long distances, a costly and difficult undertaking, as they continue to improve the amount of land irrigated and the quality of that land.

AGRICULTURAL REGIONS AND CROPPING SYSTEMS

For many years, the conventional method of defining China's agricultural regions was to delimit three main parts: (1) The Dry West, which included herding and oasis agriculture primarily; (2) North China, which depended mainly on wheat and coarse grains and which had hot, humid summers but cold, dry winters; and (3) Central and South China, a rice growing region appropriate for a humid, mild climate. The most significant division was that between warm, humid rice-growing central and south China and the dry colder wheat/coarse grain-growing north. The division between north and south China is an east-west one that parallels generally the axis of the Qinling Mountain Range, and extends eastward along the line to the Huai River, and on to the coast of the East China Sea (Fig. 6-3), a climatic-boundary noted previously. A number of scholars have observed this fundamental north-south division, and indeed, have described and mapped it based on the objective reality of primary crop types and land utilization (Hu, 1936; Buck, 1935). More recently, this definition served as a basic division between northern and southern Chinese agriculture (CIA, 1971). The division also paralleled closely Whitney's (1973) division between areas of surplus and deficit moisture, located largely between north and south China, as divided by the Qinling Mountain boundary, a division discussed in Chapter 2 (Nuttonson, 1968).

Such attempts to delimit the main agricultural zones of China are fine for descriptive purposes, but in recent years the Chinese government has sought to improve agricultural output by analyzing carefully regional environments and insuring that the most appropriate crops are associated with distinctive environments. Recent studies of agricultural regionalization have examined the entire country. Natural environmental conditions of temperature, moisture, and soils, as seen in such measures as precipitation, aridity, and accumulated temperature, have served as the basis for agricultural regions. The goal is to evaluate the influence of natural conditions on the agricultural activities, land utilization, crop combinations, and the present level and stability of production. Such evaluation then will permit a comprehensive assessment to be made of the foundations of Chinese agriculture. The physical/environmental evaluation has resulted in the division of China into eight major agricultural regions (Wu, 1981b). These regions are identified in Figure 6-3 and are described below:

A) WESTERN CHINA:

1) *Qinghai-Tibet Plateau*

Much of this great plateau is over 4,000 m high, and is cold and dry. Grazing of sheep, yaks, and horses is important, and the people are skilled herders. In

Kazak yurt in the Tian Shan Mountains of Xinjiang. Kazaks are primarily engaged in herding in these upland areas. (*L. Ma*)

valleys, communes have been organized, and subsistence agriculture has been improved. Winter and spring wheat are grown above 4,000 m along with potatoes and barley. Fruits and vegetables have been introduced.

2) *Nei Monggol-Xinjiang*

This area is north and northwest beyond the Great Wall and is one of China's largest agricultural regions. Dryness is the main environmental characteristic, and rainfall diminishes from 300 mm to 25 mm generally as one moves westward. Herding is the main activity here, although sedentary cultivation is important at oasis locations along the lowest slopes of the major ranges, rimming some of the great basins. Crops include grain, cotton, and sugar beets, usually associated with state farms. This region would benefit from more investment in irrigation and development of the more extensive water conservancy projects through tree plantings of shelter belts.

B) **NORTH CHINA**:

3) *The Loess Plateau*

The Loess Plateau is an easily defined geographic region which is enclosed by the Great Wall on the north and west, the Taihang Mountains on the east, and

Advanced gully erosion adjacent to cultivated fields on the loesslands of Shaanxi Province. This condition has been a chronic, long-term problem on the Loess Plateau. (Courtesy of Rhoads Murphey.)

the Qinling Mountains on the south. Loess covers the entire plateau. Where slope angle is steep, the loess has been eroded into badlands, and soil erosion continues to be an extremely serious problem throughout the plateau.

Chinese agriculture and civilization developed here, and man has been farming and altering this landscape for millenia. Cultivation has focused on the river bottoms and valleys, in part due to availability of irrigation water. Some uplands have been terraced, but lack of water inhibits cultivation. Millets and gaoliang are traditional dry crops, whereas cotton, wheat, and more recently corn are grown where irrigation waters are available. One of the most serious problems here is the removal of original vegetation for firewood and the degeneration of the slope land. This, of course, has exacerbated the erosional problems, and in recent years, much effort has been expended to plant trees and attempt to stabilize the soil cover.

4) *The North China Plain*

The North China Plain, bounded on the north by the Great Wall and on the south by the Huai River, is one of China's most densely populated and productive regions. The floodplain of the Huang He dominates the plain which also includes the floodplains of the Hai He in the vicinity of Peking and the Huai River to the south. Main crops include wheat, barley, cotton, corn, gaoliang, millets, and peanuts, with a wheat/barley rotation during the winter months. Forty percent of China's total cotton acreage is here, and this is also the main area for peanut production. Despite the productive agricultural environment, the North China Plain does not produce enough food to feed itself. Future plans for agricultural development include more facilities to irrigate this plain.

5) *The Northeast (Manchuria)*

This region, composed of the three northern provinces of Heilongjiang, Jilin, and Liaoning, is focused around the great Songliao or Northeastern Plain, which is rimmed by mountains on the west (Greater Hinggan), north (Lesser Hinggan), and east (Changbai). The plain is low, flat, and swampy. Except for the southern flank, the Songliao Plain has been farmed intensively only for the last 100 years. Much fertile land remains in Heilongjiang, and state farms in recent years have been engaged actively in reclaiming marsh and forestland. Cold weather and periodic drought limit crops here, but irrigation and specialized crops ameliorate the situation. Crops include annual harvests of spring wheat, millets, gaoliang, corn, soybeans, sugar beets, and flax. Some wet rice is grown in the Northeast. The Northeast has entered the domain of the Han Chinese relatively recently. Consequently, field size is larger, population density is lower, and the mechanization of agriculture has proceeded more rapidly. In Heilongjiang, especially, heavy duty equipment has become common in farming. This contrasts sharply with the very labor intensive agriculture found in densely settled parts of China. This area is one of China's last great frontiers for opening up new cropland, but the amount of potential farmland remaining is not sufficient to be a solution to the feeding of vast numbers of Chinese.

C) CENTRAL AND SOUTHERN CHINA:

6) *The Middle Lower Chang Jiang (Yangzi River)*

Although settled after the North China Plain, this region is truly the agricultural and rice producing heartland of the country. Focused around the Yangzi River, the large lakes, and the tributary streams of the Yangzi, much of this region is a low lying alluvial plain, well watered and highly productive. As Wu (1981b) noted, 20% of China's cultivated land and farm population is located here, but the region produces 60% of China's tea; 50% of the rice, rapeseed (a common oilseed), and fresh water fish; 40% of the cotton; and 35% of the pigs. Double cropping of rice and winter wheat is common. The multiple cropping index of this region is the highest in China. The yields per unit area here are the highest in the country. Concomitantly, population density is high throughout the flat alluvial plains found in this region. So, it is in no way surprising that Shanghai, the port that serves the entire hinterland of the Yangzi Basin, is China's largest city. This is also China's wealthiest region, and has traditionally provided a substantial surplus of agricultural commodities.

Drainage channel in Pearl River Delta south of Canton. Sugarcane and banana trees are in the background. (*C. W. Pannell*)

7) *South China*

China's southern area is rugged. Mountains and hills compose about 90% of the land area. Alluvial plains are found along the coasts and major rivers. The major river basin is focused on the Xi (West) Jiang and its tributaries. Where the Xi and its distributary, the Zhu Jiang (Pearl River), empty into the South China Sea is found the only large alluvial plain in the region.

The environment in southern China is humid, tropical, and subtropical. Dense agricultural populations thrive in the alluvial lowlands. In the large Pearl River Delta, rice, sugarcane, mulberries, tropical fruits, and fresh water fish are grown, and the area around the port city of Guangzhou (Canton) is rich and productive. The tropical conditions of heavy rainfall and no frost permit continuous cultivation, and two crops of rice plus a winter crop of wheat or rapeseed are common. Delta areas along China's southern flank, as well as farther north, suffer from periodic tidal surges. The development and cultivation of saline-resistant varieties of wet rice remain a high priority item for agricultural research. As in other tropical and subtropical areas, the care and proper use of soils remain significant concerns of farmers and land managers.

8) *The Southwest*

Southwest China, according to Wu (1981b), includes two main physical units–the Sichuan Basin and the Yunnan-Guizhou Plateau. Except for the relatively

Preparing land for short season winter crop after December harvest of rice in Guangdong Province south of Canton. (*C. W. Pannell*)

flat, irrigated, alluvial plain around Chengdu in the western part of the Sichuan Basin, most of this region is neither a productive nor rich agricultural area. Generally this condition results from the rough hilly or mountainous relief. Sandstone and limestone based soils also create problems locally. Climatic factors favor intensive agricultural development. Double cropping of rice is possible where irrigation waters are available, but the rugged landscape has precluded dense settlement and intensive agriculture except in valley bottoms typically along the larger streams. Native ethnic groups, many of whom practice shifting forms of agriculture, have scattered throughout the forested uplands of this part of China.

COMPARING AGRICULTURAL SYSTEMS IN NORTH AND SOUTH CHINA

Although it is difficult to generalize about Chinese agriculture, enough information exists from different areas and different farm organizations to offer a reasonable, qualitative picture of Chinese agricultural life in various locales and settings. There follow brief descriptions of the situation and conditions on two Chinese agricultural units seen in August, 1977, during a visit of an American geography delegation to China. First described is a commune outside Guangzhou in the humid, tropical Pearl River Delta. Next, the commentary describes a production brigade south of Xi'an at the northern foot of the Qinling Mountains on the Loess

Plateau. Although the scale of the units differs, it is possible to compare and contrast items such as per-unit yields and the goals of the organizations.

Xinhua Commune is a suburban commune located 40 km north of Guangzhou. The commune occupies 110 km^2 of hills and plains, about half of which is plains. The commune contained 15,700 families and 68,000 people in 1977. The people and area are divided into 20 production brigades and 313 production teams. Almost half of the entire area is cultivated, and 81% of this cultivated land is in rice production. Winter wheat is planted as a winter crop and other crops include peanuts, sugarcane, jute, soybeans, herbs, and fruits. The commune had steadily increased its crop production primarily through heavy investment and continued improvement of an extensive irrigation system, reservoirs, canals, dikes, and a pumping network. Paralleling improvements in irrigation was a well-developed system of local agricultural research and extension activities, designed to promote better knowledge and understanding of agriculture from the level of the individual peasant up through experimental institutes and universities. Per *mou* yields were reported to exceed 1,000 cattles (7,500 kg/ha) compared with a 1977 national average for rice of 3,560 kg/ha. Swine raising was also important, and 75,000 pigs were raised collectively. The commune was clearly meeting its production quotas.

Social services were focused on health and educational facilities. The commune maintained two clinics which included dental facilities, and there were health stations at each brigade. Each team had a health worker. Medical services were either free or provided for at a nominal monthly fee (3 *mao* = 16¢) per person. Free schooling is provided for children through the middle school level.

Commune officials indicated that all cadres must do manual work in addition to administration. At the brigade level, cadres must work 300 days a year. At the level of commune organization, they are required to work 150 to 200 days. In this way, the cadre maintains close contact with the peasants and the realities of their daily working environment.

Ruanshi People's Commune is located approximately 30 km south of Xi'an at the foot of the Qinling Mountains. Only one brigade was visited, the Xiaoxin Village Production Brigade, and data were provided by a brigade leader. The brigade was composed of 8 teams and 295 families. The total population was 1,600 of whom 600 were considered full-time members of the labor force. This brigade farmed 133 ha of which 10 ha were in fruit trees and orchards. Other main crops included wheat, corn, and rice in various types of seasonal rotations. Two crops a year of winter wheat and corn were normal, although some work had been done to intensify the cropping cycles.

Production had fluctuated in recent years. The fluctuation is probably due to climate variations, although it was claimed political interference had been the cause. In 1976, average grain yields, however, were reported to be 823 catties/*mou* (6,180 kg/ha), which was claimed to be 6 times greater than in 1948 and 1.3 times greater than in 1964. Much investment had been made in an elaborate irrigation system. Irrigation plus improved seed strains, fertilizing and mulching techniques, and cropping practices were believed responsible for the production increases. Swine raising was also important with its function of providing both meat and manure.

In closing, Xiaoxin Brigade had plans to reclaim 120 *mou* of new farmland and to harness a local river for irrigation water and power production. The brigade leader indicated the main goal of raising production yield figures to 1,300 cattles/*mou* (9,750 kg/ha), a 58% increase over 1976. He also indicated that this could be accomplished partly through raising three crops per year notwithstanding the harsh and cold winters and the dryness of the Loess Plateau.

CONCLUSION: ACHIEVEMENT AND CHALLENGE IN CHINESE AGRICULTURE

Chinese agriculture, as with Chinese resources, faces an enormous challenge, the feeding and support of almost one-quarter of the human race. Agriculture is called upon, moreover, to provide a surplus for capital accumulation. The soil and water resources of the country, however, have definite limits, and the Chinese people have responded traditionally with an innovative system of recycling organic wastes. Since 1949, this traditional system has been made more regular and intensive, and has been coupled with an equally intensified effort to focus more scientific research on agriculture. The results have been impressive gains in the total quantity of food grains and livestock produced in China between 1949 and 1980 (Tables 6-3 and 6-4), yet increases in per capita food grains are not nearly so impressive. The record suggests that Chinese modernization and improved well-being truly must be linked to reduced population growth and increased agricultural production. Increases in agricultural productivity can be achieved in the future, but if China wishes to provide a better life for its people, these increases should result from improvements in both land and labor productivity and the substitution of capital and energy inputs for human inputs in the agricultural sector. Only in this way will the age-old cycle of increased food production and increases in population be broken with an improved livelihood then available for all of China's citizens.

FISHERIES

The Chinese, although consuming an average of only 5 kg of fish products/per person in 1979, are among the world's leading fishermen. In 1979, China produced 4,305,000 metric tons of fish, which placed China third among the world's nations for the production of marine and fish products (Table 6-6). This total was a decline from a reported 5,020,000 tons produced in 1959, the result of stricter laws and conservation practices that relate to the management and support of fishing grounds (Hanson, 1981). Of the 1979 total of 4.3 million metric tons, some 3.1 million metric tons, or 72%, were estimated to be of marine origin. The remainder was produced in inland ponds and waterways. This is a slight percentage increase over the 67% of marine origin reported by Cressey (1955) for the annual fish harvest of 1,360,700 tons prior to the outbreak of the Sino-Japanese War of 1937.

Table 6-6. Chinese Fisheries Production, 1949–1979

Year	Quantity (metric tons)
1949	450,000
1950	911,000
1951	1,330,000
1952	1,660,000
1953	1,890,000
1954	2,160,000
1955	2,500,000
1956	2,550,000
1957	3,120,000
1958	4,060,000
1959	5,020,000
1977	4,700,000
1978	4,660,000
1979	4,305,000

Source: Hanson (1981).

China has a favorable situation for marine and freshwater fish production. The long coastline, much of which is indented and irregular, the extensive continental shelf, and the nature of the intersecting offshore ocean currents combine to give China a particularly desirable physical situation. As Hanson (1981) noted, one-quarter of the available trawling grounds of the world are found in that portion of China's continental shelf within the 100 fathom isobath. The extent of this 100 fathom shelf exceeds 1,100,000 km^2, an enormous and very productive fishing ground.

The main pelagic fishing grounds may be divided into four different areas—South China Sea, East China Sea, Yellow Sea, and Bohai (Fig. 6-4). Main species caught include several varieties of croaker, herring, mackerel, tuna, shark, squid, and octopus. Prawns and other shellfish are also very important and account for a considerable portion of the value of the fish products that are exported each year.

Inland fisheries are also very important, and China with its ancient tradition of aquaculture is the world's largest producer of fresh water fish (FAO Fisheries Mission to China, 1977). Several varieties of carp are the most common freshwater fish. One of the most interesting and productive inland fish farming areas is found in the Pearl River Delta between Canton and Macao in Shunde County. Here, an unusual ecological cycling combination of mulberry trees, sugarcane, and fishponds coexist. Droppings from silkworms are fed to the fish. The mud and guck from the fishponds are returned to the cane fields and mulberry orchards as a primary soil ingredient. All organic material appears to find its way into this highly productive cycle, and the farmers and commune members in that area are among the most prosperous in the Pearl River Delta region.

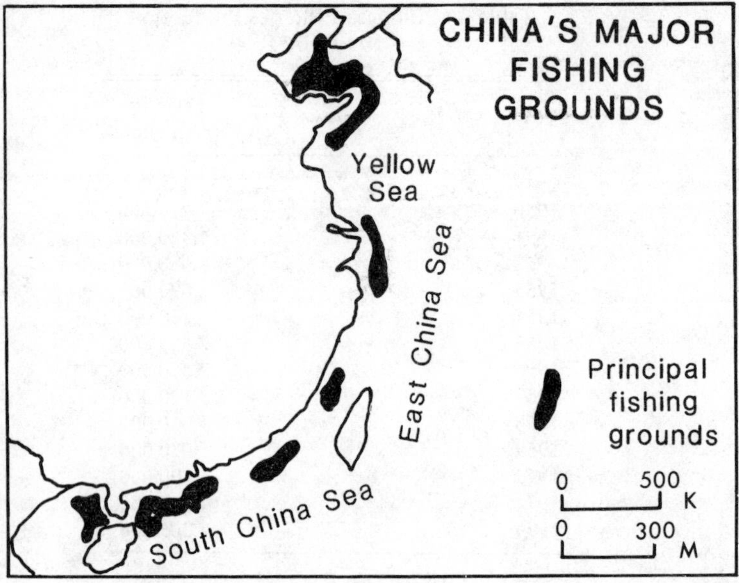

Fig. 6-4. Major fishing grounds of China.
Source: Hanson (1981).

Harvesting of carp grown in a pond in the Pearl River Delta near Canton. (*C. W. Pannell*)

Problems exist in freshwater fish cultivation, however. There is great pressure to convert fishponds, lakes, and drainage channels into land for crop production. Consequently, it has been reported that a serious decline in freshwater fish production has occurred during the last 20 years. Efforts are under way to improve scientific knowledge and better management practices for fish cultivation, but much room for improvement exists.

Exports of fish and marine products are a significant earner of foreign exchange for China. In 1978, more than $250 million of fish were exported, principally to Japan, Hong Kong, and other Asian countries. Not only is fishing important in providing valuable dietary supplements for the Chinese, but it brings in badly needed foreign exchange and can justify extensive investment in the fishing industry as a consequence. Hanson (1981) has indicated that a great deal more attention and investment will be focused on fisheries as a matter of future state policy. Perhaps most significant is the fact that in 1979 fisheries were included among the 108 leading areas, where more scientific research was needed. Also, the government has called for improvements in the nation's fisheries. Altogether, fish and marine products are very important in China's economy and as a vital supplement in Chinese diet. With more research, better understanding, and more investment in fisheries, the outlook should be promising, and China will no doubt continue to benefit greatly from its inland and marine fishery resources.

FORESTRY

China's forest resources, although never extensive, were seriously depleted over the centuries as a result of the demands of the large and growing population. Demand for firewood, charcoal, and construction material had steadily increased, and little or no attention was given to replenishing the forests that were cut or burned. Cuttings were especially severe in north China. But even in the extensive uplands in the humid south, farmers and commercial operators had cut heavily into the forest stock. The major stands of natural forests which remained in China in 1949 were in the Northeast and especially in the horseshoe composed of the Greater and Lesser Hinggan Range and the Changbai Mountains; the rugged and largely inaccessible highlands of southwest China and the eastern flanks of the Tibetan Plateau; and the northern flank of the Tian Shan Range in the far west of Xinjiang. In addition, large stands were scattered through the southern mountains and the uplands of central China (Fig. 6-5).

A considerable amount of variation exists among the estimates of the amount of forest cover in China (Table 6-7). Ross (1981) has summarized and evaluated the various estimates. His view is that in the late 1940s, probably some 8 to 9% of the total surface of the country (more than 80,000,000 ha) was in forests. This figure was based on the estimates of a respected Republican-era forester D. Y. Lin. The Communist Chinese, however, released figures, based on a 1955 survey that was apparently not too carefully done, of 5 to 5.5% of the total surface area. This figure was later revised to 7.9%, which indicates the Chinese had little

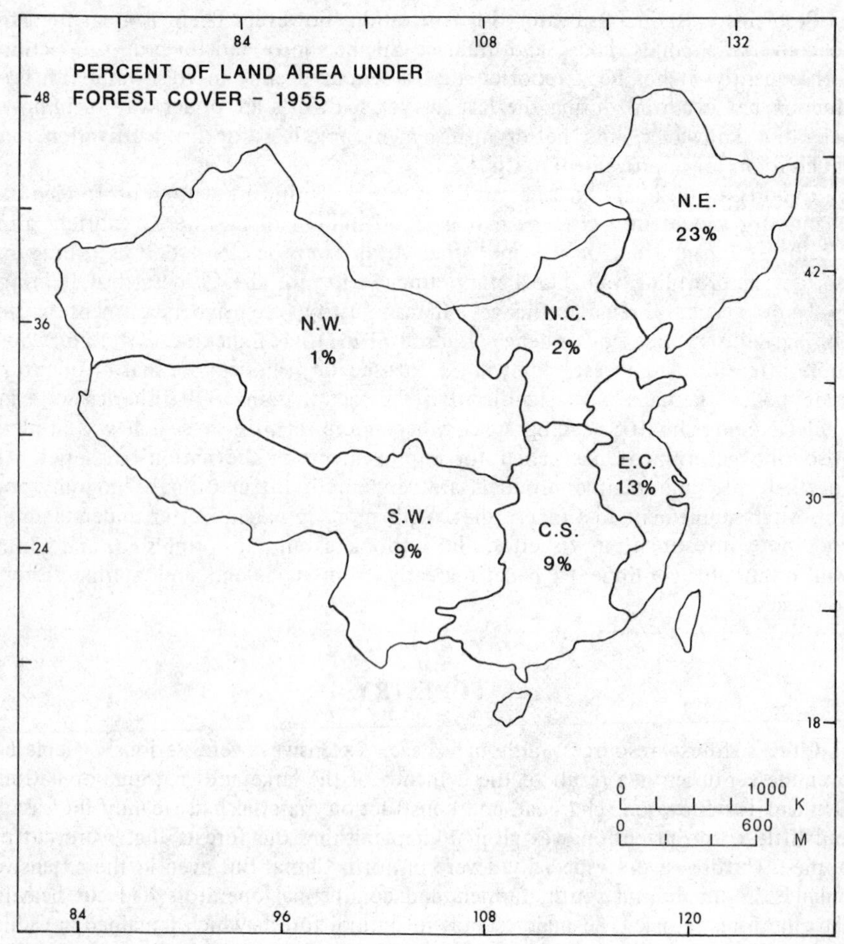

Fig. 6-5. China: Forest cover of the major regions, 1955.
Source: Ross (1981).

confidence in it. Of the total forest cover, about 60% was located in the northeast and 20% was found in the southeast. The timber in the southeast, however, was of rather poor quality and low in the stocking density[11] of the trees. The best quality and highest volume of timber was found in the Northeast and Southwest (Fig. 6-5). Richardson (1966) has concluded, based on a variety of sources, that

[11]Stocking density refers to the volume of timber per unit area and is conventionally rendered in cubic meters (m^3) per hectare (ha).

Table 6-7. Forest Resources of China

National forest area (ha.)	% of total land surface	Volumetric timber resource (million cubic meters)	Source (cited in Richardson, 1966)
46,500,000	5.0	5,150	Premezov (1955); Solecki (1964)
66,800,000	6.8	6,540	FAO (1961)
66,830,000	–	4,615	Deng (1959)
76,600,000	7.9	5,000	Messines (1958); FAO (1960)
97,000,000	10.1	6,300	Kuo et al. (1959)
100,000,000	10.0	–	NCNA, 4/7/58
96,000,000	9.9	7,460	Ministry of Forestry (1963)
–	7.0	–	*ECMM* (1956)
–	8.0	4,900	*Foreign Trade Pub.* (1959) (cited by Solecki, 1964)
–	10.0	–	Lin (1956); *Red Flag*, 12/16/58
–	7.9	4,900	Wen (1958)
–	–	5,400	Wang and Chi (1957)
–	–	6,300	*ECMM* (1959); Hsu (1959); *Red Flag*, 12/16/58
–	–	6,000	NCNA, 4/7/58; Carter (1958)
122,000,000	12.7	–	Wu (1981a)

Source: Compiled by Richardson (1966). Statistics for 1978 were taken from Wu (1981b).

about 96,000,000 ha were forested, or 9.9% of the total land area. Of this he estimated some 72,000,000 ha were accessible and could be exploited and managed reasonably.

All of these figures suggest that China is not well endowed with forests for a country with such a large land area and population. Table 6-7 indicates that only 12.7% of China's land area is under forest cover. Ross (1981) has discussed the optimum forested area for China and noted that 30% of the area is a norm sometimes used among professional foresters for large countries. The Chinese, he claimed, are aware of that figure, but Chinese foresters "have generally agreed that a target of 20% was more realistic for China given the natural and social conditions of the 20th century" (Ross, 1981, p. 115).

Richardson (1966) has described just how significant the forest sector is to the overall Chinese economy and its growth and development. He has noted that forestry is a lagging sector and impacts negatively in several important ways. Most significantly, failure to protect watersheds in the early 1950s, especially in northwest and north China, has led to disastrous increases in soil erosion. A cutback in the use of marginal farmland with renewed emphasis on afforestation, especially of shelter belts, has taken place since the mid-1950s. This shift in policy played a major role in the reduction of the amount of cultivated land between 1955 and 1980. Consequently, the best and most effective use of China's limited cropland must be viewed in the context of the protection of water resources and watersheds.

Table 6-8. Afforestation in China

Year	Total area (ha)
1949	60,000
1950	127,000
1951	451,000
1952	1,090,000
1953	1,110,000
1954	1,170,000
1955	1,710,000
1956	5,720,000
1957	4,360,000
1958	17,500,000
1959	18,700,000
1960	11,200,000
1961–62	2,000,000 (1,000,000 est. avg.)
1963	1,500,000
1964	2,380,000
1965	3,000,000
1966–70	19,500,000 (3,900,000 est. avg.)
1971–75	23,500,000 (4,700,000 est. avg.)
1976	4,500,000 (est.)
1977	4,794,000
1978	4,497,000
Total	128,869,000[a]

[a]The Ministry of Forestry appears to now calculate the total effort at 80–85,000,000 ha. The lower figure probably results in large part from a downgrading of the effort during the Great Leap Forward. "Yao zai quanguo dada di changyixia zhishu zaolin" (We Must Promote Tree Planting and Afforestation in a Big Way throughout the Country) *Renmin Ribao*, 14 Jan. 1978.

Source: Ross (1981).

Here forestry and sound forest practices impact directly on agricultural production and an integrated approach to cropland and watershed protection through afforestation must be taken most carefully.

The second impact of inadequate forest resources is seen in other sectors of the economy, most specifically in rail transport and mining. Here availability of timber for railway ties and mine props is essential to maintain present enterprises and to provide new material for future projects. Richardson (1966) has hinted at the lack of availability of railway ties to be sufficiently serious to have held up the rate of new rail construction. Apparently the Chinese have not found concrete to be a suitable substitute for such products. Whether those claims are true or not, the modest quantity of China's forests coupled with rapidly increasing demand since 1949 have indeed resulted in recognition of the deficiency of China's forest resources

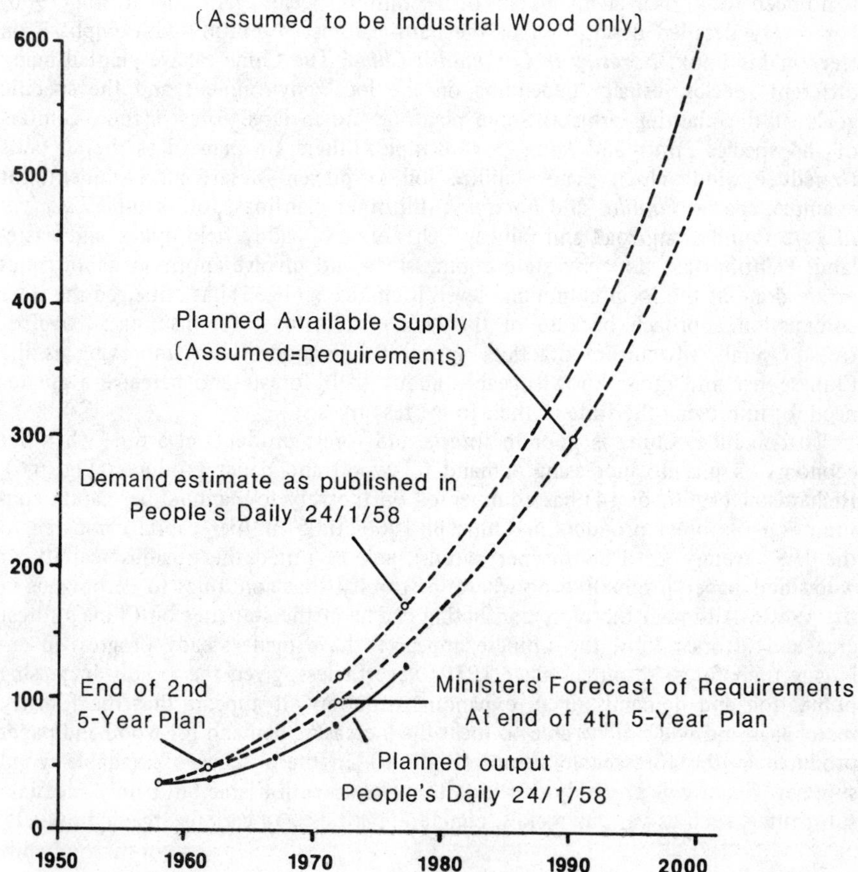

Fig. 6-6. China's estimated national wood requirements.
Source: Richardson (1966).

and the importance of it to the nation's development. A tremendous amount of attention and investment has been committed in recent years to the forest sector.

Afforestation efforts, especially since 1955, have been prodigious, although not always effective. Recent data provided by Ross (1981) indicate that a net increase of about 1 million ha per year have been added to forested land in China since 1949 (Table 6-8). Such a figure indicates China had increased its forest area by 1978 to 122,000,000 ha or about 12.7% of the total surface area. One of the major problems has been the disappointing survival rate for planted trees, a problem that has resulted from poor management practices, losses through fire, or illegal cuttings and foraging.

Tree types were discussed in Chapter 2 in the section on vegetation, and there is no need to go over all the details of the various species again. Richardson (1966) has a very detailed description of the natural forest vegetation with emphasis on trees in his book, *Forestry in Communist China*. The Chinese have planted many different species, usually depending on the local environment and the specific goals of the planting project. Some plantings are in large forest stands, conifers of the species *Pinus* and *Larix*, for example; others are planted as shelter belts to reduce wind velocity and stabilize soil or prevent desert encroachment, for example, species *Populus* and *Fraxinus*; still other plantings, for example *Eucalyptus*, are found along road and railway rights-of-way, paddy field dykes, and wasteland. Plantings are done by state commissions and involve enormous labor gangs or are done at the local communal level. Richardson (1966) has criticized the state commission approach because of the lack of incentives for insuring survival of trees. Overall, silviculture practices appear to be modest but improving as the Chinese become more knowledgeable about their forests and perceive a greater need for improving the state of their forest resources.

To conclude, China is poor in forests and forest products at a time when her economy is placing increasing demand for wood and paper products (Fig. 6-6). Richardson (1966, p. 14) has commented on the very low annual per capita consumption of forest products in China in 1966 (0.05 m^3/per capita compared to the U.S. average of 1.88 m^3/per capita), and he noted the obvious scarcity of wood and paper products everywhere, a scarcity that continues to be obvious in the 1980s. Although there are conflicting claims in the statistics on China's forest area and afforestation, the Chinese appear to have made steady progress in enlarging their forest resources since 1949. Nevertheless, given the rapidly increasing population and demands of an expanding economy, it appears that the forestry sector lags and will not be able to meet the increasing demand for wood and paper products in the foreseeable future (Fig. 6-6). In the absence of available wood supplies, China will probably continue to make do with usable but barely adequate substitutes, such as various metals, concrete, plastics, and various organic products.

LITERATURE CITED

American Plant Studies Delegation," 1975, *Plant Studies in the People's Republic of China*. Washington, D.C.: National Academy of Sciences.

Beijing Review, 1981, "Communique on Fulfillment of China's 1980 National Economic Plan," No. 19, Vol. 24 (May 11), p. 25.

Bennett, Gordon, 1978, *Huadong, The Study of a Chinese People's Commune*. Boulder, Colorado: Westview Press.

Buck, J. L., 1935, *Land Utilization in China*. Shanghai: Commercial Press.

Butler, Steven, 1978, *Agricultural Mechanization in China. The Administrative Impact.* Occasional Papers of the East Asian Institute, Columbia University, New York.

Central Intelligence Agency, 1971, *People's Republic of China Atlas.* Washington, D.C.: U.S. GPO.

Chang, Sen-dou, 1971, "China's Crop-Land Use, 1957." *Pacific Viewpoint*, Vol. 12, No. 1, pp. 75–87.

Chao, Kang, 1970, *Agricultural Production in Communist China, 1949–1965.* Madison: University of Wisconsin Press.

Chao, Shih-ying, 1972, In American Plant Studies Delegation, op. cit., p. 34.

Cressey, George B., 1955, *Land of the 500 Million, A Geography of China.* New York: McGraw Hill.

Crook, Frederick, 1975, "The Commune System in the People's Republic of China, 1963–1974." In Joint Economic Committee, *China: A Reassessment of the Economy.* Washington, D.C.: U.S. GPO, pp. 366–410.

Ding, Chen, 1980, "The Economic Development of China." *Scientific American*, Vol. 243, No. 3, pp. 152–165.

Eckstein, Alexander (ed.), 1980, *Quantitative Measures of China's Economic Output.* Ann Arbor: University of Michigan Press.

Evans, L. T., 1980, "The Natural History of a Crop Yield." *American Scientist*, Vol. 64, No. 8, pp. 388–397.

FAO Fisheries Mission to China, 1977, *Freshwater Fisheries and Aquaculture in China.* Rome: Food and Agriculture Organization of the United Nations, FAO Fisheries Technical Paper No. 168.

FAO/UNDP Study Tour to the People's Republic of China, 1977, *China: Recycling of Organic Waters in Agriculture.* Rome: Food and Agriculture Organization of the United Nations. FAO Soils Bulletin No. 40.

Groen, Henry J. and Kilpatrick, James A., 1978, "Chinese Agricultural Production." In Joint Economic Committee of the U.S. Congress, *Chinese Economy Post-Mao*, Vol. 1. Washington, D.C.: U.S. GPO, pp. 607–652.

Hanson, Jaydee, 1981, "China's Fisheries: Scaling Up Production." *China Business Review*, Vol. 7, No. 3, pp. 25–30.

Hu Huayong, 1936, "The Agricultural Regions of China." *Journal of the Geographical Society of China*, Vol. 3, No. 1, pp. 1–17 (in Chinese).

King, Frank H., 1926, *Farmers of Forty Centuries.* London: Jonathan Cape Ltd.

Kung, P., 1975, "Farm Crops of China." *World Crops*, May/June, pp. 122–132.

Kuo, Leslie T. C., 1972, *The Technical Transformation of Chinese Agriculture.* New York: Praeger.

Nuttonson, M. Y., 1968, *Agricultural Climates of China.* Washington, D.C.: American Institute of Crop Ecology.

Pannell, Clifton W., in press, "China's Shrinking Cropland." *The Geographical Magazine.*

Perkins, Dwight, 1969, *Agricultural Development in China, 1368–1968.* Chicago: Aldine.

Richardson, S. R., 1966, *Forestry in Communist China.* Baltimore: Johns Hopkins Press.

Ross, Lester, 1981, "Forestry in the PRC: Estimating the Gains and Losses." *China Geographer*, No. 11, pp. 113–127.

Salter, Christopher L., 1977, "Ta-chai Beyond Ta-chai: Some Unsuspected Lessons for the USA from a Chinese Campaign." *China Geographer*, No. 7, pp. 59–66.

Shen, T. H., 1951, *Agricultural Resources of China.* Ithaca: Cornell University Press.

Skinner, G. W., 1978, "Vegetable Supply and Marketing in Chinese Cities." *The China Quarterly*, Vol. 76, pp. 733–793.

Sprague, G. F., 1975, "Agriculture in China." *Science*, Vol. 188, No. 4188, May, pp. 549–556.

State Statistical Bureau, People's Republic of China, 1960, *Ten Great Years.* Peking: Foreign Language Publishing House.

U.S. Department of Agriculture, 1976, *The Agricultural Situation in the People's Republic of China.* Washington, D.C.: USDA Economic Research Service, ERS-Foreign 362.

U.S. Department of Agriculture, 1977, *People's Republic of China Agricultural Situation.* Foreign Agricultural Economic Report, No. 137, Washington, D.C.

U.S. Department of Agriculture, 1980, *Agricultural Situation, People's Republic of China.* Washington, D.C.: USDA, Economics, Statistics and Cooperative Service.

Welch, R. A., Lo, H. C., and Pannell, C. W., 1979, "Mapping China's New Agricultural Land." *Photogrammetric Engineering and Remote Sensing*, Vol. 45, pp. 1211–1228.

Whitney, J. B. R., 1973, "Ecology and Environmental Control." In Michel Oksenberg (ed.), *China's Developmental Experience.* New York: Praeger, pp. 95–109.

Whitton, Carolyn L., 1976, In U.S. Department of Agriculture, *The Agricultural Situation in the People's Republic of China and Other Communist Asian Countries.* Foreign Agricultural Economic Report, No. 124. Washington, D.C., pp. 18–24.

Wiens, Herold J., 1958, "China, Agriculture and Food Supply." In Norton Ginsburg (ed.), *The Pattern of Asia.* Englewood Cliffs, N.J.: Prentice Hall, pp. 168–189.

Wiens, Thomas, 1980, "Agricultural Statistics in the People's Republic of China." In Eckstein, op. cit., pp. 44–107.

Wiens, Thomas, 1981, "Agriculture in the Four Modernizations." *China Geographer*, No. 11, pp. 57–72.

Wortman, S., 1975, "Agriculture in China." *Scientific American*, Vol. 232, pp. 13–21.

Wu, Chuan-chun, 1981a, "The Transformation of Agricultural Landscapes in China." In Laurence J. C. Ma and Allen G. Noble (eds.), *The Environment: Chinese and American Views.* New York: Methuen, Inc., pp. 35–43.

Wu, Chuan-chun, 1981b, "Agricultural Regionalization in China." *China Geographer*, No. 11, pp. 27–39.

Chapter 7

Planning, Transportation and Trade in China's Development

CENTRALIZED PLANNING

Chinese development and modernization policies and practices since 1949 have followed several different models. In general, these have reflected changing official policies and events and varying approaches of the Chinese leadership to the challenge of economic growth and development (Ding, 1980). Following the success of the revolution in 1949, several options for development were available to China's leaders. These options were based on the assumption that China, like all poor and economically backward countries, aspired to industrial growth and economic modernization. This assumption appears to be fair in the case of China, inasmuch as the late party Chairman Mao Zedong and other leaders have consistently and frequently stated that China seeks to be a powerful socialist state able to defend itself and be recognized as one of the major world powers. Despite Mao's emphasis on the value of a rural peasantry, it seems clear that industrial modernization and economic growth are essential for achieving the desired status of world recognition and power. Another basic goal of economic development in China has been to reduce the gap between the various levels of income and employed groups throughout the country. Implicit has been the concept and goal of economic growth with equity and balance throughout the society and the country (Chen, 1978).

As Eckstein (1977) pointed out, three broad approaches or models of economic development and control were available for the Chinese Communists to follow in mobilizing and allocating resources. Simply put, the three were: (1) free market economy in which resource allocation is determined by consumer preferences, which also determine and reflect the adjustment of prices; (2) market socialism in which the state owns and controls the means of production and provides central economic planning, but a pricing system is allowed to control the allocation of resources; (3) command economy in which the allocation of goods, services, and factors of production are determined by central planners and an administrative bureaucratic mechanism rather than a pricing mechanism. Over the past decades, the Chinese have employed elements of all three of these models of economic growth as political events unfolded and economic conditions changed. Thus, no one specific model is satisfactory to explain fully and completely the Chinese economy under Communism.

To achieve economic and industrial modernization, capital was necessary, and a strategy and plan were required to direct and control the mobilization and allocation of resources. China in 1949–1950 had some choice of strategy, but given that the basis for the successful revolution was Marxist and drew considerable inspiration from the Russian revolution, it is not surprising that initially China followed the Soviet model of development with emphasis on centralized planning and the development of heavy industry and concentration of resources. Agriculture, by contrast, was neglected. The planning process also initially followed the Soviet model with its focus on 5-year plans. The use of these plans proved less successful in China than in the USSR, in part as a consequence of the rather dramatic shifts in politics and events. Thus, events and mass movements such as the Great Leap Forward and later the Cultural Revolution interrupted the orderly progress of carefully drawn up 5-year plans. The plans, even though developed and initially implemented, had to be shelved, altered or simply abandoned as political events overtook them and rendered their implementation and effectiveness almost meaningless. Following the cataclysmic political events of the late 1960s and the early 1970s (the Cultural Revolution), however, central planning on a 1-, 5-, and 10-year basis has been restored. Today, China's national development and economic modernization are based on such plans, and these plans are to provide the main outlines and framework for China's progress through the rest of the 20th century.

Chronology of Planning

Initially, after 1949, China was concerned first and foremost with restoring production and getting things moving again. The first few years brought only a cautious policy of economic control. Nevertheless, it was clear from the outset that the Chinese wished to follow the Soviet model of very rapid economic growth focused on industrial development at the expense of agriculture. The basis for such a strategy was a requirement for a high rate of savings, and this was institutionalized through various means, such as state ownership of means of production, price manipulation, and agricultural collectivization.

In 1953, the first 5-year plan was undertaken, and the rate of economic growth was very impressive, particularly in the industrial sector. As early as 1956, however, problems began to appear in agriculture, and leaders and policymakers began to feel the necessity for more attention to the agricultural sector as the backbone of China's economy. This shift in economic strategy implied a move away from the Soviet heavy industry model and the emergence of a new vision of economic planning, apparently more appropriate for China and endorsed personally by Chairman Mao. This new planning led to new political movements as well. In 1958, the Great Leap Forward, a mass movement with a goal to push China to the economic and industrial level of Britain in a few years, burst forth. Initially successful because of a good 1958 harvest, the Great Leap, which was Mao's vision to power China once and for all out of its cycle of poverty and economic backwardness, soon fell flat. The expectations of the Great Leap were too high, and the 1959 and later harvests declined also because of poor weather. The quality of locally produced industrial goods was also poor. Yet the concept of rural, small-scale, and local industrial production was valid, justified on the basis of a poor transportation system, large availability of underemployed rural labor, and the local demand for unsophisticated industrial goods.

Central planning also fell victim to events. In 1958 a second 5-year plan was initiated, but the failure and demise of the Great Leap rendered this plan inadequate and meaningless. Later attempts during the 1960s and early 1970s to establish and carry out 5-year plans met the same fate (Ding, 1980). The initiation of the plan would be followed by cataclysmic political events and mass movements, such as the Cultural Revolution and the emergence of the Gang of Four. Effective long-range economic planning did not reappear until the middle 1970s, as the political events of the post-Cultural Revolution and post-Mao period began to take shape (Lardy, 1978).

Following the turmoil of the Cultural Revolution, there emerged in the late 1970s a period of comparative political stability in which pragmatic leaders, such as Deng Xiaoping, became very influential. The new policies placed a strong emphasis on practical economic goals and focused around the popular program known as "The Four Modernizations" (the promotion of rapid modernization in agriculture, industry, scientific knowledge, and national defense) (Baum, 1980). A number of ambitious projects were undertaken. Many of these involved acquisition through commercial purchase of foreign technology. Foreign trade increased rapidly, and China began to finance large-scale purchases of this foreign technology through loans.

It became clear very soon that China's needs far surpassed her fiscal resources. In part, this resulted from a leveling off of petroleum production, which reduced the amount of foreign exchange earned through the export of petroleum. By 1980, some slowdown had occurred in which China began to reduce the pace of her purchases of foreign plants and technology. The State Council, the equivalent of the U.S. Cabinet, apparently decided that the country should focus resources on agricultural development and modernization, and this resulted in reducing the investment available for the purchase of industrial plant and producer goods. A slowdown followed in the development of petroleum refineries, mining projects, industrial and transportation projects. The net result was not to abandon these, but simply to place the projects in a lower ordering of priorities for development projects.

In recent years, China has been engaged in preparing annual plans to deal with the current realities of its economic production. These annual plans have been a practical supplement to the 5-year plans which were difficult to follow due to political instability and economic uncertainty. Five-year plans continue to be prepared, and it appears that these may be more important as reliable guides to actual production during the 1980s. For example, the sixth 5-year plan (1981–85) has set production targets for major industrial and agricultural production with targeted annual growth rates of 8.0% for industrial goods and 4.5% for grain production. Grain output is anticipated to reach 400 million metric tons by 1985, an increase of 26% from the 318 million m tons produced in 1980. Population growth is planned to drop from an annual rate of 1.2% in 1980 to 0.5% in 1985. A seventh plan is currently being prepared, giving a 10-year general plan package with emphasis on agriculture and light industry. Rapid growth of foreign trade is an important part of this 10-year combined plan with anticipated increased exports of crude oil, coal, and manufactured goods. The Chinese seek a balanced trade and do not wish to rely on credits for foreign purchases (*The China Business Review*, March–April, 1980, p. 6).

Institutional Framework

Centralized planning in China is highly organized and carried out through a number of important bureaus and offices. Modeled after similar Soviet organizations, the Chinese system has evolved its own structure and operational methods in response to China's particular economic and political condition. The State Council, a top level government agency staffed by important party functionaries, is responsible for determining economic goals and for laying down the main directions for all sectors of the economy. The State Planning Commission, however, actually does the work of preparing detailed plans. The Commission is supported by a variety of other agencies, the most important among which is the State Statistical Bureau, an organization responsible for providing the specific quantitative data necessary for careful and precise planning. Other important agencies that also contribute their support include the People's Bank (a national government operated bank), the State Capital Construction Commission (deals with actual construction of economic projects and oversees investments in fixed assets), the State Agricultural Planning Commission, and the State Energy Commission.

The state agencies prepare their drafts of 1- and 5-year plans. These drafts form the basis for local organizations of different administrative levels to develop their own proposals and production quotas and schedules. Officials of various units get together and discuss and revise these local plans and production schedules, and eventually the schedules are submitted to higher authority for approval or sent back for revisions or further discussion. In this way, China seeks to incorporate the views of all involved and to reconcile the needs of the state with the realities of what can be accomplished in production.

In carrying out their plans, the Chinese have a number of guiding principles that are relevant and important to their goals. As is simply and commonly stated in the Chinese economic and development literature, "agriculture is the foundation of the Chinese economy and industry is the leading factor." In promoting these two sectors simultaneously, the Chinese are quick to point out that their model of economic development is based on self-reliance and embodies the concept of "walking on two legs," of using the traditional and the modern, the old and the new, as well as the rural and the urban. Ever since 1958, China has viewed agriculture as vital to the successful development of industry and has placed considerably more emphasis on the agricultural sector than was even done in the USSR. This approach to development was confirmed in the "Four Modernizations," which was popularized in the late 1970s, included agriculture and industry, and added national defense and science and technology as two additional basic areas for rapid growth and development during the decades of the 1980s and 1990s. These four areas, supplemented by foreign trade and education, in all likelihood will form the core foci of the Chinese developmental thrust during the remainder of the 20th century.

Planning the Spatial Economy and Spatial Equity: The Regional View

The pattern of cities, industries and transport networks that the Communist government inherited in 1949 was to a great extent focused on eastern China, especially the coastal provinces, and on the northeast (Manchuria). The coastal provinces (omitting Liaoning and Zhejiang) in 1949 accounted for 80% of employment and factories and 90% of motive power (Wu, 1967). The easily understandable reasons for this shall be explained below. The point here is that the leaders of the new China found this inherited pattern to be irrational and contrary to their developmental goals. The new leaders set out to alter this pattern, and investments were allocated to that end. The stated goals of the new leaders with respect to spatial planning, according to Wu (1967), were as follows:

(1) to establish new economic and industrial centers closer to raw materials and consumer markets;
(2) to strike a proper balance between intra-regional self-sufficiency and intra-regional specialization;
(3) to enhance national security;
(4) to allow for requirements in international geopolitics;
(5) to develop medium and small cities in the interior rather than larger cities on the coast.

In support of these stated policy goals, four other guidelines were also promulgated:

(1) New industrial centers were to be built near fixed natural resources and transport links were to be expanded to serve these.
(2) Transport links could be expanded in developed, coastal regions, but, in general, only if present linkages were inadequate to permit continued economic growth.
(3) Where defense and political goals were unimportant, the transport networks should not be expanded for noneconomic objectives.
(4) Transportation should be extended into backward regions to promote development.

Implicit in this new policy direction was the idea that a strong central government should play an active role in regional development through investments in cities, industry, and transportation. The goal implied was to promote equity of wealth and well-being among China's regions. The ideological ideal of helping poor and backward areas no doubt was important. This goal logically coincided at the time with a national security goal of that era (1949-1960) of friendly Sino-Soviet relations in which military threats were believed most likely to come from the sea, i.e., the United States, Japan, and Taiwan.

Since these basic principles for spatial planning and development were laid down, it has been difficult to evaluate precisely how successfully they have been implemented. This difficulty results from the absence of detailed and accurate quantitative data on regional economic growth and incomes. Nevertheless, it is possible to piece together information to form a general picture of the pace and direction of regional economic growth and development. This may be done in a very general way through looking at expansion of the transport network, growth of cities, and development of industrial plants in various provinces and locales. Details on urban, transportation, and industrial growth are provided in other sections of this text. On the other hand, a more reliable view may be based on the allocation of resources and an analysis of Chinese fiscal policy. It is useful to describe at this point the analytical work of Lardy (1975) on center-provincial fiscal relations and economic planning.

Since the late 1950s, planners and policymakers in China have sought to decentralize economic decision making, giving more responsibility to provincial authorities in an effort to provide better management of China's large economy. The success or failure of this policy and its influence on economic growth and development in various regions of China has sparked considerable interest and debate. One view emerged which affirmed that decentralization in China advanced to the point where inter-provincial transfers of resources virtually ceased, and regional self-sufficiency became predominant as an economic growth pattern. Lardy (1975) has investigated this issue, which is analytically based on available fiscal evidence and policy. A review of his findings is useful for a better understanding of what has happened in China during the last three decades in the spatial allocation of resources and the resultant pattern of regional economic growth and development.

Lardy (1975) has argued that while considerable administrative authority was shifted to the provincial government level in China, during the 1950s, it is crucial to bear in mind that basic decision making over resource allocation remained at the national level. Consequently, according to Lardy, the argument that decentralization of planning and decision making at the provincial level led to increasing regional self-sufficiency and a greater tendency for the comparatively rich regions of China to remain rich by allocating their own resources internally is not tenable. On the contrary, throughout the 1950s, 1960s, and early 1970s, empirical evidence and statistical testing (Table 7-1) indicate that China's central government, through its fiscal powers and manipulation, continued to transfer incomes and fiscal wealth through revenue sharing and regional expenditures away from the rich, well-developed provinces and into poorly developed backward areas.

In Lardy's view, the economic planning of the 1950s in China represented an

Table 7-1. Central-Provincial Revenue Sharing

1959			
Province or city	Revenue sharing rate (%)	Province or city	Revenue sharing rate (%)
Shanghai City	-80.2	Shanxi	+7.9
Tianjin City	-69.2	Yunnan	+18.0
Liaoning	-63.9	Guizhou	+18.2
Beijing City	-51.2	Xinjiang	+25.9
Heilongjiang	-50.5	Anhui	+30.7
Jiangsu	-45.6	Qinghai	+56.7
Shandong	-44.8	Tibet	+83.5
Guangdong	-43.3	Shaanxi	+
Sichuan	-33.2	Jiangxi	+
Zhejiang	-31.0	Fujian	+
Hebei (excluding Tianjin)	-28.8	Inner Mongolia	+
Jilin	-27.4	Gansu	+
Henan	-22.0	Guangxi	+
Hunan	-19.6	Ningxia	+
Hubei	-4.2		

Post-1960		
Province or city	Period	Revenue sharing rate (%)
Shanghai	1972	-90
Liaoning	1972	-82
Jiangsu	1972	-70
Inner Mongolia	1972	
Guangxi	1972	
Xinjiang	1972	
Ningxia	1972	
Tibet	1960-73	>+50

Provinces and municipalities are listed in order of their revenue sharing rate. Negative numbers show provincial net remittances to the center as a percent of total revenues collected in the province or city. Positive numbers show net subsidies from the center as a percent of total provincial expenditures. For Shanghai, the remission rate in 1972 is inclusive of central government investment.

Source: Lardy (1975).

extension of interest in day-to-day management at the local level, while the main decision making on resource allocation remained at the national level. Two significant results were thus achieved. Control over investment was largely maintained at the national level, and a high rate of sectoral investment could be maintained or directed, for example, into producer goods. Or conversely, in the 1980s, a greater share could thus be directed into agriculture. The second result was that the national government could continue to play a vital role in maintaining an effort toward the goal of spatial equity and the equal distribution of wealth and resources. Lardy (1975) claimed the Chinese have been remarkably successful through their uniform national taxing program in seeking to establish geographic equity throughout the country by a significant redistribution of wealth accomplished through their national fiscal and planning systems.

A dual pattern of economic growth appears to have emerged in China. On the one hand, it is clear that substantial growth in interior and previously poor provinces has occurred in urban centers such as Xi'an, Zhengzhou, Taiyuan, Lanzhou, and Baotou. On the other hand, most of the large industrial centers on the eastern seaboard of China have also continued to prosper, although rates of growth in advanced industrial provinces declined in the late 1960s (Lardy, 1975). Major industrial development projects have often occurred in these locations in response to the advantageous effects of agglomeration and linkages, large markets, good transport systems, large and skilled pools of labor, and availability and ease of assembling resources and materials for processing.

Despite some recent problems and criticisms, the location of the new and soon-to-be largest steelworks in China at Baoshan, outside Shanghai, is an example of the siting decision of a major new industrial development project. The location of a major steelworks on the water to take advantage of low cost shipping costs and near the site of China's largest industrial center and market appears logical and sound, despite some problem associated with the depth of the shipping channel serving the site. Other national goals that may have been associated with an ideology of spatial equity were not allowed to override the economic logic of this locational decision, which was made when national economic growth was the goal of policy formed in the late 1970s.

Rapid growth and economic development were extended throughout most of the country. Tremendous investments in expansion of the rail system over the last 30 years have led to great improvements in accessibility in the interior of China, and this has promoted growth in interior urban centers and improved the opportunities for regional development based on nodal points of growth. Cities such as Xi'an, Zhengzhou, Taiyuan, Baotou, Ürümqi, and Lanzhou have grown rapidly under policies designed to promote interior development, and this adds further to the strength of Lardy's argument on the efficacy of Chinese fiscal and planning policies during the 1950s, '60s, and '70s. Despite the lack of firm data on which to measure economic well-being beyond the macro level, the growth of a significant number of large interior centers indicates the Chinese government has achieved a measure of success in insuring that its investments and economic opportunities are spreading by means of the urban system and hierarchy through the interior of China's densely settled area (Table 7-2). Thus, a reasonable, if by no means ideal, degree of spatial equity in the allocation of resources and economic opportunities is believed to have evolved in China during the last 30 years.

TRANSPORTATION IN CHINA

Transportation and communication in China have always been major problems that have challenged Chinese central administrations, as they sought to integrate

Hunan Province: Despite modernization, traditional methods of transportation (the wheelbarrows) continue to be used to move grain. (*C. W. Pannell*)

Table 7-2. Pattern of Growth in Industrial Output, 1957–1974 (by first order administrative units)

	1957	1974
Above average industrial output	Liaoning, Heilongjiang, Hebei, Shandong, Tianjin, Jiangsu, Shanghai, Hubei, Guangdong, Sichuan	Liaoning, Heilongjiang, Hebei, Shandong, Peking, Tianjin, Jiangsu, Shanghai Guangdong, Sichuan
Below average industrial output	Jilin, Henan, Shanxi, Nei Monggol, Peking Anhui, Zhejiang, Hunan, Jiangsi, Guangxi, Fujian, Guizhou, Yunnan, Tibet, Shaanxi, Gansu, Qinghai, Xinjiang, Ningxi	Jilin, Shanxi, Nei Monggol, Anhui, Zhejiang, Hubei, Hunan, Jiangxi Guangxi, Fujian, Tibet Guizhou, Yunnan, Shaanxi, Gansu, Qinghai, Xinjiang, Ningxi

Note: Industrial output is based on gross value in millions of 1957 *yuan*.
Source: Compiled from data in Field, Lardy, and Emerson (1976, p. 11).

the country for economic development and administrative control. Historically, various dynasties attempted to control the country administratively through a hierarchical network of administrative centers connected to one another by a crude and sporadically effective bureaucracy and postal system. Economic linkages were more difficult to establish, inasmuch as these generally involved the flow of bulky and weighty commodities or the transfer of cash in the form of valuables, like gold or silver.

The difficulties in such economic transfers were several. First, the crude and rough nature of the land transportation system meant that it was awkward, expensive, and dangerous to move either commodities such as foodstuffs or valuables in the backcountry. Even though human labor was extremely cheap, the amount of commodities and goods that an individual coolie could move in a wheelbarrow or on a carrying pole was limited to approximately 40 kilos and he could perhaps move this as far as 20 to 30 kilometers a day. Given such an inefficient mode of transportation, the cost of shipping goods was prohibitive for overland transportation throughout most of the country.

In those parts of China that possessed deep river systems, such as the central part of China, which is focused around the large and deep Yangzi River and a distributary network in the lower reaches of the river, transportation by water was both convenient and inexpensive. Under these conditions, it was possible to move agricultural commodities long distances at relatively modest costs.

Water transportation is important along the Li River in Guangxi A. R. as a convoy of river junks moves upstream. (*C. W. Pannell*)

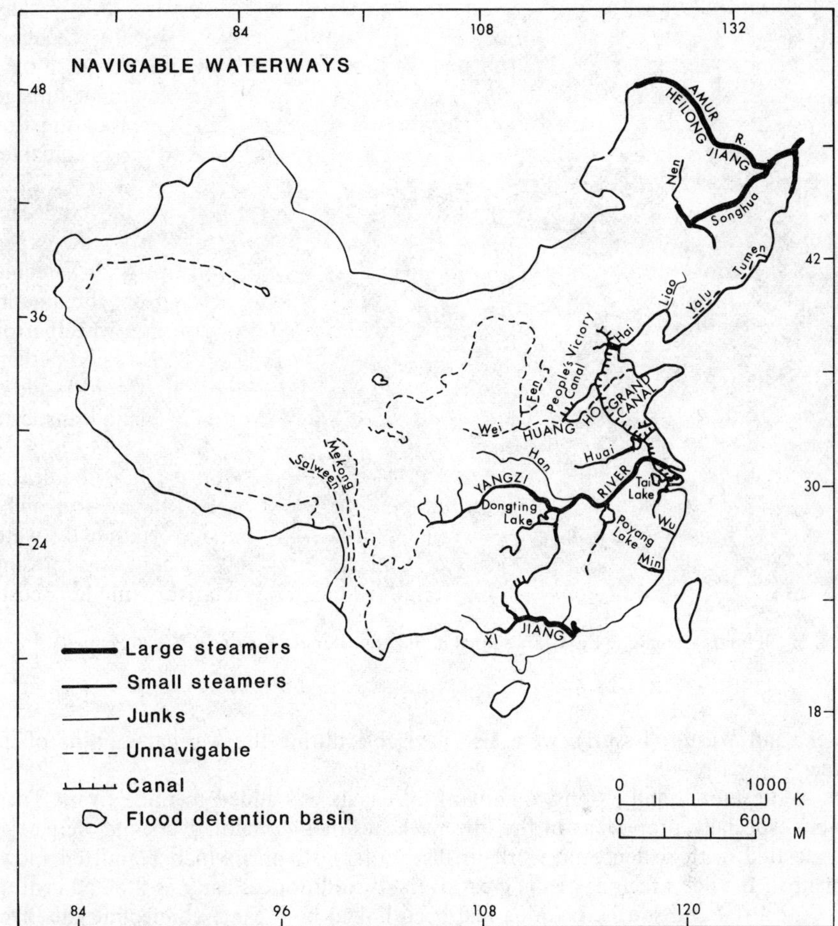

Fig. 7-1. Navigable waterways in China.
Source: Cressey (1955); Central Intelligence Agency (1971), *People's Republic of China Atlas.*

Consequently, in traditional China, river systems that provided handy and easy access corridors were integrated economically with one another and were able to transport goods in a convenient and inexpensive fashion (Fig. 7-1). It should be remembered that such areas were restricted to the middle part of China, the Yangzi River and various tributaries; the southeastern quadrant of the country, focused around its tributary network; and in the North China Plain, the Yellow River, the Huai River, and a variety of smaller tributary networks. In the northeast, the Heilongjiang (Amur) and associated tributaries, such as the Songhua (Sungari),

Small boats seen along the Grand Canal in Suzhou, Jiangsu Province. *(C. W. Pannell)*

Nen, and Wusuli (Ussuri), were also navigable during the warmer months of the year.

A substantial and extensive network of canals was added to these rivers. These were especially prominent in the lower reaches of the major rivers and were often associated with a dense network of distributary streams which permitted movement in the delta regions of the great rivers. In addition, as early as the 2nd century B.C., central and southern China had been linked by a canal connecting the Black River, south of the present city of Changsha, with the Li River, near the location of the city of Guilin in northern Guangxi. In this way, there was a limited amount of commodity shipment among the major regions of eastern China very early in historical times.

Waterways

Water transportation, as noted earlier, has always been important to China. Rivers served as the first important modes for the movement of agricultural commodities in ancient times. Canals were constructed from central China to the North China Plain and the Yellow River valley very early as the political centers, located in the north, were able to command shipments of grain from the agricultural surplus regions of central China. This pattern reached its climax in the construction of the Grand Canal in the Tang and Song dynasties. During the Yuan dynasty, this canal ran all the way from modern Hangzhou north to the Yangzi River and into the North China Plain as far north as the great political capital of Peking. The distance of the Grand Canal was approximately 1,200 kilometers. The advantage of shipping along water is that it was very inexpensive to move bulky and heavy commodities over long distances, although it had the disadvantage of being relatively slow. Thus, traditionally, it was much safer and more convenient to ship along the rivers and canals and coast of China than it has been to travel overland by horse, sedan chair, or on foot. The Grand Canal was effectively used until it was made obsolete by the railroad in the early 20th century.

Effectiveness of water transportation has been demonstrated by the ability of the Chinese to build and support large cities based on a network of waterways, canals, and streams. Such waterways bring in fresh food on a daily basis and transport the effluent of cities out to the surrounding rural areas, allowing for a kind of rough return relationship of food nutrients for organic manurial nutrients. The government of contemporary China continues to rely heavily on water transportation, and it continues to form a very important part of the transportation sector, especially for the movement of bulky commodities (Fig. 7-1).

The most important corridor of water transportation in contemporary China is the Yangzi River. Other important navigable streams include the Xi, the Heilong Jiang (Amur), and the Songhua (Sungari). Neither the Huang nor the Huai is an important river for navigation, owing to periodic flooding and the great range of average discharge of these two streams. In 1949, there were approximately 75,000 kilometers of navigable waterways in China. Within 10 years, this had been extended to approximately 145,000 kilometers of navigable waterways, of which 20,000 kilometers were open to steam vessels presumably with a draft greater than 12 feet (Whitaker et al., 1972).

The Yangzi River is of special importance as a navigable waterway in China. The major reason for this is that the Yangzi, for a good part of the year, is available as far inland as a thousand kilometers to oceangoing steam-driven vessels. A great deal of investment has been committed to improving navigation along the Yangzi and especially along the regions of the great gorges west of the city of Wuhan, to the city of Chongqing. These gorges are very scenic, but the swiftness of the current and the roughness of the bottom, coupled with frequency of shoals and dangerous rocks, have created serious impediments and dangers to shipping. With the advent of powerful steam-driven vessels, however, navigation has been extended into the interior and efforts have been made to improve the channel characteristics of the river. During the summer rainy season, oceangoing vessels as large as 15,000 deadweight tons with drafts as great as 9 meters can reach Wuhan, 1,000 kilometers inland. Beyond that, it is possible to navigate special steamships of up to 5,000 tons with shallow drafts that can serve the port of Chongqing.

In addition to the Yangzi with its deep channel as far west as Wuhan, a number of tributaries and smaller streams are also available for navigational purposes by Chinese traditional crafts and junks. Although seemingly crude and awkward, the Chinese junk is a remarkably effective and efficient draft vessel for hauling goods long distances at very cheap rates. These junks and other small craft generally have shallow drafts but are constructed in such a way that they can carry a large amount of cargo as a consequence of their wide bottoms or beams. These kinds of crafts and vessels permit the Chinese to make very effective use of a large network of smaller and more shallow streams which penetrate into the interior of China in a fine network of arms and tentacles.

Development of Railroads

Such a condition of transportation access movement persisted throughout most of China's traditional history. In the 19th century, however, associated with the arrival of Westerners and the development of the treaty ports, new transportation technologies were also introduced into China. Perhaps the most significant was the introduction of the steel railroad in 1876. The first line was constructed outside Shanghai, but the project met with opposition and fear and did not succeed. Indeed, it was only in 1894 that the first true railroad was constructed in China. This event apparently developed along with a series of significant changes in China as a consequence of the dramatically perceived threat of the modernizing Western countries and Japan, which were then gaining greater military and technological power. The first rail line opened between Peking and Shanghai in 1903, and the line extended for more than 800 kilometers.

Railroad building became very popular thereafter, and a large number of new lines were constructed in the early 20th century. In general, these lines were focused initially around several very large cities–Peking, Shanghai, Canton, and Tianjin. One major line connected Peking with the southern port of Canton and Hong Kong and traveled through the large cities of Wuhan, Zhengzhou, and Shijiazhuang. A second major line connected Peking and Tianjin with the great port of eastern China, Shanghai. In addition to these two north/south lines, a major east/west line was constructed from the port of Qingdao west along the Yellow River to the cities of Xi'an and Baoji.

Another major area of railway construction in China was in the Northeast (Manchuria). During the early part of the 20th century, both czarist Russia and imperial Japan invested heavily in the construction of railways in the Northeast, inasmuch as this part of China was a zone of very intensive geopolitical competition among Russia, Japan, and China. The Russians constructed a railroad from China through Manzhouli, Qiqihar, Harbin, and on to the Russian far eastern port of Vladivostok. The Russians also built a line due south of Harbin connecting with the large southern Manchurian city of Shenyang. This line was known as the South Manchurian Railroad and was later taken over by the Japanese after the Russo-Japanese War of 1905. In 1931, when Japan annexed all of the Manchurian region, she also took over the entire railroad network which the Russians had earlier controlled.

By World War II, approximately 26,500 kilometers of railway had been constructed in China, and it was essentially this network that was inherited by the Communists when they took over the country in 1949. The rail network, however, had suffered tremendously during World War II and the civil war that followed, and perhaps as much as one-third of the total network had been disrupted or destroyed as a consequence of the fighting and insurgency.

Recent Expansion of Rail Network

There were several basic features about the rail network that the Communists inherited in 1949 (Fig. 7-2). For example, most of the rail development and construction was focused in the eastern part of the country, and indeed, much of it was focused on the coastal provinces. Northwest China and its provinces and administrative areas of Gansu, Ningxia, Xinjiang, and Qinghai possessed no rail lines at all. In southeastern China, the coastal province of Fujian also had no rail lines. In the southwestern part of the country, the provinces of Sichuan, Guizhou, Yunnan, and Tibet also possessed no rail lines. Approximately half of

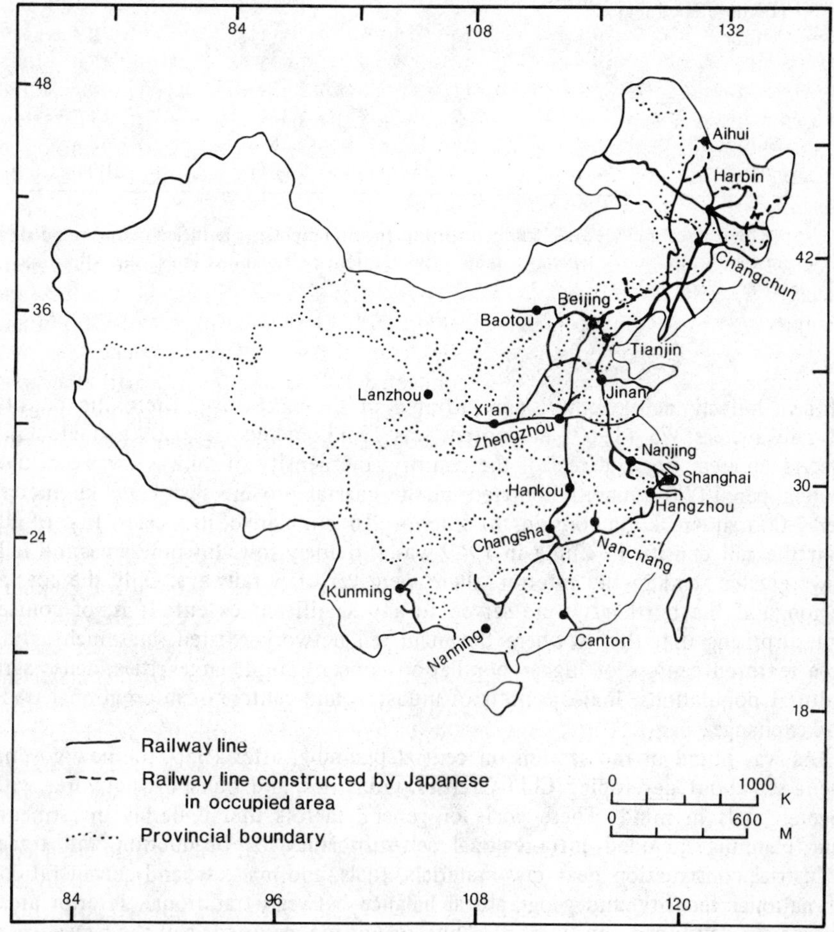

Fig. 7-2. Main rail lines in China, 1949.
Source: Leung (1979).

Table 7-3. Regional Distribution of New Railway Construction from 1949 to 1963 Year End[a]

Region	Number of new lines	Length of new lines (km)	Percentage of new lines
Developed regions			
Northeast	3	115	1.2
North	11	1,194	12.6
East	7	535	5.6
Subtotal	21	1,844	19.4
Underdeveloped regions			
Central	10	811	8.5
South	8	1,613	17.0
Northwest	11	3,839	40.4
Southwest	7	1,394	14.7
Subtotal	36	7,657	80.6
Total	57	9,501	100.0

[a]These data included all trunk lines and major branches identified, but excluded forest railways, spurs, railways under construction, and planned lines. See Appendix
Source: Wu (1967).

China's railway network was concentrated in the northeast. There the density of railways, as Wu (1967) has noted, was 12 kilometers per 1,000 square kilometers of area. For the rest of the country, the density of railways was 5.6 kilometers per 1,000 square kilometers in the coastal provinces and 3.6 kilometers per 1,000 square kilometers in the interior. To summarize, it is clear, first of all, that the rail density in China in 1949 was extremely low. In some areas, no railways existed, and in the interior, there were very few railways. Only the coastal region and the northeast were served to any significant extent. It is, of course, not surprising that this is where the main rail network existed, inasmuch as the area featured centers of higher population concentration, large cities, dense agricultural populations, major centers of industry, and centers of international trade and exchange.

As was noted in the section on central planning, after 1950, the new government set about developing China's cities, industries, and transport networks with several goals in mind. These goals or general factors that underlay investments and planning included intra-regional self-sufficiency of production and trade; industrial construction near raw materials, fuels, and markets; and considerations of national security and geographical balance between traditional, interior areas and newly developed coastal ports. Thus, one of the major goals of the new government was to focus more attention on developing the interior, while at the same time taking advantage of established urban and industrial sites. These sites were supported by an already substantial transportation network that focused on the coastal provinces and the northeast.

Much investment was committed to the development of the rail network during the first 5-year plan that got under way after 1952. Wu (1967) has rank ordered the railway development in China according to major regions (Table 7-3). His findings, based on the length of newly constructed lines, indicated that most of the rail construction after 1952 was focused in northwest China, north China, and southwest China. Following these were south China, central China, east China, and northeast China. By 1963, according to Wu, 34,235 kilometers were in operation in China, having increased from the 17,036 kilometers that existed in 1949. Of this 1963 total, 9,501 kilometers were in new construction, and the remainder were apparently accounted for by repair and overhaul of older lines. This is a substantial increase and included major lines extending from Baoji in Shaanxi Province west through Lanzhou to Ürümqi and Manas in Xinjiang. Another major line was constructed south from Baoji into Sichuan Province and connected with the cities of Chengdu, Chongqing and linked to Kunming in Yunnan Province and Guiyang in Guizhou Province in southwestern China (see also Lippit, 1976).

Two other important lines were constructed in the northwest, one following the route of the great loop of the Yellow River from Lanzhou to Baotou, and one from Xining northwest into the People's Republic of Mongolia and its capital city of Ulaanbaatar. Shorter but equally important lines were constructed in the southeastern part of the country and connected the cities of Fuzhou and Amoy (Xiamen) in Fujian Province with the Shanghai-Changsha line. In addition to these improvements and new linkages, a great deal of investment in upgrading the quality of existing lines and expanding their capacities through double trackage was also completed. The major lines from Canton north to Peking and as far to the northeast as Harbin were all double tracked. The main line connecting Peking and Shanghai was also double tracked, as was the east-west line from Suzhou west to Lanzhou.

China depends very heavily on its rail network for long-distance movement of peoples and goods. By 1970, the railroads of China had been classified into three major systems. First, there were the main north-south trunk lines which included the line from Peking to Canton, from Tianjin to Shanghai, and on southward to the ports of Fuzhou and Amoy, and the western line from Baoji south through Chengdu with one branch to Guiyang, Nanning and south to a point near the island of Hainan. The second major system was composed of the east-west trunk lines which included the line west from Qingdao along the Yellow River and the Wei River through Xi'an, Lanzhou, to Ürümqi, and from Shanghai west to Yunnan Province and the north Vietnamese border. The third system included the network of rail lines focused on the northeast. Most of these were built, as noted, either by the Japanese or Russians. This is the network that has essentially continued into the 1980s. Every province or first-order administrative region in China is now connected by rail except for Tibet. A railroad from Qinghai Province into Tibet is under construction to link the city of Xining with Lhasa. The line will be built southwest from the main Lanzhou-Ürümqi line and will link Lhasa with this main line into Chinese Turkestan. In 1980, it was estimated that the total route length of the Chinese rail system approximated 40,000 kilometers.

Table 7-4. Relative Accessibility as Determined by Kilometer Railroad Distance (all places are compared in column three with Zhengzhou, the most accessible city)

Rank	Place	Value
1	Zhengzhou	1.00
2	Xuzhou	1.05
3	Shijiazhuang	1.06
4	Peking	1.08
5	Tianjin	1.09
6	Jinan	1.09
7	Wuchang	1.15
8	Nanjing	1.21
9	Taiyuan	1.22
10	Xi'an	1.22
11	Changsha	1.23
12	Zhuzhou	1.25
13	Jinzhou	1.27
14	Shanghai	1.29
15	Shaoshan	1.30
16	Hangzhou	1.34
17	Qingdao	1.36
18	Shenyang	1.37
19	Hefei	1.42
20	Nanchang	1.43
21	Hohhot	1.44
22	Changchun	1.53
23	Dandong	1.56
24	Lanzhou	1.57
25	Liuzhou	1.59
26	Chengdu	1.60
27	Jilin	1.62
28	Dalian	1.64
29	Yinchuan	1.64
30	Erlian	1.65
31	Harbin	1.67
32	Guiyang	1.68
33	Guangzhou	1.70
34	Xining	1.72
35	Qiqihar	1.73
36	Chongqing	1.74
37	Nanning	1.76
38	Fuzhou	1.76
39	Mudanjiang	1.83
40	Pingxiang	1.91
41	Kunming	2.05
42	Manzhouli	2.20
43	Urümqi	2.86

Source: Travers (1980).

Table 7-5. Relative Accessibility as Determined by Travel Time and Train Frequency (all places are compared with Zhengzhou, the most accessible city, in column three)

Rank	Place	Value
1	Zhengzhou	1.00
2	Shijiazhuang	1.01
3	Peking	1.02
4	Tianjin	1.02
5	Xi'an	1.05
6	Jinzhou	1.06
7	Xuzhou	1.07
8	Shenyang	1.08
9	Wuchang	1.09
10	Jinan	1.11
11	Nanjing	1.12
12	Changchun	1.13
13	Changsha	1.15
14	Shanghai	1.16
15	Zhuzhou	1.17
16	Harbin	1.18
17	Hangzhou	1.20
18	Taiyuan	1.21
19	Lanzhou	1.28
20	Dalian	1.31
21	Jilin	1.35
22	Hohhot	1.35
23	Qiqihar	1.37
24	Shaoshan	1.38
25	Qingdao	1.39
26	Guangzhou	1.44
27	Chengdu	1.46
28	Xining	1.47
29	Dandong	1.48
30	Chongqing	1.68
31	Hefei	1.73
32	Nanchang	1.80
33	Yinchuan	2.00
34	Guiyang	2.00
35	Mudanjiang	2.00
36	Ürümqi	2.41
37	Kunming	2.85
38	Manzhouli	2.99
39	Fuzhou	3.38
40	Liuzhou	3.57
41	Erlian	5.01
42	Nanning	5.05
43	Pingxiang	6.43

Source: Travers (1980).

Accessibility by Rail

The most significant measure of the functioning of China's railway network is the way in which it focuses on and thus connects various urban nodes that represent the various regions of the country. The system functions to make some nodes and regions much more accessible than others. Enough data about the rail system and the frequency of train service are now available to be able to develop quantitative measures based on techniques of graph theory of the relative accessibility of various points in the country (Leung, 1979; Travers, 1980). Tables 7-4 and 7-5 and Figures 7-3 and 7-4 depict the difference in relative access among a number of major rail transport centers in China, analyzed on the basis of linear distance but, more significantly, on the basis of travel time.

Perhaps the most important point easily discernible from the schematic map and the tables indicates that the places with the highest relative accessibility are clustered on the North China Plain, with reasonably high access also found in the lower Yangzi region and the southern part of the northeast plain. South and southeast China had low indexes of relative accessibility, as did western China and the extreme northeast. Thus, the political heartland and core region of the country—the North China Plain (and part of the nearby Loess Plateau Region focused on Xi'an)—is the region of maximum accessibility for rail transport, a factor that no doubt makes it very attractive for all kinds of possible investments for development projects.

Roads and Highways

China, since time immemorial, has employed overland surface transportation. Until the 20th century, however, the road network was extremely poor. In traditional times, what passed for roads in China were more typically footpaths, trails, or narrow ways which generally were able to provide rough access for individuals carrying loads on their backs, using wheelbarrows, or on horseback sometimes followed by horse drawn carts. Overland travel was difficult, dangerous, time consuming, and very expensive. It was a most inefficient way to move people and goods, and indeed has provided a significant impediment to national integration of China throughout its very long history.

The foreigners who entered China in the 19th century eventually brought with them automobiles as they were being used in other parts of the world. The arrival of the automobile and truck created a great new demand for improvements in road construction, and indeed a great deal of effort was put into the construction of roads during the 20th century. In 1950, there were approximately 80,000 kilometers of useable highways and roads in China. By 1959, this had been expanded to 200,000 kilometers, and an official report in 1969 indicated the total highway mileage was then 800,000 kilometers. Of this 800,000 kilometers of total highway, approximately 300,000 was in all-weather roads with the remainder in secondary roads. Such rapid growth in road and highway construction indicates the tremendous emphasis that the present government places on the importance of territorial integration through the construction of transportation linkages (Whitaker et al., 1972).

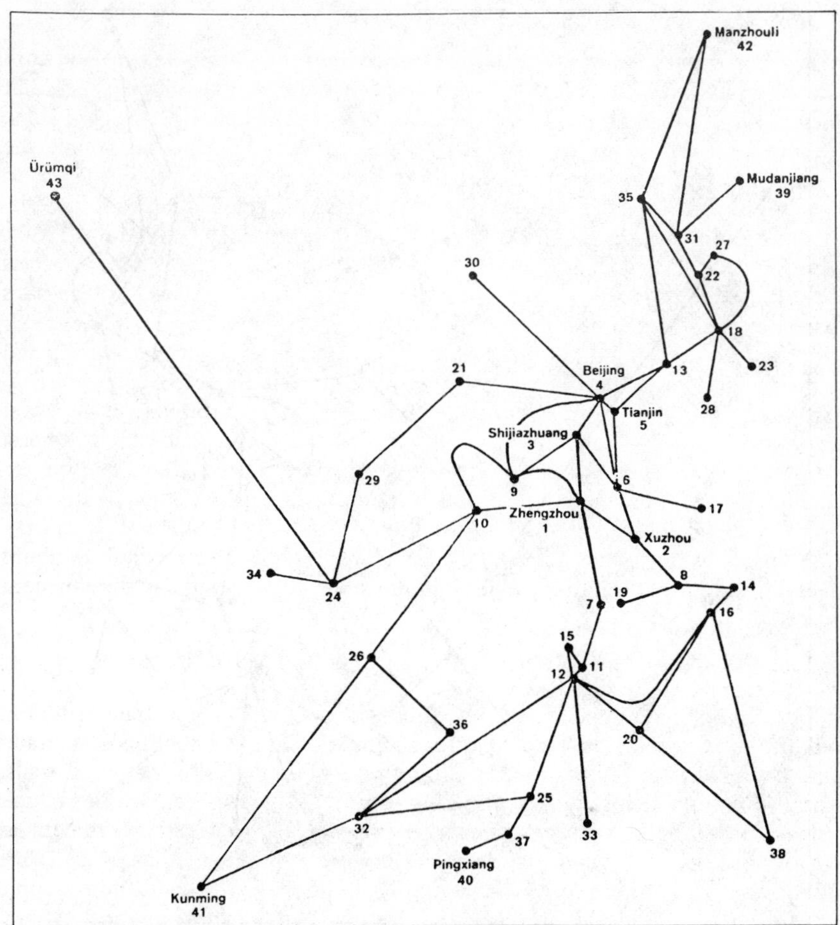

Fig. 7-3. Relative accessibility based on railroad distance.
Source: Travers (1980).

The road and highway network is a logical complementary network to the railroads (Fig. 7-5). Highways extend to areas that are not served by railroads and generally link the major cities that are served by rail with their surrounding regions that do not have rail service. In other cases, the highway and road network may parallel or supplement the rail network in filling in the interstitial areas even in the eastern part of the country where the rail network is relatively dense.

The regional view of road and highway construction in China suggests that considerably more investment had been committed to the interior and less developed regions than to the eastern more developed areas. Thus, in the period

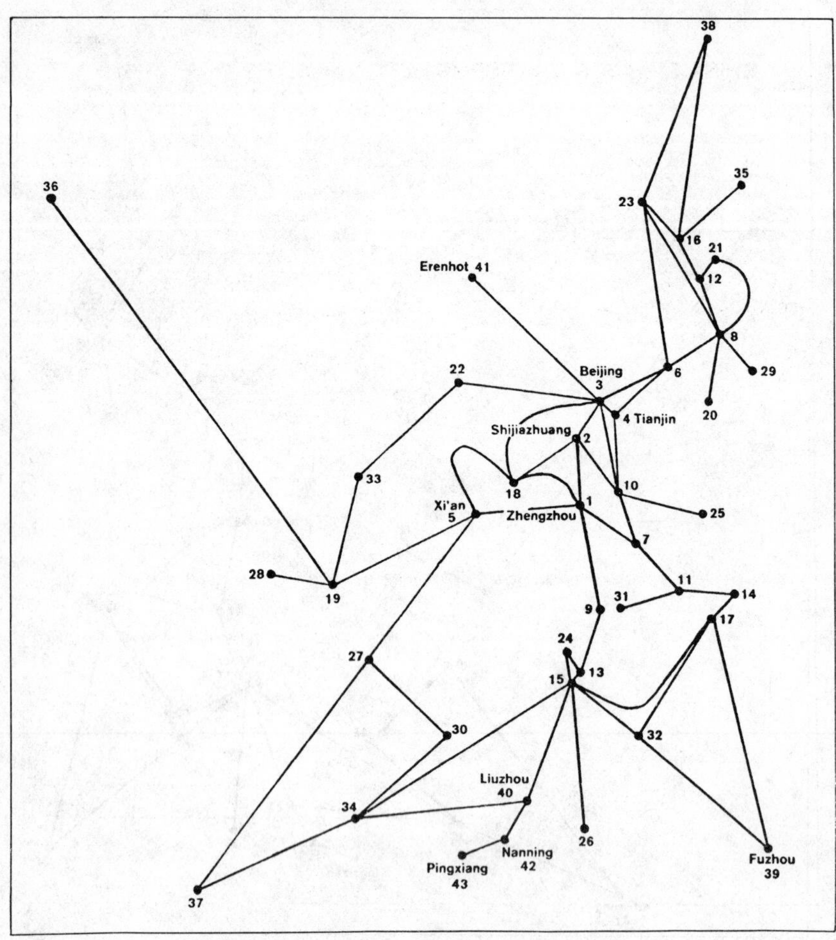

Fig. 7-4. Relative accessibility based on railroad travel time and train frequency. *Source:* Travers (1980).

from 1949 to 1960, the major new construction of roads and highways was in southwest and northwest China. The major roads have been built throughout the southwestern region and in Xinjiang, Qinghai, and Tibet. It is of considerable interest that investments in transportation, either in railroad or in highway building, have been generally highest in these same regions. It is this similarity between roads and railroads that suggests the two are viewed as complementary linkages to one another and are not seen as duplicative. If one examines why roads are built, the Chinese classify roads according to type. Trunk routes are considered to be of prime importance for either strategic or economic reasons, and are

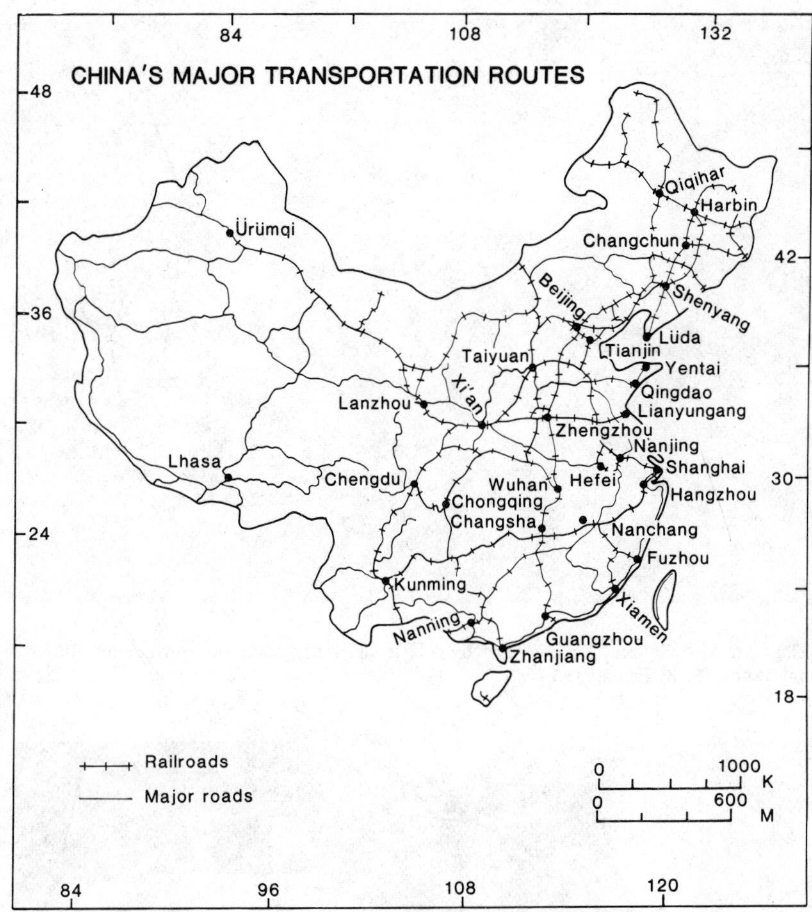

Fig. 7-5. Major transportation routes in contemporary China.
Source: Compiled from various government sources.

administered by national and provincial governments. Smaller, less important local roads may be administered by a *xian* government or indeed an individual commune. In some cases, specialized roads have also been constructed to serve specific enterprises such as a factory, a mine, or some other special purpose. In other cases, strategic roads may have been constructed by the People's Liberation Army. An example would be the important road which links western Xinjiang with western Tibet and cuts across a small arm of territory that is disputed between China and India.

Automobile and truck production in China, although still small by the standards

Tian An Men Square, Peking: The bicycle is the most common conveyance found in China's cities. (*C. W. Pannell*)

Large flexible electric buses are also a common means for moving people in cities. (*L. Ma*)

of developed countries, has grown considerably. There is new evidence, moreover, to suggest that China may increase truck production very rapidly in the years ahead. In 1980 the Chinese discussed with European automobile manufacturers the construction of a truck factory in China that would produce 150,000 new trucks every year. Even though the number is small by European standards, this is still a very important increase over past production in China and may signal a new era in automotive transportation in the People's Republic. The road network is sufficient to sustain significantly more vehicles than use it at present, despite its relatively poor quality. Thus, rapid increase in production of automobiles and trucks could be accommodated easily on the existing road structure, although it might require upgrading of the present surface of a number of roads, especially those that are likely to be heavily used in future years. Even in cities, road networks are relatively underutilized by mechanized transportation. It is likely that the use of motorized vehicles will grow sharply in the future, and a great deal more human and commodity traffic will move in cars and trucks, although the distances may be relatively short when compared with the average long haul of rail transportation.

Air Transportation

Civil air transportation began in China prior to the takeover in 1949, but most of the available aircraft were owned by the Nationalist government and were transferred to Taiwan with that government in 1949. The Communist government established an organization known as the China Civil Aviation Administration. This is the official state air carrier in China today. The carrier provides both domestic and international service, and the international service served a number of foreign cities by 1981 (Fig. 7-6). Among these were Tokyo, San Francisco, Los Angeles, New York, Moscow, Paris, Pyongyang, Dacca, and Karachi. Peking and Shanghai are the major international airports.

Domestic air service in China continues to be modest and generally is available only to party cadres and government functionaries or tourists. Major cities served by domestic air service, in addition to Peking and Shanghai, include Canton, Changsha, Kunming, Zhengzhou, Nanjing, Wuhan, Xi'an, Lanzhou, Ürümqi, Chengdu, Lhasa, Changchun, and Harbin, to name some of the most important. Where remote locations are involved, air service becomes very important in linking the country together for administrative purposes.

Many of China's passenger planes are the older piston driven and turboprop types of Soviet manufacture. In recent years, the country has purchased a variety of American, British, and French planes. In 1979, China began to manufacture its own jet passenger plane modeled, apparently, after the older vintage Boeing 707. If this manufacturing venture proves successful, it is likely that China will produce a large number of these planes to support the growth of its commercial aviation development. The demand for improved air service is obviously very great, and expansion of the air passenger fleet is a matter of high priority. Improved international and domestic service can also have a direct payoff with the foreign exchange earned from frequent tourist usage of Chinese air service.

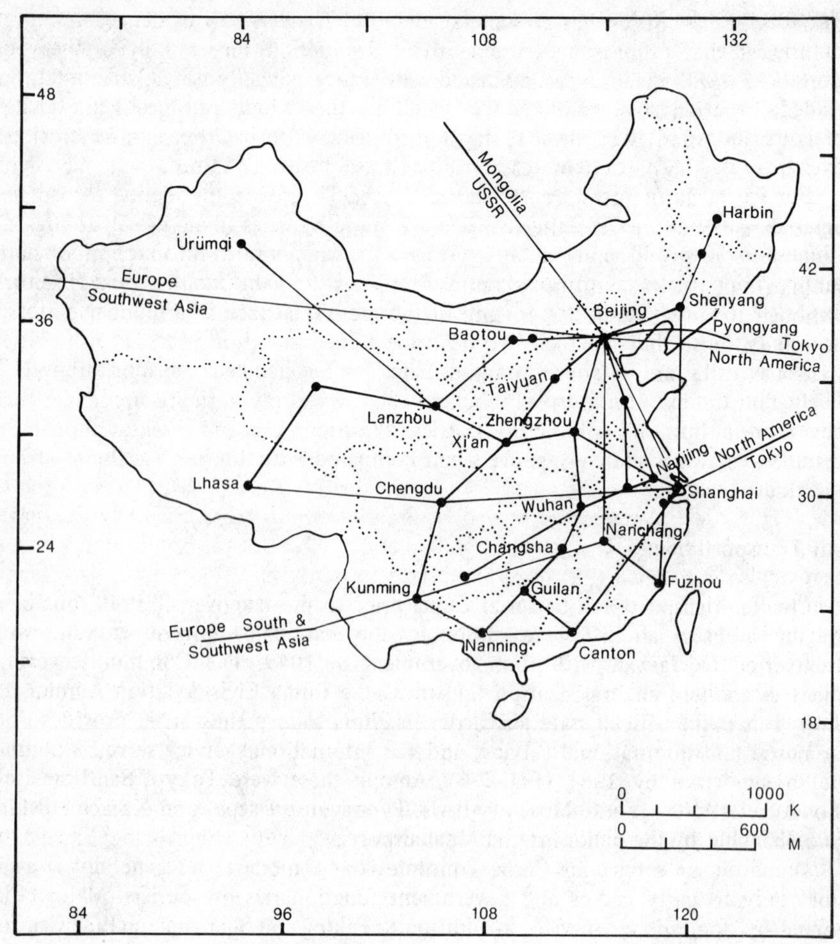

Fig. 7-6. Principal air routes in China.
Source: Ditu Chubanshe (1978).

CHINA'S TRADE PATTERNS

Trade in China, both domestic and foreign, has traditionally been under the control of governmental organizations and bureaucracies. Domestic trade has operated since antiquity on two levels or scales–local and regional. The local scale traditionally involved exchange of goods among peasants and small-time merchants through the medium of regular or periodic markets and fairs. Foodstuffs, tools, and clothing were, for the most part, produced and exchanged at the local level. A few more sophisticated or complex pieces of equipment or luxuries might be brought in from a great distance. In places where water transportation was available, e.g., the middle and lower Yangzi Basin, grain or silk was traded. Overall, most exchange was local. To the extent that regional exchange of goods occurred, the terms of trade were roughly in balance, and interregional exchanges had little effect upon traditional peasant life.

Foreign trade in dynastic times was also not a critical matter for the Chinese agrarian economy. Extending as far back as Han times (206 BC–220 AD), the Chinese exported silk and received precious goods in return. This type of specialty luxury trade persisted through the centuries, with the Chinese expanding their exports into other craft items such as porcelains and precious metals and stones, as well as tea for the most part to other Asian countries.

Western interest in China was stimulated by the accounts of Marco Polo. The Portuguese established trade as early as 1557 at the port of Macao on the Pearl River estuary near Canton. Trade with imperial Russia followed in the 17th century. By the 18th century, the Chinese imperium established a series of official merchant organizations to oversee and regulate foreign trade with Western countries. This trade was restricted to the port of Canton and was largely associated with British traders. The goods were generally the same as noted above except that opium was added to China's imports. It was this latter good that the Chinese eventually tried to control with the unfortunate consequence of initiating a brief war in 1840 that led to the humiliation of China and the opening up of the country to foreign traders and investors through treaties that began in 1842. Other treaty ports–Shanghai, Fuzhou, Ningbo, Hankou, Changsha, Nanjing, Hangzhou, and Tianjin–were opened by 1860. China was then rapidly opening to the West.

Foreign trade grew rapidly and, in addition to luxury items, China began to import such items as rice, cotton, kerosene, sugar, cigarettes, minerals, and machinery. Exports continued to be mainly agricultural goods and silk. Most of China's trade in the early part of this century was with Hong Kong, Japan, the United States, and Great Britain, a pattern that to some extent was found again in 1980.

China's Trade Since 1949

Domestic trade in China since 1949 has been carefully regulated. The main goal of the regime initially was to wrest control of wholesaling and retailing from private enterprises to state control. This goal was met during the 1950s. After 1950, the share of private commerce dropped rapidly as private functions were taken over by state ministries, trading companies, and in rural areas, supply and marketing cooperatives.

One of the major problems in a Marxist state like China is to regulate trade while at the same time to rationalize the production and consumption of goods through state directed and/or associated agencies that oversee pricing and marketing adjustments. The procedures for accomplishing this in China have fluctuated over time, and the degree of bureaucratic vs. market control has reflected the extremes of politics as they have operated in the People's Republic. Chinese leaders, it seems, have indicated some willingness to experiment and follow pragmatic policies related to trade despite the extreme control associated with the ideologically dominated mass movements (the Great Leap Forward and Cultural Revolution). For example, the restoration of rural "free markets" before and after the Great Leap indicates a willingness to allow some degree of market regulation of commodity prices and associated stimulants to local commodity production. The restoration of these free markets was associated with reestablishment of private plots to each peasant family.

Domestic trade in China, barring radical shifts in domestic policy, is viewed as a mechanism to provide adjustments in the economy and to satisfy consumer demands and thus help smooth out and rationalize production and exchange. Retail stores are operated by the government or various administrative units to provide necessary goods to the public. At the same time, production units are expected to meet their goals, which usually include some surplus that moves into a regional or national network of exchange. Given the former Vice Premier Deng Xiaoping's often quoted remark "that it doesn't matter what color the cat is as long as it catches mice," the production and exchange systems are likely to continue to operate in practical ways to satisfy consumer demands at reasonable prices as long as they continue to produce efficiently and copiously.

Foreign Trade Since 1949

Marxist countries, and particularly large ones like China and the USSR, have traditionally sought to follow policies of economic growth and development—autarky—that emphasize their domestic resources and production and rely less on foreign sources and trading partners. For this reason, as Eckstein (1977) noted, international trade has been small but nevertheless significant in maintaining economic growth and stability in China since 1949. In the 1950s, when China was following the Soviet model of development, critically needed producer goods and technology were imported, which helped accelerate the pace of industrial growth. In the early 1960s, China was experiencing food shortages that became especially critical in cities. In the early 1960s, the country satisfied the food commodity shortages by going into the international market and making large purchases of grain. Until very recently, China relied heavily on international trade to provide critically needed fertilizer, and thus mineral nutrients, for her agricultural sector. Hence, China has managed to satisfy her pressing needs and requirements through foreign trade, and her economy has benefitted and managed to maintain a satisfactory rate of growth even when crises threatened to disrupt economic stability.

China trades when it is in her interest to do so. Like other countries, she seeks gain through the mechanism of trade. The reasons for international trade are well known but may be summarized briefly to remind us of the rationale for trade among all countries. The idea underlying gains to be derived from foreign trade is that countries differ in their resource and factor endowments (natural resources, land, labor, and capital), and these differences permit varying types of specialization in production to evolve. Specialization has led to greater efficiencies and lower costs, which means that it may be cheaper to import a good than to produce it on the home territory. International trade is a mechanism whereby the most specialized and lowest cost producers can make their goods available to others and, in turn, purchase goods from others, who specialize in and deliver certain goods at low prices. China is very well endowed with labor, but the supply of arable land is limited. China has certain advantages in producing certain kinds of goods and will tend to export these because of low production costs.

The size of China's economy, despite the relative low per capita income and wealth, is enormous. This results from the large population and area and the substantial resource base. Its large size has permitted China to specialize within her own boundaries and to achieve economies of scale and efficiencies at home. Foreign trade has not been a big part of China's gross national product. As Eckstein (1977) has noted, the foreign trade turnover or trade share of the GNP in China has usually been between 4 and 8%, whereas for the U.S., it has been 10 to 15% and for the United Kingdom, 30 to 40%. Although such a measure is only approximate for China, as a consequence of sometimes unreliable data, it does present a reasonable statement on the modest size of China's foreign trade in relation to the size of the total economy.

Composition of China's Foreign Trade

In general, China has sought to provide herself with commodities and goods that are in short supply at home. The major components of China's import trade have been foodstuffs, especially grain, and inedible materials, for example such fibers as cotton; chemicals, including fertilizer; machinery and transportation equipment such as aircraft; and various manufactured goods (Table 7-6). The export picture has been similar; e.g., about one-quarter of China's exports have been foodstuffs of various types. In addition, several inedible materials, fiber, and petroleum have formed an important but slightly declining share of export trade (Table 7-7). Manufactured goods, and especially textiles, have accounted for approximately one-quarter of the exports; and the remainder has been in chemicals and assorted products. The Chinese have sought balance in the terms of trade, and overall they have achieved what may be a very modest surplus over the last three decades. In general, they have avoided getting too embroiled in credit arrangements and have sought to pay as they purchased, to the extent possible. Recent trends suggest a greater willingness to use credit and more flexibility in their approach to international trade. The composition of trade has changed over the years. For example, in 1980 the Chinese exported grain, but during the 1960s the pattern was mixed. The Chinese have imported considerable quantities of grain, but managed to export higher priced agricultural goods such as pork, vegetables, fruit, and canned goods. In both 1976 and 1977, the Chinese had a substantial surplus in the terms of trade for agricultural commodities. Other major exports include petroleum, which grew rapidly during the 1970s from no export prior to 1970, and manufactured goods, especially textiles, clothing, and handicrafts. Imports have focused on key items in scarce supply in China throughout the last three decades. During the 1970s, iron and steel imports have been large,

Table 7-6. China: Commodity Composition of Imports, by Area[a] (million U.S. $)

	1976					1977				
	Total	Developed	Less developed	Hong Kong[b] and Macao	Communist	Total	Developed	Less developed	Hong Kong[b] and Macao	Communist
Total	6,010	4,110	765	30	1,105	7,100	4,525	1,385	45	1,150
Foodstuffs	560	350	115	–	90	1,115	695	350	–	70
Of which:										
Grains	325	290	35	–	–	745	630	110	–	–
Fruits and vegetables	5	–	5	–	–	10	–	10	–	–
Sugar	200	60	55	–	85	320	60	205	–	55
Crude materials	895	245	435	15	200	1,445	415	810	20	200
Of which:										
Oilseeds	5	–	5	–	–	115	15	100	–	–
Crude rubber, natural	150	–	135	–	15	215	–	200	–	15
Crude rubber, synthetic	5	5	–	–	–	10	10	–	–	–
Wood pulp	60	60	–	–	–	55	55	–	–	–
Textile fibers, natural	190	15	175	–	–	350	50	300	–	–
Textile fibers, synthetic	115	115	–	–	–	150	150	–	–	–
Crude fertilizers, minerals	40	–	30	–	5	60	10	40	–	10
Metalliferous ores and scrap	125	25	15	–	85	110	20	35	–	55
Crude animal and vegetable materials	20	–	5	10	5	40	–	10	15	15
Petroleum and products	45	–	45	–	–	30	–	30	–	–
Animal fats and oil	15	15	–	–	–	35	35	–	–	–
Fixed vegetable oils	10	5	5	–	–	105	50	55	–	–
Chemicals	600	455	35	–	110	885	710	60	5	110
Of which:										
Elements and compounds	210	210	–	–	5	295	290	–	–	5
Dyeing materials	20	15	–	–	–	45	40	5	–	–
Fertilizers, manufactured[c]	230	100	30	–	95	345	215	55	–	75
Plastic materials	90	85	–	–	–	100	100	–	–	–

Paper and paperboard	45	40	–	–	–	60	60	–	–	–
Textile yarn and fabric	125	115	5	–	–	175	155	5	5	10
Nonmetallic mineral products	15	10	–	5	–	15	5	–	–	10
Iron and steel	1,445	1,335	5	–	100	1,570	1,470	10	–	90
Nonferrous metals	260	110	130	–	20	265	120	105	–	40
Metal products, industrial	90	80	–	–	10	55	55	–	–	–
Nonelectric machinery	1,090	905	–	–	185	455	280	15	–	160
Electric machinery	210	185	–	–	25	105	65	–	–	40
Transport equipment	470	190	15	–	265	640	365	–	–	275
Precision instruments	60	40	–	5	15	25	10	–	–	15
Watches and clocks	15	15	–	–	–	10	10	–	–	–
Other	55	10	10	–	35	100	35	20	–	45

[a]Data are rounded to the nearest \$5 million. Because of rounding, components may not add to the totals shown. Ellipsis marks indicate that imports, if any, amounted to less than U.S. \$2.5 million. Estimates are based on data reported by trading partners. Where data are incomplete, as for the less developed and Communist countries, estimates are based on fragmentary information from trade agreements and press reports and on commodity breakdowns for earlier years.

[b]Including Hong Kong reexports of third country goods to China.

[c]Excluding phosphate rock, ammonium chloride, sodium nitrate, and potassium nitrate.

Source: National Foreign Assessment Center (1978).

Table 7-7. China: Commodity Composition of Exports, by Area[a] (million U.S. $)

	1976					1977				
	Total	Developed	Less developed	Hong Kong[b] and Macao	Communist	Total	Developed	Less developed	Hong Kong[b] and Macao	Communist
Total	7,265	2,695	1,700	1,630	1,240	7,955	2,925	1,865	1,795	1,370
Foodstuffs	1,945	485	450	715	300	2,025	475	470	760	320
Of which:										
Live animals	230	–	–	230	–	250	–	–	250	–
Meat and fish	430	180	60	170	20	400	140	60	170	30
Eggs and dairy products	65	10	10	50	–	60	5	5	50	–
Grains	450	25	160	85	180	455	20	190	80	165
Fruits and vegetables	385	170	65	115	35	490	195	80	140	75
Teas and spices	140	45	65	15	10	150	55	60	15	20
Tobacco	35	15	15	5	–	30	–	20	5	5
Crude materials	1,805	1,135	145	215	310	2,045	1,280	170	245	350
Of which:										
Hides and skins, undressed	30	30	–	–	–	30	30	–	–	–
Oilseeds	85	65	5	10	5	90	55	10	10	15
Textile fibers	285	195	10	50	30	290	255	10	15	10
Crude minerals	65	45	5	10	10	75	50	–	10	15
Metalliferous ores	45	40	–	–	5	45	35	–	–	10
Crude animal materials	260	150	25	65	20	330	170	35	90	35
Coal	95	10	5	–	80	95	30	5	–	60
Crude oil	665	540	60	–	60	785	625	75	–	85
Petroleum products	175	15	25	65	75	230	10	25	110	85
Fixed vegetable oils	40	15	5	15	5	25	10	5	10	–
Chemicals	330	150	80	60	40	380	160	85	70	65
Of which:										
Medicinal products	40	10	15	20	–	50	10	10	25	5

Manufactures	3,060	890	1,015	675	535	3,415	1,000	1,135	705	575
Of which:										
Leather and dressed skins	65	50	–	10	–	65	50	–	15	–
Paper	65	5	20	30	5	60	5	25	25	5
Textile yarn and fabrics	1,115	340	325	265	225	1,300	400	380	280	240
Nonmetallic mineral products	150	30	60	60	–	170	35	55	65	15
Iron and steel	105	10	55	15	25	110	5	75	15	15
Nonferrous metals	90	40	10	5	35	65	25	5	5	30
Metal products	105	10	70	25	5	180	15	100	25	40
Nonelectric machinery	140	10	55	25	50	140	5	70	20	45
Electric machinery	75	5	40	20	10	75	5	40	20	10
Transport equipment	70	5	50	–	15	55	–	35	–	20
Clothing	420	170	105	70	80	560	210	150	105	95
Footwear	65	20	20	10	15	65	25	25	15	–
Handicrafts and manufacturers	320	155	80	55	25	370	170	115	65	20
Other	110	30	10	10	55	95	15	5	15	60

[a]Data are rounded to the nearest $5 million. Because of rounding, components may not add to the totals shown. Ellipsis marks indicate that imports, if any, amounted to less than U.S. $2.5 million. Estimates are based on data reported by trading partners. Where data are incomplete, as for the less developed and Communist countries, estimates are based on fragmentary information from trade agreements and press reports and on commodity breakdowns for earlier years.

[b]Including Hong Kong reexports of PRC-origin goods to third countries.

Source: National Foreign Assessment Center (1978).

Table 7-8. Balance of Trade[a]

	Total trade				Communist countries				Non-Communist countries			
	Total	Exports	Imports	Balance	Total	Exports	Imports	Balance	Total	Exports	Imports	Balance
1950	1,210	620	590	30	350	210	140	70	860	410	450	-40
1951	1,900	780	1,120	-340	975	465	515	-50	920	315	605	-290
1952	1,890	875	1,015	-140	1,315	605	710	-105	575	270	305	-35
1953	2,295	1,040	1,255	-215	1,555	670	885	-215	740	370	370	0
1954	2,350	1,060	1,290	-230	1,735	765	970	-205	615	295	320	-25
1955	3,035	1,375	1,660	-285	2,250	950	1,300	-350	785	425	360	65
1956	3,120	1,635	1,485	150	2,055	1,045	1,010	35	1,065	590	475	115
1957	3,055	1,615	1,440	175	1,965	1,085	880	205	1,090	530	560	-30
1958	3,765	1,940	1,825	115	2,380	1,280	1,100	180	1,385	660	725	-65
1959	4,290	2,230	2,060	170	2,980	1,615	1,365	250	1,310	615	695	-80
1960	3,990	1,960	2,030	-70	2,620	1,335	1,285	50	1,370	625	745	-120
1961	3,015	1,525	1,490	35	1,685	965	715	250	1,335	560	775	-215
1962	2,670	1,520	1,150	370	1,410	915	490	425	1,265	605	660	-55
1963	2,775	1,575	1,200	375	1,250	820	430	390	1,525	755	770	-15
1964	3,220	1,750	1,470	280	1,100	710	390	320	2,120	1,040	1,080	-40
1965	3,880	2,035	1,845	190	1,165	650	515	135	2,715	1,385	1,330	55
1966	4,245	2,210	2,035	175	1,090	585	505	80	3,155	1,625	1,530	95
1967	3,915	1,960	1,955	5	830	485	345	140	3,085	1,475	1,610	-135
1968	3,785	1,960	1,825	135	840	500	340	160	2,945	1,460	1,485	-25
1969	3,895	2,060	1,835	225	785	490	295	195	3,110	1,570	1,540	30
1970	4,340	2,095	2,245	-150	860	480	380	100	3,480	1,615	1,865	-250
1971	4,810	2,500	2,310	190	1,085	585	500	85	3,725	1,915	1,810	105
1972	6,000	3,150	2,850	300	1,275	740	535	205	4,725	2,410	2,315	95
1973	10,300	5,075	5,225	-150	1,710	1,000	710	290	8,590	4,075	4,515	-440
1974	14,080	6,660	7,420	-760	2,435	1,430	1,010	420	11,645	5,230	6,415	-1,185
1975	14,575	7,180	7,395	-215	2,390	1,380	1,010	370	12,185	5,800	6,385	-585
1976	13,275	7,265	6,010	1,255	2,345	1,240	1,105	135	10,930	6,025	4,905	1,120
1977	15,055	7,955	7,100	855	2,520	1,370	1,150	225	12,530	6,580	5,950	630

[a]Data are rounded to the nearest $5 million. Because of rounding, components may not add to totals shown.

Source: National Foreign Assessment Center (1978).

Table 7-9. Top 10 Trading Partners

	Total trade (million US $)		Rank	
	1976	1977	1976	1977
Japan	3,052	3,509	1	1
Hong Kong	1,620	1,779	2	2
West Germany	952	826	3	3
Australia	380	631	7	4
Romania	451	600	5	5
Canada	309	459	9	6
United States	351	391	8	7
USSR	417	338	6	8
Singapore	295	324	10	9
United Kingdom	277	284	12	10

Source: National Foreign Assessment Center (1978).

as well as many types of precision machines, fertilizer, grain, cotton, and aircraft. High technology items (oil drilling equipment and computers) as well as defense related equipment have also been important, but it is difficult to obtain precise information on such trade items.

Trade Flows and Partners

China's trading partners and direction of trade present a fascinating picture of the changing requirements of the economy, but more appropriately, of the changes in internal politics and related policies that may determine economic requirements. In the 1950s, China's plan for economic growth followed the Soviet model, and China's trade was heavily oriented toward the Soviet Union and other Communist countries (Table 7-8). During the 1960s, after the ideological split with the USSR, China began to trade with free market economies. This also coincided with China's need for large grain purchases. Trade with Canada, Australia, and France became important. The 1970s brought in another phase in which Japan and the USA recognized China, and trade with these two major capitalist states became very important. By 1977, China's trade with other Communist countries accounted for less than 20% of the total trade. In 1977, Japan and Hong Kong were the two most important trading partners (Table 7-9). The United States was seventh and the USSR eighth among the top 10. The geographic distribution of China's international trade by major world region is depicted in Fig. 7-7.

Growing Trade with the United States

In 1979, China and the United States signed a trade agreement, which was ratified in early 1980. Under the terms of this treaty, China and the United States granted each other most favored nation status in trade, and they agreed to the

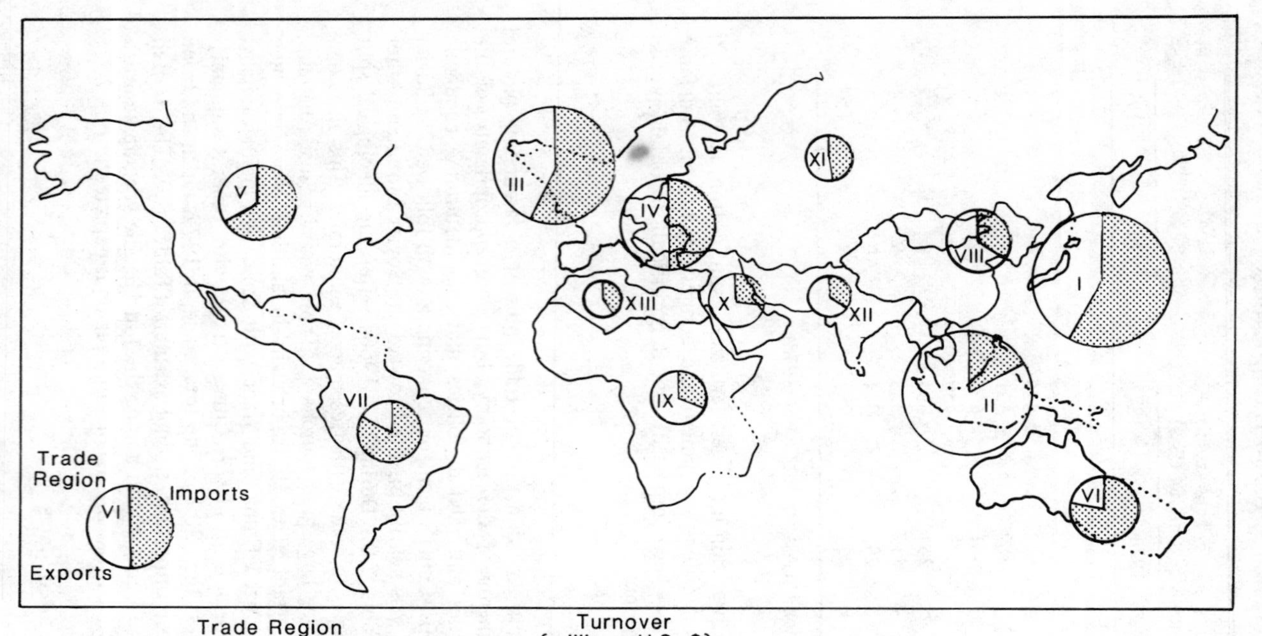

Trade Region	Turnover (millions U.S. $)	Trade Region	Turnover (millions U.S. $)
I Japan	3,510	VII Latin America (including Cuba)	635
II Southeast Asia (including Hong Kong & Macao)	2,975	VIII Far Eastern Communist Countries	635
III Western Europe	2,395	IX Sub-Saharan Africa	555
IV Eastern Europe (including Albania & Yugoslavia)	1,445	X Middle East	520
V United States & Canada	850	XI USSR	340
VI Australia & New Zealand	695	XII South Asia	325
XIII North Africa	225		

Fig. 7-7. Geographic distribution of China's foreign trade, 1977.
Source: National Foreign Assessment Center (1978).

protection of patents and copyrights. This trade agreement formalized a rapidly changing set of relations between the two countries and represented a strong recognition of the rapidly growing economic and trade ties between China and the U.S. In 1971, when then President Nixon visited China, no trade existed between the U.S. and China (see Table 7-10). By 1979, this trade had grown to more than $2 billion annually and has grown rapidly since then. In part, it reflects the increasing warmth of political relations between the two countries who perceive the working relationship and interdependence to be mutually beneficial.

The terms of trade between the two have been in the U.S. favor so far, but the Chinese have made it clear they wish the relationship to be balanced in trade flows. The U.S. sells China foodstuffs and fiber along with high technology goods, such as oil drilling equipment, aircraft, and defense related supplies. China sells the U.S. labor intensive manufactured goods, such as textiles, garments, rugs, and some handicrafts. Recently, the Chinese have promulgated new rules and regulations about foreign investments, and they have actively sought to promote foreign investment through joint ventures. Such ventures seek to take advantage of the large pool of available Chinese labor to manufacture garments, footwear, toys, handicrafts, electronics, furniture, or other goods. Export processing zones have been set up in several locations to permit the assembly of manufactured goods without encountering the red tape and expense of importing and exporting. These zones appear modeled after similar and successful zones in Taiwan, Korea, and Mexico. If successful, they may provide very strong competition for other developing countries that also seek to exploit their pools of semiskilled but industrious workers.

China as a Factor in World Trade

China accounts for a very modest part of total world trade–1 to 2%. This trade is not essential for China to survive and grow as a world power, but it is essential if China is to prosper, grow rapidly, and improve the condition of its 1 billion people. Although China's agricultural picture has been good during most of the 1970s, certain agricultural commodities and fibers (e.g., cotton) can be imported more cheaply, while China concentrates on other crops. In recent years, China has not produced enough iron and steel to meet demand. It is this type of requirement and specialization that makes trade so valuable. Other things can be obtained only through trade, and this is especially true of high technology goods, precision machinery, and certain metals. Were trade in these items not available, it appears that economic growth and technological development would be retarded. Finally, certain weapons and related military and transportation equipment can only be obtained through trade linkages. The nature and exigencies of China's military defenses require her to seek these goods on a global exchange basis. Military technology in China has lagged in recent years. This lag coupled with the increasing view of the threat from the Soviet Union have led the Chinese to seek external help through trade to improve the level and quality of weapons and military hardware.

Table 7-10. Sino–U.S. Trade, 1979

Top 15 U.S. exports to the PRC

Category	Value	% of total U.S. exports to the PRC
Cotton, not carded, and other cotton	356,763,016	20.8
Yellow corn, not donated	268,547,073	15.6
Wheat, unmilled, not donated	214,105,583	12.5
Soybeans, not specified	106,722,343	6.2
Polyester fibers	56,777,062	3.3
Seamless oil well casings	56,536,766	3.3
Parts of oil- and gas-field drilling machines	54,157,663	3.2
Seamless standard pipe other than alloy iron or steel	36,521,461	2.1
Soybean oil, crude, degummed	35,894,335	2.1
Seamless oil well drilling pipe, other than alloy iron or steel	29,937,468	1.7
Urea	27,179,233	1.6
Polyester resins, unsaturated	22,565,155	1.3
Textured yarns of polyester	22,416,073	1.3
Rotary drilling machines for oil and gas fields	17,800,320	1.0
Electric geophysical instruments and parts	17,698,320	

Total value U.S. exports to PRC: $1,716,499,905

Top 15 U.S. imports from the PRC

Category	Value	% of total U.S. imports from the PRC
Crude petroleum	71,788,895	12.1
Gasoline	21,614,894	3.7
Fireworks	15,623,799	2.6
Plain printcloth shirting	15,153,376	2.6
Ammonium molybdate	13,136,891	2.2
Antiques	12,275,794	2.1
Men's cotton or flannel sport shirts	10,551,356	1.8
Floor coverings, pile	10,253,620	1.7
U.S.-type Oxford female footwear	9,948,416	1.7
Shrimp, raw, peeled	9,731,628	1.6
Bristles, crude or processed	9,570,709	1.6
Tungsten ore	9,314,857	1.6
Cotton gloves	9,119,163	1.5
Baskets and bags of bamboo	8,908,688	1.5
Women's cotton corduroy slacks	8,166,679	1.4

Total value of U.S. imports from the PRC: $592,282,994

Source: The China Business Review (March–April, 1980).

The sum of these needs indicates that despite an ideological fondness for a policy of autarky, China needs trade; and in recent years that need has been perceived in a practical fashion. This changing perception suggests continued rapid growth of China as a factor in international trade, and for the world this means increased interdependence of China with its major trading partners. Such interdependence is believed to work in the interests of global peace, for trade is believed to bring mutual benefits, and as these benefits are seen and understood, the trading partners will seek to live and work together in greater harmony and peace.

LITERATURE CITED

Baum, Richard, ed., 1980, *China's Four Modernizations, The New Technological Revolution.* Boulder, Colorado: Westview Press.

Central Intelligence Agency, 1971, *People's Republic of China Atlas.* Washington, D.C.: U.S. G.P.O.

Chen, Nai-ruenn, 1978, "Economic Modernization in Post Mao China: Policies, Problems, and Prospects." In U.S. Congress, Joint Economic Committee, *Chinese Economy Post Mao.* Washington, D.C.: U.S. GPO, pp. 165–203.

The China Business Review, March–April, 1980, Vol. 7, No. 2, p. 6.

Cressey, George B., 1955, *Land of the 500 Million.* New York: McGraw-Hill.

Ding, Chen, 1980, "The Economic Development of China." *Scientific American*, Vol. 243, No. 3, pp. 152–165.

Ditu Chubanshe, 1978, *Zhongguo Dituce*, Shanghai.

Eckstein, Alexander, 1977, *China's Economic Revolution.* Cambridge: Cambridge University Press.

Field, Robert M., Lardy, Nicholas R. and Emerson, J. P., 1976, *Provincial Industrial Output in The People's Republic of China.* Foreign Economic Report No. 12. Washington, D.C.: U.S. Department of Commerce.

Lardy, Nicholas R., 1975, "Economic Planning in the People's Republic of China: Central Provincial Fiscal Relations." In *China: A Reassessment of the Economy.* Washington, D.C.: Joint Economic Committee, U.S. GPO, pp. 94–115.

Lardy, Nicholas R., 1978, "Recent Chinese Economic Performance and Prospect for the Ten Year Plan." In U.S. Congress, Joint Economic Committee, *Chinese Economy Post Mao.* Washington, D.C.: U.S. GPO, pp. 48–62.

Leung, C. K., 1979, "Transportation and Spatial Integration." In Lee Ngok and Leung Chi-Leung, eds., *China: Development and Challenge*, Proceedings of the Fifth Leverhulme Conference, Vol. II, "*Political Economy and Spatial Pattern and Process.*" Hong Kong: University of Hong Kong, Centre of Asian Studies, pp. 323–342.

Lippit, Victor, 1966, "Development of Transportation in Communist China." *The China Quarterly*, No. 27, pp. 101–119.

National Foreign Assessment Center, 1978, *China: International Trade, 1977–78.* Washington, D.C.: Central Intelligence Agency, ER78-10721.

Travers, Lawrence, 1980, "Railroad Travel-time Distances in China." Paper presented at the 76th Annual Meeting, Association of American Geographers, Louisville, Ky. April 13–16, 1980.

Whitaker, Donald P. et al., 1972, *Area Handbook for the People's Republic of China.* Washington, D.C.: U.S. GPO.

Wu, Yuan-li, 1967, *The Spatial Economy of Communist China.* New York: Praeger.

Chapter 8

Resources and Development of Selected Industries

Does China possess sufficient quantities of basic mineral resources and energy necessary to become a modern industrial power? The question cannot be answered satisfactorily without looking into the resource base of the country and how it has been utilized.

China, with its large land area, is well endowed with mineral resources (Wang, 1977). As a result of intensive and extensive field investigations, involving thousands of geological workers and carried out under the Communist government, new deposits of mineral resources–petroleum, coal, iron, copper, pyrites, asbestos, molybdenum, tin, lead, and zinc–have been discovered in recent years. China has long been among the world's leading producers of antimony, tungsten, mercury, magnesite, bismuth, fluorspar, and talc (Wang, 1977). In order to gain a better understanding of China's current industrial performance and its future prospect, several basic and significant resources and industries–coal, resources for iron and steel making, petroleum, and hydroelectric power–are examined in some detail in this section in terms of estimated reserves and annual production. It is these resources that will provide the necessary energy and mineral products on which China will construct her industrialization and modernization in the years ahead.

MINERAL SUPPLY AND ENERGY

Coal Supply

Among the most important resources China possesses is a very large supply of good quality coal, a major energy requirement for the drive to industrialize. China

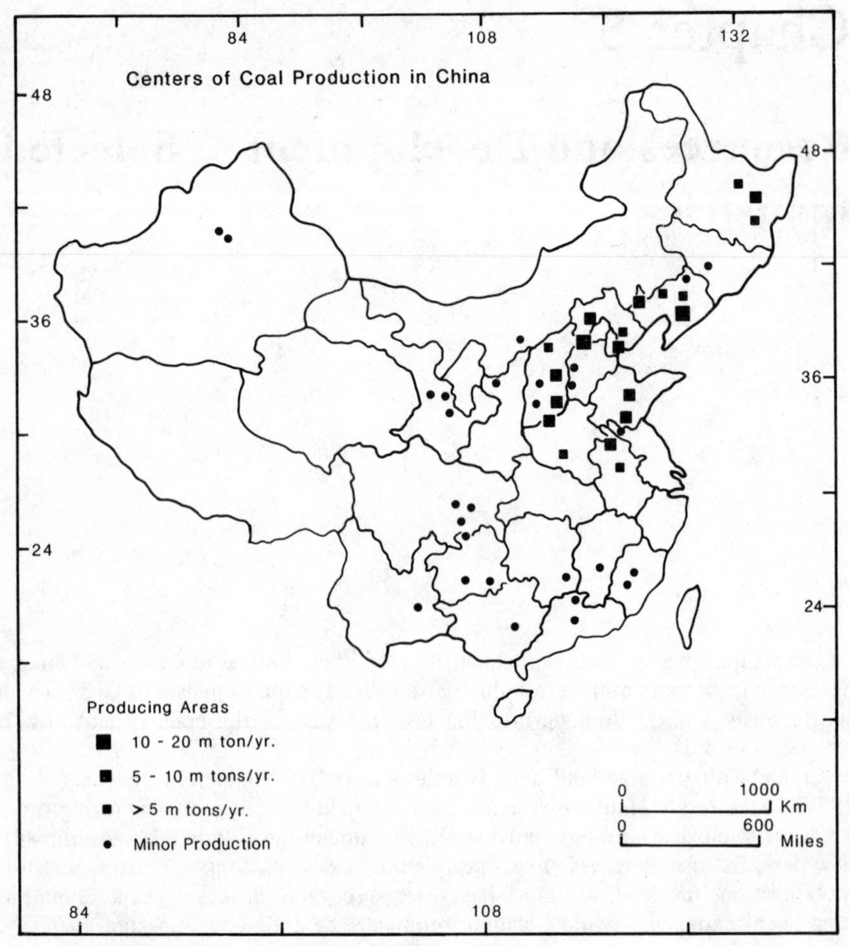

Fig. 8-1. Major centers of coal production.
Source: K. P. Wang (1977) and Central Intelligence Agency (1971).

ranks third in world coal reserves, after the Soviet Union and the United States. The amount of verified deposits was given by the government in late 1979 as 600,000 million tons (*Beijing Review*, 1979b). About 80% of the coal is bituminous and the rest is largely anthracite. Sixty-one percent of the coal is found in north China, 10% in the northwest, and only an extremely small amount is found in south China (Fig. 8-1). Shanxi Province alone contains one-third of China's verified reserves, while Nei Monggol (Inner Mongolia) Autonomous Region has 25% of the nation's total coal reserves (*Renmin ribao*, 1979).

Table 8-1. China's Supply of Primary Energy

	Total	Coal	Oil	Natural gas	Hydroelectricity
	(Million metric tons of coal equivalent)				
1952	50	48	2	Negl	Negl
1957	110	103	5	1	1
1966	207	177	17	12	1
1970	319	246	43	27	2
1974	439	305	93	38	3
1975	505	356	99	46	4
1976	530	363	113	50	4
1977	593	406	121	62	4
	Percent				
1952	100	97	3	Negl	Negl
1957	100	94	4	1	1
1965	100	85	8	6	1
1970	100	77	13	9	1
1974	100	69	21	9	1
1975	100	71	19	10	1
1976	100	68	21	10	1
1977	100	68	20	11	1

Source: National Foreign Assessment Center (1978).

Coal has always played a dominant role in China's energy supply, although its relative importance has declined since 1970 as a result of increasing use of oil (Table 8-1). Industries use approximately two-thirds of the coal produced, while residential heating and cooking consume nearly 30% of the total. Agricultural and transportation uses account for only a few percent each. In 1980, 620 million tons of coal were produced (State Statistical Bureau, 1981), a yearly total surpassed only by Soviet and U.S. production. There are more than 20,000 small coal mines in 1,100 rural counties, operated by production brigades, communes, or by the counties themselves. In 1980, output of these small mines accounted for one-third of the nation's total (*Beijing Review*, 1980c).

Large-scale production is concentrated in north and northeast China (Fig. 8-1). The largest coal mining center is located at Kailuan, Hebei Province, where the annual output before the major July, 1976 earthquake, which severely damaged the mines, exceeded 25 million tons. It was reported that in 1977 its production level had returned to that experienced before the earthquake. China has called for an increase to 50 to 60 million tons per year at Kailuan. Other large mining centers include Fushun, Tiefa, and Fuxin in Liaoning Province; Hegang in Heilongjiang; Yanzhou in Shandong; Fengfeng in Hebei; Datong and Guijiao in Shanxi;

Table 8-2. Raw Coal Production in China, 1949-1978
(million tons)

Year	Total	Small mines	Large mines
1949	32.43	1.45	30.95
1950	42.92	1.91	41.01
1951	53.09	2.37	50.72
1952	66.49	2.96	63.53
1953	69.68	3.11	66.57
1954	83.66	3.73	79.93
1955	98.30	4.70	93.60
1956	110.36	4.44	105.92
1957	130.73	7.50	123.23
1958	230.00	51.34	178.66
1959	300.00	66.07	233.93
1960	280.00	66.54	213.46
1961	170.00	26.00	144.00
1962	180.00	26.00	154.00
1963	190.00	28.00	162.00
1964	200.00	30.00	170.00
1965	220.00	32.00	188.00
1966	240.00	36.00	204.00
1967	190.00	29.00	161.00
1968	200.00	36.00	164.00
1969	250.00	55.00	195.00
1970	300.00	75.00	225.00
1971	320.00	83.00	237.00
1972	340.00	92.00	248.00
1973	365.00	102.00	263.00
1974	390.00	112.00	278.00
1975	440.00	–	–
1976	490.00	–	–
1977	550.00	–	–
1978	618.00	–	–
1979	635.00	–	–
1980	620.00	–	–

Source: 1949–1974: Smil (1976, p. 18); 1975–76: estimated; 1977–78: *Beijing Review* (1979a, p. 37); State Statistical Bureau (1981).

Huaibei in Anhui; and Liupanshan in Guizhou, each producing more than 10 million tons per year. A major new open-cut mining center, the Huolinhe Coal Field, located in the Horqin region of Inner Mongolia, has been designed by two West German companies with a capacity of 20 million tons per year. It is now under construction (*Beijing Review*, 1980c). In early 1980, the Chinese press reported that three major coal deposits were discovered. The Yunlian Coal Fields in Yibin, Sichuan have verified reserves of 2,400 million tons (*Huaqiao ribao*, 1980); the Zhangji Coal Field in Anhui has 2,200 million tons of verified coal (*Beijing Review*, 1980c); and the Binxian Coal Field in Shaanxi has verified deposits of 9,100 million tons (*Renmin ribao*, 1980). Their development would unquestionably help industrial growth in east China, the northwest, and in Sichuan.

China's coal output has shown steady growth in the last three decades (Table 8-2). Chinese coal supply, however, faces major problems. The level of mechanization in the large mines remains low. Although there are some relatively advanced collieries, less than 50% of China's coal is mechanically extracted, loaded, and conveyed. In the United States and the Soviet Union, by contrast, such operations are almost 100% mechanized (Smil, 1978).

Another problem is that China south of the Chang Jiang is deficient in coal reserves and must depend on the northern mines for supply. The total verified reserves in the eight southern provinces (Hunan, Hubei, Guangdong, Guangxi, Jiangsu, Zhejiang, Fujian, and Jiangxi) and in Shanghai Municipality, mostly south of the Chang Jiang with major industries, account for only 1.8% of the nation's total, and 66.5% of the verified reserves have already been extracted (*Renmin ribao*, 1979). The exploration and extraction of coal in these nine areas have been costly because the reserves are scattered and complex in geological structures, many deeply buried. In the period 1950–1977, the nine areas used 18.7% of the nation's investment in coal but produced only 10.8% of the national output. It has been calculated that if the same amount of investment that has been allocated to the southern provinces had been diverted to the coal fields in north China, the return would have been three times greater. It is clear that the future of China's coal industry lies in the north, particularly in Shanxi Province, and that the development of the southern industries will depend on northern coal to an even greater extent than has been the case in the last three decades. This increasing dependence will undoubtedly place greater burdens on the already heavily used railway system.

Resources and Iron and Steel Production

No nation can be expected to become a major industrial power without a well-developed metallurgical industry. To build industrial enterprises such as machine-building, transportation, and energy systems requires large quantities of iron and steel. Although China's steel output has been on the rise, it is still inadequate to meet the nation's needs.

China possesses large resources needed for the nation to become a major steel producer. The total reserves of iron ore have been estimated to range from 8 to 100 billion tons. In any event, the reserves are sufficient for continued extraction well into the 21st century. The reserves near Anshan in Liaoning and near Baotou in Inner Mongolia, two of China's leading centers of steel production, can be used for at least 50 more years at the annual production rate of 4 million tons of pig iron. The Benxi plant near Anshan also has deposits nearby to last for about a century at the rate of 1 million tons of pig iron per year. One major weakness

Table 8-3. Recent Increases in Chinese Steel Production (in million metric tons)

1965	12.5
1970	17.8
1971	21.0
1972	23.0
1973	25.5
1974	23.8
1977	23.7
1978	31.7
1979	34.4
1980	37.1

Sources: 1965–1974; Usack and Egan (1975, p. 276); 1977–78: *Guangming ribao* (1981, p. 1); 1979: *Beijing Review* (1980b, p. 4); 1981: State Statistical Bureau.

of China's iron ore is its inferior quality, and China has been slow to invest in beneficiation for treatment. This has retarded the growth of the steel industry. In recent years, substantial amounts of iron ore and pig iron have been imported to meet domestic needs.

Other resources needed by the steel industry, including coal, limestone, manganese, molybdenum, vanadium, and tungsten, are found in many areas. Cobalt, chromium, nickel, and steel scrap, however, must be imported. Coking coal is found primarily at Kailuan, Fushun, Huainan, Pingdingshan, and Shizuishan (Ningxia). Much of the coal used for coking appears to have an ash content of more than 15%, considerably higher than the level of 8% or less that has been considered the maximum by other nations to produce good quality coking coal. On the other hand, China has claimed technological breakthroughs in the use of anthracite and local coals for steel production. This development is said to have reduced the demand for coking coal by 20% in some places.

The output of China's crude steel has been rising steadily, as the tabulation in Table 8-3 shows. The last three figures are from official Chinese sources, whereas the earlier figures are estimates. China in 1979 produced only about one-fourth as much crude steel as the United States. About 40% of China's crude steel is produced at Anshan in Liaoning and in Shanghai. In 1973, Anshan, China's largest integrated steel complex, produced 5.9 million tons, whereas Shanghai's individual plants collectively produced 4.2 million tons. A large, integrated steel complex is under construction at Baoshan in Shanghai Municipality with Japanese equipment. When completed, it will greatly enhance the role of Shanghai as a steel producer. The project has been very expensive, however, and certain technical problems have arisen (Fountain, 1980). Other leading steel centers [and their

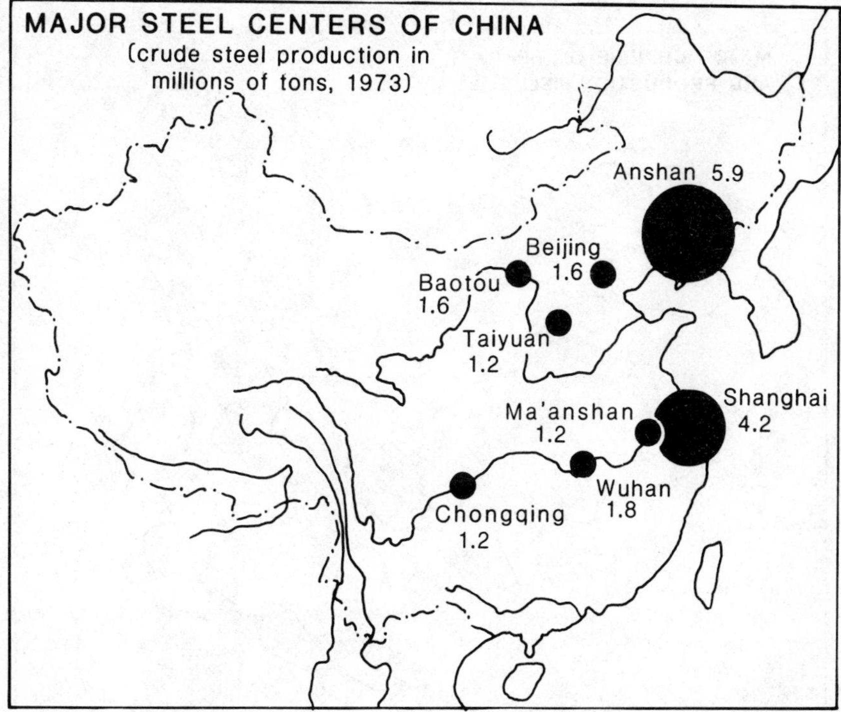

Fig. 8-2. Major steel production centers in China.

1973 output in million tons] include Wuhan (1.8) in Hubei; Baotou (1.6) in Nei Monggol; Beijing (1.6); Chongqing (1.2) in Sichuan; Ma'anshan (1.2) in Anhui; and Taiyuan (1.2) in Shanxi (Fig. 8-2).

The amounts of steel products produced in China are inadequate to meet domestic demands. The nation now faces the difficult choice of importing large quantities of raw, semifinished, and finished steel products, or increasing the capacity of domestic production by importing advanced equipment. Both approaches are expensive, and neither would work without sufficient supplies of energy to operate the nation's steel plants. China hopes that a rapid development of the petroleum industry will generate a large portion of the foreign exchange needed for economic growth.

Petroleum

Before 1950, some Western geologists considered China to be very poor in petroleum reserves and expressed doubt that China would ever become a large oil producer (Harrison, 1977). The production of oil was very modest; the national

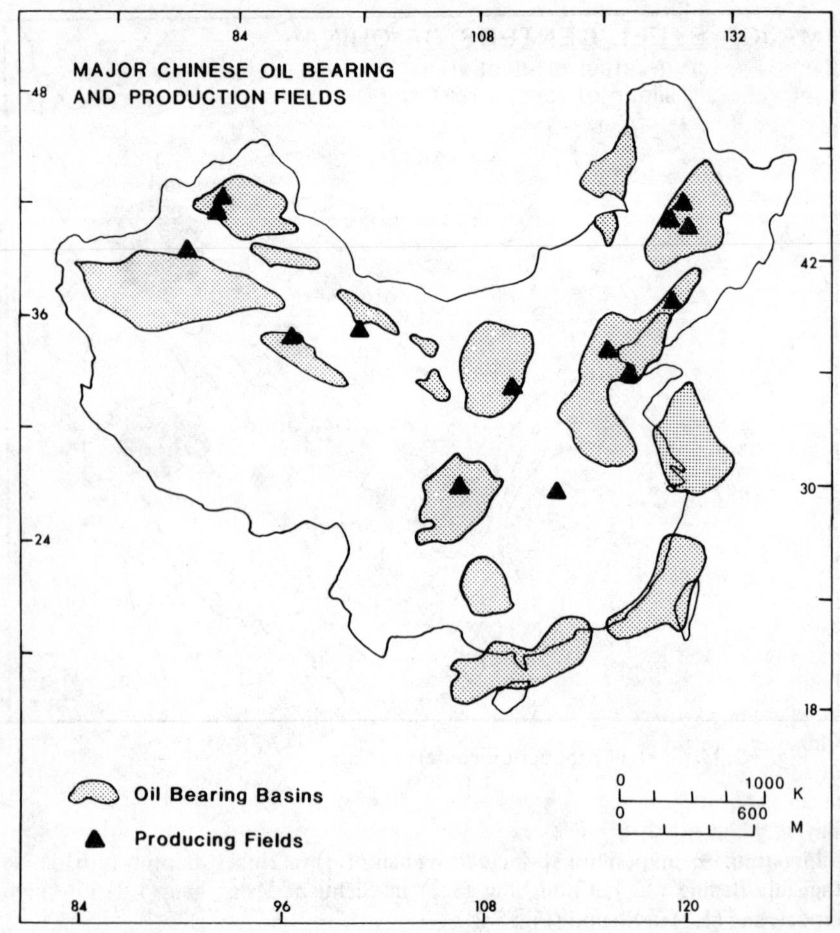

Fig. 8-3. Major oil bearing basins and production fields in China.

total rarely exceeded 100,000 tons per year. Over 85% of the nation's needs (largely kerosene) had to be imported, and oil was never an important source of energy. Since the 1960s, China has become a net exporter of oil, and the country is rapidly becoming a major oil producer. There are, however, serious problems in oil exploration and extraction which must be overcome before China produces a large surplus for export.

No one is sure of the amount of oil reserves in China, and Western estimates vary widely. In terms of production, about one-half of the nation's crude oil comes from the Daqing fields in Heilongjiang Province (Fig. 8-3). The Shengli fields in Shandong and the Dagang fields in Hebei together produce about another

Table 8-4. Petroleum Production of Major Chinese Fields, 1975

Field	Province	Production (million metric tons)
Daqing	Heilongjiang	40.03
Shengli	Shandong	14.90
Dagang	Hebei	4.34
Qianjiang	Hubei	4.10
Panshan	Liaoning	4.05
Fuyu	Jilin	3.25
Karamay	Xinjiang	1.07
Yumen	Gansu	0.78
Anguang	Jilin	Less than 1
Dushanzi	Xinjiang	Less than 1
Lenghu	Qinghai	Less than 1
Nanchong	Sichuan	Less than 1
Tash-arik	Xinjiang	Less than 1
Yanchang	Shaanxi	Less than 1

Source: Central Intelligence Agency (1977, p. 10).

one-fourth. The major oil fields and their production are listed in Table 8-4. New fields include Renqiu in Hebei; Nanyang in Henan; Zhenwu in Jiangsu; and Liaohe in Liaoning. Details about them, however, are lacking. The reserves of northwest China are not fully developed, mainly because of transportation problems. No offshore oil is known to have been produced because offshore exploration is still in an early stage of development. So far, it has been concentrated in the Bohai Bay and the South China Sea. In 1979, a large oil-bearing basin, 150,000 square kilometers in size, and located about 200 kilometers south and southwest of the Zhujiang (Pearl River) Delta, was discovered, but no production has been reported (Figs. 8-3 and 8-4).

Crude oil production has risen at a rapid rate in the last three decades, especially since 1960 (Table 8-5). In 1979 China produced 106.1 million tons of crude oil (*Beijing Review*, 1980a). This rapid increase, however, is likely to slow down in the immediate future because the production in Daqing has already reached its peak. In the 1980s, barring unexpected production breakthroughs, the rate of increase is likely to be between 10 to 15% annually instead of the 20% rate of the 1970s. In 1978, China was the world's seventh largest producer of crude oil, as is indicated in Table 8-6.

In terms of export, China is not doing as well as the other major producers. In the late 1970s, China exported between 10 to 20 million tons of crude oil annually, largely to Japan. This is a very small amount. The prospect of a significant expansion of the volume of export depends largely on whether China can obtain advanced oil exploration and production equipment from abroad, including seismic devices, computerized field units, and drilling and casing pipes. Also,

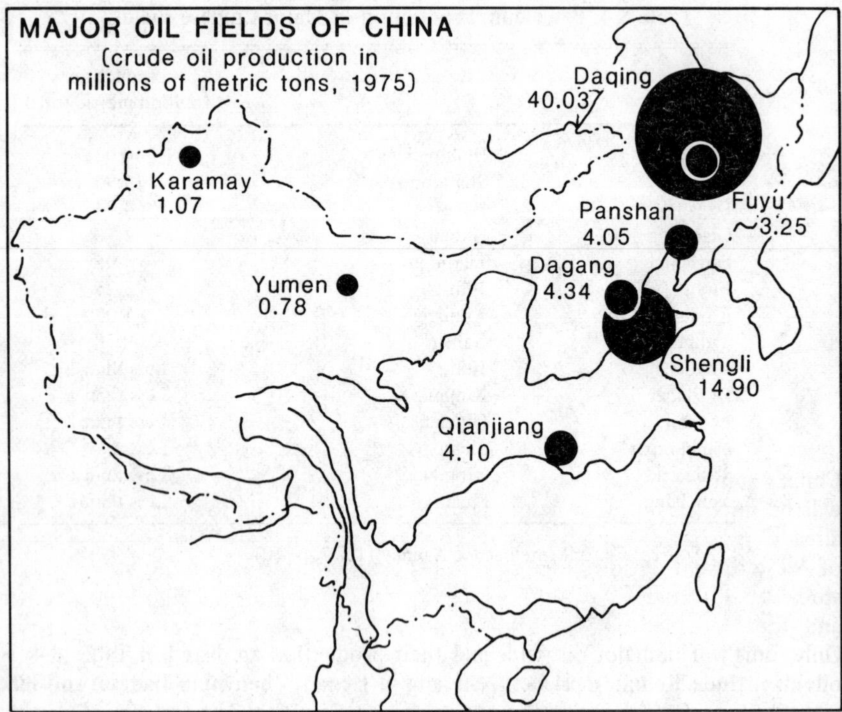

Fig. 8-4. Production at major oil fields in China, 1975.
Source: Compiled by authors from Central Intelligence Agency (1977) data.

Table 8-5. China: Crude Oil Production (million metric tons)

1950	0.2
1960	5.1
1970	28.2
1977	93.6
1978	104.0
1979	106.1
1980	106.0

Source: Central Intelligence Agency (1977); State Statistical Bureau (1981).

Table 8-6. Major Petroleum Producing Countries, 1978 (million metric tons)

Soviet Union	675
United States	432
Saudi Arabia	423
Iran	258
Iraq	130
Venezuela	107
China	*104*
Libya	99
Nigeria	95
Kuwait	93

Source: The World Almanac and Book of Facts (1980, p. 101).

China's ability to enlarge its refining capacity, pipeline network, and port facilities will be important factors determining if large-scale export is possible. China has already purchased some sophisticated equipment from the West, and a number of Western and Japanese oil companies are working with China to do seismic studies of offshore reserves. China has the determination to expand its oil supply, and there are substantial onshore as well as offshore reserves for production. Only time will tell if China can succeed in becoming a major oil supplier. If so, oil may provide the impetus to break the cycle of poverty and slow economic growth that has long plagued China (Fountain, 1980).

The level of petroleum use in China is still relatively low, and the pattern of consumption differs greatly from that of developed nations. Chinese oil is used mainly for truck transportation, farming operations, shipping, and by the military. Since there are no privately owned automobiles in China and the number of passenger cars, used by Chinese officials and foreigners only, is extremely small, cars use only a limited amount of petroleum. Household consumption for heating is insignificant, because coal is the only important source of heat in most places.

To facilitate transportation, new oil terminals have been completed recently at two ice-free ports, one in 1975 at Qinhuangdao in Hebei and the other in 1976 at Dalian in Liaoning. A 1,144-kilometer, large-diameter pipeline was completed in 1974 connecting the Daqing fields with Qinhuangdao, and from there the pipeline has been extended to Peking where a modern refinery turns out a wide variety of petroleum products. The facilities at Dalian are capable of accommodating oil tankers of up to 100,000 tons. A parallel pipeline connecting Daqing with Dalian was also completed in 1975. In 1978, a pipeline extending from Linyi in Shandong to Nanjing was laid and put to use. This pipeline brings crude oil from the Shengli fields to the Nanjing oil harbor, from where it is shipped to provinces and cities along the Chang Jiang. These pipelines have significantly reduced the burden on the railways in east China and boosted industrial and farm production.

Table 8-7. Major Hydroelectric Stations of China, 1980

Station	Province or autonomous region	River	Designed capacity (1,000 kilowatts)	Construction status
Gezhouba	Hubei	Chang Jiang	2,700	Under construction
Longyangxia	Qinghai	Huang He	1,600	Under construction
Liujiaxia	Gansu	Huang He	1,225	Completed in 1974
Danjiangkou	Hubei	Han Shui	900	Completed in 1973
Baishan	Jilin	Songhua Jiang	900	Under construction
Gongzui	Sichuan	Dadu He	750	Completed in 1979
Xin'an	Zhejiang	Xin'an Jiang	652.5	Unclear
Wujiangdu	Guizhou	Wu Jiang	630	Under construction
Fengman	Jilin	Songhua Jiang	600	Compelted in 1958
Yanguoxia	Gansu	Huang He	595	Completed in 1974
Dahua	Guangxi Zhuang	Hongshi He	400	Under construction
Xinfengjiang	Guangdong	Xinfeng Jiang	290	Completed in 1960
Qingtongxia	Ningxia Hui	Huang He	272	Completed in 1974
Xierhe	Yunnan	Nanpan Jiang	255	Under construction
Sanmenxia	Henan	Huang He	200	Completed in 1973
Shizuishan	Ningxia Hui	Huang He	200	Under construction
Bapanxia	Gansu	Huang He	180	Completed in 1975

Source: National Foreign Assessment Center (1980).

Hydroelectric Power

China leads the world in hydropower potential. The theoretical aggregate generating capacity has been estimated by the Chinese at 580 million kilowatts, and at least 300 million kilowatts of this total are found in regions suitable for large-scale industrial development. If fully developed, the total potential could generate electric power equivalent to 14 billion tons of coal. The current level of hydropower development, however, is extremely low. In the mid-1970s, hydroelectric power accounted for only 1% of China's total energy supply (Table 8-1).

The greatest hydropower potential lies in southeastern Tibet in the area of a sharp bend of the Yarlung Zangbo Jiang (Brahmaputra River), where a station could be built to generate 27 million kilowatts of power. This site, however, has no chance of being built in the near future because of its remoteness and isolation from major industrial centers. Another large station with the same capacity could be constructed in the Three Gorges section of the Chang Jiang, but due to technical and financial difficulties, it has not been built (Ludlow, 1980a). However, a nearby station to the east of the gorges is under construction–the Gezhouba Hydropower Station, located near Yichang, Sichuan. Under construction since 1974, it will have 2.7 million kilowatts of installed capacity and will be the largest station in China when it is completed in 1986 (Ludlow, 1980b). A series of stations have been built on the Huang He and more are under construction (Table 8-7).

Although the current modernization drive has emphasized the development of large-scale hydropower stations, small rural stations will continue to play a

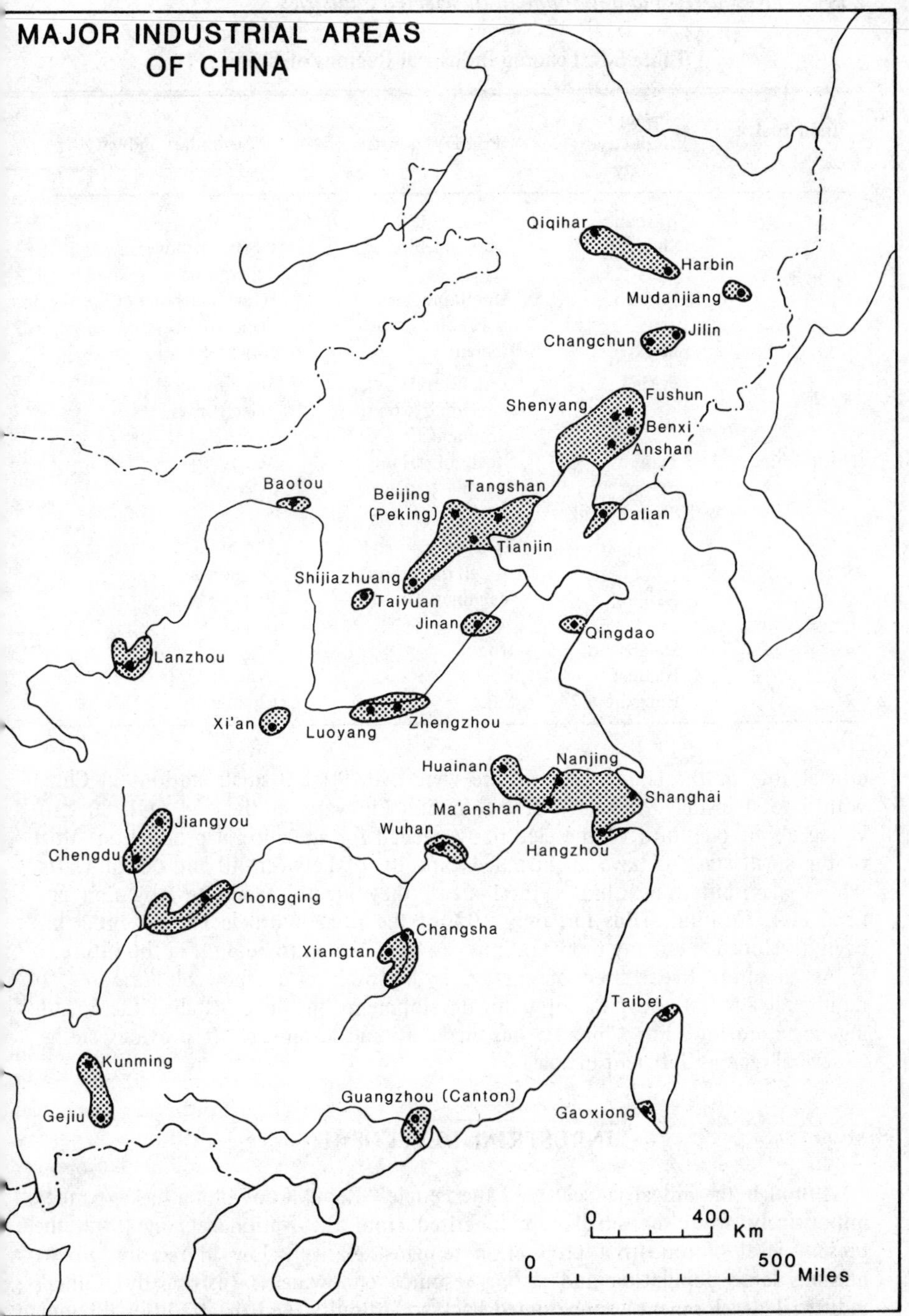

Fig. 8-5. Major industrial regions of China.

Table 8-8. Leading Industrial Regions of China

Industrial region	Major industrial city	Primary industry	Secondary industry
Northeast	Anshan	Iron and steel	
	Shenyang	Steel, machine tools	Heavy machinery, chemicals
	Fushun	Aluminum, steel, oil refining, coal	Heavy machinery, cement
	Benxi	Cement	Iron and steel
North China	Peking	Agricultural machinery, textiles, iron and steel	Machine tools, electronics
	Tianjin	Steel, oil refining, textile, paper	Machinery
	Shijiazhuang	Steel	
Lower Yangzi	Shanghai	Textiles, iron and steel, oil refining	Shipbuilding, electronics, chemicals
	Nanjing	Machinery, oil refining	Precision instruments
	Ma'anshan	Iron	
	Huainan	Coal	
	Hangzhou	Silk	Chemicals

crucial role in the countryside. There were over 90,000 small stations in China with a total installed capacity of 6.8 million kilowatts at the end of 1980, providing about one-third of the electricity needed for agricultural production. Most of the small stations have an installed capacity of between 40 and 60 kilowatts. Widely distributed in China's rural areas, they greatly facilitate irrigation and rural electrification. Thus far, only 10% of the rural hydroelectric potential has been developed and many more stations can be expected to be built in the future.

As an alternative source of energy, hydropower is a renewable resource. It requires heavy initial capital input for development, but once installed the operating costs are low. For China, it has an additional advantage. It provides energy to several regions deficient in coal.

INDUSTRIAL DEVELOPMENT

Although the industrial sector of the People's Republic of China has expanded impressively from the small base inherited from the Nationalists in 1949, the present level of industrial production remains relatively low in relation to the nation's large population and strong resource endowment. Historically, China's industrial development can be dated back to antiquity, and the traditional handicraft industries remained strong even in the century following the Opium War

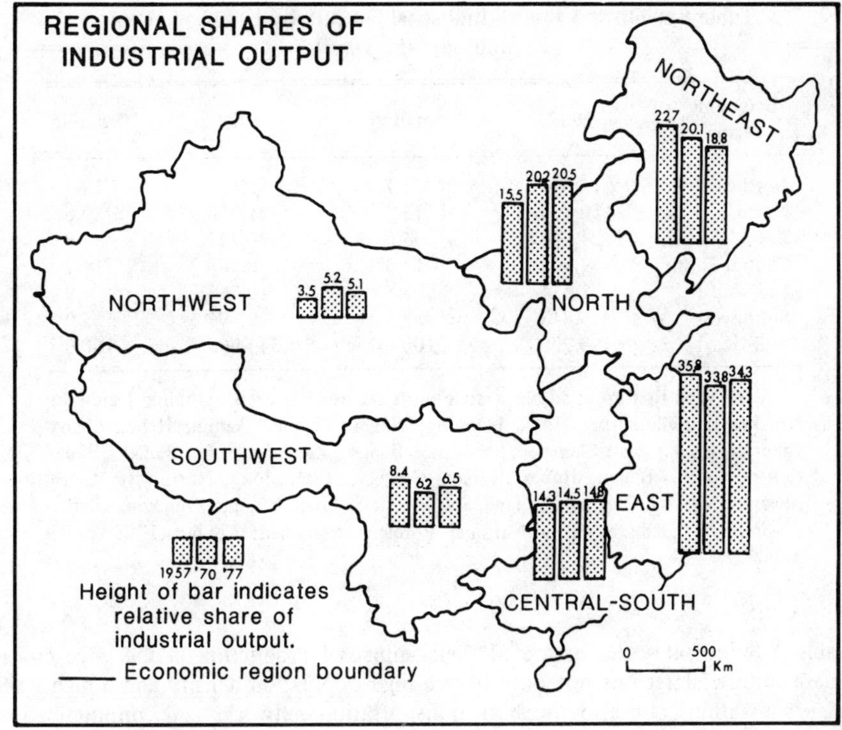

Fig. 8-6. Regional share of industrial output in China.
Source: Compiled from data in National Foreign Assessment Center (1978).

of 1840. During the 19th century, foreigners imported Western consumer goods as well as modern means of production to produce goods in China. The largest industries established by Westerners included cotton textiles, flour milling, cigarettes, and pressing of vegetables for oil. These factories were located largely in the eastern third of China, especially in such coastal cities as Tianjin, Qingdao, Shanghai, and Guangzhou (Canton).

Regional Distribution of Industry

The Japanese, who occupied and intensively developed heavy industries in Liaoning and Jilin Provinces of northeast China to support their wartime efforts in the 1930s, stimulated industrial development in that region. Elsewhere, the coastal as well as inland treaty ports, where Western commercial and industrial activities were based, played a major role in shaping the present geographical pattern of industrial distribution (Fig. 8-5). The largest leading industrial regions of China are all located along the coast, each including several industrial cities.

Table 8-9. Gross Value of Industrial Output, by Economic Region (million 1957 *yuan*)

Economic region	1957	% nation	1974	% nation
Northeast	15,874	22.7	65,890	19.1
North	10,806	15.5	71,023	20.6
East	24,846	35.6	120,222	34.8
Central-South	9,995	14.3	50,568	14.7
Northwest	2,434	3.5	16,765	4.9
Southwest	5,843	8.4	20,497	5.9
Total	69,798	100.0	344,965	100.0

Note: The first-order administrative units included in each economic region are: Northeast: Heilongjiang, Jilin, Liaoning; North: Peking, Tianjin, Hebei, Shanxi, Inner Mongolia; East: Shanghai, Shandong, Jiangsu, Zhejiang, Anhui, Jiangxi, Fujian; Central-South: Henan, Hubei, Hunan, Guangxi, Guangdong; Northwest: Gansu, Shaanxi, Ningxia, Qinghai, Xinjiang; Southwest: Sichuan, Yunnan, Guizhou, Tibet.

Source: Calculated from National Foreign Assessment Center (1978, p. 19, Table 12).

Table 8-8 indicates the nature of their industrial production in the large cities. These industrial regions not only have a high population density and a high level of urbanization, but also the best transportation networks and communication systems as well as extensive fertile farmland. Thus, the three areas listed in the table–the northeast, north China, and lower Yangzi region–may be considered the key economic regions of China today.

In 1952, three fourths of China's total industrial production were from the coastal regions of the northeast, north, and east (Fig. 8-6). Although serious efforts were made in the First Five-Year Plan (1953–57) to develop the economy of the inland regions at a greater speed, the spatially unbalanced pattern of industrial growth persisted. As Fig. 8-6 shows, the relative shares of industrial output in terms of gross value of the six regions in China's overall growth have not changed significantly, although the regions have all increased industrial output by several times (Table 8-9). The east leads all other regions by a large margin. The city of Shanghai, with a population of about 10 million, continues to be the single most productive industrial center of China. The gross value of industrial output of Shanghai in 1974 exceeded that of the central-south, northwest, and southwest regions. The north, centered on Peking and Tianjin, has become a much more important industrial region than in earlier times, while the relative role of the southwest has declined somewhat.

Shanghai's gross industrial output far exceeds that of any other province, as is indicated in the following ranking of China's 10 most productive industrial provinces and cities in 1974 (Table 8-10). In contrast to these industrial provinces and cities, the mountainous and arid minority areas in the northwest and southwest

Table 8-10. Ten Most Productive Industrial Provinces and Cities, 1974

Province or city	Gross value of industrial output (million of 1957 *yuan*)
Shanghai City	52,892
Liaoning	40,727
Jiangsu	23,435
Hebei	22,648
Shandong	20,374
Peking City	18,569
Tianjin City	17,524
Guangdong	17,195
Heilongjiang	15,785
Sichuan	13,852

Source: National Foreign Assessment Center (1978).

did poorly in industrial production. In 1974, the five least industrialized areas were Xizang (Tibet), Ningxia, Qinghai, Xinjiang, and Guizhou, all in the northwest and southwest, and none of which produced more than 3.4 billion *yuan* of gross value of industrial output. Such a spatially unbalanced pattern of industrial development results from historical as well as environmental factors. The physical differences between the eastern half of China and the rugged and arid regions of the west are too sharp for the latter to catch up economically with the former.

China, with a large population and a relatively weak economy, does not yet have a large amount of developmental resources which could be used to equalize imbalances in the space economy. Investment of resources for economic growth in the more developed eastern regions can always be expected to produce a more rapid economic return, and thus the present pattern is likely to continue. While it would be premature to state that the western provinces and autonomous regions could never be developed to the same level as that of the eastern regions, it would be extremely difficult to do so in the foreseeable future without sustained state support and large investment. Such support and investment, however, are not likely to come any time soon, and it appears certain that the more developed coastal areas will continue to dominate the industrial landscape of China for many years to come. As was noted in Chapter 7, however, the national government is committed to the goal of spatial equity in developmental priorities, and some investments in lagging areas are likely despite their low rates of return.

Rural Industrial Development

In an attempt to achieve spatial equity in economic development, China in the last three decades placed a great deal of emphasis on small-scale rural industries.

Production of buckets on a commune outside Shanghai. (*L. Ma*)

Production line in older silk spinning factory in Suzhou. (*C. W. Pannell*)

This development strategy, initiated in the Great Leap Forward period (1958-1960), is carried out at the county and commune levels where the industries are financed, constructed, and managed locally. Special attention is directed toward the development of the so-called "five small industries"–agricultural machinery, chemical fertilizers, cement, iron and steel, and coal mining.

Simple farm tools are manufactured locally, including small pumps, one-man threshers, small harvesters, rice transplanters, and simple tractors. Equally important to agricultural growth is the repair and maintenance of farm machinery to sustain a high level of utilization. Relatively simple farming implements are repaired and maintained by the production teams and brigades, leaving the more complicated maintenance jobs to the communes and counties. At present, 96% of the counties and many people's communes have factories making and repairing farm machinery. Large tractors and harvesters are usually manufactured at the provincial level.

One important way to increase agricultural productivity is to use more chemical fertilizers. Since 1960, small fertilizer plants have been built in many small cities. In 1975, there were more than 2,000 small fertilizer plants which supplied more than 50% of the nation's chemical fertilizers. An average small plant can produce between 3,000 to 5,000 tons of synthetic ammonia annually.

Small cement plants with capacities ranging from several thousand tons per year to a maximum of about 32,000 tons are also widely found in China's countryside. In Guangdong Province, for example, 95 of the 107 counties and cities have built a total of 106 small cement plants. In 1975, these small plants produced 70% of the province's cement.

Small coal mines with a capacity of less than 1,000 tons a year produce about one third of China's total coal supply. Much coal is mined by commune members for household use, but a substantial portion is for industrial use, especially for metallurgy. Small-scale ironworks are widely distributed in the small cities of the countryside, and their capacities range from several hundred tons to 50,000 tons of products annually. The level of mechanization at the small iron factories is much higher than that of their counterparts during the Great Leap Forward, and their products are also of higher quality. Locally produced iron and steel are indispensable for the manufacturing of small agricultural machinery.

Western scholars who have examined China's small-scale industry unanimously consider it a feasible and positive means of furthering the goal of agricultural development in China. Capital requirements for rural industries are considerably lower than large industries located in the cities where a portion of the capital must be diverted from immediate production to housing and transportation. In addition, small rural industries can be built quickly and can use inferior raw materials unsuitable for large and modern industries. Although rural industries can create employment opportunities for no more than a few percent of the population of any given rural locality, the profits from local factories are usually reinvested or contributed to the agricultural sector for the purchase of better farm equipment and more fertilizers (American Rural Small-Scale Industry Delegation, 1977).

Rural small-scale industry plays a key role in linking the modern industrial sector of the nation more closely to the rural economy by introducing more

Kiln of local brick works on Lile Commune south of Canton. (*C. W. Pannell*)

Cutting clay bricks before firing on Lile Commune brick works south of Canton. (*C. W. Pannell*)

advanced industrial technologies into rural areas. This link provides the vast rural labor force with the opportunity for becoming familiar with various aspects of the processes of industrial development and contributes much to skill formation in rural areas. Numerous how-to technical handbooks on establishing or maintaining small plants are prepared by the more advanced industrial units and distributed to the rural population, thus spreading the knowledge of modern technology. Since the late 1950s, large numbers of technicians have been sent to the countryside to perform specific technical tasks, and lower level personnel are sent to the cities to receive special training in factories or in colleges.

It should be pointed out that the Chinese model of rural development is not intended to bring industries ubiquitously to all the villages. Rather, a concerted effort has been made to locate rural industries in selected county capitals or in relatively wealthy communes where the economic base is suitable for industrial development. Small-scale industry increases the level of local control of local economic affairs, reduces the administrative burdens of the central government, makes local economic planning more practical, and fosters regional self-sufficiency. It helps local income and raises the standard of living of the rural population. As a result, it contributes greatly to the narrowing of the gap between city and countryside.

Stages of Industrial Development

In the last three decades, Chinese leaders have followed several different approaches to industrial development at different times, but not all of them were successful. These approaches reflect the changes in China's domestic political patterns and changing attitudes toward foreign countries. Since 1949, seven periods of industrial development with varied emphases can be differentiated.

1. *Rehabilitation and Recovery (1949–1952):* At the end of China's civil war between the Communists and the Nationalists, from 1945 to 1949, immediately following World War II, the economy of the nation was in disarray. The new leaders, the Communists, quickly took control of all sectors of the economy and instituted fundamental changes. While factories, transportation lines, and raw material bases were being repaired and restored, positive measures were taken to nationalize private industries. By 1952, the capacity of industrial output had returned to the pre-revolutionary level, and the nation was ready to undertake long-term programs to develop the economy.

2. *The First Five-Year Plan (1953–57):* The economy as a whole registered sharp gains at a high speed during this period. The performance of the industrial sector was particularly impressive. Existing plants were used intensively and new industrial projects were constructed. The plan was designed with the assistance of the Soviet Union, emphasizing the construction of heavy industries, including iron and steel, machine-building, and mining. Over 80% of the nation's total industrial investment during this period went to heavy industries, while some 55% of the plan's industrial investment and approximately three-quarters of all new plant investments were allocated to inland areas for defense purposes and to

stimulate inland development. Consequently, many industrial centers in the interior grew rapidly, including Baotou, Wuhan, Lanzhou, Taiyuan, Xi'an, and Luoyang.

While the First Five-Year Plan itself was carried out successfully, its emphasis on heavy industry at the expense of light industry and agriculture was not entirely appropriate for China, an agrarian nation. During the First Five-Year Plan period, agricultural development was slow. By 1955, its poor performance began to undermine the goals of industrial growth. In 1955, Mao Zedong decided to accelerate the development of agricultural cooperatives and at the same time called for early collectivization of industry and trade. This policy change was based on Mao's belief that a much faster rate of economic growth could be achieved by complete public ownership of the economy, by more decentralized planning, by developing both modern and indigenous industries, and by encouraging the masses to work harder through spiritual rather than material incentives.

3. *The Great Leap Forward (1958--1960):* The methods to boost economic production during the First Five-Year Plan were subsequently incorporated into the Great Leap Forward, during which millions of people were mobilized to meet increasingly higher goals of industrial production set by the state. The intensive drive for a higher rate of economic development without careful planning did not prove workable. Many of the industrial goods, especially iron and steel which were produced by "backyard furnaces" using local resources and indigenous methods, turned out to be of poor quality. Human exhaustion, industrial accidents, and misuse of materials were common problems. The Great Leap fell short of the goals that Mao had hoped to achieve.

In 1959–1960, the economic crisis further intensified because of serious natural disasters which greatly reduced the level of agricultural production and resulted in localized shortage of food. The sudden withdrawal of Soviet assistance in June 1960 as a consequence of ideological conflicts with the Soviet Union left China with many unfinished industrial projects. When the Soviet technicians returned home, they took with them the blueprints of the industrial projects which they were helping the Chinese to build. This unexpected Soviet action dealt an additional serious blow to the already troubled economy.

The Great Leap Forward, however, was not without positive contributions to China's long-term economic development. As mentioned earlier, China's planners in the last three decades have not relied exclusively on any single model of economic growth. They hoped in the 1950s that China could become a modern industrial power after a series of 5-year plans. By 1958, however, it was clear to the Chinese that foreign technological assistance was not forthcoming and that an indigenous approach to economic development must be designed. As a result, the Great Leap placed a special emphasis on the development of local industries. Ideologically, such an emphasis was in line with Mao's desire to upgrade the level of economic growth in rural areas. The introduction of the rural commune system in 1958 marked the completion of the nation's rural collectivization program, which provided an effective vehicle of administration to carry out the projects of rural industrialization. It may be said that the Great Leap Forward nourished the beginning of a uniquely Chinese approach to modernization, which has brought about significant changes in China's rural areas ever since and has attracted considerable attention in foreign nations. The significance and implications of rural industrial development have been discussed in more detail in an earlier section.

4. *Recovery and Readjustment, (1961–65):* The Great Leap Forward was a daring attempt conceived by Mao to develop China's economy in a short period of time. Fundamental policy changes were made after the Great Leap. Agriculture, described as "the foundation of the national economy," was assigned top priority for development. Industrial growth, based on systematic and cautious planning, returned to normal, with heavy emphasis given to those sectors which could support agricultural development. The entire economy recovered slowly but steadily, and consumer goods, especially those for peasant consumption, were produced in greater quantity. This recovery was based mainly on a fuller use of existing facilities rather than on the construction of new projects. There was serious difficulty in the sector of heavy industries where progress was greatly retarded by the withdrawal of Soviet technicians. Chinese engineers found that they could not operate many of the plants built by the Soviets and had a hard time trying to complete the unfinished projects without blueprints.

By 1964, the economy had made sufficient progress to prompt Premier Zhou Enlai to announce in December of that year at the Third National People's Congress that the economy had recovered and that it was time to modernize the nation based on the "four modernizations" of industry, agriculture, national defense, and science and technology. The term "four modernizations," however, was never mentioned in the following decade because of the interruption by the Cultural Revolution. It reappeared in 1975 and became a national policy shortly after the death of Mao in 1976.

5. *The Cultural Revolution (1966–69):* China's economic development has closely followed the ups and downs of domestic political events. The Cultural Revolution brought profound and often violent changes to China, and the nation's industrial performance was also adversely affected. The extent to which the economy was disrupted by the politically turbulent years of the Cultural Revolution, however, was not as great as one might have expected. Large-scale disruptions of industrial enterprises, transportation networks, and raw material supply were confined largely to isolated areas in the early phase of the movement, and by 1967, efforts were made to prevent the fervently excited Red Guards from further damaging the economy. By 1969, the economy had returned to the 1966 level.

On the other hand, outbreaks of anti-foreignism gave rise to an almost complete self-imposed national isolation. Foreign trade stagnated, and the importation of foreign technology was discouraged. Western culture was not only avoided but also frequently denounced as decadent or otherwise undesirable. Many scientists were forced to abandon their jobs and sent to the countryside to do ordinary manual work. Basic research was virtually nonexistent, and the severely disrupted scientific community was completely cut off from the outside world.

6. *Reorientation (1970–76):* During this period, a precarious balance of power was maintained between the pragmatists led by Zhou Enlai and the radicals led by the now infamous and purged "Gang of Four," with the former group enjoying greater power. With the consent of Mao, Zhou engineered a foreign policy which

sought to establish a more friendly relationship with Western powers. One important reason for this change of national policy was clearly China's desire to obtain Western technology to speed up her economic development. On the other hand, much progress was also made in the rural areas where small industries continued to expand. On the whole, national economic growth registered impressive gains during this period, and by 1974 the nation's industrial production had more than doubled that of 1967. Efforts were made to enlarge the capacity of oil production to generate more foreign exchange for national development. For the first time since 1949, credit was used in foreign trade to purchase advanced but expensive Western technology. The living standards of the people gradually improved. Since the death of Mao and the arrest of the "Gang of Four" in 1976, the policy of China's economic development has again been guided by the slogan of "four modernizations" which Zhou Enlai had envisioned and initiated as early as 1964. China now hopes to achieve the goal of modernization by the year 2000.

7. *The Four Modernizations (1976–2000):* The Chinese economy in the post-Mao period has been characterized by a series of drastic changes initiated to speed up the growth of the economy. A highly ambitious but unrealistic 10-year plan (1976–1985) was annnounced in February 1978 which called for the attainment of the following major goals: (1) the value of industrial output would increase by more than 10% per year during the 10-year period; (2) the completion of 120 large-scale industrial projects by 1985, including 10 iron and steel complexes, 9 nonferrous metal complexes, and a number of coal mines, oil and gas fields, new railroads and harbors, which together would help create 14 fairly large and strong industrial bases; (3) the level of farm mechanization in all major areas of farming would reach 85% by 1985; and (4) the nation's total production of grains would increase from 285 million tons in 1977 to 400 million tons in 1985.

The 10-year plan soon proved to be too ambitious and impossible to achieve with the tight developmental resources available to China. The problems of implementing the plan were discovered less than a year after it had been announced, and a 3-year plan (1979–1981), announced in July 1979, was launched to "readjust, restructure, consolidate, and improve the national economy." In early 1981, many projects that were not urgently needed or were ill-conceived were canceled or postponed. Factories that were operating at a loss were closed down. The investment in basic capital construction projects, which must be supported by large amounts of energy or a more efficient transportation system, two of the weakest links in the Chinese economy, was curtailed.

Chinese planners are searching for a new economic order that would accelerate the development of the economy without the problems of earlier approaches caused by the lack of foreign technological input, suffocating control of the economy by the central government, and excessive development of heavy industries without the support of adequate energy and transportation. The 1976–1985 10-year plan has been abandoned, and in 1980 a new 10-year plan (1981–1990) was being created, which will give priority to agriculture, energy, communications, and transportation as well as cultural, educational, and scientific undertakings.

The general goals of China's "four modernizations" program are clear. Chinese planners hope that the national economy can be in the front ranks of the world by the end of the century. In the development of science and technology, China hopes to catch up with the advanced world level in a number of areas and surpass it in selected fields. In terms of per capita gross national product, the target is to reach $1,000 by the year 2000, almost four times higher than the per capita income of $253 for the year 1979 calculated by the Chinese government (Yu, 1980).

RECENT CHANGES IN THE ECONOMIC SYSTEM

Given the present level of technology in China, the large population, and the lack of sufficient capital resources, it would be very difficult to reach the goals of modernization without fundamental changes in the economic system. Since 1976, the need for new strategies of economic development has been clearly recognized and a series of innovative measures has been adopted to transform the economic system. The experience of Western nations is being studied by Chinese planners for partial adoption, and capitalist countries are no longer viewed with contempt or hostility. Although the capitalist system as a whole is still seen as unplanned and chaotic, the system's individual firms are considered highly efficient in terms of both production and distribution as well as profit making. There is little question that China admires the current level of economic development of the West with which China is often compared. Western visitors to China frequently hear: "Compared with the advanced capitalist countries of the West, China is still behind." The hostility toward the West before 1976 has been replaced by admiration for the West.

At the present time, China is actively seeking foreign assistance to step up the tempo of economic growth. In addition to adopting the most advanced Western technology, which is frequently obtained by importing complete factories, China has also solicited long-term credits to pay for it. Foreign investment in China is encouraged, as are joint ventures to build economic projects in China. The extent to which China has been seeking foreign technology and credit represents a drastic departure from the policy of isolation from the outside world during the periods of the Great Leap Forward and the Cultural Revolution.

Domestically, a number of new policies have also been initiated to stimulate the economy. The new policies have been carried out on an experimental and limited basis since early 1979, and they suggest that China is moving away from the rigid, centrally planned economic model inherited from the Soviet Union three decades ago and is embracing a daring new economic order that includes some elements of Western capitalism. It appears that China's planners fully intend to restructure the entire economic system to allow flexibility of decision making at various administrative levels and to enable the production enterprises to increase their profits.

The search for a new economic order is manifested in a number of experimental changes made in the economic system. It should be pointed out first that Chinese economic enterprises have always been managed as administrative organs of government ministries and that they are owned, operated, and supported entirely by the state regardless of their economic performance. Every stage of the production process, from the setting of production quotas to raw material acquisition and product distribution, is rigidly controlled by an extremely large and sluggish state bureaucracy, which is not only slow in making decisions but is also insensitive to market forces. The production units must turn over all profits to the state. Factories that are run at a loss are always subsidized by the state. Such a system of management without incentives and penalties discourages productivity and breeds inefficiency.

The new economic system, which is being tried, calls for greater power of self-management for the enterprises. As of mid-1980, about 6,600 industrial enterprises had been given more management power. After they have fulfilled the state production quotas, they can now produce goods needed on the market at home and abroad and sell them at prices fixed by the state. They can also retain part of the profits, including foreign exchange earned from exports, for equipment purchase, for expanding production, and for the workers' welfare and bonuses. The more income an enterprise generates, the more profit it can retain. On the other hand, these factories must also be fully responsible for any financial losses. In addition, competition among enterprises, once forbidden, has been endorsed. Such support will certainly spur factories to improve management, strengthen cost accounting, raise product quality, and generate greater profit.

The results of these fundamental changes of the economic system have been highly encouraging, and the state is planning to enlarge the scope of the experiment to include more enterprises. The enterprises will be run not as mere administrative adjuncts of government ministries, but as economic units to be operated on the basis of effective cost accounting and profit. China's top planners are clearly willing to unleash market forces and flirt with the laws of supply and demand. They have found that profits can fuel enthusiasm of both workers and management better than anything else can. If the experimental changes in the economic system are adopted as national policies for large-scale implementation, which will require as long as a decade to complete, then what is most likely to evolve is a new economic order characterized by a hybrid of socialism and capitalism. This new order is likely to be similar to the economic systems already in place in such Eastern European countries as Yugoslavia, Romania, and Hungary from which China has learned a great deal since 1976. In this system, the state will continue to own all industrial enterprises ("the means of production," in Communist jargon) but will loosen the reins on management to make room for the enterprises to seek profits, a powerful force that can stimulate economic development in any society. Of course, whether or not the new economic order will appear depends heavily on political stability in the next decade.

LITERATURE CITED

The American Rural Small-Scale Industry Delegation, 1977, *Rural Small-Scale Industry in the People's Republic of China.* Berkeley: University of California Press.

Beijing Review, 1979a, Vol. 22, No. 27 (July 6).

Beijing Review, 1979b, "Fuel and Power Industries." Vol. 22, No. 43, (Oct. 26), p. 27.

Beijing Review, 1980a, "Coal and Petroleum Targets Met." Vol. 24, No. 2 (Jan. 12), p. 7.

Beijing Review, 1980b, Vol. 24, No. 2 (Jan. 12) p. 4.

Beijing Review, 1980c, "Eight Coal Bases under Construction." Vol. 23, No. 26 (June 30), pp. 4–5.

Central Intelligence Agency, 1971, *People's Republic of China Atlas.* Washington, D.C.: U.S. G.P.O.

Central Intelligence Agency, 1977, *China: Oil Production Prospects.* (ER77-100 30U). Washington, D.C.

Fountain, Kevin, 1980, "The Development of China's Offshore Oil." *The China Business Review*, Vol. 7, No. 1, pp. 22–36.

Guangming ribao, Jan. 23, 1981, p. 1.

Harrison, Selig A., 1977, *China, Oil, and Asia: Conflict Ahead?* New York: Columbia University Press.

Huaqiao ribao (Overseas Chinese Daily), 1980, April 24, p. 9.

Ludlow, Nicholas, 1980a, "Harnessing the Yangzi." *The China Business Review*, Vol. 7, No. 3, pp. 16–21.

Ludlow, Nicholas, 1980b, "Gezhouba on the Yangzi." *The China Business Review*, Vol. 7, No. 3, pp. 11–14.

National Foreign Assessment Center, 1978, *China: Economic Indicators.* (ER 78-10750, December). Washington, D.C.: Central Intelligence Agency.

National Foreign Assessment Center, 1980, *Electric Power for China's Modernization: The Hydroelectric Option.* (ER-80-10089U, May). Washington, D.C.: Central Intelligence Agency.

Renmin ribao (People's Daily), 1979, Feb. 26, p. 3.

Renmin ribao (People's Daily), 1980, Jan. 22, p. 1.

Smil, Vaclav, 1976, *China's Energy.* New York: Praeger.

Smil, Vaclav, 1978, "China's Energetics: A Systems Analysis." In U.S. Congress, Joint Economic Committee, *Chinese Economy Post Mao.* Washington, D.C.: U.S. GPO, pp. 323–369.

State Statistical Bureau, 1981, *Communique on the Fulfillment of the 1980 National Economic Plan*, Xinhua, Apr. 29, 1981.

Usack, Alfred H. and Egan, James D., 1975, "China's Iron and Steel Industry." In U.S. Congress, Joint Economic Committee, *China: A Reassessment of the Economy.* Washington, D.C.: U.S. GPO, pp. 264–288.

Wang, K. P., 1977, *Mineral Resources and Basic Industries in the People's Republic of China.* Boulder, Colo.: Westview Press.

The World Almanac and Book of Facts, 1980. New York: Newspaper Enterprise Association.

Yu, Youhai, 1980, U.S. "$1,000 by the Year 2000." *Beijing Review*, Vol. 23, No. 43 (Oct. 27), pp. 16–18.

Chapter 9

Urban Development

Urban development in China since 1950 has resulted from three major factors: (1) the large population of China, (2) the extremely rapid growth of China's population since 1950, and (3) the increasing number of rural migrants moving into cities where traditionally only a small percentage of the country's population has lived. These three factors are not only the cause of urban growth in China since 1950, but they indicate that in the future China's cities will grow and develop enormously. Consider China's population growth from 588 million in 1953 to approximately 1 billion in 1981, while keeping in mind that the percentage of China's total population residing in cities was a modest 12 to 14% in 1953. Today, that percentage, or urbanization index, remains low, somewhere between 13 and 20%.[12] Although initially the urbanization index appears small, 13 to 20% of China's total population is 130 to 200 million people (Table 9-1). These totals indicate almost as many people are living in China's cities as live in cities in the United States. By the turn of the century, China could have as many as 200 to 300 million people in cities, although the exact number is difficult to predict. Viewed in this manner, China already is one of the great urban nations on earth,

[12]The variance in the percentage results from the kind of administrative definition that the Chinese use in describing the jurisdictional boundaries of their cities. For example, China's medium-sized and larger cities often include, within their administrative boundaries, agricultural workers in adjacent suburbs and counties. The rural activities and products of these peasant suburbanites support the urban populations, and a good argument can be made that these peasants function in part as urbanites.

Table 9-1. Cities and Urban Population in China, 1948-1980

	Number of urban places			Urban population (in thousands)			
Year	Municipalities	Other urban	All urban places	Built-up areas	% of nation	All urban places	% of nation
1948	150[a]						
1953	164[b]	5,404	5,568	43,523	7	77,257	13.2
1978	189[c]	3,261	3,450	112,000	13.4	167,164**	20
1980	216[a]	3,200*	3,416				

Source: [a]*Beijing Review*, 1980, Vol. 23, No. 16, April 21, p. 27.
[b]Ullman (1961).
[c]Yao, Shen, and Chang (1981).
*Includes 2,000 county towns with populations from 10,000-50,000.
**Including agricultural populations residing in suburbs.

and the impending scale of the developing Chinese urban experience is without precedent.

The enormity of these population statistics pinpoints the need, even urgency, of learning more about China's cities, their growth and development processes. There is nothing of a comparable scale in past human experience to help us envision the nature of developments in this enormous country, as its economy modernizes and its population begins to shift from a predominantly rural, farming population to an urban-based service and manufacturing population. It is with this challenging prospect of a scale and magnitude rarely dreamed of that we develop our discussion and analysis of China's cities and urban system. The challenge of housing and supporting such vast numbers of people confronts China's leaders and planners as they hasten their modernization efforts. As a preface to China's contemporary urbanization, a brief review of urbanization and the rise and development of China's urban network is useful.

BACKGROUND OF CHINESE CITIES AND THEIR INDIGENOUS HISTORICAL DEVELOPMENT

China has an ancient and well-established tradition of city building. For more than 2,000 years, China, through its highly centralized government, has engaged in building administrative centers. These included in every time period a major national capital and a number of smaller provincial and regional administrative and economic centers. Probably most important in the development of a national urban system in China was the administrative function at the county or *xian* level. By the end of the 3rd century A.D., a national urban system based around *xian* capitals had come into being (Fig. 9-1) (Chang, 1963). These local centers were administrative outposts of the central government and in large part provided the

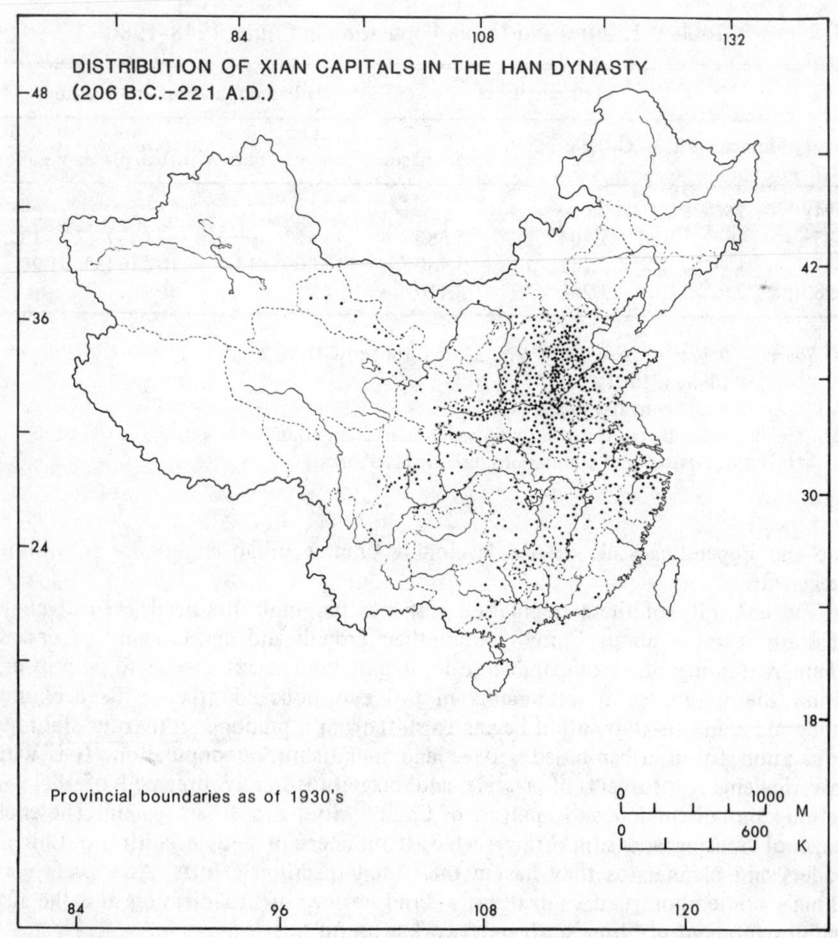

Fig. 9-1. Distribution of county capitals in the Han Dynasty (206 B.C.–221 A.D.).
Source: Chang (1963).

political linkages which held the very large territory together in a political/administrative sense. This network of urban centers has survived to the present day. Thus, the basic outline of the Chinese urban system is almost 2,000 years old.

In addition to this administratively based set of urban centers, over the centuries there also developed a set of local and regional marketing and commercial centers which became increasingly important and which paralleled and overlapped the administrative centers (Rozman, 1973). Related to the rise and development of commercial and marketing centers, there developed within China a series of great economic regions which resulted from the nature of the traditional transportation system, it has been argued. These systems developed within the great river basins since the constraints of the physical geography of China impeded overland transportation (Skinner, 1977). But the regions were poorly connected with one another. Skinner (1977) has asserted that the economic functions, based on the traditional transportation systems, resulted in a series of regional urban networks, and the large territory of China was poorly integrated economically as a consequence of the physical impediments to nationwide overland transportation linkages and the high cost of overland transportation.

Consequently, it is useful to view the emergence of a national Chinese urban network during the last 2,000 years as a set of administrative centers sometimes paralleled and overlapped especially at the regional and local level by marketing and commercial centers. In many cases, particularly at the provincial level, the combining of administrative with economic functions led to rapid growth of specific urban centers. In other cases, the economic activities of the small administrative centers, such as the *xian* capitals, were underdeveloped, and the growth of the individual urban places was stunted.

Such a pattern persisted for many centuries. Indeed, China's urban system evolved in the manner of the combination of economic and administrative activities. Periods of rapid economic growth and commercial development were paralleled by equally dynamic growth in the urban system. For example, growth of commerce in the Song Dynasty (960–1279) was followed by a rapid flourishing of urban centers (Ma, 1971). Despite such periods, the overall growth of the urban network remained relatively low until the 19th century. During the 19th century, a fundamental change took place in the development of the urban system. Improvements were made in transportation and the farm economy became more commercialized. In part, the change resulted from the arrival of Western colonialists, and the development of new technological innovations, especially those related to industrialization. This new phase of economic growth and development and its concomitant phase of urban progress has been labeled conventionally a treaty port phase. The term, treaty port, refers to the partially colonialized status of a number of China's coastal and river towns and cities, which became associated with Western countries and which had within them extraterritorial zones of foreign influence.

CHINESE CITIES AS TREATY PORTS

China's treaty ports differed strikingly from the cities of China's imperial past (Murphey, 1974). The treaty ports grew and developed because of their associations with foreigners–British, French, Germans, Russians, Americans, and Japanese –and the new ideas, technologies, and capital that these foreigners introduced to China. The new technologies and capital brought into the treaty ports resulted in a number of new opportunities for local people, and approximately 100 towns and cities located along the coasts and rivers of China were allocated treaty port

Reconstructed city gate in the heart of Xi'an. (*C. W. Pannell*)

status and attracted many migrants from neighboring rural areas. The more important of these are depicted in Fig. 9-2. Consequently, the treaty port cities grew very rapidly. Several related developments took place. First, a series of new transportation linkages was established both with the interior of China and with the external world. A major consequence of the presence of foreigners in China was an improved spatial integration of the national territory and its better connection with an international economy. This improvement in the national transportation network, however, was superficial. Initially, it related primarily to water transportation, although by the end of the 19th century railroads were being built in China.

In the 19th century, new capital and commercial relationships were available in China. In order for the foreigners to take advantage of China both as a market and as a supplier of goods for export, new opportunities for local people were created. After several decades of increased commercialization of the domestic economy and increased involvement with foreign businessmen, a whole new class of Chinese entrepreneurs and related businessmen emerged who provided a linkage between the foreigners and the large population of China. These people became known as compradores or Chinese agents of foreign capitalists, and they served an extremely important role during the late 19th and early 20th centuries. Many of them became wealthy and developed their own commercial firms and industrial establishments. The combination of foreign capital and local entrepreneurs signaled

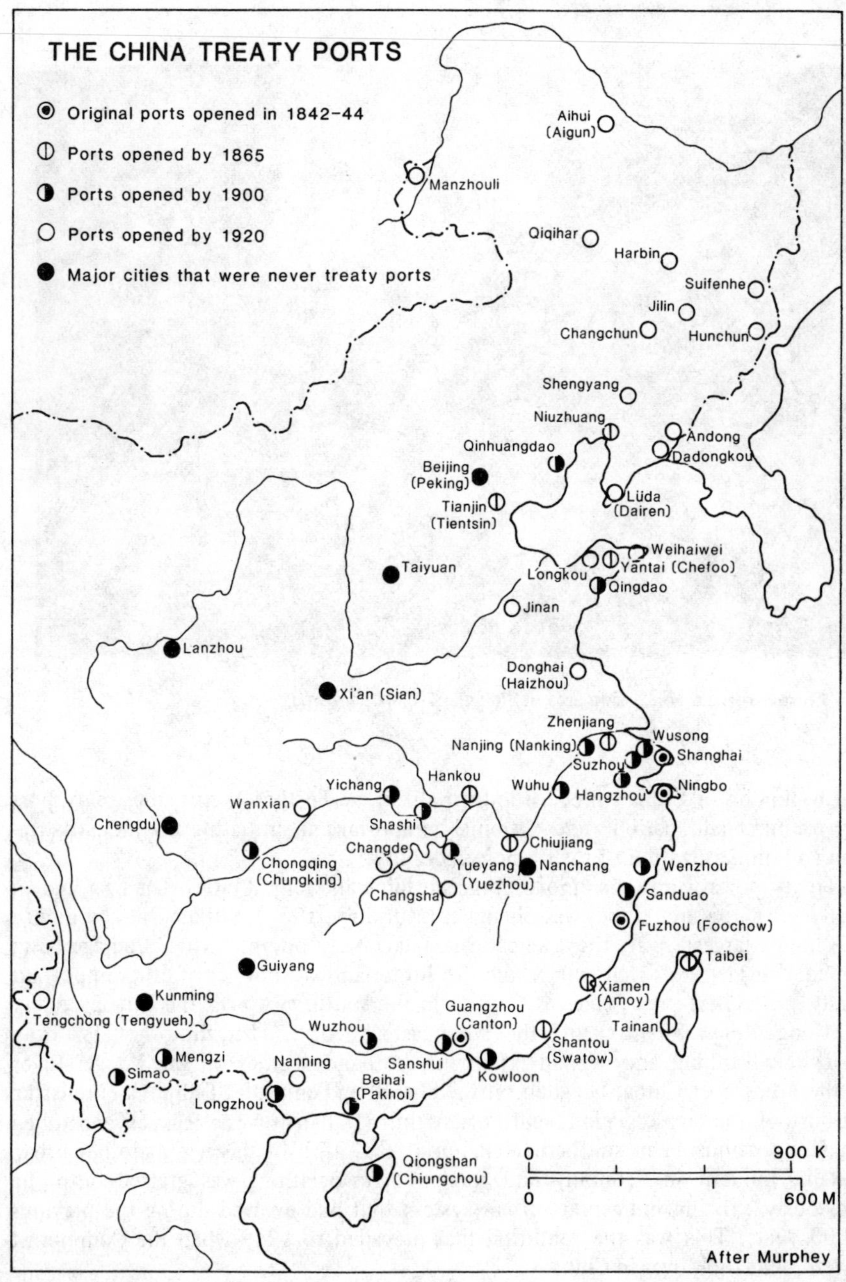

Fig. 9-2. The treaty ports of China.
Source: Murphey (1980).

Former foreign concession area in Shanghai. (*C. W. Pannell*)

the beginning of China's modern industrialization. To that extent, the treaty port development and period were extremely important in initiating the industrialization and modernization of the Chinese economy.

Treaty ports were soon among China's leading and largest cities. The best known treaty port, the archetype, was Shanghai (Murphey, 1954). Situated at the mouth of China's largest river, the Yangzi, Shanghai, drew on the entire drainage basin of the Yangzi for its rich and productive hinterland. A number of other important treaty port cities grew, such as Canton in the south very near the British colony of Hong Kong; Shantou off the southeastern coast; Hangzhou not far from Shanghai; Nanking and Wuhan (Hankou), both large cities on the Yangzi River in the interior of China; Qingdao on the Shandong Peninsula; Tianjin, an industrial outport of the city of Peking and Port Arthur (Dalian) on the Russian controlled Liaodong peninsula in southern Manchuria (Fig. 9-2). In this way, another urban system, modern in economy and foreign in association, was grafted onto the previously existing indigenous urban system that had evolved during the previous 2,000 years. This was the condition that prevailed to 1949 when the Communist government took over in China.

Murphey (1974) has argued that during the treaty port era a dual pattern of Chinese urbanization developed. The first pattern was the traditional, indigenous system that was focused on the interior of China and that was, to a large extent, spatially isolated from the coastal areas and poorly integrated in the context of

Drum Tower Square with Drum Tower in the background, Nanking. (*C. W. Pannell*)

modern transportation. These interior centers were based on local commercial and administrative functions and, in Murphey's view, formed the basic stratum of China's urban network. The second urban system was the new treaty port system that was composed of commercial and industrial centers associated through external contact with a modern, global economic system. Murphey has argued that the treaty ports, located as they were along the major rivers and coastal areas, had little effect on the large residual economy of China's interior. Chang (1976), by contrast, placed greater emphasis on the treaty ports. He indicated it was these treaty ports that provided significant developmental growth impulses to propel China's 19th and early 20th century economic growth and modernization. Buck (1978) completed a thoughtful study of one city, Jinan, and the processes of change it underwent during the 20th century. Studies such as this contribute a great deal to our understanding of the nature of Chinese urbanization during the last century.

CITIES UNDER COMMUNISM

Since 1950, it is clear, a new phase in the development of China's urban system has emerged. Although it is difficult to give a careful and precise description of this phase, owing to deficiencies in data on city growth, enough information is available to provide a sufficient picture of the major developments in the growth of China's urban network. Two main points at the outset are worth noting: (1) China's urban policy since 1950 has been to discourage the growth of large "super" cities and to encourage the development of medium and small cities; (2) locational policies of the government have focused on developing industrial centers away from vulnerable coastal areas and nearer to resources. These policies have stimulated the growth and development of interior centers. Examples of the latter would include Zhengzhou, Xi'an, Wuhan, and Lanzhou, all having experienced very rapid growth and increased significance since 1950. Offsetting this stated policy and desire to promote growth in the interior nearer resources, however, has been the hard fact that the largest pool of skilled labor and the largest consuming markets are found along or near the coast in the large former treaty port cities, such as Shanghai, Canton, Lüda, Nanking, and Tianjin. Large, industrial, former treaty port cities have continued to grow, despite sporadic efforts to counter their population growth and in some cases to force migration of city residents to surrounding rural areas (Wu, 1967; Ma, 1977).

Enormous investments and resources were involved in already existing large cities along the coast and major rivers. Government policy has been to recognize the value of these existing investments and resources and to continue to use them in a worthwhile and practical manner. There has been no policy aimed at destroying already existing urban centers. Indeed, several of the former treaty ports, such as Canton, have grown rapidly under the guidance of Communist policy and pragmatism (Lo, Pannell, and Welch, 1977). Most recently, Chinese policy is to create export processing zones, locally called special economic or export zones. Foreign investment has been encouraged in export oriented industries in selected locations in the vicinity of Hong Kong and Macao, as well as along the coasts of Guangdong and Fujian provinces opposite Taiwan (Kamm, 1980).

Despite the fact that these former colonial and foreign influenced coastal cities have grown rapidly, it is clear that the ideological basis for their existence has undergone a radical shift. All cities in China, including the capital, Peking, have had to alter their economic bases and activities in order to demonstrate their contributions to the national economy as industrial "producer" cities. Producer cities are those with substantial industrial activities which can contribute to the national economic well-being by virtue of exporting their industrial products throughout the nation as well as abroad. Such cities contrast with the older, service oriented "consumer" cities, including the former treaty ports.

Such policies confirm that there is a strong ideological current that underlies contemporary urban policy with reference to the nature of the economic activities and patterns that take place in China's contemporary cities. This ideological base has had a dramatic influence on the policies to promote city growth, and especially on the former treaty ports. The treaty ports have the serious ideological and political problem of their former commercial and service status associated with the presence of foreigners and the use of the native population in a service and consumer role. Consequently, in reordering China's urban system, Communist policy has focused directly on altering the economic activity patterns of all cities. This change has been most dramatic in the former treaty ports where policy has sought to rid these cities of their past foreign associations and so-called improper economic bases, and correct those losses as appropriate to the nature of a socialist economic system.

URBAN POPULATIONS: DEFINITION AND ADMINISTRATIVE ORGANIZATION

China's highly centralized administrative system includes cities at several different levels in its hierarchical structure. Cities are classified both on the basis of administrative as well as functional roles (see Chapter 5, Fig. 5-2). The three largest cities–Shanghai, Peking, and Tianjin–administratively rank as independent municipalities or national cities, and they are equivalent in status to China's 21 provinces and 5 autonomous regions. Other cities may rank independently within their provinces or at the same level as the prefectures (*diqu*) and counties (*xian*); smaller urban clusters rank as townships or towns (*zhen*). Large cities as spatial administrative units are composed of districts (*qu*) (see Chapter 5, Fig. 5-2). Growth of cities involves expanding the areal size by absorbing neighboring rural counties, townships, and towns. Administrative boundaries of the city will coincide areally with the boundaries of these counties and towns that have been absorbed.

Chinese cities are also classified according to the size of their populations. Indeed, it is the population that generally determines the administrative status of the cities. The cities, according to Yao, Shen, and Chang (1981), are classified into three groups based on population: large cities (over 500,000), medium sized cities (200,000 to 500,000), and small cities (less than 200,000). The latter category is called "minor cities or towns (*xiao chengzhen*), and many of these typically have populations between 50,000 and 60,000 inhabitants (Yao et al., 1981).

Definitions are less clear for urban places smaller than 50,000 although it appears that the Chinese in the past have made clear distinctions between urban and rural based on the occupation of the inhabitants of urban clusters. As Ullman (1961) noted,

> According to the definition given in the 1955 resolution of the State Council, urban places in China are those with 2,000 inhabitants or more, of whom at least half are engaged in nonagricultural pursuits. Places of 1,000 to 2,000 population may also be classified as urban if not less than 75 percent of the population is nonagricultural, provided also that these places are industrial, commercial, rail, educational, or research centers, or are residential areas for workers. Places with sanitarium facilities in which patients constitute more than half of the local permanent population may also be classified as urban. Finally, the location of a municipal people's committee or of a people's committee of the county level or above is considered urban, except for mobile administrative units in the pastoral areas.

In addition to this kind of definition, administrative distinctions are made between suburban districts (*jiaoqu*) and those districts in the densely built-up

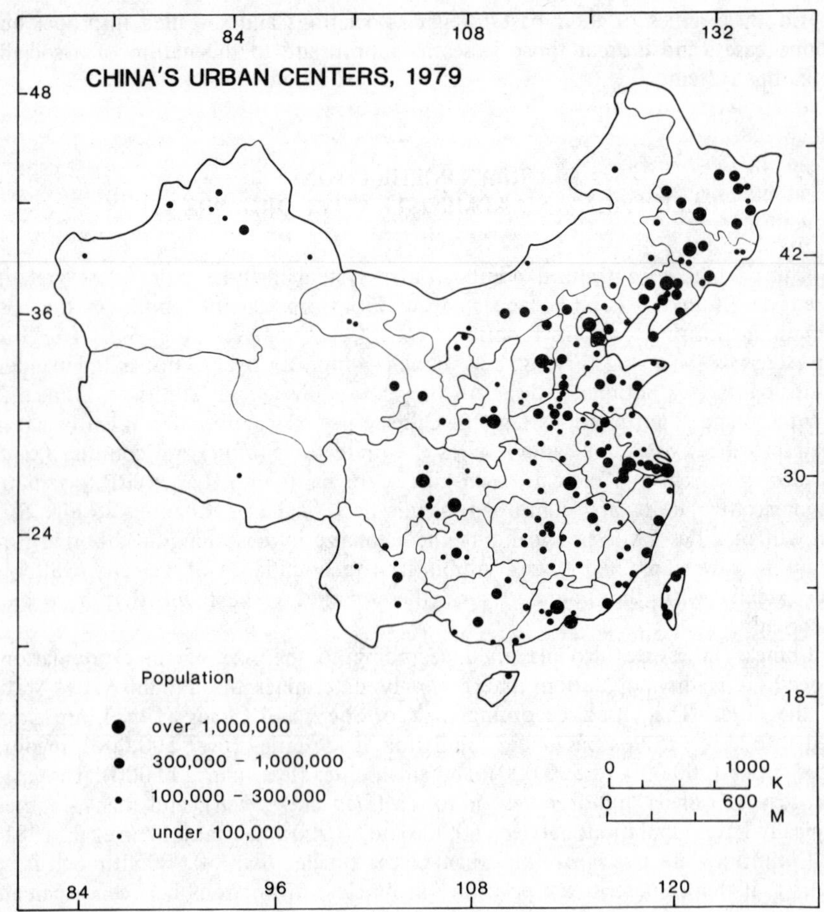

Fig. 9-3. China's urban centers, 1979.
Source: Zhongguo Dituce (1980).

section of the city (*shiqu*). As will be discussed below, this administrative distinction and definition have their analogue in the morphology and physical structure of the cities as well (Pannell and Welch, 1980).

In 1953, according to Ullman (1961), 13.2% (77,257,000) of China's 587,960,000 people lived in 5,568 cities and towns (Table 9-1). This figure included those living in market towns and in the suburbs of cities, but excluded those living in villages. Yao et al. (1981) reported that 112,000,000, or 13.4%, of the total population in 1978 lived in 3,450 cities and towns. According to Yao, if the agricultural population residing in suburbs were also included, the urbanized population would rise to 20%. Yao further noted that of the 3,450 cities and towns, 189 were incorporated municipalities of which 94 were places with more than 200,000 people (Fig. 9-3). This compares with 1953, when there were 164 municipalities of which, according to Ullman's data, only 53 had 200,000 people or more (see Table 9-1). Despite serious efforts to restrict the number of people in cities, the available evidence indicates that China's cities have grown rapidly and that the percent of the population living in cities has also increased, although slowly. There are, as noted above, varying definitions as to what constitutes a city and urban population, and this is examined in the next section.

Population Growth and City Growth

Two major trends have shaped the development of China's urban network and the growth of cities since 1950. First is the continued growth of China's population, and some of these people have moved legally into cities because of their jobs. The major consequence of this trend is that China's cities, as our figures indicate, have grown rapidly since 1950. The urban fraction of the total population has not increased a great deal, and most rural people remain on the communes. Nevertheless, the rural population base is so large that even a modest flow represents a substantial number of migrants to cities. The rapid population growth is simply reflected in part by an equivalent natural increase in the urban population and in part by a modest migration of ruralites into urban centers in the 1950s. This trend is seen in cities of all sizes, and there is no indication that larger cities are growing any more rapidly than are smaller cities (Pannell, 1981).

Second, the nature of the city growth has changed the structural outlines of the cities. For example, recent government policy has focused on decentralizing urban growth to the suburban and outlying smaller satellite cities and towns commonly located around the peripheries of the large cities (Ma, 1979). This policy apparently results from the strong desire of China's leaders to avoid the problems that have been encountered in many other developing countries in which the twin forces of rapid population growth and rapid urbanization have led to excessive concentrations of people in large cities. The resulting congestion and crowding have led to very serious social, economic, and political problems in these Third World cities. Calcutta and Djakarta are two of the frequently cited bad examples of urbanization in developing countries. Planners and policymakers in China hope to avoid such urban problems by not allowing excessive concentrations of peoples in the inner cities within their urban system and by decentralizing city populations to outlying locations where the problems of economic development and social evolution can be managed more easily (Pannell and Welch, 1980).

Another and somewhat draconian method of restricting urban population growth during the Cultural Revolution was the policy of sending or transferring urbanites to rural areas (*xia fang* and *xia xiang*). Several techniques were used, but the main goal was to transfer urban residents, mainly young people, to rural areas, where they would take up rural occupations or practice their trades and skills in a rural setting. In some cases, these were youths who had little or no marketable skills and who could not contribute greatly to the urban economy. In other cases, urbanites with expertise and talent were sent to the countryside

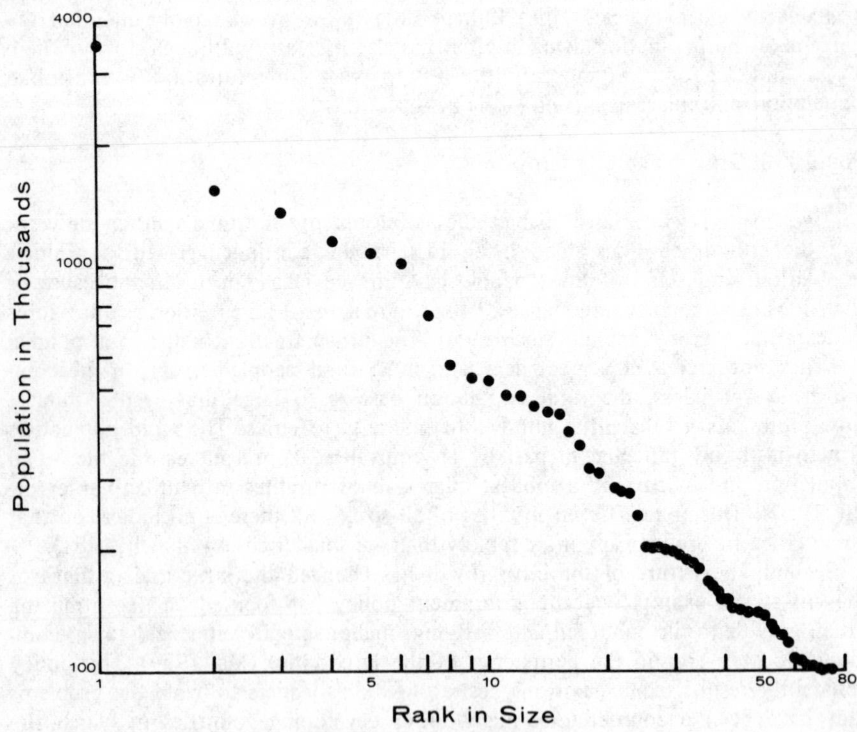

Fig. 9-4. Size distribution of China's cities, 1937.
Source: Skinner (1977).

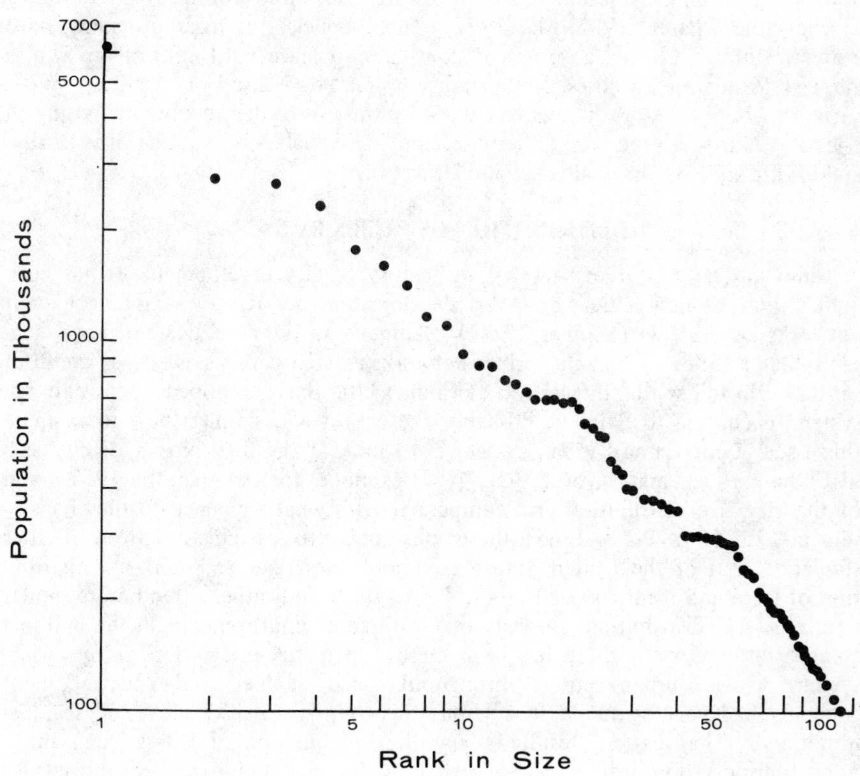

Fig. 9-5. Size distribution of China's cities, 1953.
Source: Pannell (1981).

to try to help correct rural/urban imbalances in technical levels and to help promote industrial development and modernization in rural areas. Such policies were never popular, and many individuals who were transferred worked avidly to return to the cities (Salter, 1972; Ma, 1977). These policies, as mass programs, have ceased, although China's government continues to place tight control on who is allowed to migrate to cities. In general, one must have a job or specific purpose, such as schooling (together with a work permit), in order to obtain housing in one of China's large cities. Otherwise, the individual is not in the city legally, and his life-style becomes sub rosa and almost fugitive.

DISTRIBUTION OF CITIES BY SIZE

China, as noted earlier, has a long history of city development. It has been argued that Chinese cities, however, developed as a series of semi-independent networks or systems (Skinner, 1977). Skinner's work, as indicated above, suggests that a series of regional urban networks existed perhaps as late as the 20th century. No full spatial integration of China's cities had developed into a national system, according to Skinner. Probably the easiest and simplest way to examine this issue about China's urban system is to look at the distribution of city size in China through graphs, over time. If we examine, for example, the 1937 graph of the city size distribution and compare it with what happened to the city system in 1953 (Figs. 9-4 and 9-5), the graphs appear to resemble a pattern of cities similar to that of the United States, commonly described as a rank-size distribution of large and medium sized cities.[13] The graph, indicating a trend more similar to a rank-size distribution, suggests that with some improvements in the national transportation system there has been increasing spatial integration of the urban system. China's urban centers throughout much of their earlier development generally had been scattered throughout the country to serve local and regional hinterlands. That pattern resulted from the combination of a large area and a poor transportation system, as suggested by Skinner and described above. Our graphs indicate this condition is giving way to a national system of cities, as China modernizes its economy.

An examination of city size distribution graphs for 1953 and 1970 indicates that China's urban system has a remarkably smooth profile (Figs. 9-5 and 9-6). In both years, the number of cities in various size classes is evenly distributed, and there is not an excessive concentration of population in one very large primate city with a resulting lack of cities in smaller size categories. In recent years, there appears to have been more growth in the medium sized cities, say those in the 250,000 to 2 million class range. The graphs suggest that these cities are growing in a balanced fashion. Significantly, the graphs also indicate that the largest cities, e.g., Shanghai, Peking, and Tianjin, are growing at a steady but unspectacular pace.

[13]Rank size, when referring to an urban system, is a condition in which ideally the second ranking city in a system is one-half the population of the largest city and the third ranking city is one-third the population of the largest, etc. When graphed on double logarithmic paper, the slope of a line representing such a system of cities should be linear.

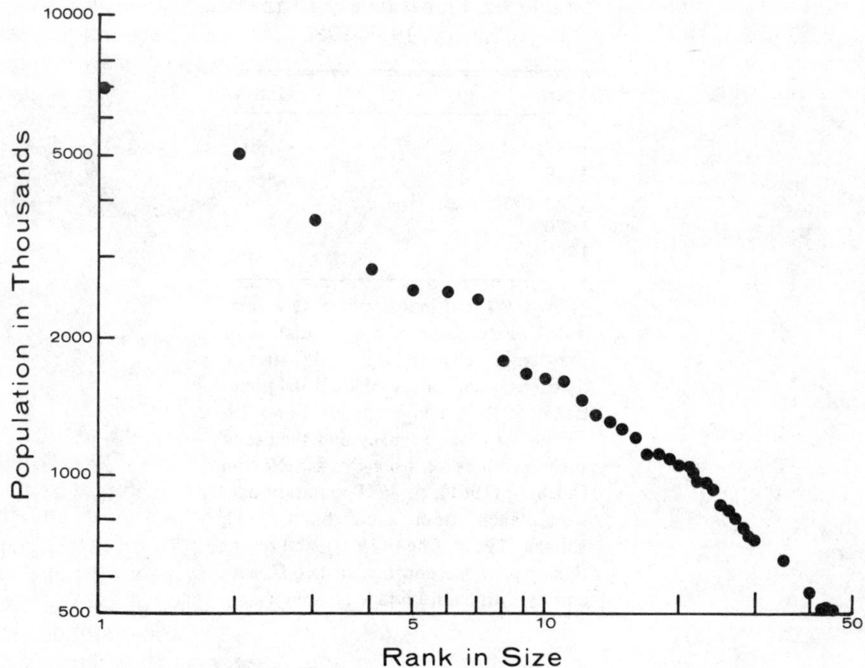

Fig. 9-6. Size distribution of China's cities, 1970.
Source: Pannell (1981).

These patterns of growth further indicate that the governmental policy of containment of very large cities appears to be having some effect, and that the Chinese government is succeeding in keeping people out of the largest cities and restricting the urban immigration of its population. Another way to look at and confirm this pattern is to compute and analyze the index of urban primacy. The index of urban primacy is a measure, or ratio, of the extent to which the largest city in a system is larger or smaller than a specified number of next largest cities (10 in this case) in the system. China's index of primacy looked at over a 25-year period from 1937 to 1977 (Table 9-2) suggests that the index or ratio of Shanghai as a primate city has in fact declined. The decline would suggest that the government policy of spreading growth to other urban centers in the system has succeeded. The evidence discussed above indicates that a serious and effective effort is underway to disperse growth to regional centers and thus to reduce inequalities among regions within China.

It would be a mistake to suggest that there has been a total involution of the pattern of urbanization and urban development. Indeed, the large cities continue to be important, and they continue to grow. But it is also clear that increasing efforts to focus investment and growth policies on developing cities in the interior of China are working. For example, since 1976, a new urban policy has been developed which requires that newly designed heavy and large-scale industries

Table 9-2. China: Index of Urban Primacy, 1937-1980

Year	Index
1937	.30
1949	.28
1953	.28
1970	.23
1980	.19

Note: These index values were computed on the basis of the population of the largest city (Shanghai on all five dates) as a percentage of the total population of the 10 largest cities. For a discussion of urban primacy and the use of such measures of primacy, see Norton Ginsburg (1961), p. 36. Population data were taken from Trewartha (1951), Ullman (1961), Chen (1973), and recent figures provided courtesy of Leo Orleans and Ly Burnham, Library of Congress.

can be located only in small and medium sized cities and in the suburbs of the large cities. Such policy, if implemented over a period of a decade or more, may retard significantly the growth rates and economic importance of the large cities. It is likely that the government will continue to focus attention on some of these interior centers and to try to promote faster growth and economic opportunities in the interior of China in such locations as Zhengzhou, Xi'an, Lanzhou, Taiyuan, Shijiazhuang, and Wuhan. The 1953 through 1970 growth pattern of these cities indicates that most have grown at least as rapidly (many have more than doubled their populations) as the overall national population growth, and several have grown much more rapidly (Table 9-3). The internal transportation system, based primarily on railroads, reinforces this development, and such key junction points as Zhengzhou reflect the importance of high accessibility in their growth.

Recent trends of economic growth, however, have been focused on outward looking policies and greater involvement with the global economic system and foreign trading partners selected from noncommunist countries (see Chapter 7). This recent orientation has created new economic opportunities, primarily along the coastal areas and largely focused near previous treaty port cities. Such new opportunities will no doubt create new conditions for urban growth. It will be important to watch closely the developments and growth patterns in cities like Canton, Fuzhou, Shanghai, Tianjin, and Lüda, as well as in the smaller adjacent centers where the export zones are located.

Table 9-3. Estimated Population of Large Chinese Cities

	1953*	1970**	1977***	1980–81****
Shanghai	6,204,417	7,000,000	10,810,000	12,000,000
Peking	2,768,119	5,000,000	8,300,000	8,800,000
Tianjin	2,693,831	3,600,000	6,280,000 (1976)	7,400,000
Shenyang	2,299,831	2,800,000	4,200,000	4,700,000
Chongqing	1,722,500	2,400,000		6,200,000 (1979)
Guangzhou	1,598,900	2,500,000	4,970,000	5,400,000 (1979)
Wuhan	1,427,300	2,560,000	3,670,000	3,800,000 (1979)
Harbin	1,163,000	1,670,000		4,000,000
Nanking	1,091,600	1,750,000	3,200,000	3,600,000
Qingdao	916,800	1,300,000		1,400,000 (1969)
Chengdu	856,700	1,250,000		4,000,000 (1979)
Changchun	855,200	1,200,000		5,000,000
Xi'an	787,300	1,600,000	2,500,000	2,800,000
Lüda	766,400	1,650,000	4,000,000 (1975)****	4,000,000 (1975)
Taiyuan	720,700	1,350,000	1,800,000****	1,800,000 (1977)
Kunming	698,900	1,100,000	1,500,000 (1976)	1,900,000 (1979)
Hangzhou	696,600	960,000	5,000,000****	5,000,000 (1979)
Tangshan	693,300	950,000		1,200,000
Jinan	680,100	1,100,000	1,100,000 (1974)	3,200,000 (1979)
Fushun	678,600	1,080,000	1,800,000 (1976)****	1,800,000 (1976)
Changsha	650,600	825,000	800,000 (1973)	2,600,000 (1979)
Zhengzhou	594,700	1,050,000	1,700,000 (1976)	1,300,000 (1979)
Wuxi	581,500	650,000	1,000,000 (1973)****	1,000,000 (1973)
Fuzhou	553,000	680,000		2,500,000
Anshan	548,900	1,050,000		2,500,000 (1961)
Suzhou	474,000	730,000	1,050,000	900,000
Benxi	449,000	600,000		1,200,000 (1970)
Jilin	435,400	720,000		2,200,000 (1975)
Nanchang	398,000	675,000		2,400,000 (1979)
Lanzhou	397,400	1,450,000	2,000,000+	2,300,000 (1979)
Shijiazhuang	373,400	800,000	800,000+	1,000,000 (1979)
Xuzhou	373,000	700,000		800,000
Qiqihar	344,700	760,000		1,000,000 (1972)
Huainan	286,900	600,000		
Guiyang	270,100	660,000		1,300,000 (1979)
Nanning	194,600	550,000		600,000 (1979)
Zebo	184,200	850,000		
Hefei	183,600	630,000		1,500,000 (1979)
Luoyang	171,200	580,000		1,100,000 (1978)
Baotou	149,400	920,000		2,000,000
Hohhot	148,400	530,000		1,000,000 (1978)
Urümqi	140,700	500,000		1,200,000
Xining	93,700	500,000		900,000 (1979)

Sources: *Ullmann (1961).

**Chen (1973).

***Compiled by authors from field data provided by various urban planning officials and leading members of local revolutionary committees to Ohio Academy of Sciences, Geography Delegation, August, 1977, and from various published sources.

****Courtesy of Leo Orleans and Ly Burnham, Library of Congress (see also Orleans, 1959).

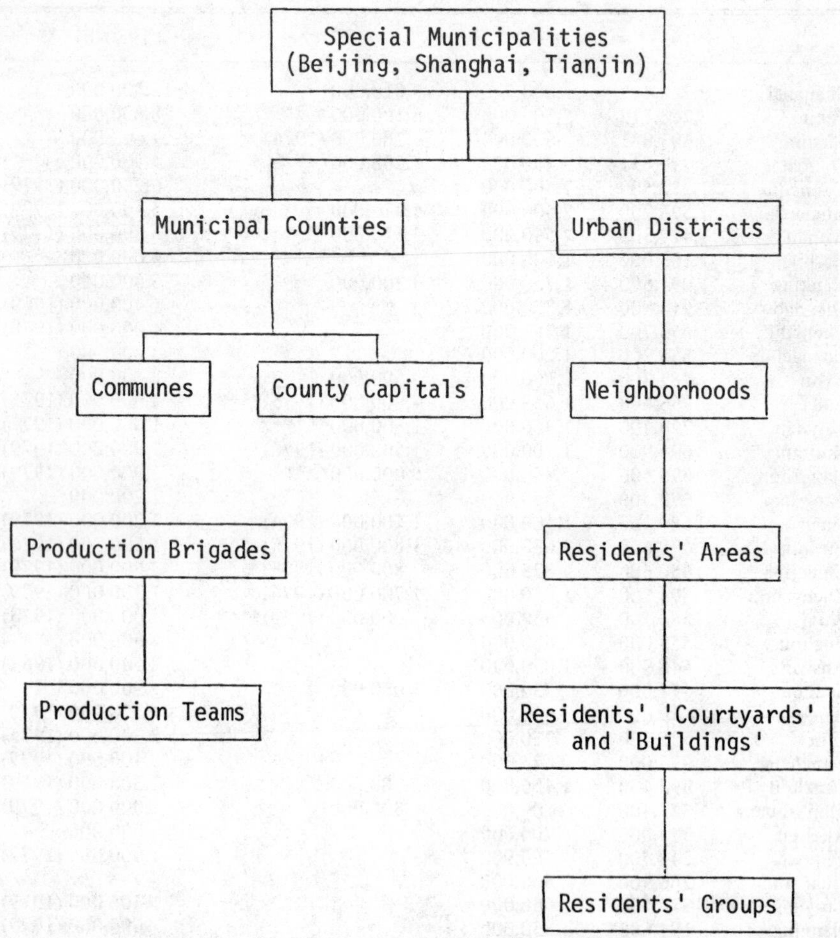

Fig. 9-7. Administrative organization of Chinese municipalities.
Source: Ma (1979).

INTERNAL STRUCTURE

As previously stated, China's cities are organized administratively into districts (*qu*) for carrying out national and local urban policies and programs. The districts, as Ma (1979) noted, are further broken down into neighborhoods and residents' areas, each with its own tasks, functions, and administrative areas nested inside the space of the larger administrative units (Fig. 9-7). An important principle of this organizational framework is the more dense the urban population, the smaller

Town center of Minhang, an industrial satellite of Shanghai. (*L. Ma*)

the area of the administrative unit. For example, the urban districts of Peking's continuously built-up area are smaller in area than agriculturally oriented communes in the suburbs with less densely crowded populations.

Land Use Organization

Cities in China, as in other socialist countries, are designed to reflect ideologically based concepts of urban form. For this reason, Chinese cities should be different in form from cities that develop under conditions of free market economies. One important feature of this has been the transformation of the old morphological pattern of China's cities, especially the former treaty ports, because they reflect the putative "dysfunctions" of a capitalist economy and society. The older cities were service oriented and "consuming" in their economic patterns. Chinese cities under the new order were to abolish the old patterns and in this way become "producer" cities that contributed to the national well-being through their industrial production.

Major goals of socialist city planning, according to Fisher (1962), include four tenets: (1) standardized land uses and social areas; (2) development of neighborhood self-sufficient units; (3) ceremonial role for the city center; and (4) an optimum size for each city. Based on what has happened in China's cities in recent years, it is clear that the Chinese take these idealized urban planning precepts very seriously.

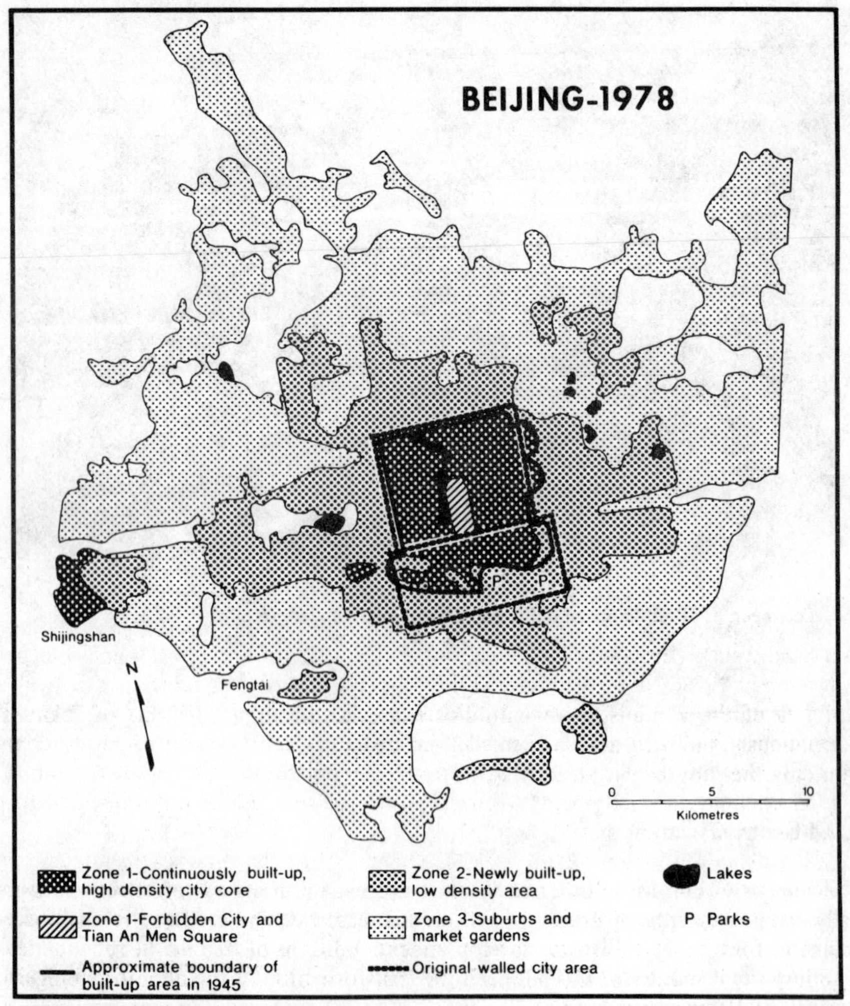

Fig. 9-8. Land use zones in Peking, derived from interpretations of 1978 Landsat Return Beam Vidicon (RBV) and Multispectral Scanner images, indicate growth and land use changes that have occurred since 1945.
Source: Pannell and Welch (1980).

The structure of land use in China's large cities is generally consistent. However, several different types of cities have resulted from size, location, and historical development (Tien, 1973). One distinctive type would be the indigenous city, usually walled and located in the interior of the country and largely unaffected by the 19th and 20th century presence of foreigners. Xi'an and Taiyuan represent

Table 9-4. Land Use in Chinese Cities Based on Building Density

Zone 1:	Continuously built-up, high density city core Building density is compact and crowded. Land uses include residential, commercial-service, roads, and public-administrative. Historical parks and public assembly areas (Tian An Men Square) also are included in this category.
Zone 2:	Newly built-up, low density area Building density is continuous but reduced. Land use is primarily residential with associated government employment centers and industries mixed in. This zone also includes service facilities such as schools, clinics, and markets for residents. Limited vegetable production occurs here.
Zone 3:	Suburbs and market gardens Building density is low and not continuous. Major land use is intensive vegetable cultivation and farmland.

Source: Pannell and Welch (1980).

this category. A second classification would be the treaty port, often beginning as a small walled administrative center but owing its great commercial and industrial development and population growth to the association with foreigners. Shanghai and Tianjin are good examples of this type. A third, special type of city with some special situational or historical condition may also be identified: cities that usually were smaller, with no special change envisioned for them. Suzhou is a good example of a city with a special historical role, and is not scheduled to be changed to fit the idealized pattern.

Basic policies of urban planning are made at the national level and their implementation has resulted in structural similarity in Chinese cities. Generally, however, they have not altered the older traditional core areas, and the Chinese planners have concentrated their attention on the newer areas of the cities. Pannell and Welch (1980) used recent satellite data to identify three land use zones in Peking (Fig. 9-8) and Tianjin based on the density of buildings (Table 9-4). It is believed that similar structural patterns of land use are found in most of China's large cities that have grown rapidly in recent years.

Zone 1, the old continuously built-up high density city core, has changed least in these cities. Zone 2 is a new zone of lower but more or less continuous buildings. Residential land predominates, but it is interspersed with employment centers, such as government offices, educational activities, some factories, and green space. This is the main area of city growth. Beyond this is a third zone of suburban land composed of agricultural land (especially urban market gardens), housing estates, and nucleated industrial development. Building patterns are not continuous, although growth and development in this fringe zone are rapid. In the largest cities, the limits of Zone 3 are difficult to establish, but the zone

Wangfujing, a busy commercial center in Peking. (*L. Ma*)

correlates most closely with the market garden belt discussed by other observers (Skinner, 1978; Lo, 1979). The main structural pattern associated with these changing zones of land use is that the newly developing areas of the city are less densely populated than the older core areas. The new areas have lower building density and more green space.

The above new zones are supported through a very specific land use classification coding system (Table 9-5) that city planners use in their work and in designing the structure of land use for China's cities. Chinese policymakers and planners seemed determined to avoid crowded, congested cities with extremely high building densities and the attendant social and public health problems commonly found in cities in developing countries. The use of the land use classification code coupled with the ideologically based goals of socialist urban planning appear to be successful in creating a new and common morphological pattern among the larger cities in China.

Zoning and Land Use Classification

Functional land use zoning as practiced in China seeks to create homogeneous zones of land use in different parts of cities. Ma (1979) has suggested this approach to land use zoning resembles the concept of a series of multiple nucleated land use zones in cities that the geographers Harris and Ullman (1945) introduced some years ago. A 1976 urban planning draft regulation proposed seven major

Table 9-5. Urban Land Use Classification

I. Land for daily living
  1. Residential
  2. Public buildings
  3. Public green space and parks
  4. Streets and public squares

II. Industrial
  1. Industry
  2. Mining
  3. Special railways for industry

III. Storage
  1. Warehouses
  2. Stockpiles

IV. Public utilities
  1. Water works
  2. Sewage treatment works
  3. Gas plants
  4. Power station
  5. Transmission lines and pipelines
  6. Parking, maintenance and engineering facilities for the above

V. Buffer belts for public health and safety
  1. Buffers for public health
  2. Buffers to protect water sources
  3. Buffers to reduce wind and sand damage

VI. External transportation
  1. Railways
  2. Highways
  3. Stations, wharves, and airports

VII. Special
  1. Military
  2. Public security

Source: Chengshi yangdi xuance ji fangan bijiao (The Selection of Urban Land Use and Comparative Plans), 1976.

categories of land use (Table 9-5). Of these, four categories and subcategories had been generally identifiable previously–residential, industrial, cultural, and public open space. Despite such classification, it has not been easy to distinguish clearly zones of land use in China's cities, inasmuch as the policy of functional zoning is relatively recent. This difficulty exists despite the fact that the broad precepts of socialist town planning apparently have been accepted and implemented for three decades.

Among the more significant consequences of land use zoning is the concentration of industries in clusters that reduce the impact of pollution on the nearby city. Serious efforts have been made to reduce the impact of air pollution on

New apartments gradually replace the spontaneous dwellings in Xi'an. (*C. W. Pannell*)

cities by locating industries downwind and to decentralize locations to adjacent industrial satellite towns. The Peking industrial satellites of Fengtai and Shijingshan are good examples. The populations of such satellite towns and industrial centers are frequently housed in large residential estates, another feature of functional land use clustering and planning (Fig. 9-8). Such planning supports the concept of reducing population and building density in the central city and indicates the significance of industrial locational planning as an element in determining the future pattern of urban growth.

Housing

One of the greatest challenges facing urban planners in contemporary China is housing. There are two major aspects of this challenge. The first is to build sufficient new housing to provide adequate space and amenities for the rapidly increasing city populations, especially in conjunction with the construction and growth of new industrial centers. Second, great investments are required to improve the housing stock of dilapidated and congested areas within the large central cities. Although cities have been cleaned and environmental conditions made sanitary, a large supply of older, less desirable housing remains in the densely crowded cores of the larger cities. This existing investment will no doubt continue to house inner-city populations for many years, although deteriorating

Workers' apartments in Peking. (*L. Ma*)

slums are replaced or renovated all the time. For example, Ma (1979) noted that 10% of Shanghai's total housing stock still consists of shacks or simple houses (*jianlou fangwu*).

The major pattern of constructing new urban housing areas is linked closely with the development of new centers of employment, especially industrial centers. Housing estates are commonly located close to the factory, office, or research center in order that the workers and cadres may be within walking distance or a short ride away. Housing estates are developed with a broad set of available local goods and services. Large residental estates, which comprise administrative units and urban residents' committees, would include schools, a medical clinic, a post office, and a variety of low level consumer services. Larger and more populous administrative units (the district or *qu*) would include larger stores and markets as well as more recreational facilities. The main goal is to satisfy demand for goods and services at the neighborhood or local level and so reduce the need for people to travel throughout the city for schooling, medical attention, food, clothing, and other services. The supply of urban transportation is poor. Thus, the planning strategy incorporated in China's urban housing appears to be logical and appropriate for current income levels.

The factory or bureau of a local housing administration usually operates and maintains the housing estate, and the monthly rent is usually very modest–5% of a family's income is a standard figure. Design of these housing estates is frequently standardized and stereotyped. Most are four- and five-story buildings

New high-rise apartments in Shanghai. (*L. Ma*)

Table 9-6. Average Living Space Per Dwelling Unit in Selected Countries

Country	Time of survey	Average living space (m^2)	
		2-room unit	3-room unit
Sweden	1967	65	–
France	1972	–	63–55
Hungary	1970	53	–
USSR	1970	50–43	63–58
Nicaragua	1969	–	52.2
Honduras	1969	–	50.3
China	1977	50	–
Guatemala	1969	–	40.3
El Salvador	1969	–	39.8

Sources: European countries: Fuerst (1974, pp. 4, 100, 114, 128). Central American countries: United Nations, Department of Economic and Social Affairs (1973, p. 106, Table 2). The figure for China is based on Peking, given by city planners of Peking, August 15, 1977, as reported in Ma (1979).

composed of flats. The older ones are often rather crowded and compact in location, although more recently constructed housing compounds appear to place more stress on green space and amenity values. Varying figures have been suggested for floor space per resident, and living space varies from 6 to 17 m^2 per inhabitant (Ma, 1979). Towers (1973) reported that the average flat size is between 30 and 40 m^2 for a family of five, a figure that compares favorably with the resettlement estates in Hong Kong and the apartments of the Singapore Housing and Development Board. Recently in Peking, the average flat size has been increased to 50 m^2 and includes two rooms, kitchen, and bathroom. By Western standards, this would appear crowded; however, it is considered adequate for contemporary conditions, and compares reasonably with other socialist countries (Table 9-6). Each apartment unit has its own toilet facilities but generally shares a kitchen and shower with a neighboring family.

CIRCULATION AND TRANSPORTATION

Movement and circulation within China's cities remain at a low level and are constrained by the modest supply of available transportation facilities. Three major modes of transportation are involved–walking, bicycles, and buses–and the number of buses and electric buses in China's large cities is small when seen in the context of the populations of these cities. For example, as late as 1977, Shanghai, with an inner-city population of 5.5 million, had only 2,600 buses and a daily ridership of 6 million person trips. City residents owned more than 1 million bicycles, but these are inadequate to relieve the enormous demand for bus transportation (Table 9-7). Peking has a one-line subway, but it is not yet a major factor in the urban transportation of the city. Plans exist for expanding this line, and in the future it may come to be a significant facet of intra-city movement.

Roads in China's cities are generally adequate to handle the flow of people on bicycles, buses, and the few cars, trucks, and carryalls seen. There is no private

Table 9-7. Bus Ridership in Urban Peking and Shanghai, 1977

	Peking	Shanghai
Estimated number of potential riders	2,000,000	4,840,000
Year ridership (person trip)		
Entire city	1,400,000,000	2,190,000,000
Each potential rider	700	452
Average daily ridership (person trip)		
Entire city	3,840,000	6,000,000
Each potential rider	1.92	1.24

Source: Ma (1979).

On the way to work in an older area of Guilin. (*C. W. Pannell*)

ownership of cars in China other than those possessed by foreigners. Consequently, auto traffic is modest, even in the largest cities. The road networks in China's large cities are designed to handle a substantial volume of traffic (mostly bicycles) and to provide a pleasant, tree-lined vista. Thus, the cities are designed to be attractive and to enhance the livability for urban inhabitants. Obviously, all areas of cities do not yet meet these goals, but gradually the goals are being met. The cities more and more are being opened up and designed to reflect amenity values associated with contemporary town planning.

Urban transportation in China's great cities will require a great deal of planning and investment in future years. At this point, transport supply is severely restricted, and urban residents are afforded limited transportation services. As modernization and income levels increase, urban residents likely will exhibit demand preferences for increased travel and more commodious modes of transportation within cities. Policy may begin to shift toward improvements in the mass transit systems in the largest cities. It is unlikely that China will permit much private auto ownership in the coming decades, although motorcycles and mopeds may come into more widespread use. The impact of such limited transportation service on urban structure will continue to mean that cities will be of comparatively high densities, even though these densities may be contained in smaller, clustered satellite centers. Personal travel will be highly restricted and localized, and China's cities will offer only limited opportunity for the exercise of individual mobility and movement.

VEGETABLE GARDENING AND URBAN FOOD SUPPLY

One of the most remarkable things about China's cities is that they produce their own food, or at least most of it. For many years, scholars have observed and remarked on the intensive vegetable belts that surround China's cities (King, 1926; Murphey, 1954). It was known that a substantial amount of a city's fresh produce for daily consumption was grown on an adjacent circular belt of intensively farmed land, some of which penetrated the city where vacant plots of land were available. The reasons for the existence of this urban horticultural belt are clear. First, the crude and limited nature of the transportation system meant that cities could not rely on long-distance transportation to provide fresh foodstuffs. Urban food demand was heavy and had to be met locally for the most part. Second, the city as a large concentration of people was producing a large quantity of organic manure. This night soil was available to sustain and improve soil nutrients. Because of transport and handling costs, its movement had to be highly localized. Thus, there evolved a remarkable symbiosis in which night soil was systematically collected, transported to the adjacent suburbs, decomposed through a brief aging process, and then applied in various forms to local fields. Inasmuch as the available quantities were great, the ability of local fields to sustain continuous, high level crop production was thus enhanced, and the production of vegetables provided a supply of fresh foods to meet local urban demand (Salter, 1976).

Private vendors hawking goods in Canton. (*C. W. Pannell*)

A quiet lane in Peking. (*C. W. Pannell*)

In 1977, a delegation of American agricultural scientists visited China to study vegetable farming. One of their most significant findings was that more than 85% of the fresh vegetables consumed in cities are produced within the administrative boundaries of the cities, in sharp contrast to the regional specialization of vegetable production common to cities in Europe and North America (Skinner, 1978). In addition to the various ecological factors involved in urban vegetable farming, it was discovered that the main compelling reason for continuing to satisfy urban food needs locally was the cost of transportation. Despite improvements and continuing investments in transportation, the transport network remains inadequate to provide timely, efficient, and low cost movement of perishable commodities.

Organizationally, as Skinner (1978) noted, the advantage of municipal self-sufficiency in vegetable production is that it simplifies planning. The adjacency of production and consumption within the same urban administrative unit reduces administrative interference and facilitates the management of adjusting urban food supply and demand. This explains, in part, the increase in the administrative boundaries of many of China's cities. To incorporate sufficient agricultural land to supply its needs, the city achieves self-sufficiency in food production. Thus, the goals of urban administrative organization are both economic and political.

The system of urban self-sufficiency in vegetable production is a highly complex yet remarkably practical system which, as Skinner (1978) points out, is usually adapted to local circumstances and management techniques. For urban dwellers, it ensures a good supply of fresh vegetables at a reasonable price, although prices will fluctuate seasonally. For the peasants from the adjacent suburban communes and production brigades that specialize in vegetable production, a stable market is provided for their produce, and a good price is assured on a steady basis. Linkages between specific production brigades and urban markets are maintained, and the relationships between city and suburb become long-term. Operations of the vegetable marketing system vary from city to city. Generally, the approach is to allow the city to develop its own particular production, marketing, and distribution system; and the results appear to be successful. Given existing levels of technology, the present system of vegetable production and distribution seems both efficient and effective.

URBAN QUALITY AND ENVIRONMENT

Efforts have been made by Chinese planners to make the cities better places in which to live. Two major improvements in environmental quality have occurred since 1949. The cities have been cleaned, and policy has been to reduce the density of people and buildings in order to make the urban environments attractive and comfortable places in which to live and work. Despite the efforts and successes in reducing the crowding and congestion, by the standards of cities in the industrial West, China's cities (both large and small) remain densely populated.

Other efforts to improve the quality of China's cities involve extensive plantings of trees and shrubs to "green" the urban environment. The idea is to provide shade and to help reduce the intense summer heat as well as to increase the beauty of the cities. The Chinese also believe that increases in urban plants help to muffle the noise level and to reduce the amount of air pollution, all of which will improve the quality of life in cities.

Recreation is a serious matter, too. First, park space is available but not in every area of each city. Residents of China's cities frequently may be seen early in the morning taking exercises, such as Chinese *taiji* (slow rhythmic exercises somewhat inappropriately analogized to shadow boxing), in local parks or the compounds of factories, schools, or offices. Some space for athletic activities, e.g., basketball courts, soccer fields, or swimming pools, is available, but again not a sufficient amount for all those who wish to play. Many urban residents use sidewalks and streets as a means for gathering to talk with friends, play checkers, play ball, or simply watch others go by. Such urban watching provides entertainment enough, as there always seems to be something going on. In the contemporary environment of China's cities, cleaned and with plenty of attractive shade trees along the broad boulevards, taking a stroll late on a summer afternoon that provides a variety of sights, sounds, and smells is recreation and entertainment.

In some large cities, however, there are acute air and water pollution problems. Despite efforts to locate industries away from residential areas, air pollution is evident in many large industrial cities. In Lanzhou, heavy concentration of chemical industries coupled with poor atmospheric circulation due to local topography have made the city one of the most polluted in China. Widespread urban air

Sunday is a busy market day for many citizens in Canton. (*C. W. Pannell*)

pollution is due partly to the fact that the importance of environmental quality was simply not considered in China's industrial planning and location prior to the worldwide awareness of environmental degradation in the late 1960s. Many old urban industries are simply not equipped with any pollution-control devices, and new environmental regulations established in the 1970s which require such devices appear to affect new industries primarily.

The burning of coal is another reason for urban air pollution. Coal is not only the chief source of energy for the industries, it is also widely used for cooking and heating by most urban residents. Except for such large cities as Peking and Shanghai, where gas is available for some residents, alternative sources of energy for cooking and heating will not be available for many years to come, simply because investment in utilities and in urban housing construction or rehabilitation is not a profitable way to use the nation's limited financial resources.

The pollution of urban waters is also serious in some cities. In Shanghai, the Suzhou Creek, an open sewer before 1949, has hardly been improved, while the Huangpu and Wusong Rivers, which used to be fairly clean, have become increasingly polluted as a result of heavy concentration of industries in the city proper and in the industrial satellite towns. Even in such nonindustrial cities as Suzhou, the lack of sewage treatment facilities and modern sewer systems has cut down the ability of the slow-flowing rivers and canals to carry sewage. In Shanghai, excessive tapping of the ground water for industrial and residential uses has resulted in general land subsidence and slow incursions of the sea water.

These problems have been recognized by the government and measures have been taken to alleviate them. A few polluting factories have been fined, but since the factory leaders are not penalized financially, such an approach has had little effect. In the scenic city of Guilin, a few factories have been shut down by the government for polluting the Li River, but for the nation as a whole the total number of factories so affected is very small.

A basic factor contributing to the pollution problems stems from the nation's planning ideology of stressing "production first" that has dominated the thinking of China's top planners in the last three decades. This planning doctrine has led the industries to pay attention only to the fulfillment of higher production quotas each year. Until the late 1970s, environmental quality simply did not come into the planning picture. Unless and until the long-term impact of environmental changes due to urban economic growth is fully recognized and adequately dealt with by China's top economic planners, the problems of air and water pollution in the cities will continue.

PLANNING AND POLICY

In organizing and planning China's urban and rural development, to serve best its people and the country, three main ideologically rooted principles are followed (Ma, 1979). In sloganized form, these are: to serve proletarian politics, socialist production, and the livelihood of the working people. In addition to these broad and general principles, four goals of city planning have been set. These goals, presented in terms of the popular slogans used to advance their objectives among the populace, are: (1) combine industry with agriculture; (2) combine city with countryside; (3) enhance production; and (4) facilitate the people's livelihood.

Although expressed as popular devices, the principles underlying these slogans are firmly rooted in Marxism and are basic to understanding the manner in which Chinese planners approach cities and how they plan for urban change. For example, Marx, in the context of the 19th century, saw cities as centers of commerce and capital, where capitalists sought to exploit rural peasants as well as urban workers. The late Communist leader, Party Chairman Mao Zedong, believed these same urban-rural and social class contradictions existed in China during the first half of the 20th century. Mao viewed China's cities as parasitic and "consumer" oriented. Thus, he believed the economic systems should be overturned and the social order reconstituted. The cities, according to Mao, should be made into socialist "producer" cities, which would help to break down contradictions and contribute greatly to socialist construction in China. This was Mao's vision for the cities of the new China. While this vision has faded somewhat, a portion has been embraced in operational planning for contemporary cities (Murphey, 1980).

In urban construction, such a planning ideology and approach gives a certain and sometimes boring sameness to housing construction in which row after row of similar apartment buildings are constructed for workers. Livability means a few parks; even so, extensive efforts have been made to create green space through tree and shrubbery plantings. The main objective of central planning and policy in China today is for cities to produce for the national good. Cities should produce their own food (or at least most of it, as discussed above), and should, through their industrial and service activities, serve the nation by exporting goods and services beyond their own administrative boundaries. This means providing industrial goods to the rest of the country and possibly selling some of these goods on international markets. Services such as education, planning, and research must also be provided, and these, too, must be oriented toward the national well-being and not simply for local consumption.

Such then are the broad goals of contemporary Chinese urban policy and planning. Although the Chinese frequently point to agriculture as the foundation of their country, it is clear that cities are vitally important to the country's economic growth and development. Cities are centers of industry, transportation, commerce, education, and research. Most of China's elite–its intellectual talent, leaders, and policymakers–live and work in cities. Despite their own disclaimers, it is clear the Chinese will use their urban centers extensively and depend on them heavily as the country continues its titanic effort to modernize and develop. Any alternative path would not only be unwise but also impractical and unlikely to produce satisfactory results. Ginsburg (1980), in a recent essay on China's latest efforts to modernize, evaluated the role of cities in national development. He concluded that the broad program of the "Four Modernizations" and other evidence increasingly coming to light indicate that China is beginning to make greater use of its cities as centers of innovation and engines of economic growth. The imperatives of rapid industrialization and technological improvements have necessitated this shift in emphasis, according to Ginsburg. Such patterns indicate the urban path to modernization is emerging in China as it has in other countries. Whether or not China can retain its own distinctive style of urbanization consistent with past traditions and contemporary socialist planning policies remains to be seen. The more rapid growth of cities and towns that will inevitably accompany a stronger emphasis on practical policies that promote an accelerated modernization and national development, with less attention and emphasis on ideology, should prove an interesting test case of the meaning as well as the fundamental nature of urbanization in the world's most populous country.

LITERATURE CITED

Beijing Review, 1980, Vol. 23, No. 16 (April 21), p. 27.

Buck, David, D., 1978, *Urban Change in China, Politics and Development in Tsinan, Shantung, 1890–1949.* Madison: University of Wisconsin Press. 1978.

Chang, Sen-dou, 1963, "Historical Trend of Chinese Urbanization." *Annals of the Association of American Geographers*, Vol. 53, pp. 109–143.

Chang, Sen-dou, 1976, "The Changing System of Chinese Cities." *Annals of the Association of American Geographers*, Vol. 66, pp. 398–415.

Chen, C. S., 1973, "Population Growth and Urbanization in China, 1953–1970." *The Geographical Review*, Vol. 63, pp. 55–72.

Fisher, Jack C., 1962, "Planning the City of Socialist Man." *Journal of the American Institute of Planners*, Vol. 28, pp. 251–265.

Fuerst, J. S. (ed.), 1974, *Public Housing in Europe and America.* New York: John Wiley & Sons.

Ginsburg, Norton, 1961, *Atlas of Economic Development.* Chicago, Ill.: University of Chicago Press.

Ginsburg, Norton, 1980, "Urbanization and Development: Processes, Policies and Contributions." In C. K. Leung and Norton Ginsburg (eds.), *China, Urbanization and National Development.* Chicago: University of Chicago, Department of Geography, Research Paper No. 196, pp. 259–280.

Harris, C. and Ullman, E., 1945, "The Nature of Cities." *Annals of the American Association of Political and Social Sciences*, No. 242, pp. 7–17.

Kamm, John, 1980, "Importing Some of Hong Kong . . . Exporting Some of China." *The China Business Review*, Vol. 7, No. 2 (Mar.–Apr.), pp. 28–35.

King, F. H., 1926, *Farmers of Forty Centuries.* London: Jonathan Cape Ltd.

Lo, Chor-pang, Pannell, Clifton W., and Welch, Roy A., 1977, "Land Use Changes and City Planning in Shenyang and Canton." *Geographical Review*, Vol. 67, No. 3 (July), pp. 268–283.

Lo, C. P., 1979, "Spatial Form and Land Use Patterns of Modern Chinese Cities: An Exploratory Model." In Lee Ngok and Leung Chi-Keung (eds.), "China: Development and Challenge." *Proceedings of the Fifth Leverhulme Conference.* Hong Kong: Centre of Asian Studies University of Hong Kong, pp. 233–272.

Ma, Laurence J. C., 1971, *Commercial Development and Urban Change in Sung China 960–1279.* Ann Arbor: University of Michigan, Department of Geography, Publication No. 6.

Ma, Laurence J. C., 1977, "Counterurbanization and Rural Development: The Strategy of Hsia-Hsiang." *Current Scene*, Vol. 15, Nos. 8 and 9, pp. 1–12.

Ma, Laurence J. C., 1979, "The Chinese Approach to City Planning: Policy, Administration and Action." *Asian Survey*, Vol. 19, pp. 838–855.

Murphey, Rhoads, 1954, *Shanghai, Key to Modern China.* Cambridge, Mass.: Harvard University Press.

Murphey, Rhoads, 1974, "The Treaty Ports and China's Modernization." In M. Elvin and G. W. Skinner (eds.), *The Chinese City Between Two Worlds.* Stanford, Calif.: Stanford University Press, pp. 17–72.

Murphey, Rhoads, 1980, *The Fading of the Maoist Vision.* New York: Metheun.

Orleans, Leo A., 1959, "The Recent Growth of China's Urban Population." *Geographical Review*, Vol. 49, pp. 43–57.

Pannell, C. W., 1981, "Recent Growth and Change in China's Urban System." In Laurence J. C. Ma and Edward Hanten (eds.), *Urban Development in Modern China.* Boulder, Colo.: Westview Press, pp. 91–113.

Pannell, C. W. and Welch, R., 1980, "Recent Growth and Structural Change in Chinese Cities." *Urban Geography*, Vol. 1, No. 1, pp. 68–80.

Rozman, Gilbert, 1973, *Urban Networks in Ch'ing China and Tokugawa Japan.* Princeton: Princeton University Press.

Salter, Christopher L., 1972, "Hsia-Fang: The Use of Migration by the Chinese in Their Quest for a Classless Society." *Proceedings of the Association of American Geographers*, Vol. 4, pp. 96–99.

Salter, Christopher L., 1976, "Chinese Experiments in Urban Space: The Quest for an Agrapolitan China." *Habitat*, Vol. 1, No. 1, pp. 19–35.

Skinner, G. W. (ed.), 1977, *The City in Late Imperial China.* Stanford, Calif.: Stanford University Press, pp. 3–31; 211–249.

Skinner, G. William, 1978, "Vegetable Supply and Marketing in Chinese Cities." *The China Quarterly*, Vol. 76, pp. 733–793.

Tien, H. Yuan, 1973, *China's Population Struggle, Demographic Decisions of the People's Republic, 1949–1969.* Columbus: Ohio State University Press.
Towers, Graham, 1973, "City Planning in China." *Journal of the Royal Town Planning Institute*, Vol. 59, pp. 125–127.
Trewartha, Glenn T., 1951, "Chinese Cities: Numbers and Distribution." *Annals of the Association of American Geographers*, Vol. 41, No. 4, pp. 331–347.
Ullman, Morris B., 1961, *Cities of Mainland China: 1953 and 1958.* Washington, D.C.: Bureau of the Census, International Population Reports, Series No. 59, p. 95.
United Nations Department of Economic and Social Affairs, 1973, *Pilot Housing Project in Central America.* New York: United Nations.
Wu, Yuan-li, 1967, *The Spatial Economy of Communist China.* New York: Frederick Praeger.
Yao, Shihmou, Shen, Daoqi and Chang, Fubao, 1981, "The Development of Minor Cities and Towns in China." In Laurence J. C. Ma and Allen Noble (eds.), *The Environment: Chinese and American Views.* New York: Metheun, pp. 243–252.
Chengshi yongdi xuance ji fangan bijiao (The Selection of Urban Land Use and Comparative Plans), 1976. Beijing: Architecture Publishing House.
Zhongguo Dituce, China Map Folio, 1980. Shanghai: Atlas Publishers.

Chapter 10

Changing Taiwan

Contemporary Taiwan offers many contrasts and much internal diversity. Progress and poverty, modern methods and traditional manners, urbane Chinese scholars and diplomats and backward tribal mountain people, booming cities and stagnating villages, mainland Chinese nationalists and independent Taiwanese loyalists are some of the many contrasts of contemporary Taiwan. One is surprised by so much diversity and so many contrasts, for Taiwan is a small island, about the size of Maryland and Delaware combined, with a considerable degree of physical homogeneity.

Located 160 kilometers off the coast of southeast China (Fig. 10-1) and densely populated by the descendants of Chinese migrants, Taiwan would be expected to be cohesive and homogeneous, for it is a small and accessible place. Yet an accessible location and international politics have made Taiwan an unusual and highly distinctive place. Its role as a refuge for Chinese nationalists following Communist ascendancy on the mainland in 1949 has promoted a cultural mosaic of great variety among the population. Today the island is in some ways a microcosm of mainland China. The mainland's troubles and successes are mirrored in contemporary events on this small island and in the lives of the island's 18 million inhabitants.

Taiwan cannot logically be divorced from China, for the two are linked by geography, culture, and history. Contemporary politics and relations between China and Taiwan indicate that Taiwan's destiny is associated intimately with China's

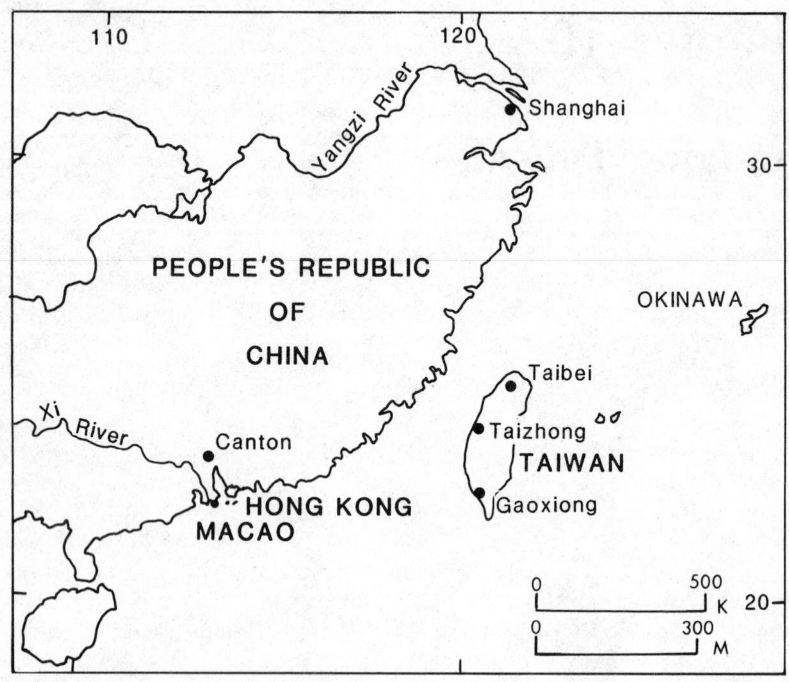

Fig. 10-1. Location map of Taiwan, Hong Kong, and Macao.

HISTORICAL BACKGROUND

Chinese from the southern provinces of Fujian (Fukien) and Guangdong (Kwangtung) have been migrating to Taiwan and the adjacent Pescadores Islands for many centuries, although only in the last three and a half centuries have the numbers of such migrants been significant enough to justify the incorporation of Taiwan as a part of the Chinese polity.[14] As early as the 9th century A.D., historical records indicate Chinese were migrating to the Pescadores, the stepping stone to Taiwan. A permanent colony of Chinese was established. The name Linchiu (Liu-ch'iu), the same name as that for the neighboring Ryukyus, had long been used to describe Taiwan as well as other islands in the East China Sea. All of these islands were to some extent territory shared and sometimes contested by three groups: Chinese immigrants, Japanese pirates, and Taiwanese natives (Davidson, 1903; Kuo, 1973).

Probably the first settlers of Chinese origin to establish permanent habitation on Taiwan were refugees, who in the 13th century were seeking to escape from

[14]For a good, comprehensive historical geography see Knapp (1978, 1980).

the scourge of invading Mongols. In that century, the first imperial administrative office was established in the Pescadores. This political fact may be interpreted as legitimizing the inclusion of the Pescadorean and Taiwanese archipelago as distinctly Chinese territory. Despite the early administrative claims, conditions of piracy in 1388 forced the closing of the local administrative office and resulted in the waning of Chinese influence for two centuries. It was not until 1558 that the Chinese reestablished an administrative presence in the Pescadores.

Only in the late 16th or 17th century did significant permanent Chinese settlement take place on the island of Taiwan. From 1620 on, Chinese commercial figures and entrepreneurs began to visit Taiwan regularly and to promote settlement on the southwest coast in places such as Beigang (Pei-kang), Anping (Tainan), and farther south. For nearly half a century, European colonial powers were influential. The Dutch controlled Taiwan from 1624 to 1662. In fact, their control was focused on a few key places—the major coastal settlements along the southwest periphery and the northern port city of Jilong (Keelung). The interior uplands of the island were inhabited by native tribes, who were independent of any but their own control. The larger interior plains and basins were in the process of agricultural colonization by Chinese (Hsieh, 1964).

Internal politics and the overturn of the Ming Dynasty by the Manchus resulted in far-reaching changes in Taiwan. It was a Chinese Ming loyalist exile, Cheng Cheng-Kung (Koxinga), who was able to marshal sufficient military strength to cast out the Dutch colonials and establish Taiwan as a refuge for Ming loyalists. Cheng was also able to promote extensive immigration of Chinese exiles to Taiwan and was important in peopling the island with those of Chinese origin. At no time since Cheng's rule has there ever been a question that Taiwan's population is not predominantly of Chinese origin.

Beginnings of Modernization

The Ming loyalists held out for two decades, but in 1683 the island was incorporated into the Manchu Empire. For two centuries thereafter, Taiwan remained a prefecture of Fukien Province and a frontier of Chinese settlement; the island occupied a strategic Pacific location, but with China's inward orientation of that period, it was not critically important. By the late 19th century, with the increasing threat of foreign intervention of Europeans and Japanese and the establishment of treaty ports, Taiwan's special importance and vulnerability had become obvious to the Manchu court. Consequently, in 1888, the Manchu Emperor established Taiwan as a separate Chinese province and upgraded its administrative position to keep pace with the island's commercial and strategic significance (Kuo, 1973, pp. 171-240).

A new governor, Liu Ming-ch'üan, was appointed in 1885, and he set about promoting a number of reforms and development projects aimed at the modernization of the island. These new efforts continued the many development projects initiated a decade earlier by the then commissioner of Taiwan, Shen Baozhen (Shen Pao-chen). Shen's projects had been aimed primarily at expanding the road network in order to integrate the island spatially and to permit the pacification of the native tribes. One part of this policy further encouraged the opening of interior areas to Chinese settlement and the promotion of increased Chinese agricultural colonization (Davidson, 1903).

Liu continued not only to improve the military defenses of Taiwan, but, more importantly, to extend the projects of Shen Pao-chen. New roads and a railroad were built, more interior settlement was encouraged, a new land survey was ordered, and fiscal reform in the tax system was instituted. This was a brief but progressive period for Taiwan. Unfortunately, the Sino-Japanese War of 1894-1895 interrupted the rapid Chinese development based on the new reforms. The Chinese lost the war. The terms of the Treaty of Shimonoseki, which settled the conflict, transferred the island of Taiwan from China to Japan. The effect of this transfer was to relegate all Chinese citizens to the status of Japanese colonial subjects. A short-lived uprising by the residents of Taiwan to oppose this transfer of authority was met with force by the Japanese, and the Taiwan loyalists were quickly subdued. By the end of the year, resistance had been crushed, and Taiwan entered a period of 50 years as a colony of Japan.

The Japanese Period: Economic Growth and Political Stagnation

Japanese colonialism of Taiwan was not a happy time for Taiwan's people, for the Taiwanese, like colonials everywhere, were disenfranchised politically and forced into a sort of second-class status, which largely excluded them from the same educational and administrative opportunities available to Japanese. The colonial period was not, however, without benefit for Taiwan. There is considerable evidence that the Japanese efforts at economic modernization and development were successful in setting the stage for later gains achieved in the post-World War II period (Ho, 1978). Examples of Japanese enterprise and direction were most dramatic in two sectors–capital improvements and agriculture. Capital improvements in the Taiwanese infrastructure, completed during the Japanese colonial period, included a series of route network expansion projects associated with the north-south railway and highways that gave the island a modern and integrated transportation system by the mid-1920s (Hsu, Pannell, and Wheeler, 1980). Closely linked with these transportation projects were the construction of modern deep water ports at the northern Keelung (Jilong) and southern Kaohsiung (Gaoxiong) ends of the island, and the provision of supportive cargo handling equipment. Interior cites were also developed. Modern town planning was introduced as cities were redesigned and, in some cases, rebuilt with modern street layouts. A modern power grid was developed, and major investments in hydroelectric power production were made.

A fundamental alteration of the agricultural system was an equally important contribution. This was made possible by investments in large irrigation projects. Such projects plus advances in agronomy, marketing, and distribution of commodities led to rapid increases in production and the commercialization of the agricultural system (Myers and Ching, 1964; Lee, 1971). The evidence, as indicated in Figure 10-2, suggests that Japanese-directed efforts in the agricultural sector were successful in transforming the traditional cellular structure of rural economic

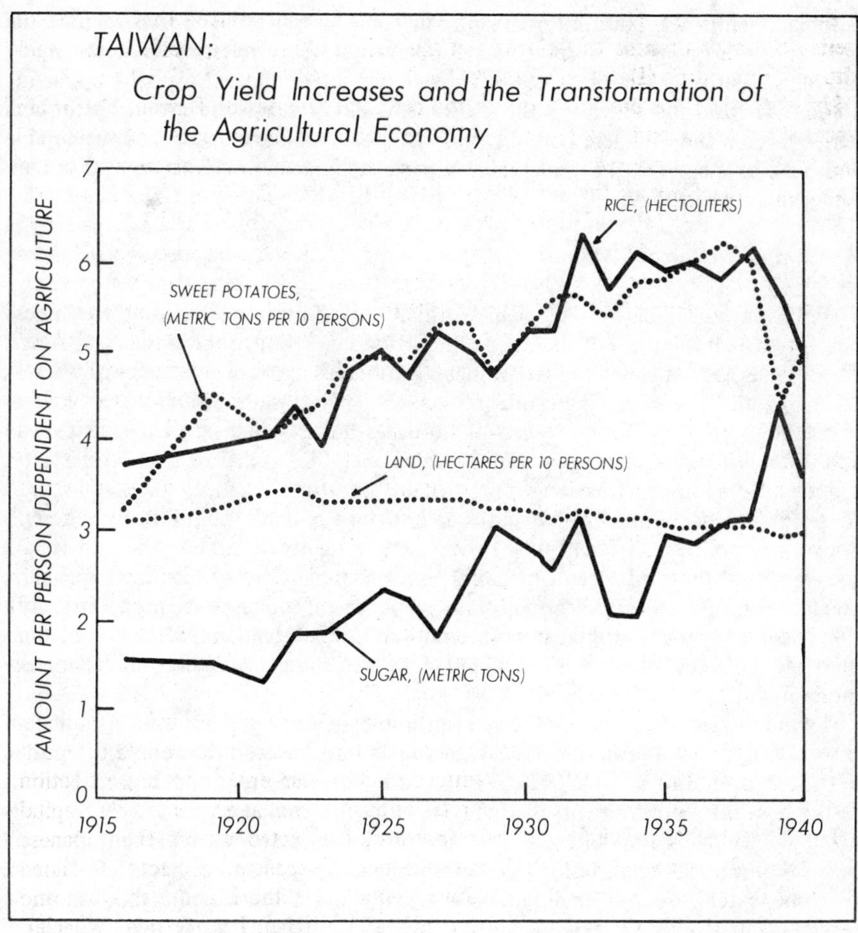

Fig. 10-2. Historical development of Taiwan's agricultural economy. *Source:* Barclay (1954, p. 55).

activities into a commercial agriculture that involved the island-wide transfer of commodities and foodstuffs.

Another significant aspect of colonialism was the introduction of new techniques in medicine and public health and the resulting rapid decline in the island's death rate. Without a concomitant decline in birth rates, the net effect was to produce a rapidly growing population. More on this dramatic population growth will follow in a succeeding section. The point is that the underpinnings for a modern economy were laid down during the 50 years of Japanese colonial rule. This was accomplished at some cost to the Taiwanese population, for the Japanese colonial regime was authoritarian and, in some cases, even oppressive. But the developmental gains were solid and fundamental. The investments were largely internally derived, for after 1908 Taiwan was predominantly a self-supporting colony. It was not easy, for the Taiwanese, but it seems clear that there were benefits from the Japanese colonial period. The economic gains were considerable and set the stage for the remarkable growth and rapid modernization that continues in Taiwan today.

Restoration to China: 1945

Following the Japanese defeat in World War II, Taiwan was restored to Chinese control as part of the Potsdam Agreement for a postwar order among the Allies. The island has remained under Chinese Nationalist control ever since. In 1949, following the Communist ascendancy on the mainland, the Nationalist government, supported by almost 1 million refugees and soldiers, retreated to Taiwan and established an exile government in Taipei (Taibei), Taiwan's largest city. The first decade of restoration was a difficult one for Taiwan, as the island sought to restore its economic growth patterns and find a viable political environment. Social and political differences between local residents (Southern Min and Hakka speakers) and those of recent mainland Chinese origin (largely Mandarin speakers) created considerable stress initially. In some cases, violence resulted. But with the passing of time, compulsory instruction in the Mandarin dialect, the intermarriage between local and mainland Chinese, these differences have become more muted.

Economic growth since 1960 has been impressive and perhaps even spectacular. But recently, new international political trends have favored the People's Republic of China over Taiwan. In 1971 Taiwan was expelled from the United Nations as the legitimate government of China. In 1979 the United States officially recognized the People's Republic of China and no longer recognized Taiwan, although a close unofficial relationship was established. These actions have left Taiwan to some extent isolated and with few friends and allies. Despite these political reverses and the uncertainty of future events, Taiwan continues to prosper economically, and the Nationalist government prides itself on its record of modernization. The modernization of the island forms the main theme of this chapter. An evaluation of Taiwan's future prospects will be provided in the concluding summary.

THE PHYSICAL ENVIRONMENT

Most of the islands that rim the eastern flank of the Eurasian landmass are mountainous, and Taiwan is no exception. Lying 160 km east of the Chinese province of Fukien across the shallow Taiwan Strait, the egg-shaped island resembles a giant block tilted up on its eastward margin to form a sharp dip into the Pacific. A series of north-south trending ridges form the interior of the island (the Central Mountains) and slope more gently westward blending into a series

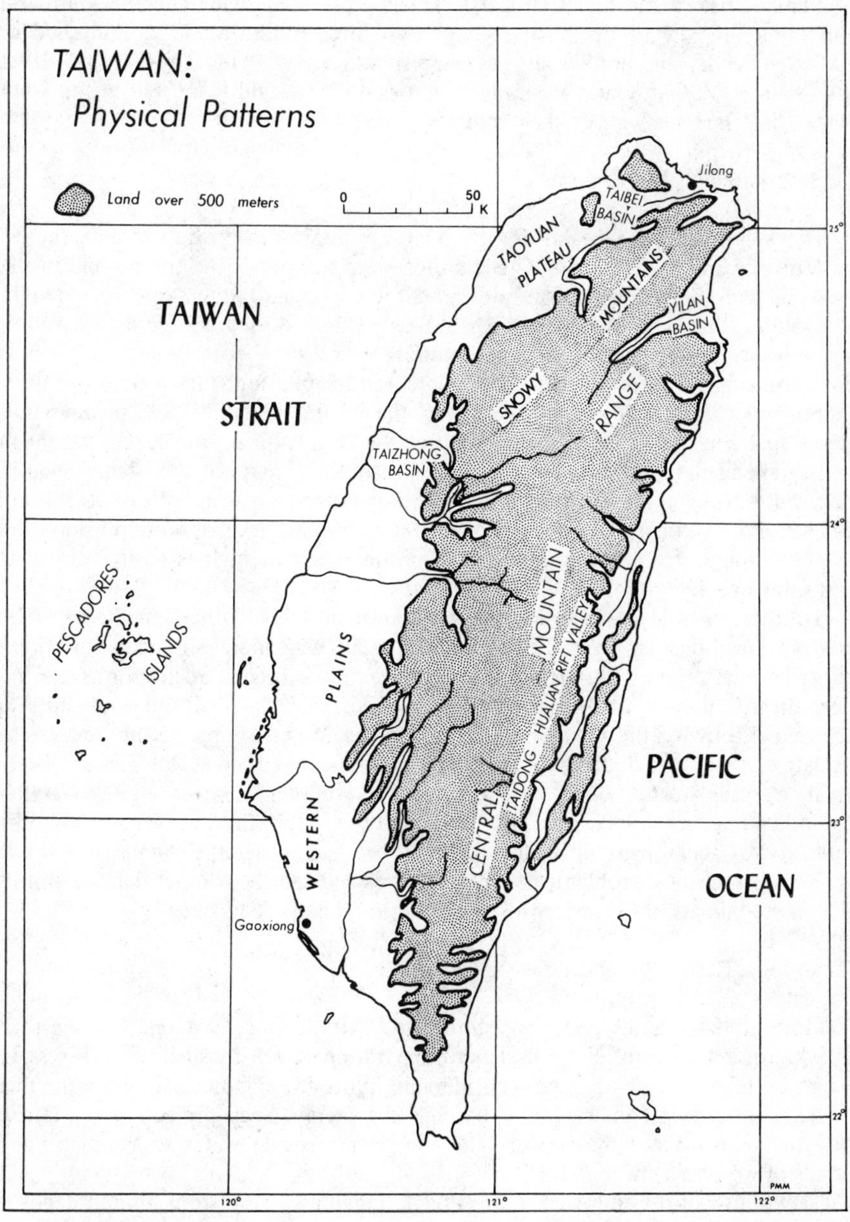

Fig. 10-3. Physiography of Taiwan.
Source: Chang (1972).

of flanking basins and plains (Fig. 10-3). These plains are widest in the southwest and taper off toward the north. About two-thirds of the island is composed of rugged uplands, and numerous peaks crest above 3,000 m. The island's tallest mountain is Yushan (Jade Mountain). It rises 4,000 m and is located inland from Jiayi (Chia-i), almost astride the Tropic of Cancer.

Climate Variables and Patterns

The location of the island and its main mountain range result in a distinctive pattern of climate. Taiwan lies on the northeast margin of the tropics and in the path of prevailing East Asian monsoon-influenced air circulation patterns. In general, weather is influenced by northeasterly winds during the winter and southwesterly winds during the warmer, summer months. In both cases, these winds are marine influenced and bring considerable precipitation; many stations report 2,560 mm or more of rainfall. However, the locational variation in precipitation is seasonal (Fig. 10-4). The northern tip of the island, for example, receives much of its rain in the winter, while the west and southern parts of the island, lying in the winter orographic shadow, have a comparatively dry and pleasant autumn and winter. By contrast, the south and west commonly receive more precipitation in the summer from the southwest monsoon. Only at high elevations do frost and snow occur.

To this general pattern of circulation must be added other climate variables common in monsoon Asia. The summer months, with increased insolation, often experience afternoon thunderstorms of convectional origin. Such storms are important, for they contribute needed rainfall to those agricultural landscapes in the rain shadow of the prevailing southwesterlies. More striking are the characteristic late summer and autumn typhoons which annually sweep across Taiwan. These great tropical storms, originating east of the Philippines, bring enough rainfall to indicate a secondary seasonal peaking of precipitation. Unfortunately, the intensity of accompanying winds and rain wreak considerable damage. Flooding is the most serious problem, and past records indicate occasional massive storms that cause human and property losses in both rural and urban areas.

Hydrology, Resources, and Soils

Most of the island's rivers are short and swift flowing. Not one is more than 105 km in length, and all are useless for navigation except by shallow draft vessels. Some of these streams possess considerable hydropower potential, and a number of dams have been constructed to harness this energy. Such projects are generally tied to irrigation systems as well, and the rivers provide water to the plains and basins of western Taiwan.

Taiwan is poorly endowed with valuable minerals. Aside from limited deposits of coal, copper, sulphur, and gold, all of which have been mined heavily since Japanese colonial times, only very modest quantities of petroleum (oil and gas) and salt exist for commercial exploitation. The extent of offshore petroleum resources is still uncertain, but preliminary surveys suggest promise for the Taiwan

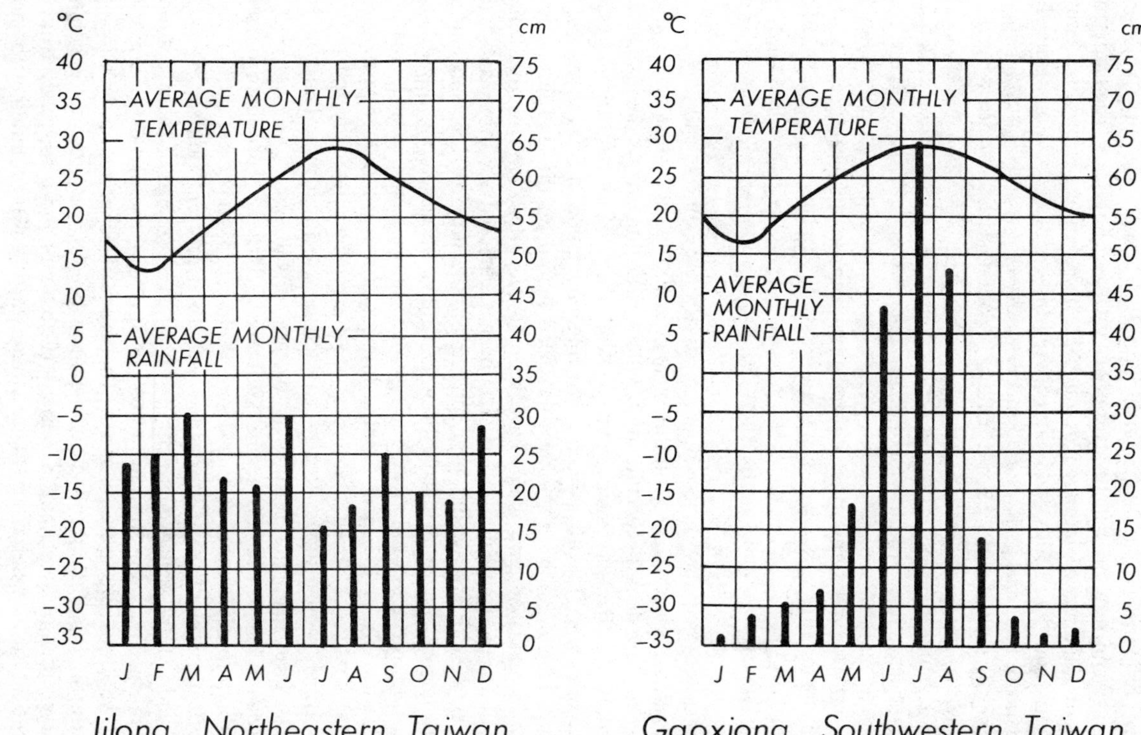

Fig. 10-4. Climate patterns of north and south Taiwan.
Source: Statistics compiled from Taiwan Provincial Government, *Taiwan Statistical Abstract*, No. 28, 1969.

Strait and East China Sea, both areas that Taiwan, China, and Japan have laid claim to.

Among the most valuable assets found on the island are the young azonal alluvial soils and planosols found throughout the western plain and basins. Although not extremely fertile or rich in nutrient materials, these soils are easy to manage and respond well to a variety of different fertilizers. The labor-intensive nature of Chinese rice farming, in which great quantities of organic material are frequently added to paddy fields, has altered the original condition of the alluvium and planosol materials and resulted in the ability of the soils to sustain high yields over long periods of time. Such a pattern is common in many other riverine areas of East Asia.

The resource base of Taiwan is very modest. The mineral supply of the island is almost negligible, although natural gas deposits in the Xinzhu (Hsin-chu) and Miaoli regions may be important, as in the manufacture of petroleum-derived fertilizers. The most important natural resources are soil, water, and forests, although the latter are insufficient to meet domestic demand.

Human Adjustments and Modification

Taiwan entered the Chinese polity relatively late, but like so many other parts of the Middle Kingdom, the imprint of man is everywhere. Most of the low-lying, level areas have long been cultivated. Where irrigation waters are available, most commonly wet rice has been grown. Since the turn of the century and especially since World War II, with a rapidly growing population and increased per capita domestic consumption, great stress has been placed on the land resources of the island. Increases in crop yields have been forced intensively. At the same time, much of the best agricultural land has been preempted for urban and industrial purposes. New emphasis has been placed on the interior slopeland and a great deal of effort and money have been expended on developing mountain lands for grazing, orchards, and tree farming. Man's impact on the landscape is everywhere, and only in the most isolated interior mountains is there a suggestion of primeval conditions. Even these locations have been altered by the presence of native tribal people known locally as Kao-shan-tsu (high mountain people) who live in enclaves analogous to American Indian reservations.

Taiwan is small (35,960 square kilometers). With its 18 million people, it is incredibly crowded—more so than Japan. As in Japan, its people, with their distinctive cultural system, have husbanded well their meager resources. Through diligence and careful management, they have taken advantage of their location, their accessibility, and their soil and water resources. A prosperous economy has resulted, yet it is precariously based. The costs of economic growth in localized environmental pollution and crowding have been great. Foul air is common in the large cities of Taipei and Kaohsiung (Gaoxiong) and increasingly troublesome in some of the smaller cities. Many streams are heavily polluted with industrial effluents, and flooding is common in low-lying areas of the largest city.

Chinese people have grappled with nature and attuned their activities to harmonize with their surroundings for many centuries. Yet the industrial experience, as seen in Taiwan, with its prosperity and mass benefits followed by the inevitable dirt and environmental degradation, is relatively new. In a place as small and congested as Taiwan, such problems are especially conspicuous and troublesome. Here, then, is another challenge for planners, politicians, and ordinary citizens to add to the chronicle of modernization in a Chinese context. How can Taiwan's natural environment be preserved and husbanded under conditions of increasing consumer demand and economic progress?

POPULATION AND POPULATION GROWTH

Taiwan's population in 1981 was approximately 18 million, a very large number of people for such a small land area (Table 10-1). Such a large population has not come about overnight, but the rapid growth of the population has taken place in this century. When the Japanese took over the island in 1895, there were about 2 million inhabitants. Japanese policy forbade the continuation of Chinese in-migration from the mainland, but a trickle of Chinese managed to sneak into Taiwan. Of greater importance, however, were Japanese efforts at curbing the traditionally high death rate. Through the introduction of modern practices of sanitation and public health, the rate of death declined sharply over several decades, while the birth rate throughout the Japanese colonial period remained high (4.4% higher per annum).

The decline in death rate continued, and during most of the Japanese period the population growth rate was above 1.0%. Indeed, from 1925 on, the annual growth rate commonly exceeded 2.0% and, by 1940, had reached 2.5% (Barclay, 1954). The final Japanese census was taken in 1943, at which time there were about 6 million Taiwanese. Since restoration, Taiwan has received an estimated 1 to 2 million immigrants from mainland China, and the population of the island has continued to grow at a rapid rate. Only since the late 1960s, with the establishment of a serious family planning organization, have the birth and growth rates begun to decline. In 1979, based on a birth rate of 2.5% and a death rate of 5%, the rate of population growth had declined slightly to 2.0%. This continued high birth rate suggests that Taiwan has had only limited success in population planning. With a population base as youthful as Taiwan's and so many potential child-bearing women still to reach marriage age, it is likely that considerable additions to the island's population will continue. At least one projection estimates the island's population at the end of the century will be about 24 million people (Population Reference Bureau, 1980).

Family Planning

The family planning program was initiated in Taiwan during the 1950s in a low-key manner. Initially, a number of influential figures opposed family planning, as they believed it contrary to Chinese customs and the thinking of the national father, Dr. Sun Yat-sen. Moreover, many thought that in the absence of modern technology, Taiwan's only hope for military strength was through rapid population

Table 10-1. Taiwan's Population Growth

Year	Total population
1905	3,039,751
1915	3,479,922
1925	3,993,408
1935	5,212,426
1940	5,872,084
1946	6,090,860
1951	7,869,247
1960	10,792,202
1965	12,628,348
1970	14,676,000
1975	16,150,000
1980	17,800,000 (est.)

Source: Taiwan Provincial Government, *Fifty One Years of Statistical Abstracts in Taiwan: Taiwan Statistical Abstract, No. 28, 1969*, Population Reference Bureau, *1975 and 1980 World Population Data Sheet*, and *Industry of Free China* (1980).

growth. In 1961, a collaborative effort uniting several Chinese and Western institutions established a Population Studies and Family Planning Center in Taichung (Taizhong). This center serves as a research and experiment center for monsoon Asia. Since its establishment, more vigorous effort has followed, and since the mid-1960s public educational efforts at family planning have been under way. Coupled with the availability of new and older techniques of birth control, the result has been a drop in the rate of birth, with the hope that this will continue until a rough replacement level has been achieved. Attitudinal changes are also involved, and a strong educational campaign has been promoted which encourages people to consider a two-child family as the most desirable norm. Nevertheless, the continuation of the high rate of birth (2.5%) indicates this campaign has had only limited success.

Training, Manpower, and Employment

The changing demographic picture in Taiwan has implications for future economic growth trends. One dimension shows up in the educational and training programs. In 1973, there were 4.34 million students at all levels in the educational system and in 1978, approximately 4.5 million.

Since 1967, free education through grade 9 has been guaranteed to every child. About two-thirds of those who finish grade 9 advance to senior high school, based on a competitive examination. Of those who graduate from high school, about three-fourths enroll in various colleges and universities. Such great emphasis on education results in a literate and highly trained population. A large number of professionals are trained in engineering and in the medical and natural sciences, accounting for more than 40% of the college and university graduates. The social sciences account for about 32%. The point is that Taiwan has developed a good system of public and private education, one that is probably more than adequate to supply the needs of the economy for skilled manpower. An extensive program of vocational training supplements the university training and helps produce skilled clerical and industrial workers. Only at the highest graduate level is Taiwan lacking training programs, and in these, the demand levels are too low, generally, to justify developing such programs.

Manpower needs and employment structure to a large extent will continue to parallel changes in the island's economic structure. The main change in that structure has been a progressive shift from an economy dependent on agriculture to one that depends more on industry and commerce (Fig. 10-5). As depicted in the graph, the share of the labor force engaged in agriculture is projected to continue declining through the end of the decade, a drop of more than one-half in the share of employment accounted for by agriculture. Such a pattern corresponds well with the growth of the island's economy and the modernization process under way within that economic system, although the real figures for 1978 indicate that industrial employment was running at a higher rate than predicted and the service sector at a slightly lower rate.

Locational Distribution and Migration of People

People in Taiwan are concentrated predominantly in the alluvial plains and basins of the western part of the island (Fig. 10-6). A remarkable association between a particular physical setting and concentration of people exists that is common throughout monsoon Asia (Hsu, 1969). These are the areas of early Chinese settlement and agricultural development, and here have been built the major transportation networks and cities (Fig. 10-7).

Major cities are spotted at intervals from Keelung and Taipei in the north through Tainan, Kaohsiung, and Pingtung in the south. The largest concentrations of people are found in the Taipei Basin in northern Taiwan and in the large plains in the southwest that contain Tainan and Kaohsiung. To the extent that people have been migrating in recent years, these movements have been primarily rural to urban in nature, with the largest cities of Taipei and Kaohsiung acting as the major attracting magnets.

Within Taiwan, population has tended not only to move to the largest cities but also to move out of the central and western plains and basins to the largest cities. One exception would be the rapid growth of Taichung in the west central part of the island. Taichung is now the island's third largest city. South of Taichung all the way to Tainan is an area from which a large out-migration has occurred, in part to larger cities within the region, i.e., to Changhua and Chia-i, but more commonly to Taichung, Tainan, or Kaohsiung.

Reasons for migration, as indicated by Speare (1972), appear to be rational economic decisions. The search for a better job takes place usually in one of the large cities. The link to occupation has been confirmed in a study by Wang (1977).

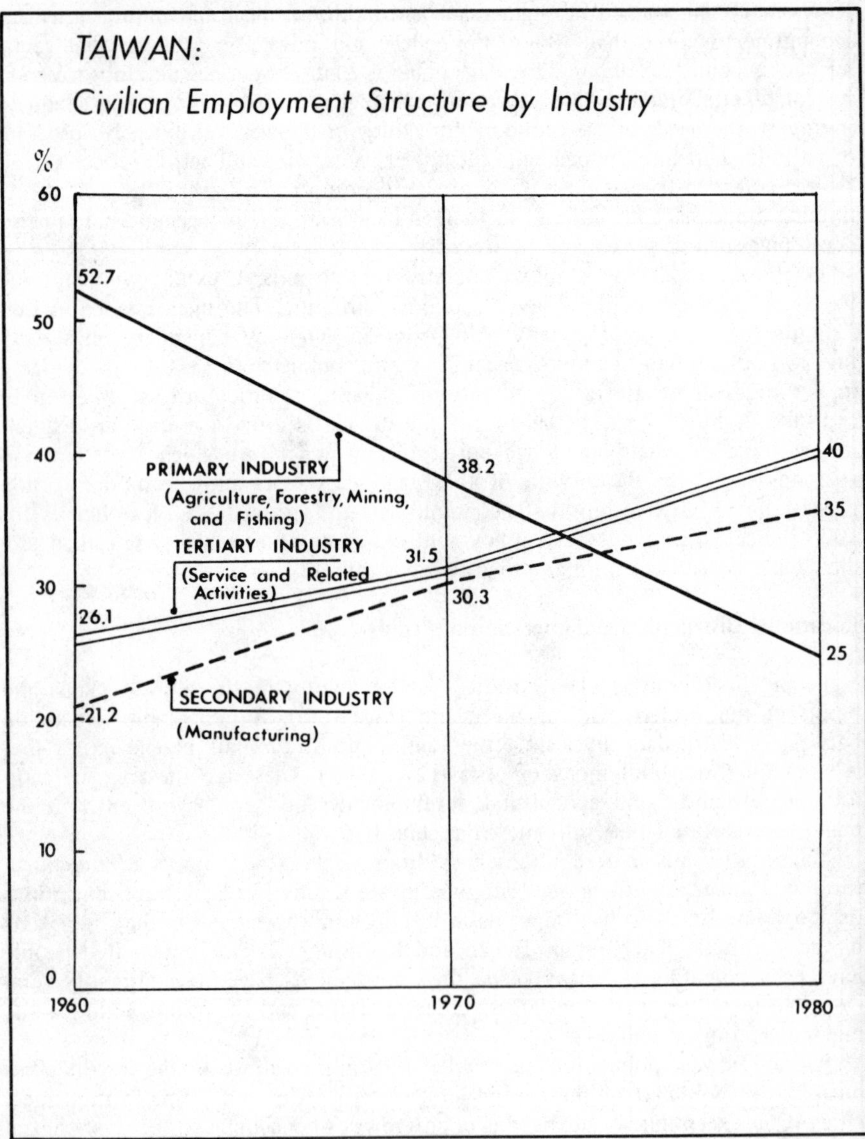

Fig. 10-5. Sectoral employment in Taiwan.
Source: Council for International Economic Cooperation and Development (1972).

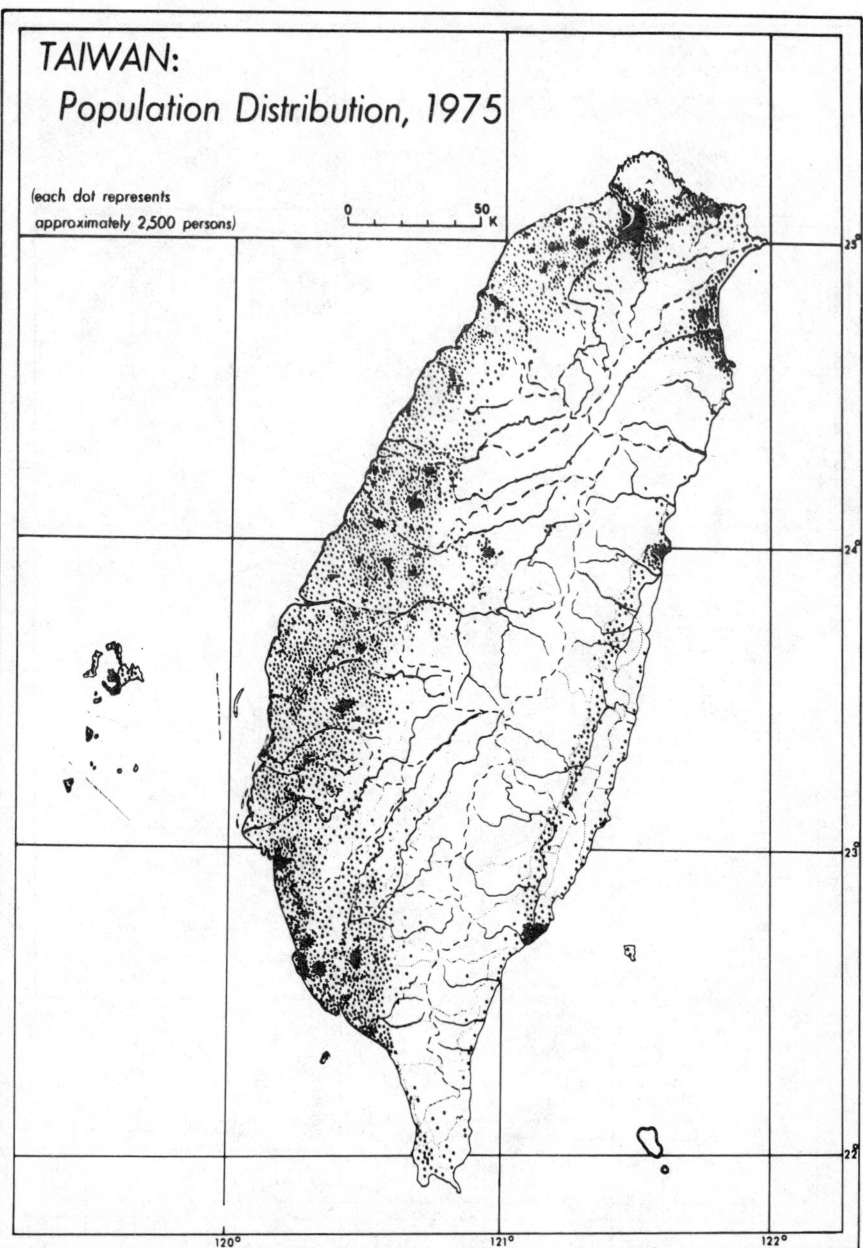

Fig. 10-6. Taiwan population distribution, 1975.
Source: Modified from Chang Chi-yun (1972). *Atlas of Taiwan.*

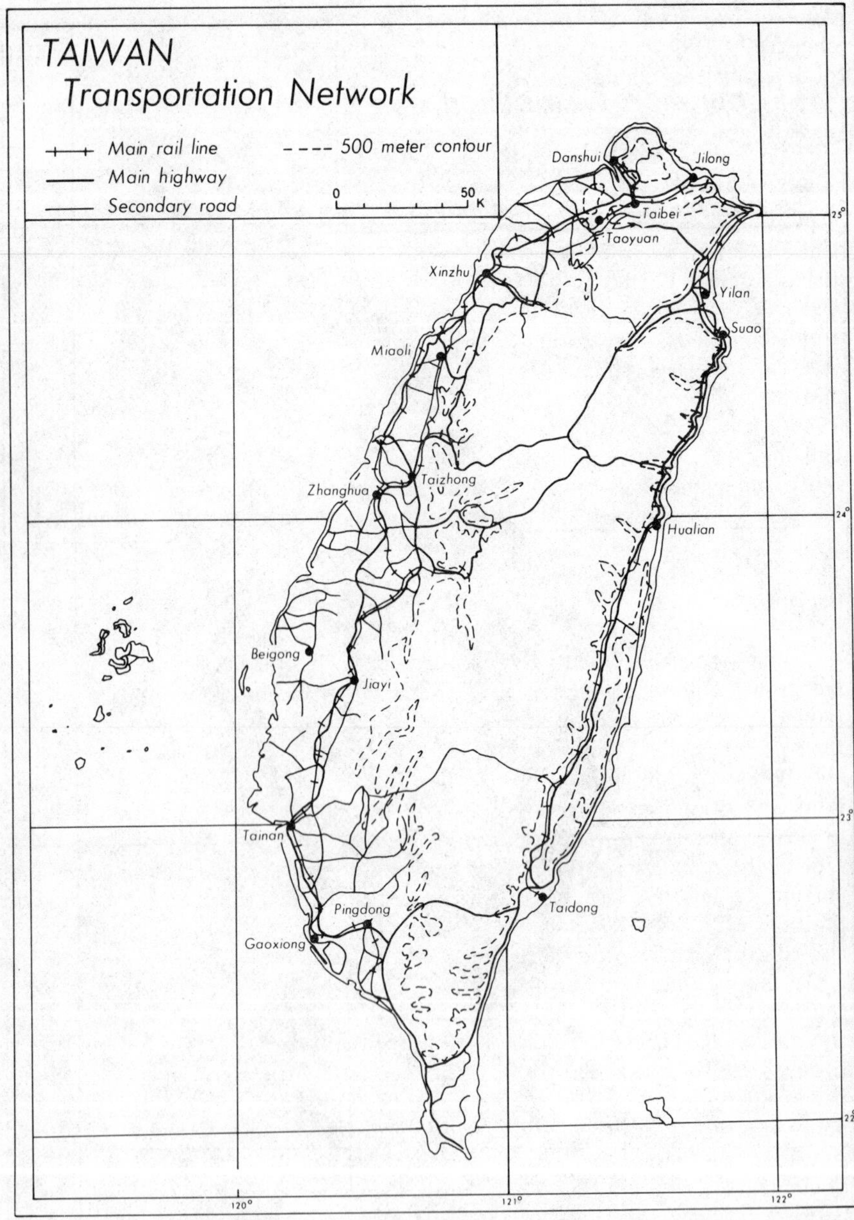

Fig. 10-7. Taiwan transportation network.
Source: Modified from Chang Chi-yun (1972).

Another important factor in such moves is the presence of close relatives (Gallin and Gallin, 1974). Such determinants of migrational behavior are representative of developing economies.

SOCIETY AND CULTURE

Taiwan's society and culture, it has been argued above, are Chinese in origin and character. Yet there are certain features that make Taiwan a separate, identifiable segment of the Chinese settled part of the earth. For example, Taiwan was a relatively recent addition to China, and prior to this century it was a crude frontier receiving Chinese immigrants, largely from Fukien and Kuangtung provinces in southeast China. A number of different dialect groups were involved, and many different religious customs and practices were brought to Taiwan. Since 1949, a new group of Chinese, largely from north and central China, have arrived, and they too brought new dialects, habits, and traditions. Fragmented tremendously and embracing refugees from every province on the mainland, this group has added a new and complicating dimension to the already varied and complex social mosaic of contemporary Taiwan.

Social Groups

Among the many identifiable ethnic and social groups on Taiwan, two groups are probably most significant: Taiwanese and Mainlander, with place of origin rather than place of birth the controlling fact. Mainlanders, although they or their parents come from every province on mainland China, came to Taiwan probably because they were involved with the Guomindang political party or Nationalist army and thus were refugees from the Communist-led takeover of the mainland in 1949. Mainlanders speak Mandarin Chinese. This group, composing roughly 19% of the population, continues to be more or less distinct, despite a considerable amount of intermarriage with Taiwanese. Mainlanders continue to occupy key positions and thus dominate the military, security, and police apparatuses, and also control the national government assembly and bureaucracy.

To assume that the remaining 81% of Taiwan's population is a cohesive, homogeneous group potentially in opposition to the mainland dominance of the island is too simple and facile, however. The remaining group is largely composed of so-called native Taiwanese, including perhaps one-quarter of a million indigenous people living in isolated mountain areas. The Taiwanese are by no means a cohesive group, and they are divided into several dialectical groups (Fig. 10-8).

Of the Taiwanese, the largest segment, 68% was reported to be of Fukienese origin. Among this group, certain minor dialectical and ethnic differences exist between Hokkien and Hoklo; the distinction is minor, and the two can be treated as a common group. Another 13% of the Taiwanese are composed of the descendants of migrants from Kuangtung (Guangdong) Province. Most of these people were Hakka-speaking (K'e-chia or Kejia ren), and in the past never got along well with Taiwanese citizens of Fukienese origin.

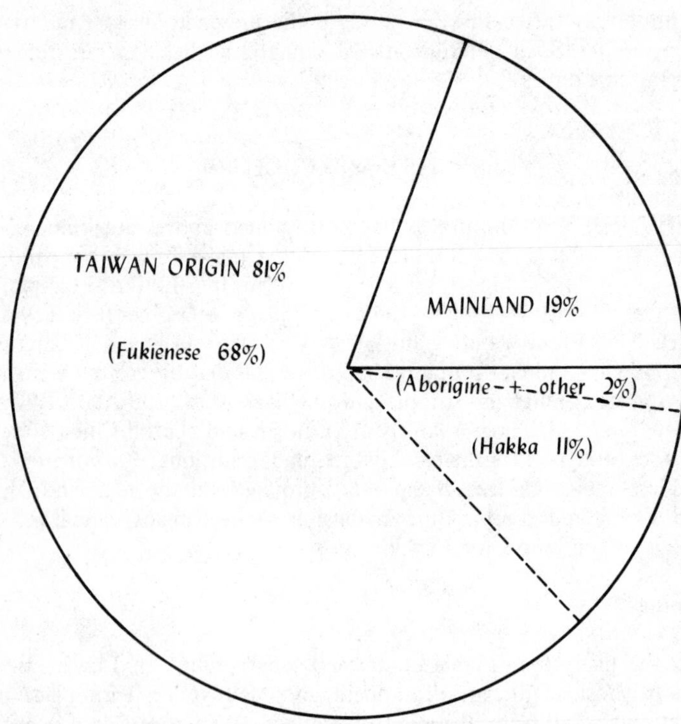

Fig. 10-8. Ethnic origin of Taiwan's population, 1975.

Note: Several sources were consulted and all are believed reliable. Discrepancies among these, however, suggest the above figures are estimates and should be treated carefully.

The Hakkas have located traditionally in the foothills of northwestern and central Taiwan, with a small group in the southern foothills near the city of Pingtung. The Taiwanese of Fukienese origin have traditionally occupied the plains and basins along the west coast. Where the two groups were in close proximity and competing for agricultural land, as in the area around Hsin-chu or Feng-yuan, hostility and animosity were endemic. Much of the rebellion and social turmoil of 19th century Taiwan was likely related to this. In fact, disputes and fighting occurred between these two ethnic groups, although such local uprisings might have been described historically as fighting against the Manchu regime (Pasternak, 1972).

Religion and Religious Practices

In contemporary Taiwan, religious freedom is a constitutionally guaranteed right. Taipei, in addition to its traditional Confucian, Buddhist, Taoist, and folk temples, contains a large mosque and a number of Christian churches of many different sects. Religion for most of the inhabitants of Taiwan is like traditional Chinese religion as practiced in other places, a blend of assorted forms and customs in which worship of ancestors and locally important deities are most important. In addition, as specific occasions demand, veneration of Buddhism, Taoism, or Confucianism may take place and supplement the more commonplace forms of worship.

Chinese religion and religious practices as they exist today in Taiwan are fundamentally different from western religions. First, religious beliefs involve a number of different deities, many of which may be local in character. The exclusive monotheistic nature of the three great Western religions of Judaism, Christianity, and Islam is alien to this traditional polytheistic Chinese approach. Second, Chinese religious adherence is often not formalized through weekly attendance and regular participation in the affairs of a temple or church. Participation is sporadic and depends more on annual occurrences tied in usually to a lunar calendar or to some crisis in the life of the individual. Thus, if a person is having difficulty of some sort, he may seek relief through a religious soothsayer or shaman; he may go to a temple and seek guidance through traditional methods of divination, such as casting divination blocks or sticks. Objects of special veneration may often be associated with nature, particularly large or unusually shaped trees or boulders, for example. Chinese peasants have always been in close contact with nature and its vagaries. Nature and natural forces as objects of worship and veneration are logical to Chinese peasants (Wolf, 1974; Kramer and Wu, 1970).

Particularly important in Taiwan is the goddess Matsu (patroness of the sea and seafarers), but there exists a large number of other local deities. Temples tend to be largely local in scope and attraction. The informality of Taiwanese folk religion results in considerable overlap of temple deities, and many of the same well-known gods will appear in large temples. Another critical factor in temple origin and support is the presence of a specific clan or common surname association. Powerful and wealthy clans have traditionally developed their own temples, and many of these have managed to survive even in large urban areas.

Among the more interesting features of contemporary Taiwanese religions is the activity associated with ritual festivals or *baibai* (pai-pai), as they are termed locally. Such festivals involve great and expensive preparations and often include the sacrifice of a large hog. Parades and celebrations focused around the temple being ritualized bring together great numbers of people. Large offerings of food and wine are presented. Incense fills the air, and quantities of paper money are burned as offerings to ancestors. Despite governmental efforts to tone down the energy and money consumed in the numerous *baibai*, the custom persists and forms an important aspect of Taiwanese culture in both urban and rural areas.

Social Organization and Customs

The primary unit of social organization in Taiwan, as in China, traditionally has been the family. The Nationalist Government, which sees itself as the legitimate bearer of Chinese civilization based on the Confucian ethic, pursues social policies that continue to emphasize the primacy of the family and family life. Despite such policies, some change in traditional social relations is under way. These changes are more obvious in urban areas, but it is the urban areas that increasingly dominate the society.

Among the most significant challenges to traditional family norms is the shift away from the idea that a large family with many sons is most desirable. Policies of family planning coupled with crowded conditions in urban areas have resulted in a trend toward two or three children as a desired norm. Moreover, many families in urban areas exist as nuclear units composed of parents and children only. It is true that certain areas of cities contain small clusters of related individuals, usually based on common surnames, and recent migrants to the city will often seek shelter with a brother or sister. However, modernization and urbanization are powerful forces, and tendencies toward smaller familial groupings seem well established.

Rural society is also changing, for modern mass media (including television) extend everywhere in Taiwan. The ideal of a smaller family with greater benefits to all members is a powerful message. Greater economic opportunities in the neighboring cities and towns have drained off many people. During planting and harvest season, labor shortages appear in many rural areas. Traditional customs persist, however. The extended family unit, in which the senior male presides over a dwelling unit that contains the families of several sons, is still common in small villages.

Taiwan's rural society today differs from the image of traditional village life in China; in no way can villages in Taiwan be considered isolated and cellular units cut off from the mainstream of the island's modernizing economic, political, and social forces. Few places are without modern means of communication. The transportation network promotes the rapid and efficient circulation of people, goods, money, and information.

Cultural Impact on the Landscape

Taiwan is an extremely crowded place. With about 18 million people in 1980 occupying a land area a little larger than New Hampshire, the average population density is more than 500 per square kilometer. In fact, as noted previously, the population is concentrated in the western third of the island, and effective densities are considerably higher. In places, Taiwan's rural population density is higher than suburban densities in the United States. Under conditions of such crowding, the effects of man are ubiquitous.

Although the island has been settled relatively recently in China's history, the agricultural imprint of peasant farmers is heavily stamped throughout the alluvial plains and basins of western Taiwan. The paddy fields replicate, in remarkable degree, patterns common in southeastern China. Everywhere streams have been dammed and canalized. Irrigation systems are common, and large bulwarks have been constructed to protect against periodic wet season flooding. Accessible uplands have been cleared and tea, sisal, citronella, banana, orange, or acacia trees planted. In more remote, higher locations, forests have been cleared to be replaced by pastures and orchards, although a large reserve of forests remains in the Central Mountains. Grave sites are common. In the Pescadores, an early site of Chinese colonization, more than 10% of the total arable land is taken up in burial mounds. This is obviously a serious impediment to agricultural production and economic progress (Pannell, 1973).

During the few centuries Chinese settlers have been in Taiwan, they have been very active in exploiting good agricultural land intensively. The very nature of the agrarian society and its dynamic demographic situation led quickly to great stress being placed on the limited land resources, for the island offered scant resources other than its productive agricultural environment for so many people.

Throughout China, traditional social behavior provided for equal inheritance of the family's land among all surviving sons. Such an equal division resulted in ever smaller landholdings among each succeeding generation. In areas settled for a long time, a serious problem of land fragmentation occurred. Out-migration was one solution that provided a safety valve where population densities were great. In recent decades, rapid population growth has aggravated this difficulty, for fragmented landholdings are inefficient to farm. Out-migration is no longer a satisfactory solution, because little new land for agricultural colonization is available. Moreover, rapidly growing cities and their supporting transportation systems, situated as they are on the most productive agricultural land, have been consuming land for urban uses as rapidly as new farmland could be created.

Such a situation, common throughout other modernizing areas in East Asia, has been especially serious in Taiwan. New approaches to land management and new policies for urban growth are being studied. One alternative considered in Taiwan is the more intensive development of previously neglected slope and plateau land (Williams, 1981). Recent projects, such as the new international airport at Taoyuan and the north-south expressway, aim to consume more marginal land and avoid the best agricultural land (Fig. 10-9). In part, this may be accomplished, but the necessity of serving the already sited cities works at cross-purposes to the policy goals. A major challenge thus exists to planners and policymakers to monitor carefully the productive land resources and seek new solutions to modernization and urban growth in the adjacent uplands.

POLITICAL AND ADMINISTRATIVE GEOGRAPHY

The location of Taiwan on the eastern flank of China has resulted in a somewhat tenuous political situation for the island. As with so many of the peripheral areas of China, Taiwan has been a frontier for agricultural colonization and has often been contested territory between China and its neighbors (Knapp, 1980). Only about a century ago did the island become a full-fledged, effective political territory, and that status was cut short as a result of Japanese military activity.

The Island as Chinese Political Territory

The political history, thus, has been checkered. Taiwan was first settled by tribal people of proto-Malay origin and later colonized by Chinese peasants. A

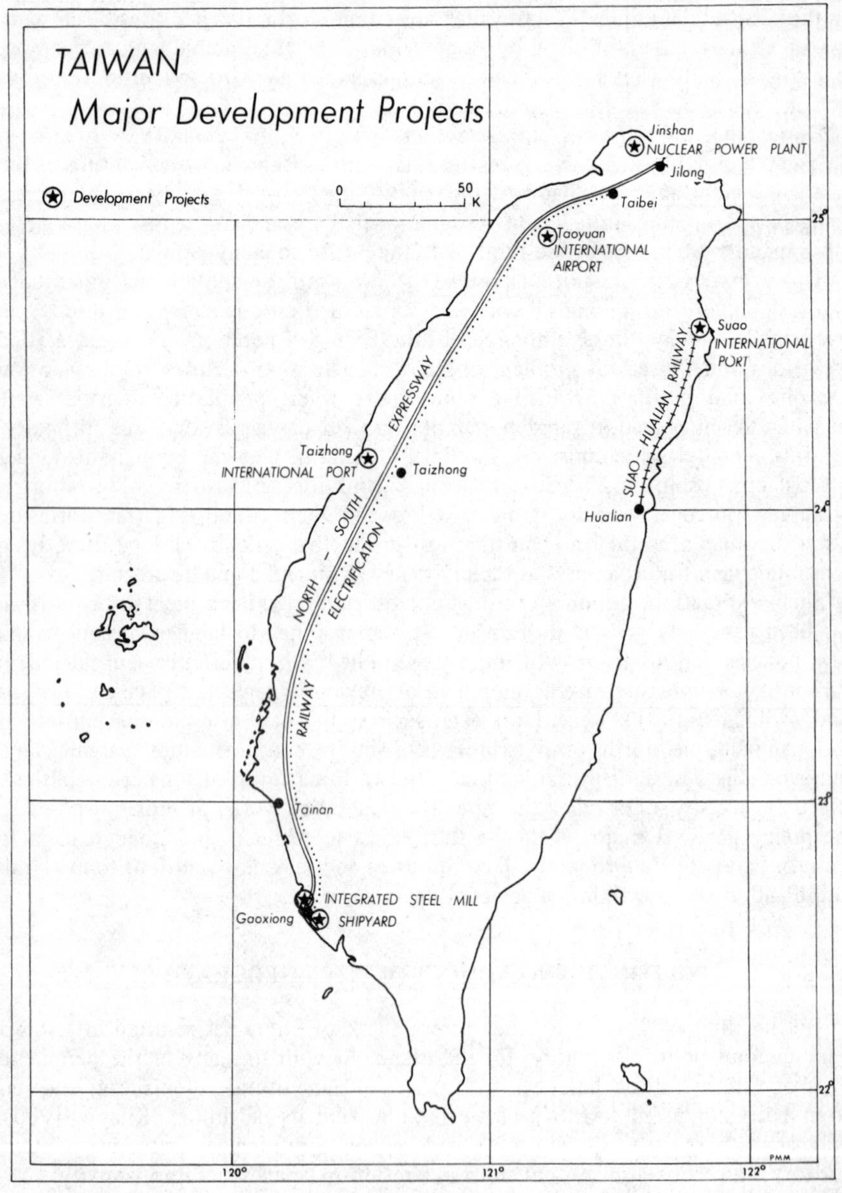

Fig. 10-9. Recent major development projects. Some have been completed; others are in progress; while some are still under study.

Source: Compiled from government sources.

half-century of European colonial control followed in the early 17th century, and this was succeeded by restoring the island to Chinese control. Until 1888, the island was administratively attached to Fukien province as a subunit. In 1888, the imperial authority apparently became convinced of the seriousness of foreign threats and upgraded the status of the island. Taiwan became a province with an imperially-appointed governor. Fifty years of Japanese colonial rule began in 1895 and interrupted Chinese sovereignty. The Japanese imposed a different type of administrative organization. However, in 1945, with restoration of a Chinese government over the island, a Chinese-style administrative organization was reimposed. This system and its territorial units of organization continue today and give political unity and coherence to the operations and effectiveness of the government.

The Administrative Apparatus: Space and Function

Political systems rely to a large extent on their supporting administrative structures and organizations for successful preservation of control of the territory of the state. While the Chinese system of political control and governance as maintained in Taiwan may not be specifically unique, it is distinct from certain other forms of administrative and political organization.

First, the nature of Chinese political administration as practiced in Taiwan is comprehensive in scope and organizes all the territory of the province into functional units. Administrative units extend from the province and major cities and counties (hsien, *xian*) down to individual neighborhoods in urban and rural areas. From those neighborhoods, it is possible to extend political contact and responsibility directly to the family and its individual members. Although this system of extending responsibility and political and police control all the way to individual citizens is not an obvious and articulated aspect of political control today, the mechanism for such control exists and could be used anytime the political situation necessitated its use.

At every level of this detailed administrative structure and its territorial component (Fig. 10-10), there is an office or individual who exercises some degree of control over that territory and is responsible, at least for informational purposes, for affairs and events that take place within that territory. In this way, the territory of contemporary Taiwan is governed and functions as effective political space.

Figure 10-10 indicates that in 1968 Taiwan had many different spatial units of political organization at several different levels in the tiered hierarchy. Areas of greatest population concentration and density have more smaller units of political administration. It is an established truism that such areas function better as politically effective territory than do, for example, remote and sparsely populated mountain areas. The detailed nature of the administrative structure insures that this will be so, for in the inaccessible, sparsely settled mountain areas of Taiwan, administrative units are large and tend to be cohesive only insofar as common physiographic patterns prevail.

Contemporary Taiwan is like so many other parts of the world. The politically

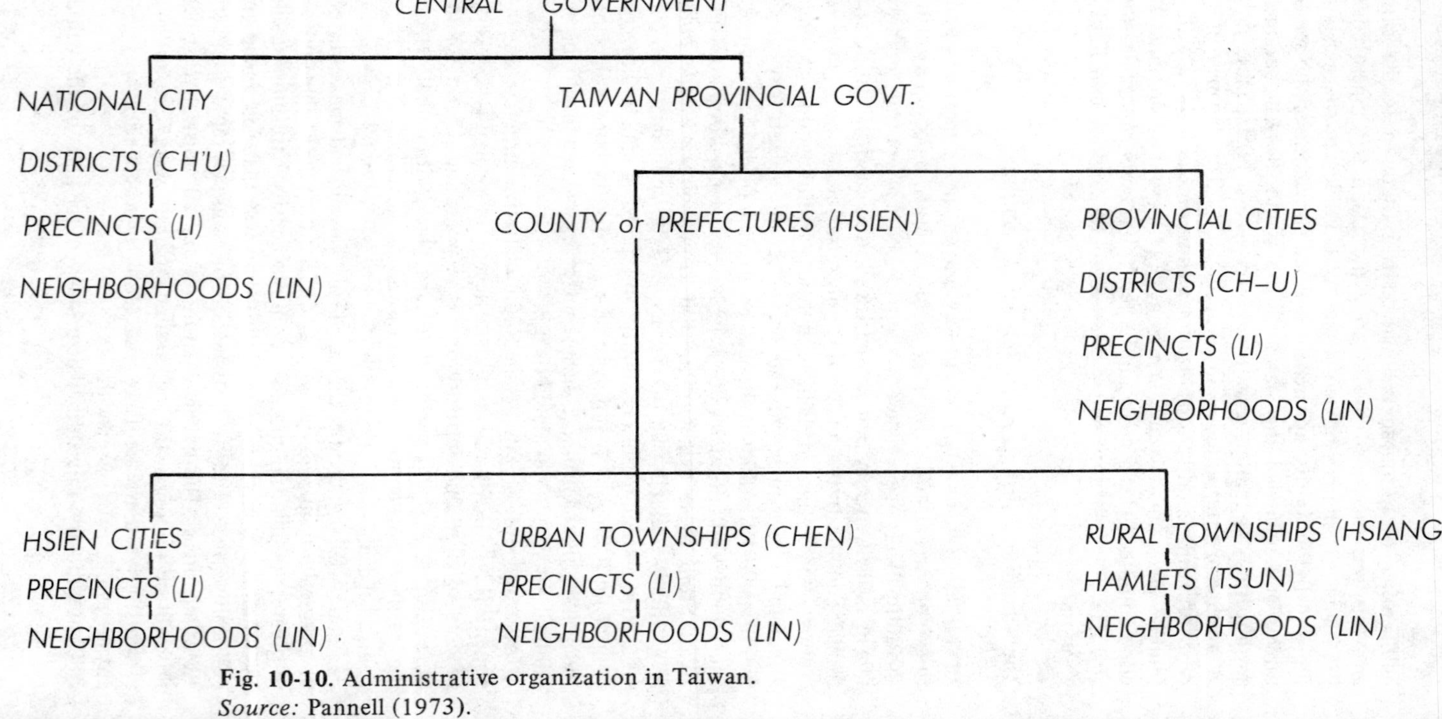

Fig. 10-10. Administrative organization in Taiwan.
Source: Pannell (1973).

effective space tends to be the densely settled, spatially integrated, economically productive segment of the total territory of the state. Such an area includes the capital and core region as well as the intensively effective areas. Less effective politically is that area that does not meet the above definition and consequently is neglected both administratively and economically. In Taiwan, this area tends to be the rugged mountainous interior of the island, although the small area and compact shape of the island render all of it reasonably accessible for purposes of political governance and management. This may be one of the reasons why subversive political elements were unable to challenge Kuomintang political and police power on Taiwan which had been so ineffective in countering Communist-inspired rural revolution on the mainland.

Taiwan's Future as Political Territory

That Taiwan's governmental apparatus operates effectively to integrate and manage the island's territory seems well established. The island functions well as politically effective and economically productive territory of the Nationalist government. Yet the island republic has not been able to project its power beyond to the mainland and establish its claim as the legitimate government of the Chinese people. Indeed, it has been argued that were it not for U.S. influence and power, Taiwan would not be defensible from the Chinese Communists. The question is a moot one, and the U.S. must await some future amicable settlement which the two Chinese groups work out between themselves.

A number of options and possibilities may be envisioned, and these will be discussed at the conclusion of the chapter. The Communist government on mainland China grapples with its own problems of internal territorial administration (as discussed previously). Changes in the territorial structure of administration suggest that it too has problems of control and governance. Traditional Chinese approaches to geopolitics suggest the Chinese, although not much interested in foreign extension of power, are much concerned with their neighbors and flanking territory. Such past trends would suggest that peace and happiness will not prevail until the claims of the Middle Kingdom to its island province of Taiwan have been satisfied and the territory reestablished as Chinese in the strict sense.

AGRICULTURAL DEVELOPMENT

Agricultural production in Taiwan is the foundation of the stable and prosperous economic system, and steady gains in agriculture have provided both the means to feed a rapidly growing population and enough surplus to finance other developmental projects. Indeed, Taiwanese agriculture has often been cited as a model of productiveness under conditions of extreme crowding. Techniques of rice and fruit cultivation, vegetable growing, and animal husbandry have been studied and diffused to other tropical and subtropical environments in developing parts of the world. So much progress has been achieved in the past that future gains in agricultural productivity will become increasingly difficult and expensive.

Good, level land is used intensively throughout the island, and there is little that can be done to give rapid increases in production. Taiwan, as it industrializes and modernizes, must curb its population growth, for it is problematical if its food production will be able to keep pace with rapid population growth in the future.

The Nature of Taiwan's Agriculture

The subtropical environment of Taiwan, characteristics of which were sketched above, is well suited for production of a variety of different foodstuffs. The high average temperatures, abundant rainfall, long growing season, and manageable soils combine to provide an attractive setting for producing a number of different grains, vegetables, and fruits. Among these, the production of wet rice far exceeds in importance, both in acreage and value, all other crops. Its production is concentrated heavily in the plains and basins of the western third of the island and is commonly associated with flatlands, alluvial and planosol soil conditions, and available irrigation waters. Two areas in the east possess limited rice field cultivation—the Ilan Basin in the northeast and the Hualien-Tai-tung (Hualian-Taidong) Rift Valley. Otherwise, the island's rugged uplands restrict agricultural development to special uses, such as pastures, orchards, tea, and other specialty crops (Williams, 1981).

Land Use and Agricultural Change

Despite Taiwan's rugged interior, almost one-quarter of the land area is suitable for agricultural purpose and is under cultivation. This compares favorably with equivalent figures of 11% for mainland China and 16% for Japan, although it is considerably less than India's 35% and France's 46%.

In the early part of this century, the cultivated area expanded rapidly. In 1910, 674,089 hectares were cultivated. By 1940, as indicated in Table 10-2, this had increased to 859,919. The figure was 922,778 in 1978, and as Table 10-2 indicates, little increase in farm acreage has taken place in the last four decades. Population

Table 10-2. Agricultural Land in Taiwan

Year	Farm land in hectares	Population (millions)	Population arable land ratio, people/hectares
1910	674,089	3.25	4.82
1940	859,919	5.87	6.83
1959	877,740	10.43	11.89
1965	889,563	12.63	14.21
1970	905,263	14.68	16.22
1978	922,778	17.10	18.53

Source: Taiwan Provincial Government, *Taiwan Statistical Abstract, No. 30, 1971* and *Industry of Free China* (July, 1980).

Table 10-3. Taiwan: Farm Households

Year	Farm households	Total number of people in farm households
1956	745,318	4,698,532
1965	847,242	5,738,503
1970	880,274	5,996,889
1978	870,000	5,570,000

Source: China Yearbook, 1980.

growth, by contrast, was very rapid. When compared with growth in cropped land (the population/arable land ratio), the number of people that must be supported from a given unit of land has increased almost threefold between 1940 and 1978. The critical question becomes how much longer can gains in land productivity keep pace with population growth.

Table 10-3 suggests another significant aspect of agricultural change has taken place in the expansion of farm families from the period 1956–1970 and the slight decline that occurred between 1970 and 1978. It appears that a basic change is now under way. Farm families averaged 6.4 people per family in 1978, although it may be that many recent migrants to Taiwan's cities continue to be enumerated as residing on farms as a result of household registration procedures in gathering census data. The average farm size was 1.06 hectares. Such small holdings make it clear that off-farm employment and income are very important.

The point of all of this is that a lot of change has taken place in Taiwan, and the nature of the agricultural economy is a good place to examine this change. In brief, a technical transformation of the agricultural economy has taken place which has been well documented. For example, production averaged 1.3 metric tons of rice per hectare in 1895, a figure comparable to yields in India in 1960. By 1968, this had more than doubled to 3.21 metric tons/hectare and had increased to 3.40 tons/hectare by 1979 (Table 10-4). Although there has been great population pressure on the island, the agricultural system has responded through increased total and per-unit yields and a modernization and commercialization of the agricultural economy. The question is whether such improvements can continue with future population growth (Selya, 1981). The 1979 data suggest the main improvements have come about in vegetable production.

Details of the Japanese efforts at modernization of Taiwan have already been outlined. Part of that effort was focused on the agricultural sector. Construction of large-scale irrigation systems and the introduction of new cropping practices, fertilizers, seeds, and insecticides were also important. Another significant contribution was the development of cash crops such as sugarcane and investments in processing facilities to refine the cane and prepare a product for market.

Table 10-4. Taiwan: Maincrops, Acreages and Yields, 1968 and 1979

	Area (hectares)		Yield (metric tons)		Unit yields (metric tons/hectare)	
	1968	1979	1968	1979	1968	1979
Food crops						
Wet paddy	778,016	720,612	2,499,993	2,449,817	3.21	3.400
Sweet potato	239,652	74,336	3,437,508	1,224,759	14.34	16.470
Soybeans	49,461	19,333	72,995	31,782	1.48	1.646
Corn	21,385	33,778	51,483	98,514	2.41	2.917
Cash crops						
Tea	33,999	27,259	24,238	27,055	.71	.993
Horticultural crops						
Peanuts	95,248	53,812	106,408	85,881	1.12	1.596
Sugarcane	95,902	105,370	8,085,465	9,120,750	84.31	86.559
Banana	43,795	9,910	645,331	226,769	14.74	22.883
Citrus fruit	18,439	32,830	170,827	398,828	9.26	12.148
Vegetables	116,250	226,675	1,184,313	3,029,722	10.19	13.307

Source: Taiwan Provincial Government, ***Taiwan Statistical Abstract, No. 28, 1969***, and *Industry of Free China* (July, 1980).

Land Reform and Land Tenure

The Japanese did little to alter established patterns of landholding, although they were careful to insure that farmland was surveyed accurately and platted correctly. It remained for the Nationalist government in 1953 to carry out a thorough program of land reform and redistribution of the land to those who were responsible for tilling it. In brief, this program involved the breaking up of large estates and creating a financial system that permitted tenants to purchase small holdings. Table 10-5 presents data that are instructive and indicate the efficacy of this program. From 1946 to 1968, the number of owner-cultivators jumped dramatically, while the number of tenants declined equally dramatically.

The Nationalists were able to accomplish that which had eluded them on the mainland, the breakup of a feudal system of land tenure and redistribution of landholdings to small farmers. It may be that the political implications of this went far beyond the economic aspects, for the net effect was to create an enfranchised yeoman peasantry with a stake in preserving the established order. This may well have been the most far-reaching achievement of land reform in promoting social and political stability on Taiwan. Paradoxically, redistributing land in mini-parcels to tens of thousands of peasants resulted in further fragmentation of fields and farms, a condition that has inhibited production efficiency. In recent years, government policy has encouraged land consolidation aimed at increasing efficiency of production.

Table 10-5. Taiwan: Effects of Land Reform and Redistribution

Year	Number of farm households affected	
	Owner-cultivator	Tenant
1946	172,314	206,122
1952	262,065	240,572
1956	448,157	124,573
1961	517,182	113,193
1968	593,405	100,132

Source: Taiwan Provincial Government, 1969, *Taiwan Statistical Abstract, No. 28, 1969.*

Crop Types and Agricultural Regions

The mild climate and suitable environment permit a diversified agricultural base that involves both cash and food crops. Rice is the main staple and accounts for the most acreage. In addition, a rich variety of fresh vegetables is grown. The production of the vegetables correlates with the presence of large consuming urban populations. Other food staples are sweet potato, soybean, and corn. Cash crops are of several types. Sugarcane, tea, peanuts, and bananas have long been important. More recently, citronella, tobacco, pineapples and specialized production of mushrooms and other Chinese specialty edibles have been popular. Table 10-6 enumerates the major crops, acreages, and yields for the island.

Crop regions are dominated by rice, which accounts for about half the cropped acreage. In general, rice is double-cropped. Only in the southwest coastal plains does this pattern change. Here the long dry season during the cooler months has made it difficult to grow more than one crop of rice a year. Sugarcane, thus, occupies a considerable area, although nowhere does it challenge rice as the dominant crop. Table 10-6 indicates the extent of these crops by *xian* (county) administrative division. Enough sugarcane is produced to suggest the presence of a distinctive region, as indicated by Chen (1963). Tea is produced in the foothills of northern Taiwan along with a variety of citrus crops. Bananas and pineapples are concentrated heavily in the Taichung and Nantou areas of central Taiwan. Soybeans are grown mainly in the south, while sweet potatoes and peanuts are grown everywhere. Main crop patterns and land uses are depicted in Figure 10-11.

The Taiwanese Village in Transition

A theme that recurs frequently in this chapter suggests that great change has been under way in Taiwan and the process of modernization is well advanced. This is true. At the same time, however, tradition lingers and old habits persist. One way to examine the nature of recent changes is to consider briefly village

Table 10-6. Major Crops in Taiwan by Area in County Units, 1969
(in hectares)

Hsien	Wet rice	Sweet potato	Sugarcane	Soybeans	Peanuts	Vegetables	Tea and citrus fruits	Bananas and pineapples
Taipei	39,200	7,241	–	28	1,340	7,880	14,528	161
Ilan	115,982	4,659	114	597	3,021	3,224	1,646	34
Taoyuan	224,617	6,762	–	33	552	7,333	7,782	229
Hsinchu	101,870	8,651	679	16	1,771	5,112	17,828	1,248
Miao-li	104,633	11,338	437	44	5,060	6,177	4,669	1,292
Taichung	200,022	9,169	3,520	386	4,601	10,936	1,961	4,769
Chang-hua	371,336	25,568	5,245	1,487	10,015	16,406	553	3,444
Nan-tou	88,052	9,460	1,768	351	2,076	4,098	2,793	14,199
Yun-lin	254,817	28,059	11,690	1,080	37,065	9,671	171	844
Chia-i	162,841	22,974	12,373	2,305	11,926	9,051	2,177	1,671
Tainan	172,887	43,463	25,480	1,237	3,256	8,979	1,002	3,158
Kaohsiung	130,946	15,963	11,935	7,918	3,617	8,051	162	8,906
Pingtung	289,651	15,245	10,400	30,031	1,356	7,291	247	11,388
Taitung	57,622	8,814	4,335	757	5,326	3,542	1,033	2,825
Hualien	64,515	13,245	5,473	2,096	8,080	3,619	677	926
Pescadores	–	3,216	–	–	4,993	449	–	–
Major urban centers and their environs	93,652	5,821	2,453	1,095	2,353	4,431	205	545

Source: Taiwan Provincial Government, 1971, *Taiwan Statistical Abstract, No. 30, 1971.*

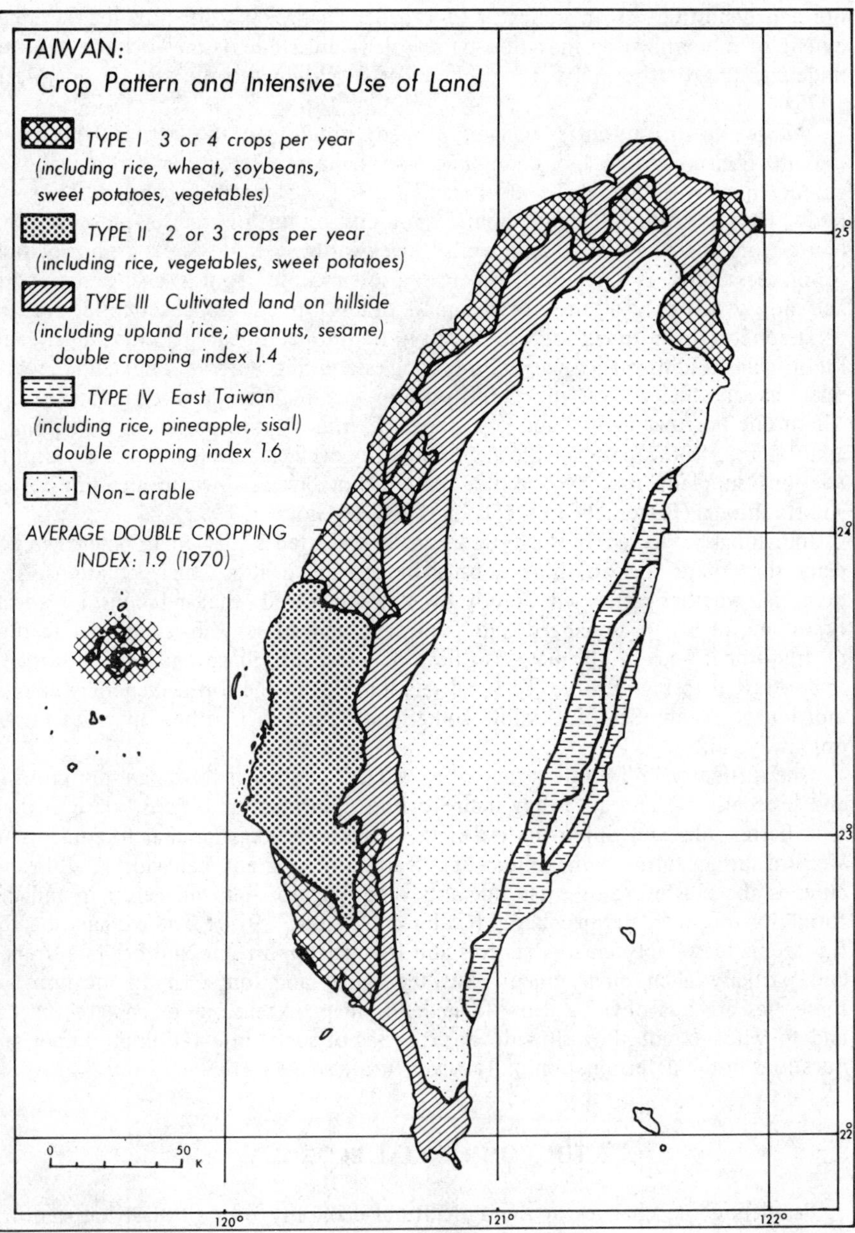

Fig. 10-11. Agricultural land use in Taiwan.
Source: Courtesy of the Government of Taiwan.

life and conditions as an indicator of broader change. Insights into the pace and extent of modernization may thus be revealed, and students may achieve a better understanding of the multifaceted nature of development processes (VanderMeer, 1975).

Village life in Taiwan is changing. Already noted were the efficient and omnipresent transportation and communication linkages. Television and telephones extend to every village, and pocket transistor radios are available cheaply to everybody. Few are more than one hour from a city by bus or train or more than six hours from their capital. Consequently, backwardness that results from isolation or inaccessibility is rare. Such linkages also promote rapid exchange of goods and money that draw all the citizenry more or less into a national economic system.

Despite a high index of accessibility, traditional social patterns linger, and life in villages and small towns follows long-established norms. For example, social relations are focused on the family–whom one marries, how one votes, from whom one borrows money and buys goods. The family is important in determining all of these. These patterns are determined by well-established forms of kinship relations supplemented by accepted patterns of behavior which are time tested and traditional (Pasternak, 1972; Gallin, 1966; DeGlopper, 1972).

Individuals involved in such traditionally oriented social environments might deny that there was anything unusual or controlled about such situations. The point is, whether perceived or not by those involved, that relationships of all types are highly personalized and family influenced, a well-established feature of traditional society. It may also be a hallmark of village and small town life as contrasted to big city life. Personal relationships in the former generally involve individuals or families who know something about each other. In cities this is not always so.

One difficulty in Taiwan is that many villages and small towns are not growing and prospering. Many are losing their brightest and most ambitious youth as they seek better jobs and opportunities in the cities, a process familiar to students of Western urbanization. One interesting feature of migrant behavior in Taiwan's cities is the clustering of these migrants according to their village origin and the formation of small urban villages (Gallin and Gallin, 1974). The explanation for this seems reasonably clear. Relatives and friends support one another in a strange and partially alien environment. But the short- and long-term implications of these ties are less obvious. How long these village extensions or enclaves persist and to what extent they slow down processes of social integration are important questions in the determination of Taiwan's future society.

THE COMMERCIAL ECONOMY

Paralleling the changes in the agricultural economy over the last half-century have been a series of equally far-reaching changes in the nature of commerce and industry on Taiwan. Although set in motion six decades ago, the most spectacular changes in industry and commerce are very recent; most have occurred in the last two decades (Raper, 1953; Pannell, 1974). Earlier progress in industrialization under the Japanese was more closely associated with extractive industries–smelting, for example, and the processing of agricultural commodities and forest products. Recent industrialization, by contrast, has focused on modern forms of manufacture that seek to take advantage of Taiwan's low cost but productive labor force (Lin, 1973; Ho, 1978).

Contemporary Industry Mix

In recent years, textiles, garments, appliances, electronics components, toy and furniture manufacturing, shoes, sporting goods, and handicrafts have developed rapidly along with tobacco, food, and beverage processing and other consumer-oriented manufacturing. These are among the more important industries associated with the export to foreign markets. Heavy industries aim primarily for domestic consumption, and major heavy industries include oil refining, chemical fertilizer and plastics production, iron and steel making, cement manufacture, shipbuilding, machinery and metalworking, and others. Although Taiwan followed import substitution and protectionist policies for a number of years and attempted to develop a full range of industrial and consumer goods, recently tariff reductions were carried out on more than 2,000 items. Policymakers on the island recognize that an autarkic economic policy for a place as small as Taiwan with a very restricted resource base is folly. Foreign trade is essential for Taiwan, and this trade

Heavy traffic along Taipei's Chung-hua Road, one of the city's main commercial areas. (*C. W. Pannell*)

Paddy land (seen at left) is quickly being converted to urban apartments and shops along the peripheries of Taiwan's rapidly growing cities. This scene was taken on the southern edge of Taichung. (*C. W. Pannell*)

has permitted the rapid and vigorous expansion of the manufacturing and modernizing sector of the economy. The key for Taiwan is to insure that her export goods are competitive on world markets.

Export Processing Zones

Among Taiwan's contributions as a model of a developing economic system has been the creation and development of successful export processing zones. The first one was developed at the large southern city of Kaohsiung in the mid-1960s. Two others, near Tainan and Taichung, followed 5 years later. Established as processing centers to exploit the low labor costs in Taiwan without incurring import and export tariffs, these zones have been successful in attracting a variety of industries that seek the advantages of the low-cost and skilled Taiwanese labor. Textiles, shoes, sporting goods, toys, electronic components and instruments, and furniture are among the products of these processing zones. The concept of the export processing zone has spread to other parts of Asia and is now being used in the United States as well.

Commercial and Financial Development

Associated with the rapid growth of Taiwan's industries has been a remarkable growth in commercial and financial institutions that support the island's economic modernization. Since 1965, more than five American banks have opened Taiwan offices, and several other foreign banks operate in Taipei as well. These banks not only have assisted in facilitating the exchange and transfer of money involved with the rapidly growing foreign trade, but they also provide examples of new methods, innovations, and techniques of banking for the Chinese to study and learn from in developing their own indigenous banking system.

Large insurance firms, customs brokers, shippers, and jobbers further support the bustling commerce of the island. Virtually no necessary commercial service is absent. Other sources of capital are provided through ancillary financial institutions, such as the numerous local credit societies and savings and loan companies. A small but active stock market provides a source of finance for corporate enterprise. Unfortunately, the stock exchange has been beset with speculators and gamblers, and the market has proved too volatile to be a consistent and reliable source of capital financing.

Cities and Economic Progress

One commonly agreed on index of modernization in developing states is the level or degree of urbanization. Hence, the larger the percentage of the population living in cities, the more modern and advanced the society and economy are believed to be. Taiwan, with about 77% of its inhabitants in cities in 1980, appears to support this contention well. A 1980 per capita gross national product of US $1,400 makes it one of East Asia's richest and most modern countries. There are many cities, and several of these are large. In 1975, two, Taipei and Kaohsiung, contained more than 1 million inhabitants; two others, Tainan and Taichung, each had more than 500,000; while a fifth, Keelung (Jilong), was approaching 400,000. Another six cities had more than 100,000 people (Fig. 10-12).

Most of the industrial growth and commercial progress described above has taken place in and near those cities, and especially in the larger ones. Fortunately, the cities are scattered throughout the western half of the island, and the centers of innovation and progress have not been concentrated. The productive resources and wealth of the island have not been clustered spatially in only one location, a feature commonly observed in the great primate cities of Southeast Asia.

The Transportation Network

The glue holding together this dynamic urban and regional system is the extensive and well-developed network of surface transportation. An island-wide system of roads and railways (already described) integrates the compact island and allows it to function as a united economic and political system. Historically, the network developed incrementally and focused on local urban centers. The number of transport linkages each center or node shared, in part, determined its importance to the island-wide economic system and then its pattern of subsequent growth (Lin, 1973; Hsu et al., 1980).

Over time, those city and town centers with the better transport connections have tended to grow and prosper. Such a growth pattern is also supplemented

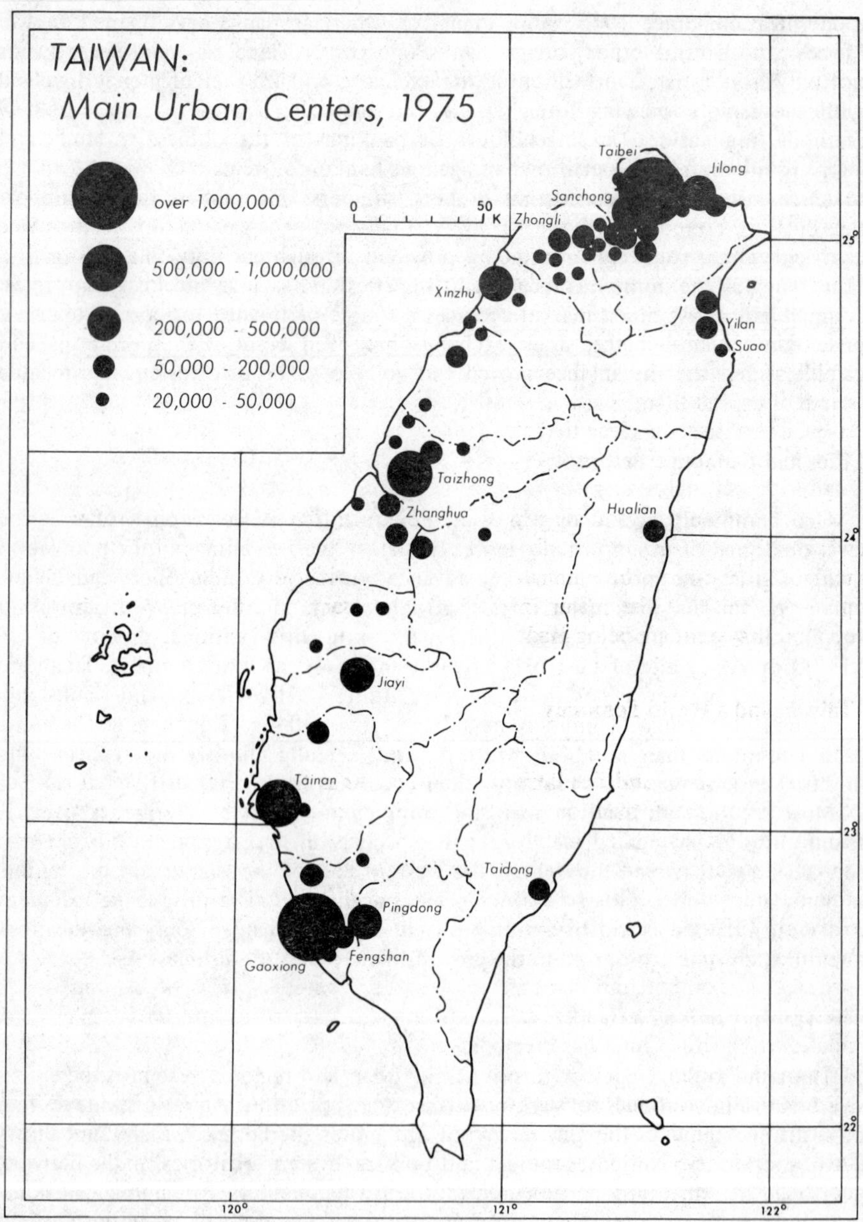

Fig. 10-12. Main urban centers in Taiwan, 1975.

with other factors, such as administrative and economic decisions of where to locate major bureaucratic, commercial, and industrial projects. However, no major activity could be sited without consideration for the accessibility and external linkages it possessed.

It is instructive to examine Taiwan as a compact area with a dense and well-articulated transport network, because this may suggest something about the factors underlying its success as a developing state. Planners in recent years have continued to recognize the value of good transport linkages and have persuaded the government to construct a north-south expressway (Fig. 10-9) linking all the major cities along the island's western flank. In 1978, this expressway was completed. Now that the entire route is finished, the driving time from north to south has been halved from 10 to 5 hours. Expansion of the rail network has also been under way in recent years to link eastern Taiwan into the island-wide network.

Already it seems clear that the western plains and basins of Taiwan, containing a number of large and growing cities that are interlinked by efficient and good highway and rail systems, are developing into a conurbation or megalopolitan system. The indications suggest a Taiwanese analogue to the type of urban agglomeration familiar in Japan's southern Honshu region. How rapidly this develops remains to be seen, but already there are signs in the growth of cities and transport systems that the major investments necessary to a fully modern, integrated economic system are being made.

Taiwan and a World Economy

Taiwan is small and has limited resources. As is true in Japan, Taiwan has constructed her modernization and recent economic growth on foreign trade. In doing this, she has relied mainly on the discipline, industry, and skills of her labor force, coupled with the advantage of a highly central location and good ties with the outside world. This reliance on foreign trade has both helped and hindered Taiwan. Difficulties exist, since the vigor of the economy, tied in closely with world trade patterns, is precariously based. The recent rise in world petroleum prices, for example, hit hard in Taiwan and created a series of disruptive price increases. Political alliances and changing currents also interfere. Japan's new relationship with China has created some economic and trade difficulties between Taiwan and Japan.

Taiwan must trade to survive and prosper, and the island must trade with countries other than the United States. The new political realities of China's entry into the United Nations have forced Taiwan to seek more pragmatic economic policies that disregard or de-emphasize political alliances. If Taiwan is able to continue to worry less about changing political currents and concentrate more on pragmatic economic policies that promote increased trade and exchange, prosperity may continue despite political differences. Indeed, there is really no other acceptable direction if Taiwan is to remain a viable political entity (see Figs. 10-13a and 13b).

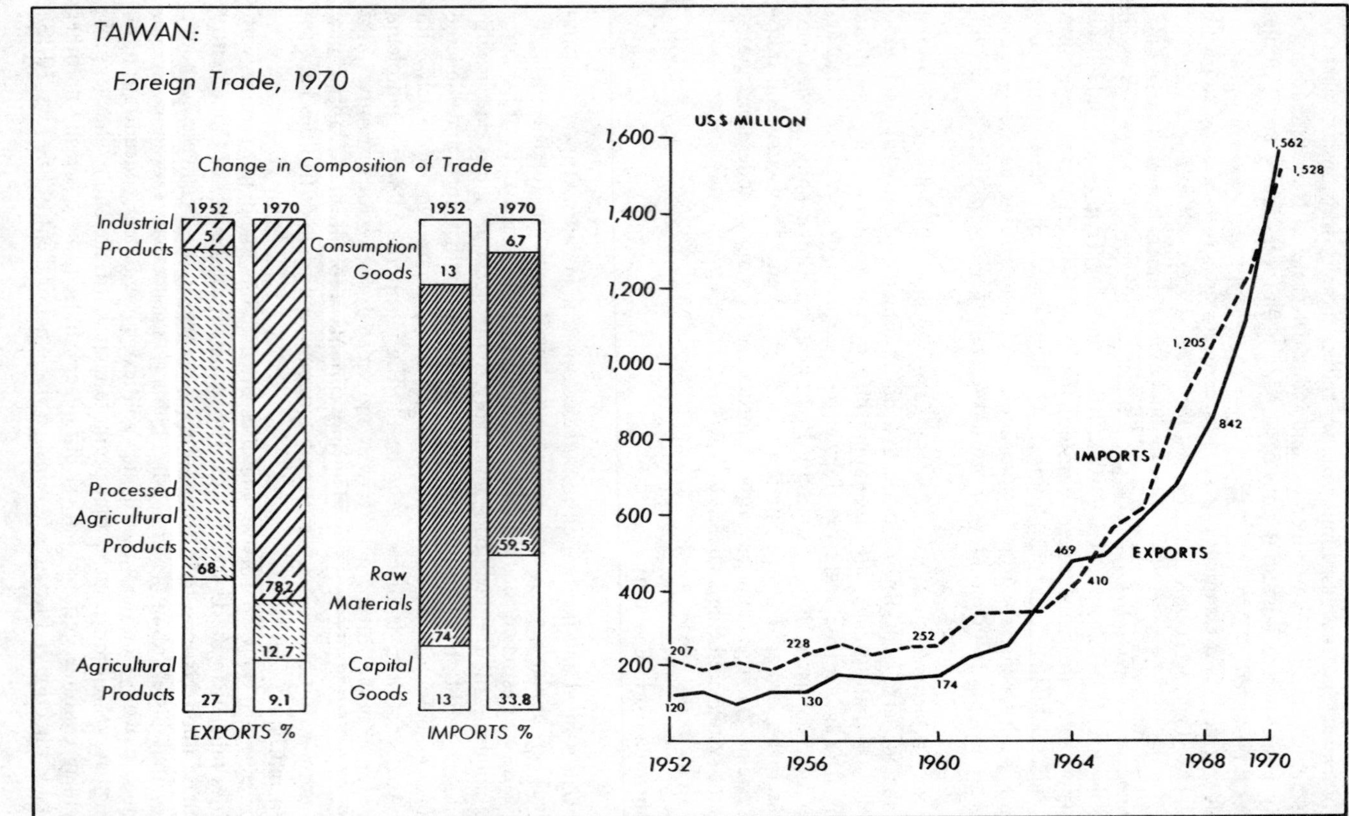

Fig. 10-13a. Foreign trade in Taiwan, 1952–1970.
Source: Courtesy of the Government of Taiwan.

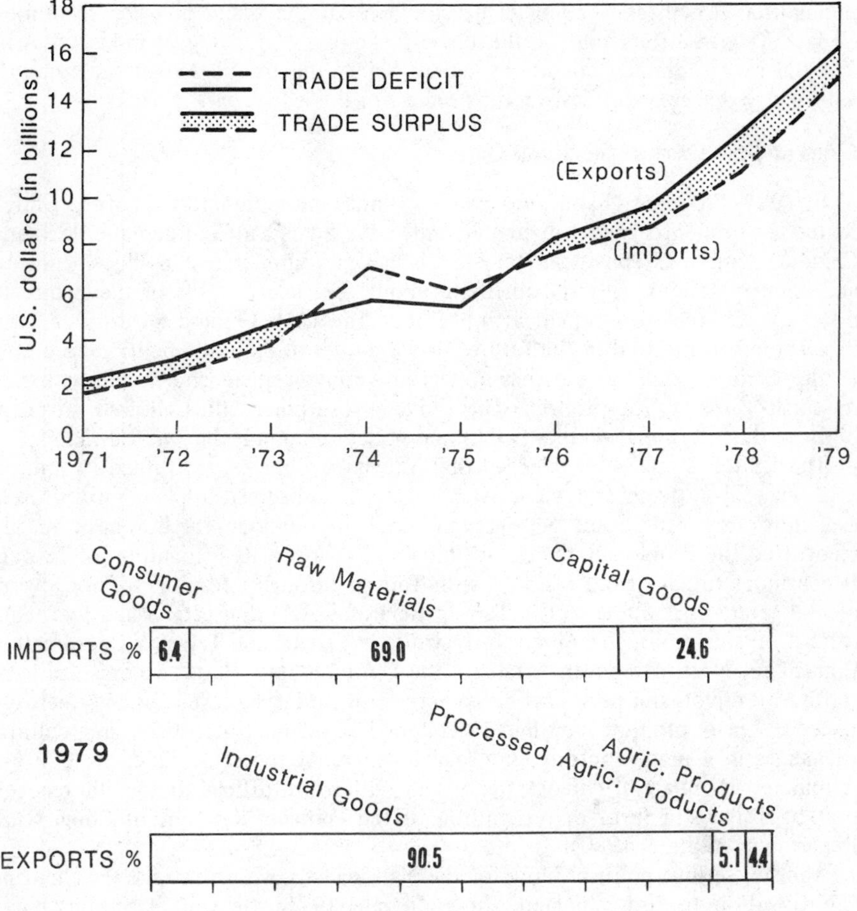

Fig. 10-13b. Foreign trade in Taiwan, 1971–1979.
Source: China Yearbook, 1971 and 1980.

CONCLUSION

Taiwan is a place of great promise as well as a place of pressing uncertainties and problems. The island in many ways is fortunate and blessed with advantages. Its location along the southeastern flank of the China mainland is highly accessible and lies across the main shipping and air lanes connecting East Asia with Europe, South and Southeast Asia, and North America. The subtropical marine location yields a physical environment well suited for intensive cultivation of a variety of food grains, vegetables, and fruits. Such a location and situation have led to rapid population growth and economic development of the island in recent centuries. Today, Taiwan offers one of the highest standards of living in monsoon Asia. Yet the rosy economic conditions cannot shield the troubled political situation, a difficulty that may yet destroy the progress of the recent past.

China and the Crisis of the Status Quo

In 1972, President Nixon journeyed to China, and representatives of the United States government signed a document called the Shanghai Communique. U.S. and Chinese Communist positions toward Taiwan are enumerated in this document, and these positions suggest something about the future status of the island. In brief, the Chinese government affirmed that Taiwan is Chinese territory and will be returned to the fold in the future. It is a matter of domestic politics, according to the Chinese, and the U.S. has no legitimate involvement and should withdraw its small garrison from Taiwan. The Chinese government thus allowed no possibility of the interpretation of a two-Chinas policy or an independent Taiwan.

The United States acknowledged that Taiwan is Chinese, reaffirmed its interest in a peaceful settlement of the Taiwan question, and agreed to phase out its forces as conditions permit. Since the signing of that communique, the U.S. has officially recognized the People's Republic of China and dropped its recognition of Taiwan. It continues to have close relations with Taiwan through a formula for nongovernmental relations and a law (The Taiwan Relations Act) that established two semi-official organizations, the American Institute in Taiwan and Taiwan's Coordination Council for North American Affairs in the United States. These two organizations, staffed by diplomatic personnel either retired or on leave, have worked effectively since 1979 to promote continued economic, academic, scientific, and cultural exchanges in a pragmatic but unofficial manner. At the same time, the U.S. has terminated its bilateral defense treaty and withdrawn official diplomatic recognition of Taiwan in favor of recognition of the People's Republic of China (U.S. Department of State, 1980).

Another serious political blow for the Nationalist government was the changing U.N. position toward mainland China. In late 1971, the United Nations voted to expel Taiwan, and installed the Communist government as the legitimate occupant of the China seat and as a permanent member of the Security Council. Since then, Taiwan has been excluded from participation in activities of the United Nations and its related agencies. A number of countries formerly represented in Taipei have closed their embassies and sought to establish diplomatic contacts with the Communist government in Peking. Such are the vagaries of international political currents for Taiwan; the period since 1971 has been extremely difficult and troublesome. Whatever the foreign views of Taiwan, the island is in practice a sovereign state in that no mainland Chinese Communists govern Taiwan. In the practice of its internal governmental affairs, the island is independent.

Alternatives for Change and the Future

There is little Taiwan can do to affect the politics of other countries. For herself, there is much more. First, it is unlikely that either the government, as presently constituted, or the people (both Taiwanese and Mainlanders) would support political reintegration with the Communist controlled mainland China at this time. Second, Taiwan is strong and rich enough to defend itself against any kind of attack except full-scale assault. Moreover, it is unlikely the Communist government could develop the amphibious force necessary to invade the island in the near future. Thus, a military solution to the question, at least in the short term, appears unlikely.

Other alternatives are few. A separate Taiwanese state is unlikely without a change in government, and even under Taiwanese political control, many would oppose such a creation. An independent but Chinese Taiwan is conceivable; in fact, that is what exists today. From an American point of view, one can affirm the Chineseness of Taiwan, as did the State Department in the Shanghai Communique. In what form or guise this Chineseness is manifested and articulated politically remains to be determined. The American position appears to be a wait-and-watch posture in which the United States plays a passive role in allowing the Chinese of different political outlooks to decide and resolve their own political destinies (U.S. Department of State, 1980).

LITERATURE CITED

Barclay, George, 1954, *Colonial Development and Population in Taiwan.* Princeton: Princeton University Press.

Chang, Chi-yun, 1972, *National Atlas of China* (4th ed.). Yangmingsham, Taipei: National War College, Republic of China.

Chen, C. S., 1963, *Taiwan: An Economic and Social Geography*, Vol. 1, Taipei: Fun-Min Geographical Institute of Economic Development, Research Report No. 96, pp. 269–299.

China Yearbook, 1980 and annually, Taipei: China Publishing Co.

Council for International Economic Cooperation and Development, 1972, *Manpower Development in Republic of China.* Taipei Manpower Development Committee.

Davidson, James W., 1903, *The Island of Formosa, Historical View from 1430–1900.* New York: Macmillan.

DeGlopper, Donald R., 1972, "Doing Business in Lukang." In W. E. Willmott (ed.), *Economic Organization in Chinese Society*. Stanford: Stanford University Press, pp. 297–326.

Gallin, Bernard, 1966, *Hsin Hsing, Taiwan: A Chinese Village in Change.* Berkeley: University of California Press.

Gallin, Bernard and Gallin, Rita, 1974, "The Integration of Village Migrants in Taipei." In Mark Elvin and G. William Skinner (eds.), *The Chinese City Between Two Worlds.* Stanford: Stanford University Press, pp. 331–358.

Ho, Samuel P. S., 1978, *Economic Development of Taiwan.* New Haven: Yale University Press.

Hsieh, Chiao-min, 1964, *Taiwan-Ilha Formosa, A Geography in Perspective.* Woburn, Mass.: Butterworth.

Hsu, Mei-ling, 1969, "Taiwan Population Distribution, 1965," Map Supplement No. 19. *Annals of the Association of American Geography*, Vol. 59, pp. 611–617.

Hsu, Yi-rong Ann, Pannell, Clifton W., and Wheeler, James O., 1980, "The Development and Structure of Transportation Networks in Taiwan." In Ronald Knapp (ed.), *China's Island Frontier*, pp. 167–202.

Industry of Free China (monthly), "Taiwan Economic Statistics." Taipei.

Knapp, Ronald, 1978, The Geographer and Taiwan. *The China Quarterly*, No. 74, pp. 356–368.

Knapp, Ronald (ed.), 1980, *China's Island Frontier.* Honolulu: University of Hawaii Press.

Kramer, G. P. and Wu, George, 1970, *An Introduction to Taiwanese Folk Religions.* Taipei: Published by authors.

Kuo, Ting-yee, 1973, "Early Stages in the Sinicization of Taiwan, 230–1683," pp. 21–57 and "The Internal Development and Modernization of Taiwan, 1863–1891," pp. 171–240. In Paul K. T. Sih (ed.), *Taiwan in Modern Times.* New York: St. Johns University Press.

Lee, Teng-hui, 1971, *Intersectoral Capital Flows in the Economic Development of Taiwan, 1895–1960.* Ithaca, N.Y.: Cornell University Press, pp. 32–65.

Lin, Ching-yuan, 1973, *Industrialization in Taiwan, 1946–1972.* New York: Praeger.

Myers, Ramon and Adrienne Ching, 1964, "Agricultural Development in Taiwan Under Japanese Colonial Rule." *Journal of Asian Studies*, Vol. 23, pp. 555–570.

Pannell, Clifton W., 1973, "Recent Change and Stagnation in the Pescadores Islands, Taiwan." *Philippine Geographical Journal*, Vol. 7, No. 2, pp. 31–45.

Pannell, Clifton W., 1974, "Development and the Middle City in Taiwan." *Growth and Change*, Vol. 5, No. 3, pp. 21–29.

Pasternak, Burton, 1972, *Kinship and Community in Two Chinese Villages.* Stanford: Stanford University Press.

Population Reference Bureau, 1980, *1980 World Population Data Sheet.* Washington, D.C.: Population Reference Bureau, Inc.

Raper, Arthur, 1953, *Urban Taiwan, Crowded and Resourceful.* Taipei: Joint Commission on Rural Reconstruction.

Selya, Roger, 1981, "Food for the Cities of Taiwan." *The China Geographer*, No. 11, pp. 73–87.

Speare, Alden Jr., 1972, *The Determinants of Migration to a Major City in a Developing Country: Taichung, Taiwan.* Taipei: Institute of Economics, Academia Sinica, Population Papers, June.

Taiwan Provincial Government, 1980 and annually, *Taiwan Statistical Abstract* (various numbers). Taipei: Bureau of Accounting and Statistics.

U.S. Department of State, 1980, *Review of Relations with Taiwan.* Washington, D.C.: Bureau of Public Affairs, Current Policy No. 190 (June 11, 1980).

VanderMeer, Paul, 1975, "Pacifying Space in a Chinese Village." *The China Geographer*, No. 2, pp. 27–39.

Wang, I-shou, 1977, "The Recent Patterns of Internal Migration in Taiwan." *The China Geographer*, No. 6, pp. 37–47.

Williams, Jack, 1981, "The Use of Slopeland in Taiwan's Agricultural Development." *The China Geographer*, No. 11, pp. 89–111.

Wolf, Arthur, 1974, *Religion and Ritual in Chinese Society.* Stanford: Stanford University Press.

Chapter 11

Hong Kong and Macao

HONG KONG

Hong Kong is a British crown colony located on the southern coast of China, adjacent to the Province of Guangdong. The colony was first established in 1842 as a result of the settlement of the Opium War in which Hong Kong island was ceded to the British in response to British demands for trading rights. At that point, the colony was composed of approximately 80 km^2 of Hong Kong island and adjacent small islands. In 1861, the peninsula of Kowloon on the mainland was also ceded to the British by China, an additional 10 km^2 of colonial territory that gave the British colony good control over the deep water natural harbor which lies between Hong Kong island and the adjacent Kowloon peninsula. In 1898, another large section of territory was leased to the British that added to the 90 km^2 of British colonial Hong Kong. This new lease amounted to 930 km^2, and the additional lands ever since have been called the New Territories. This land was leased to the crown colony of Hong Kong by the Imperial Chinese Government for a period of 99 years; the lease is due to expire in 1997. The area of the New Territories has a distinct legal status from the colony of Hong Kong and Kowloon, and its legal status may be viewed in a different light. At this point, it is difficult to predict what will happen in 1997 or indeed even before then with regard to the status of both the New Territories and Hong Kong.

Hong Kong, then, is a small, foreign controlled enclave located just south of the Tropic of Cancer on the southern coast of China. The location is ideal for international trading purposes. It lies along the main shipping lines between Japan and Southeast and South Asia. Both the port and the airport at Hong Kong are

View of Hong Kong skyline and harbor taken from the peak on Hong Kong Island. Kowloon is seen across the water.

very important stopovers for trans-Pacific and trans-Indian ocean traffic. Hong Kong's most significant asset is its location and high degree of accessibility, and its early growth from the period of initial British colonial development has been as a trading and transshipment center for the China trade. By World War II, Hong Kong was one of the most important entrepots in Asia, and shipping, trade, and related activities have always been a mainstay of the economy.

The Chinese Communist Revolution in 1949 brought great change to Hong Kong, however, and resulted in radical changes in the nature of the colony's economic system. First, Hong Kong's role as a transshipment center and entrepot for the China trade was abruptly cut. Consequently, new economic activities had to develop if the colony was to survive and prosper. The response to the new political realities was very rapid. Hong Kong, with its large population and little more than its assets of accessibility and a hardworking and industrious people, turned quickly to industrialization. Sources of capital from overseas Chinese and local entrepreneurs, from the United Kingdom, from Japan, and from the United States provided the wherewithal to invest in a variety of different kinds of petty and larger scale industrial establishments. Among the most important of these were textiles and garment making, traditionally a major industrial and manufacturing activity for the colony. Textiles and clothing were followed soon by a variety of other labor intensive kinds of manufacturing activities, such as the manufacture of furniture, toys, sporting goods, and, in more recent years, the assembly of electronic components and optics. More details will be provided on the nature of the modern economy in a succeeding section.

Physical Geography

The physical geography of Hong Kong and the New Territories is very similar to that of the related adjacent hills of southeastern China. Essentially composed of folded mountains made up of volcanic and metamorphic material, the lay of the land and the relief are characterized by several ridgelines of rugged and often precipitous hills. Generally the strike or axes of these ridges is northeast to southwest, and the tallest peak is Tai Moa Shan (957 m) in the heart of the New Territories. The island of Hong Kong is also characterized by a peak more than 300 m in elevation. The only large area of flatlands is in the alluvial plain of the northwestern part of the New Territories in the area around Deep Bay. Generally the lithology of Hong Kong is composed of both older rocks of igneous and metamorphic origin and more recent folded sedimentary strata. Among the more common are crystalline or granite-like rocks, many of which have been heavily weathered as a result of the high average temperatures and very extensive precipitation and humidity throughout much of the year (Tregear, 1980).

The climate of Hong Kong is characteristically monsoonal. Rainfall totals about 2,250 mm and is concentrated heavily during the summer months, especially from May through September. During these months, winds typically blow from the south and southwest, giving to the colony a monsoonal pattern of onshore breezes. Another significant feature of this climate is the late summer concentration of precipitation, typically in the month of September, as a result of the frequent large tropical storms known as typhoons which sweep across the region every year. The months from October through April tend to be much drier, as is characteristic of monsoonal climates during the cool season. The winds commonly blow from the east and northeast during this period, and there is usually little rainfall. The autumn months are an especially pleasant time to visit, when the climate is dry and cool. The pattern described above is a general pattern only. It should be remembered that there may be extreme variability within this overall pattern, and that the nature of the general climate characteristics is based on averages compiled over many years during which records have been kept on the climate. The location is in the tropics, and frost is unknown at lower elevations. On the peaks, however, frost at elevations greater than, say, 300 m may occur sporadically during the winter months. The summers, by contrast, are hot and muggy, and the climate in this part of Asia is similar to the climate in the southeastern United States during the summer months.

The natural vegetation of Hong Kong has been mostly destroyed by the works of human beings. Today, only about 12% of the land area of Hong Kong and the New Territories is composed of woodlands and forest (Table 11-1). In general, most of the trees found in Hong Kong have been planted, and they are composed primarily of local pines, causarina, and eucalyptus varieties. One of the major environmental problems that has resulted from the excessive activities of human

Table 11-1. Land Utilization in Hong Kong

Class	Approximate area (square kilometers)	Percentage of whole	Remarks
Built-up (urban areas)	130	12.4	Includes roads and railways.
Woodlands	124	11.8	Natural and established woodlands.
Grass and scrublands	616	58.9	Natural grass and scrub, including Plover Cove Reservoir.
Badlands	44	4.1	Stripped of cover. Granite country. Capable of regeneration.
Swamp and mangrove lands	13	1.2	Capable of reclamation.
Arable land	104	9.9	Includes orchards and market gardens.
Fish ponds	18	1.7	Fresh and brackish water fish farming.
Total	1049	100	

Source: Hong Kong, 1977, p. 51.

beings over many years is the destruction of some of the steep slopelands and forestlands to the point that they have eroded and become badlands. This land has generally been lost to any effective use. Much of the original woodlands has now given way to coarse grasses and scrubby vegetation, and its usefulness may be limited to grazing. This type of ground cover occupies half of the total land area. Hong Kong thus has a serious land problem, and the available land has not been well cared for in previous years.

The soils of Hong Kong reflect mainly the nature of the climate. The combination of heavy summer rains and high temperatures with the accompanying heavy chemical and mechanical weathering in the widespread sedimentaries and granites has resulted in thin, clay lateritic type soils. Soils everywhere are generally acidic. The rather poor quality of local soils combined with the limited expanse of alluvial lowlands results in a small quantity of farmland and limited development of agriculture. Indeed, Hong Kong has very little suitable land for growing crops in order to support its very large population, and is heavily dependent on China for its food.

Rural Economy

The rural economy of Hong Kong is composed of two major sectors: fishing and agriculture. There are less than 65,000 people involved in these two activities and neither of them is critical or essential to the continued viability of the colony. Of the 62,975 people involved in the primary sector of the economy (Table 11-2), the largest number–approximately 40,000–are involved either directly or indirectly in fishing. Fishing involves both deep-sea and near-shore fishing, although the

Table 11-2. Employment in Hong Kong

	1971*		1976
	Number	Percent	
Manufacturing	677,498	42.8	773,746
Services	312,173	19.7	
Commerce	208,604	13.2	
Construction and engineering	168,773	10.7	
Transport and communication	114,722	7.2	
Agriculture, forestry and fishing	62,975	3.9	
Public utilities	8,879	0.6	
Mining and quarrying	4,518	0.3	
Other	24,716	1.6	
Total	1,582,858	100.0	

*Based on 1971 census as reported in *Hong Kong, 1977.* Percentages added.

tremendous amount of near-shore fishing in recent years has seriously depleted the fishery resources in and around the crown colony. In addition to the ocean and near-shore fishing, pond aquaculture has developed considerably in the northwestern part of the New Territories and this has evolved as a very important form of agricultural activity.

Farming in Hong Kong is focused around several major enterprises. Probably the most important is the production of fresh vegetables, flowers, and fruits for the large urban consuming market in nearby Kowloon and Hong Kong Island. The other major agricultural activity is, of course, the production of wet rice, which is common throughout much of this part of southeastern China. The production of wet rice, however, does not provide good marginal rates of return to the farmers, and more of the land previously given over to wet paddy has in recent years been converted into vegetable production. About 10% of the total land area is cultivated (Table 11-1). The nature of farming in this part of tropical, southeastern China means that crops can be grown year-round. Generally where rice is produced, two crops of wet paddy are produced from each unit of land. Only a small amount of the cropland is now given over to rice production; however, where vegetables are grown, there is a constant cycling of different vegetables on the same plot of land, and this rotation goes on year-round. A variety of different vegetables are grown, and in some cases as many as eight crops a year may be produced from a given unit of land. According to the annual *Hong Kong*, 1977 the main vegetables grown are white cabbage, flowering cabbage, leaf mustard cabbage, radishes, chives, Chinese kale, watercress, onions, and Chinese lettuce. Other crops would include sweet potatoes, yams, taro, peanuts, and a limited amount of sugarcane. Poultry and swine production are also very important sideline activities in the rural economy.

Walled town and farmland in the New Territories. (*C. W. Pannell*)

Vegetable farming in the New Territories can be quite a profitable enterprise. However, land is so valuable and there are so many alternative forms of employment available locally that agriculture is a declining aspect of the economic system of Hong Kong and the New Territories. The nature of the relationship between the People's Republic of China and Hong Kong has promoted an increasing dependence of Hong Kong and the New Territories on China for its fresh food. This exchange is a very important aspect of the mutually beneficial trading relationship between China and Hong Kong, and may help explain the willingness of the Chinese to permit Hong Kong to continue as a colony on their very doorstep. Each year China sells more than $1 billion worth of fresh commodities in order to help feed the 5 million people of Hong Kong as well as the large number of tourists that visit the colony. The foreign exchange earned by China as a consequence of this trading relationship is very vital, and Chinese leaders in the PRC have shown themselves flexible and willing to allow this kind of relationship to continue.

People and Society

Most of the population of Hong Kong are ethnically Chinese (about 98%), and most of the Chinese are native speakers of Cantonese. There are other Chinese ethnic groups, however. These include prominently both Hakkas and Hoklos; the latter is primarily a fishing group. The population of Hong Kong has grown steadily in recent decades. At the end of World War II the population was approximately 1 million people in 1945. By 1971, this population had increased to about 4 million, and the increase was attributable to improvements in health care and a high birth rate in Hong Kong itself as well as to periods of very rapid immigration from mainland China. The population is youthful, and about 60% of the total were born locally. In the last decade, another million have been added, many of whom are migrants. In 1981, the population of Hong Kong and the New Territories was approximately 5 million. Today, the birth rate has declined to a modest level (1.7%), and the government of Hong Kong has worked vigorously to reduce the birth and growth rates. Refugees and immigrants from mainland China and also from other Southeast Asian countries, such as Vietnam and Kampuchea, however, have added large numbers of people to Hong Kong in recent years, as many as 100,000 in some years.

Hong Kong is crowded. The major problem from the point of view of demography is that the land area is simply too small for the large number of people. A land area of slightly more than 1,000 km^2 housing 5 million people means that these people are crowded in an incredibly dense situation. About 12.4% of the total land area is built up. Approximately 90% of Hong Kong citizens are clustered in the major urban areas, e.g., Kowloon, Hong Kong Island itself, and adjacent urban centers (such as Shatin in the New Territories). In some of these areas (e.g., Kowloon's Mongkok District), population densities are probably as high as anywhere in the world. It has been suggested that in the tenements of Kowloon and Hong Kong, population density may be as high as 5,000 people per hectare, probably the highest population density of any place on earth. Hong Kong, therefore, is faced with a very serious problem of how to provide for its people on the modest land resource. Here is a place with a population the size of Norway's or slightly larger, yet which exists on a quantity of land that is not much larger than the area of Norway's largest city.

Modern Economy

Hong Kong traditionally had served as a port of entry for the China trade. Consequently, its functions of commerce and trade were heavily dependent on its role as an entrepot and break-of-bulk port for international shippers desiring to enter the China market and the southern part of that country. In 1949, with the ascendancy of a new political regime in China, Hong Kong suddenly found that its major economic reason for being had been abruptly shattered. The decade of the 1950s was a difficult one for the crown colony. The China trade was interrupted, and Hong Kong's traditional economic functions and activities were sharply curtailed. Nevertheless, gains were made. A basic shift in the nature of economic activities underway in the colony was set in motion in the 1950s.

The new shift in economic activities focused around replacing commerce and trade with the production of manufactured goods and especially consumer goods. On the one hand, such production sought to take advantage of the abundant and hard-working labor force available in Hong Kong. On the other hand, industrialists

Shipping remains a major economic activity, and Hong Kong is a major container shipping port. (*C. W. Pannell*)

sought to take advantage of the good accessibility of Hong Kong along the major shipping lanes. In this way it was hoped to put Hong Kong in a good position to make its products available on world markets (Table 11-3).

Associated with this shift in basic economic orientation was a shift in trading partners. The colony began to place much greater emphasis on its export trade with the United States and with Great Britain. Thus, a fundamental change in the nature of the economic structure of Hong Kong was set in motion from commerce to industry. This change has continued up to the present decade of the 1980s. Despite the fact that Hong Kong has again strongly increased its trading relationship with China and become a major factor in the China trade once more, nevertheless its role as a manufacturing and industrial production center has become a basic one. Today, industry is the mainstay of economic activities in Hong Kong.

The nature of manufacturing in Hong Kong is primarily oriented around consumer goods and light industrial products for export. About 70% of the total industrial work force in the colony is employed in the production of light industrial goods, such as textiles and garments, plastic products, toys, watches, clocks, and electronics. Textiles and garments are unquestionably the most important of the industrial products and account for approximately 50% of the total work force in industrial activities. A small amount of heavy and service

Table 11-3. Hong Kong's Foreign Trade (in millions of US dollars)

Exports, 1976		Imports, 1976	
Food	120	Food, beverages, etc.	1527
Fibers and raw materials	59	Fibers and raw materials	666
Fuel	–	Fuel	536
Chemicals	47	Chemicals	684
Manufactured goods	5326	Manufactured goods	3688
Machinery and transport equipment	958	Machinery and transport equipment	1540
Other goods	16	Other goods	17
Gold and coins	–	Gold and coins	457
Total exports	6526	Total imports	9115

Dollar conversions at the rate of $1 US for $5 Hong Kong.
Source: Hong Kong, 1977.

industries is located in Hong Kong, and most of this is focused around the maintenance and manufacturing of boats and ships as well as the manufacture of steel, machinery, and machine tools and some aircraft engineering maintenance. Hong Kong's exports go primarily to the United States, the Federal Republic of Germany, Great Britain, Japan, and Australia. These five countries account for almost two-thirds of Hong Kong's domestic exports.

Trading is essential for the survival of Hong Kong. Just as important as the export trade is, of course, the import trade. Hong Kong must import most of its foodstuffs as well as a variety of other goods ranging from fuel, airplanes, subway cars, buses, automobiles, down to very small things such as computers and appliances (Table 11-3). The major trading partners in terms of imports to the crown colony are Japan, the People's Republic of China, and the United States. Other significant trading partners from whom Hong Kong imports a considerable amount of goods are Singapore, the United Kingdom, Taiwan, and the Federal Republic of Germany.

One of the interesting aspects of Hong Kong's trade with the People's Republic of China is that a large share of the fresh, edible commodities that the population of Hong Kong consumes is brought in on a daily basis from adjacent counties in Guangdong Province. It is estimated that China gains more than 2 billion U.S. dollars per year as a result of its exports to Hong Kong. These exports include not only food, but a large variety of consumer and handicraft goods as well. The latter are sold principally at the famous Chinese emporiums and department stores that operate in the main shopping districts of Hong Kong and Kowloon. China's exports to the colony are a very important source of foreign exchange for the People's Republic. Such a favorable trading pattern for the People's Republic may also help explain the willingness of leaders in China to allow, and in fact encourage, continued progress and growth in the crown colony in which China is able to gain a major share.

Shoppers crowd the sidewalks along Queen's Road Central. Hong Kong is well known as an emporium for the world. (*C. W. Pannell*)

A final significant item in Hong Kong's economy is tourism. Tourism remains the second largest source of foreign earnings for the colony. In 1980, the amount of money generated by the tourist trade was approximately 1 billion U.S. dollars, and the growth rate of this tourist trade has been extremely rapid. One needs only look at the large number of hotels, restaurants, taverns, emporiums, and shops to understand the importance of tourism to the overall economy. In 1980, there were almost 2 million tourists who visited Hong Kong. The annual increase in tourists continues to be very rapid, and the colony is one of the most popular spots for tourists in monsoon Asia. Many visitors to China also like to spend time in Hong Kong before and after entry to the PRC. This popularity stems from the high quality of Hong Kong's facilities and the excitement of its fancy stores, hotels, boutiques, restaurants, and nightlife as well as its proximity to China. Shopping in the colony is unsurpassed, and the names of many famous stores from Paris, London, Tokyo, and New York are found in Hong Kong as well. Tourism will no doubt continue to grow and occupy an important niche in the economic structure of the colony.

Prospects for the Future

No analysis or discussion of Hong Kong is complete without some attempt to discuss what the prospects for future developments in the colony are likely to be. As indicated previously, the lease on most of the land area of the colony–the New Territories–is due to expire in 1997. A major question thus becomes: will the People's Republic of China request the reintegration of most of the land area of the colony into the PRC? In recent years, the government in Hong Kong has been investing a great deal of money in the construction of new town development in the New Territories. Employment centers and major industries have been located in the New Territories, and these have been surrounded by large housing estates, schools, markets, hospitals, and various types of service centers for the local populations. Hence, the colony has committed itself to the development of the New Territories and to the relocation of a large segment of the population out of the crowded Kowloon Peninsula and Hong Kong Island into the New Territories. Such a developmental direction would indicate that the British colonial government is acting in good faith in attempting to promote the best development of the island irrespective of the long-term future political status.

The question which follows, however, is more difficult to answer. That is, should the New Territories revert to China in 1997, what will become of Hong Kong Island and the Kowloon Peninsula? Hong Kong and Kowloon are the focus of most of the built-up urban land and indeed the area where most of the people are concentrated. Will the British also be willing to return this land to China? Will the Chinese and the British attempt to negotiate a settlement in which some British presence will be maintained, and the colony will continue to function as a center of free trade and free market economic activities? An arrangement such as the latter would appear to be in the best interest of the People's Republic of China. Moreover, at this time pragmatic philosophies of economic management prevail in China, and the best logic would indicate that the Chinese are likely to want to encourage Hong Kong to prosper in order that China may be a beneficiary from the economic progress of Hong Kong. Nevertheless, we must remember that domestic politics in China have changed frequently in recent years. A return to politically oriented policies led by leaders who place greater emphasis on Communist ideology and care less about the practical aspects of the economic growth might indicate that there could be problems in the long-term future of Hong Kong. Such leaders might be much more interested in reintegrating all of China's territory along the coast into the administrative territory of the People's Republic. It is clear that the British would be unable to hold out against China should the Chinese elect simply to take all of the colony and reintegrate it into the mainland.

At this point it seems likely that the Chinese and the British will negotiate some kind of settlement. One possibility might be for the New Territories to revert to China, although they might be allowed to continue some relatively close association with the British colony of Hong Kong and Kowloon. Another status might be preserved for Hong Kong island and the 11 square kilometers of the Kowloon Peninsula in which a joint Chinese and British presence would be maintained, and the concept of a dependency or some related kind of status would be maintained. Such a condition would permit the continuation of the tremendous economic dynamism that exists in Hong Kong, which may serve as an inspiration and a model for economic planners on the mainland. Clearly it is perceived as in

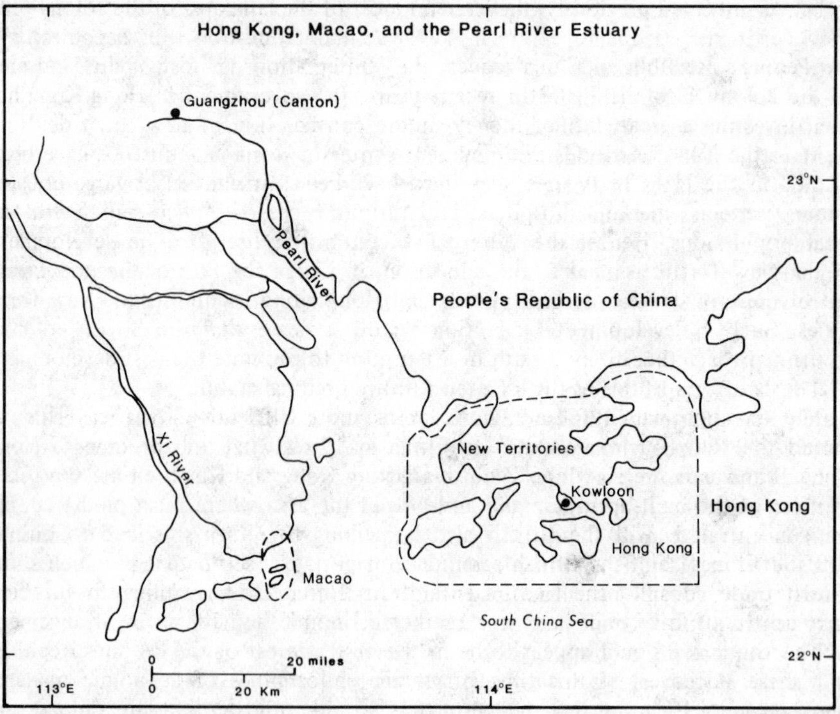

Fig. 11-1. Location of Hong Kong and Macao.

China's best interest to have this model of economic growth nearby as well as to have some of the advantages of selling Chinese goods in a center where there are a great many local Chinese as well as tourists with plenty of money to spend. For these reasons, it seems likely that whatever the legal status of Hong Kong in future years, its continuation as an example of dynamic, free market processes of economic growth will continue to be available to local people and tourists alike, and it will continue to be an attractive and exciting spot for the foreign visitor ("Hong Kong," *Asia Yearbook*, 1980).

MACAO

Macao, located 60 km west of Hong Kong across the mouth of the Pearl River, was established in 1557 as a Portuguese base for trade and missionary activity with China and Japan. Macao thrived for some years, but began to decline as a result of Japan's self-imposed isolation and the aggressive trading competition of the Dutch and other Europeans in East Asia. Rent was paid by the Portuguese on the territory until 1849 when the Portuguese declared Macao a free port. In 1887, a treaty was signed between Portugal and China whereby Macao and the two adjacent small islands of Coloane and Taipa (a total of 16 km^2) were ceded to Portuguese rule, although under the terms of the treaty, Portugal agreed not to alienate the territory without China's consent.

Macao in 1951 was made an overseas province of Portugal. In 1974, as a result of political changes in Portugal, the territory was redefined as Chinese territory under Portuguese administration with an elected minority on the local legislative assembly. Macao, despite its somewhat awkward and unusual political status, remains useful economically both for the Chinese and the Portuguese. It is likely to continue in its present form as long as it benefits both countries. China earns an estimated $100 million a year from Macao, including sales of food and water to the territory.

The territory of Macao is miniscule, composed of about 16 km^2. Approximately one-quarter of this land area is built up. Its 1981 population was approximately 300,000, of whom about 11,000 were Europeans and the remainder Chinese. The major economic activity of the territory is tourism and service activities (hotels, restaurants, shops, taxis, etc.) related to tourism. More than 2,000,000 tourists visit Macao each year, mainly to gamble at its casinos and dog track. It is also possible to visit China from Macao, and this has further stimulated the tourist trade. Most of the tourists enter from Hong Kong, and there is excellent ferry and hydrofoil service between Macao and Hong Kong.

The other main economic activity is the production of textiles and garments, and these goods, along with fireworks, account for most of Macao's exports. Those exports, however, have had problems in recent years due to the more severe restrictions on importation of garments and textiles, especially to the United States. Most recent investment has gone to improve tourist and harbor facilities. It seems clear that tourism is the only vibrant sector of Macao's economy.

Macao's future, like that of Hong Kong, is difficult to forecast. At this point the Chinese and Portuguese are getting along well, and both seem happy with the current status of Macao. The territory remains something of a stagnant backwater when compared with the growth of Hong Kong, but there is little anxiety over this situation. Moreover, slow growth is a well-known aspect of Macao's history and has not resulted in dramatic change in the past.

LITERATURE CITED

"Hong Kong," *Asia Yearbook*, 1980. Hong Kong: Far East Economic Review.

Hong Kong, 1977 (report of the previous year). Hong Kong: Hong Kong Government Press.

Tregear, T. R., 1980, *China, A Geographical Survey*. New York: John Wiley & Sons.

Chapter 12

Prospects for China's Modernization: A Geographical Appraisal

During the 18th and 19th centuries, many Western commentators and statesmen regarded China as poor and underdeveloped, on the one hand, but with enormous potential for growth and power, on the other hand. A common cliché was that China, with its large population and area, would someday awaken from its isolation and slumber and would shake the world. Since the mid-20th century, it has been conventional to observe that recent events in China–the Communist revolution and the drive to modernize–have indeed been earthshaking. This volume has attempted to examine and to evaluate the recent planned developmental efforts from the perspective of the geography of China–its physical and human resources and its spatial layout and interconnections.

More than 30 years have passed since the Communist revolution, and a great deal has been accomplished. China has become an important political power and the world's largest producer of food grains. China's domestic economy is large despite the relatively low level of annual per capita national income (estimated at $253 in 1979). The population is reasonably well fed and clothed, and modest housing and shelter have been provided. A base level of health care and education is available for all citizens, and it is either free or very inexpensive. Basic needs are being taken care of for the approximately 1 billion people of China (Ding, 1980). At the same time, all of China's people who are able are expected to work. Life is satisfactory, but conditions may be regarded as spartan.

An evaluation of the performance of the economy indicates a satisfactory record of economic growth; nevertheless problems remain. Some of these problems, especially some of the challenges that face the agricultural economy, may be traced to physical conditions of the country. Other problems stem from the large and growing population that places great demands on the economic system to provide employment. Although China has not been able to keep everyone employed, the rate of unemployment for the nation as a whole is believed to be low. The level of individual productivity remains low, however, and most people remain poor. It is useful to summarize and review some of the major physical and spatial impediments to development in contemporary China and to comment on efforts to overcome these obstacles. In this way, we may begin to arrive at a reasonable prospectus for future development and growth in China.

First, China's location and large land area present both advantages and obstacles to economic growth. It is clear that China's middle latitude location and long coastal exposure on the western Pacific basin give it enormous advantages of accessibility. China benefits from many of the same locational advantages that Japan has used so effectively to propel its development. Recent domestic political events in China suggest that more pragmatically focused policies will permit the country to become more outward looking in its economic and political orientation and thus take much greater advantage of its geographic position and situation, as it strengthens its trading and financial linkages with overseas partners and as it extends its maritime and international air linkages to more Pacific and southeast Asian locations. Such a reorientation can only be seen as a positive, growth-inducing factor in China's economic development and modernization.

Second, the large and diverse land area of China offers many prospects for a substantial mineral resource base, and China today has sufficient quantities of most minerals necessary to sustain its drive to modernization. Recent petroleum discoveries indicate China has important inland and offshore reserves. A modest quantity of petroleum was exported in recent years, but it is uncertain if China will be able to continue exporting petroleum. At least the country appears to have sufficient reserves to support its own rapidly expanding consumption (Wang, 1978).

Examples of obstacles to development that result from China's location and large size are the closure of western China by high mountains and the resulting spatial isolation and poor environmental conditions in that part of the country. Development has proceeded slowly and erratically in western China, where environmental conditions are not favorable for farming and the population is sparse. The combination of a high and dry environment that is typically either too hot or cold, with few people, and little advanced transportation has resulted in continued poverty and backwardness in western China.

LAND, ITS USE, AND PRODUCTIVITY

The land and physical resources of the country pose tremendous challenges. The supply of cultivated land is limited to 11% of the total surface area and may be declining. China in the future will face continuing problems over the availability of land for intensive row cropping (Pannell, in press). "Agriculture is the foundation" is a slogan that must be taken seriously. Although China in the 1950s followed the Soviet model of heavy industrial development, the emphasis has shifted away from that approach. Today it is clear the agriculture must be seen as the linchpin of the entire economic system. The agricultural sector of the economy must be nurtured carefully if progress, prosperity, social stability, and peace are to prevail.

Other related problems persist. North China has a serious shortage of water, and gigantic schemes have been conceived to remedy this by transferring water north from the Yangzi River. The scale of this project is enormous, but it is not entirely certain if the Yangzi really has sufficient water for transfer to the north. In addition, serious problems of soil salinization and alkalization may result from using the water for irrigation in North China. Water diversion may also lead to undesirable ecological consequences in the lower Yangzi area, including the damage to aquatic life and salt water incursion along the coast. The scheme of water transfer is still under study, and many scholars have urged the Chinese government to be cautious in making any decision on the project.

Recent events to modernize China must be seen in the light of China's history and cultural traditions as well as its contemporary politics and society. Here the enormous and growing population casts a long shadow, for the task of organizing and controlling such an enormous number of people is formidable indeed. The history of China's peasants working to wrest a living from the soil underpins the stability of the society and enables the system to continue even where conditions allow only a modest return on the effort invested. To this tradition, the Communist government has added its more far-reaching system for administering both urban and rural areas. The spatial units of administration were largely taken over from traditional existing units, such as hamlets and villages. But the functions, activities, and control were strengthened to the point where the new government has made its presence and authority known down to the level of the individual. This is a new achievement in China and one that has many implications.

Initially, this achievement signaled an important increase in the level of political integration both in spatial as well as functional terms. Additionally, since the units of political administration were usually also units of economic production, such as communes, a higher level of economic integration resulted. This improved level of economic integration logically grew out of the preexisting spatial as well as functional system of production. Today China is better organized and operated in a functional and spatial sense. Aggregate production, as our statistics have indicated, has also increased greatly. The human resources of China have been marshaled as never before, and the efforts of the population have been channeled to contribute to the well-being of the entire country. What remains is to raise the levels of individual productivity, so that the per capita contributions also rise rapidly. In this way the entire country will benefit, and eventually the level of individual well-being will reflect the productivity gains.

One of the best places to examine this relationship between production and productivity is in the agricultural sector. The quantity of irrigated land has tripled in the last 30 years and almost half of China's cropland is now irrigated, clearly an enormous investment in the agricultural sector, but more investment is needed. Food grain output has risen steadily during the last 30 years, and since 1979 has exceeded 300 million metric tons annually. The productivity of land has also increased steadily. Population growth, however, has offset much of the gain in food production, and China faces a very serious problem of improving the standard of living of its people if population growth is not slowed down. The per capita grain production figure has increased only slightly from 282 kg/capita in 1952 to 324 kg/capita in 1980. In brief, this modest gain in agricultural productivity summarizes the critical nature of the problems facing China as she looks toward the elusive goals of modernization by the year 2000.

NEW SOLUTIONS AND CONTINUING PROBLEMS

Several approaches to solve some of these critical problems are being followed. For example, since the excesses of the Cultural Revolution and Gang of Four era in the late 1960s and early 1970s, more practical policies that stress individual incentives and rewards have been followed. Free markets for farm products produced on private plots are a good indication of this, with the goal of producing more food as well as insuring a better availability of food for city dwellers. By 1980, it was clear that the market share distributed through free markets had increased substantially since the mid 1970s.

Decentralization of decision making in what to plant and where to plant is occurring, and such decisions are being increasingly turned over to the production teams. Teams are being encouraged, moreover, to negotiate production contracts with individual households. Recently, indications point to an encouragement of regional specialization in agriculture based on local environmental conditions. The production of more gains used to be the only concern in China's agricultural planning during the Maoist era, and grains were planted everywhere in China regardless of local conditions. This resulted in very poor yields in areas unsuitable for grains, including Tibet and the Loess Plateau. Since 1976, agricultural planning has increasingly permitted local areas to develop a diversified or specialized agrarian economy. At a more localized scale–the *xian* (county) level–specialization in a variety of commodities (to include timber, livestock, fish, and industrial crops) will be promoted. These commodities will be determined based on local needs and resources. Cities will increasingly be supplied from their immediate hinterlands. All of this increased specialization at local and regional scales indicates the result of geographical analysis of the conditions and needs of the country and a spatial approach to problem solving.

Other efforts indicate the use of new and different incentives even to the point of encouraging foreign capital and technology to come into China in order to make use of Chinese labor. The direction of centralized planning today encourages policies designed to attract external capital, technicians, and high technology equipment, especially to coastal areas in Guangdong and Fujian. Joint Chinese and foreign manufacturing ventures are being encouraged and set up. The goal is to learn from the Western style of technical development in order to provide more for China, a flexible and practical approach to the current goals of national development. Foreign trade and technical exchange are vitally important to these goals, and current policies have been to promote the growth of both of these areas.

Other problems abound. China's transportation system is poor. The rail system is insufficient to support the needs of such a large country and space economy. The rail system is expanding, but it is still insufficiently dense to serve many areas. The road system is poor, although perhaps it is adequate for the limited number of motorized vehicles available and likely in the near future. Air travel remains very limited, and is available primarily for officials and foreign tourists. Altogether the level of spatial integration is low, and enormous investments will be required to build the transportation system required for a modern economic system.

Industrial growth in China has been sporadic and much remains to be done. A major problem has been the lack of sufficient energy for industrial use, although China's coal, petroleum, and hydropower reserves are substantial. Thirty-seven million tons of steel production for 1980 was insufficient for the enormous demands of an economy that generated roughly $282 billion in 1980 in gross national product. Planning for new plants has not always been good, and the example of the problems of the Baoshan project, discussed previously, raise serious questions about the degree of care in planning that occurred when the push to modernize got under way in the late 1970s.

At the same time, one must look again at the great size of China to be aware of the enormous potential for economic growth that exists. For years, proponents have been urging China to undertake some of the great development projects. For example, the Yangzi River has enormous potential to produce hydroelectricity. One project is under way at Gezhouba and others are being planned. Yet the scale of these projects and the costs are enormous. The Chinese cannot afford poor decisions and investments, and they must be extremely careful to insure a good marginal rate of return on their investment. They also must try to avoid environmental problems that may lead to hidden future costs. Another great project, already noted, is the Yangzi River diversion to provide irrigation waters to drier areas in the North China Plain. Here again the costs are high and the consequences of such a project are difficult to forecast. The scale is large and the stakes are high. Indeed, all the world is watching to see what kind of performance takes place in China.

One of the major problems that results from the large size and poorly developed system of transportation and communications is the problem of spatial equity of economic well-being and opportunity. According to recent data, China suffers from a serious problem of regional inequality in per capita income levels (Fig. 12-1). If the data mapped in Figure 12-1 are accurate, they indicate that certain regions, especially those in the eastern part of China and several of the larger cities such as Shanghai and Peking, have average incomes remarkably higher (almost 20 times) than other areas. Conversely, the large, sparsely population provinces in western China, with average annual per capita incomes under $100, remain very poor.

Some development economists would argue that such inequalities are normal and should be expected in a large developing country. Over time and with continued economic growth, such inequalities may be expected to decline, as the effects of economic growth spread throughout the space economy. Such an

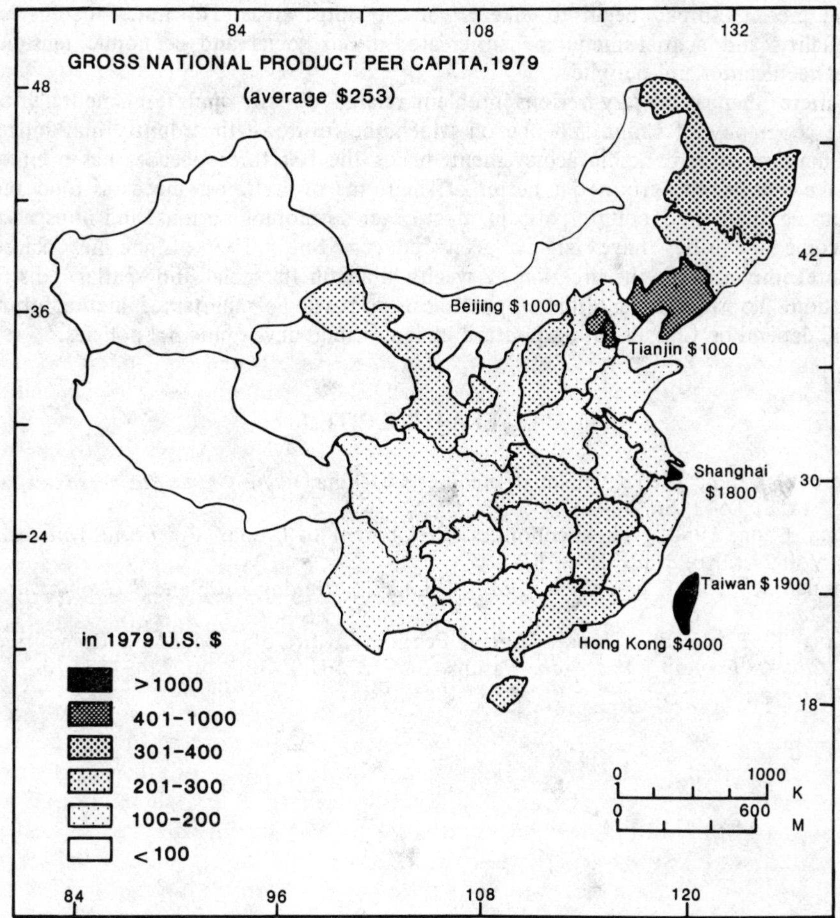

Fig. 12-1. Personal income in China, regional distribution and inequality.
Source: Official National Council Provincial files (as reported in Berney, 1981).

argument is probably unsatisfactory in China, for the country has indicated a strong commitment to spatial equity of well-being and to the reduction of differences between city and countryside. Yet the size of the country and the scale of the investments required for transportation and development projects to change these conditions suggest regional inequality of income and economic well-being are likely to continue to be an important aspect of the human geography of the country for many years. The crucial question may well be how great will the extremes of inequality and income become before the forces of regional balance and income spread begin to take effect over large areas. Too much income inequality and spatial inequity can create serious social and economic tensions between center and periphery.

Here then is a very serious problem related directly and fundamentally to the geography of China and one on which the future of the country may hinge. China's most remarkable achievement during the last three decades has been to make low-income groups far better off in terms of such basic needs as food and housing than their counterparts in most other developing nations, and nonspatial income inequities have largely been reduced. Since 1976, China has placed more emphasis on the creation of wealth than on its social and spatial redistribution. To what extent this emphasis can and will be maintained in the future will depend on China's future political ideologies and developmental policies.

LITERATURE CITED

Berney, Karen, 1981, "Personal Incomes in China." *The China Business Review*, Vol. 8, No. 2, pp. 19–20.

Ding, Chen, 1980, "The Economic Development of China." *Scientific American*, Vol. 243, No. 3, pp. 152–165.

Pannell, Clifton W., in press, 1982, "China's Shrinking Cropland." *Geographical Magazine*, Vol. 53.

Wang, K. P., 1978, "China's Mineral Economy." In Joint Economic Committee, *Chinese Economy Post Mao*. Washington, D.C.: U.S. GPO, pp. 374–407.

Appendix 1

Wade-Giles/Pinyin Conversion Table

Wade-Giles to Pinyin

Wade-Giles	Pinyin	Wade-Giles	Pinyin	Wade-Giles	Pinyin	Wade-Giles	Pinyin
a	a	ch’ü	qu	hsin	xin	ko	ge
ai	ai	chua	zhua	hsing	xing	k’o	ke
an	an	ch’ua	chua	hsiu	ziu	kou	gou
ang	ang	chuai	zhuai	hsiung	xiong	k’ou	kou
ao	ao	ch’uai	chuai	hsü	xu	ku	gu
		chuan	zhuan	hsüan	xuan	k’u	ku
cha	zha	ch’uan	chuan	hsüeh	xue	kua	gua
ch’a	cha	chüan	juan	hsün	xun	k’ua	kua
chai	zhai	ch’üan	quan	hu	hu	kuai	guai
ch’ai	chai	chuang	zhuang	hua	hua	k’uai	kuai
chan	zhan	ch’uang	chuang	huai	huai	kuan	guan
ch’an	chan	chüeh	jue	huan	huan	k’uan	kuan
chang	zhang	ch’üeh	que	huang	huang	kuang	guang
ch’uang	chang	chui	zhui	hui	hui	k’uang	kuang
chao	zhao	ch’ui	chui	hun	hun	kuei	gui
ch’ao	chao	chun	zhun	hung	hong	k’uei	kui
che	zhe	ch’un	chun	huo	huo	kun	gun
ch’e	che	chün	jun			k’un	kun
chen	zhen	ch’ün	qun	i	yi	kung	gong
ch’en	chen	chung	zhong			k’ung	kong
cheng	zheng	ch’ung	chong	jan	ran	kuo	guo

Wade-Giles	Pinyin	Wade-Giles	Pinyin	Wade-Giles	Pinyin	Wade-Giles	Pinyin
ch’eng	cheng			jang	rang	k’uo	kuo
chi	ji	en	en	jao	rao		
ch’i	qi	erh	er	je	re	la	la
chia	jia			jen	ren	lai	lai
ch’ia	qia	fa	fa	jeng	reng	lan	lan
chiang	jiang	fan	fan	jih	ri	lang	lang
ch’iang	qiang	fang	fang	jo	ruo	lao	lao
chiao	jiao	fei	fei	jou	rou	le	le
ch’iao	qiao	fen	fen	ju	ru	lei	lei
chieh	jie	feng	feng	juan	ruan	leng	leng
ch’ieh	qie	fo	fo	jui	rui	li	li
chien	jian	fou	fou	jun	run	lia	lia
ch’ien	qian	fu	fu	jung	rong	liang	liang
chih	zhi					liao	liao
ch’ih	chi	ha	ha	ka	ga	liah	lie
chin	jin	hai	hai	k’a	ka	lien	lian
ch’in	qin	han	han	kai	gai	lin	lin
ching	jing	hang	hang	k’ai	kai	ling	ling
ch’ing	qing	hao	hao	kan	gan	liu	liu
chiu	jiu	hei	hei	k’an	kan	lo	luo
ch’iu	qiu	hen	hen	kang	gang	lou	lou
chiung	jiong	heng	heng	k’ang	kang	lu	lu
ch’iung	qiong	ho	he	kao	gao	lü	lü
cho	zhou	hou	hou	k’ao	kao	luan	luan
ch’o	chuo	hsi	xi	kei	gei	lüan	lüan
chou	zhou	hsia	xia	k’ei	kei	lüeh	lüe
ch’ou	chou	hsiang	xiang	ken	gen	lun	lun
chu	zhu	hsiao	xiao	k’en	ken	lung	long
ch’u	chu	hsieh	xie	keng	geng		
chü	ju	hsien	xian	k’eng	keng	ma	ma
mai	mai	pao	bao	so	suo	tseng	zeng
man	man	p’ao	pao	sou	sou	ts’eng	ceng
mang	mang	pei	bei	ssu	si	tso	zuo
mao	mao	p’ei	pei	su	su	ts’o	cuo
mei	mei	pen	ben	suan	suan	tsou	zou
men	men	p’en	pen	sui	sui	ts’ou	cou
meng	meng	peng	beng	sun	sun	tsu	zu
mi	mi	p’eng	peng	sung	song	ts’u	cu
miao	miao	pi	bi			tsuan	zuan
mieh	mie	p’i	pi	ta	da	ts’uan	cuan
mien	mian	piao	biao	t’a	ta	tsui	zui
min	min	p’iao	piao	tai	dai	ts’ui	cui
ming	ming	pieh	bie	t’ai	tai	tsun	zun
miu	miu	p’ieh	pie	tan	dan	ts’un	cun
mo	mo	pien	bian	t’an	tan	tsung	zong
mou	mou	p’ian	pian	tang	dang	ts’ung	cong
mu	mu	pin	bin	t’ang	tang	tu	du
		p’in	pin	tao	dao	t’u	tu

Wade-Giles	Pinyin	Wade-Giles	Pinyin	Wade-Giles	Pinyin	Wade-Giles	Pinyin
na	na	ping	bing	t’ao	tao	tuan	duan
nai	nai	p’ing	ping	te	de	t’uan	tuan
nan	nan	po	bo	t’e	te	tui	dui
nang	nang	p’o	po	teng	deng	t’ui	tui
nao	nao	pou	bou	t’eng	teng	tun	dun
nei	nei	p’ou	pou	ti	di	t’un	tun
nen	nen	pu	bu	t’i	ti	tung	dong
neng	neng	p’u	pu	tiao	diao	t’ung	tong
ni	ni			t’iao	tiao	tzu	zi
niang	niang	sa	sa	tieh	die	tz’u	ci
niao	niao	sai	sai	t’ieh	tie		
nieh	hie	san	san	tien	dian	wa	wa
nien	nian	sang	sang	t’ien	tian	wai	wai
nin	nin	sao	sao	ting	ding	wan	wan
ning	ning	se	se	t’ing	ting	wang	wang
niu	niu	sen	sen	tiu	diu	wei	wei
no	nuo	seng	seng	to	duo	wen	wen
nou	nou	sha	sha	t’o	tuo	weng	weng
nu	nu	shai	shai	tou	dou	wo	wo
nü	nü	shan	shan	t’ou	tou	wu	wu
nuan	nuan	shang	shang	tsa	za		
nüeh	nüe	shao	shao	ts’a	ca	ya	ya
nung	nong	she	she	tsai	zai	yai	yai
		shen	shen	ts’ai	cai	yang	yang
o	e	sheng	sheng	tsan	zan	yao	yao
ou	ou	shih	shi	ts’an	can	yeh	ye
		shou	shou	tsang	zang	yen	yan
pa	ba	shu	shu	ts’ang	cang	yin	yin
p’a	pa	shua	shua	tsao	zao	ying	ying
pai	bai	shuai	shuai	ts’ao	cao	yu	you
p’ai	pai	shuan	shuan	tse	ze	yü	yu
pan	ban	shuang	shuang	ts’e	ce	yüan	yuan
p’an	pan	shui	shui	tsei	zei	yüeh	yue
pang	bang	shun	shun	tsen	zen	yün	yun
p’ang	pang	shuo	shuo	ts’en	cen	yung	yong

Selected Bibliography

Academy of Sciences, USSR, 1960, *Soviet-Chinese Study of the Geography of Sinkiang* (Prirodnyye usloviya Sinitszyana). Moscow: Publishing House of the Academy of Sciences (JPRS 15084, 31 Aug. 1962).

Ahn, Byung-Joon, 1975, "The Political Economy of the People's Commune in China: Changes and Continuities." *Journal of Asian Studies*, Vol. 34, No. 3, pp. 631–658.

Aird, John S., 1978, "Population growth in the People's Republic of China." In *Chinese Economy Post-Mao*, Vol. 1, *Policy and Performance*. Papers submitted to the Joint Economic Committee, 95th Congress, 2nd Session. Washington, D.C.: U.S. Government Printing Office, pp. 439–475.

American Plant Studies Delegation, 1975, *Plant Studies in the People's Republic of China.* Washington, D.C.: National Academy of Sciences.

The American Rural Small-Scale Industry Delegation, 1977, *Rural Small-Scale Industry in the People's Republic of China.* Berkeley: University of California Press.

An, Keshi, 1980, "Thermal Spring in China." *Geojournal*, Vol. 4, No. 6, pp. 507–513.

Andersson, J. G., 1934, *Children of the Yellow Earth.* London: Kegan Paul, Trench, Trubner.

Banister, Judith, 1977, "Mortality, Fertility, and Contraceptive Use in Shanghai." *China Quarterly*, No. 70, June, pp. 255–295.

Barclay, George, 1954, *Colonial Development and Population in Taiwan.* Princeton: Princeton University Press.

Baum, Richard, editor, 1980, *China's Four Modernizations, The New Technological Revolution.* Boulder, Colorado: Westview Press.

Beijing Review, 1978, "Meeting on Family Planning," Vol. 21, No. 29, p. 4.

_______, 1979, "Communique on Fulfillment of China's 1978 National Economic Plan," Vol. 22, No. 27 (July 6), p. 41.

_______, 1979, "Fuel and Power Industries," Vol. 22, No. 43 (Oct. 26), p. 27.

_______, 1980, "Coal and Petroleum Targets Met," Vol. 24, No. 2 (Jan. 12), p. 7.

_______, 1980, "Eight Coal Bases Under Construction," Vol. 23, No. 26 (June 30), pp. 4–5.

_______, 1981, "Communique on Fulfillment of China's 1980 National Economic Plan," Vol. 24, No. 19 (May 11), p. 25.

Bennett, Gordon, 1978, *Huadong, The Study of a Chinese People's Commune.* Boulder, Colorado: Westview Press.

Berney, Karen, 1981, "Personal Incomes in China." *China Business Review*, Vol. 8, No. 2, pp. 19–20.

Buchanan, Keith, 1966, *The Chinese People and the Chinese Earth.* London: G. Bell and Sons.

_______, 1970, *The Transformation of the Chinese Earth.* London: G. Bell and Sons.

Buck, David C., 1977, "Ta-Ch'ing: A Model Industrial Community in the People's Republic of China." *The China Geographer*, No. 7, pp. 17–36.

_______, 1978, *Urban Change in China, Politics and Development in Tsinan, Shantung, 1890–1949.* Madison: The University of Wisconsin Press.

Buck, John L., 1935, *Land Utilization in China.* Shanghai: Commercial Press (atlas and text).

_______, 1937, *Land Utilization in China: A Study of 16,786 Farms in 168 Localities, and 32,256 Farm Families in 22 Provinces in China, 1929–1933.* Nanking: University of Nanking.

Butler, Steven, 1978, *Agricultural Mechanization in China. The Administrative Impact.* Occasional Papers of the East Asian Institute, Columbia University, New York.

Central Intelligence Agency, 1972, *Atlas of China.* Washington, D.C.: U.S. Government Printing Office.

_______, 1977, *China: Oil Production Prospects.* (ER77-100 30U). Washington, D.C.

Central Meteorological Bureau, Office of Climatological Data Research, 1960, *An Atlas of Chinese Climatology* (Zhongguo Qihou Tu). Beijing: Map Publishing Society (JPRS 16321, 23 Nov. 1962).

Chang, Chi-yun, 1962, *National Atlas of China.* Yangmingshan: Taipei, National War College, Republic of China.

Chang, K. C., 1977, *The Archeology of Ancient China*, 3rd ed. New Haven and London: Yale University Press.

Chang, Kuei-sheng, 1975, "The Geography of Contemporary China: Inventory and Prospect." *The Professional Geographer*, Vol. 27, No. 1, pp. 2–6.

Chang, Sen-dou, 1963, "Historical Trend of Chinese Urbanization." *Annals of the Association of American Geographers*, Vol. 53, pp. 109–143.

_______, 1971, "China's Crop-Land Use, 1957." *Pacific Viewpoint*, Vol. 12, No. 1, 75–87.

_______, 1976, "The Changing System of Chinese Cities." *Annals of the Association of American Geographers*, Vol. 66, pp. 398–415.

_______, 1981, "Modernization and China's Urban Development." *Annals of the Association of American Geographers*, Vol. 71, pp. 202–219.

Chao, Kang, 1970, *Agricultural Production in Communist China, 1949–1965.* Madison: University of Wisconsin Press.

Chao, Shih-ying, 1963, "Searching the Direction of China's Agriculture." *Kexue Tongbao* (*Science Bulletin*), No. 8.

Chen, C. S., 1963, *Taiwan, An Economic and Social Geography*, Vol. 1. Taipei: Fu-Min Geographical Institute of Economic Development, Research Report No. 96, pp. 269–299.

Chen, Cheng-siang, 1967, "Ups and Downs of 'Acta Geographica Sinica': Some Personal Observations." *Geographical Review*, Vol. 57, No. 1, pp. 108–111.

Chen, C. S., 1973, "Population Growth and Urbanization in China, 1953–1970." *The Geographical Review*, Vol. 63, pp. 55–72.

Chen, Kao Tang, editor, 1980, *China Yearbook.* Taipei: China Publishing Co.

Chen, Nai-Ruenn, editor, 1969, *Chinese Economic Statistics, A Handbook for Mainland China.* Chicago: Aldine Publishing Co.

_______, 1978, "Economic Modernization in Post Mao China: Policies, Problems and Prospects." In U.S. Congress, Joint Economic Committee, *Chinese Economy Post Mao.* Washington, D.C.: U.S. Government Printing Office, pp. 165–203.

Chen, Pi-chao, 1976, *Population and Health Policy in the People's Republic of China.* Washington, D.C.: Interdisciplinary Communications Program, Smithsonian Institute.

Chi, Chao-ting, 1936, *Key Economic Areas in Chinese History.* London: George Allen & Unwin.

The China Business Review, 1980, "The Three Gorges Controversy Rages On," Vol. 7, No. 3, May–June, p. 23.

China Reconstructs, 1972, "About National Minorities in China," Vol. 21, No. 12 (Dec.), p. 8.

_______, 1978, "At the Hsishuangpanna Tai Autonomous Prefecture," Vol. 27, No. 12, p. 31.

_______, 1978, "The Yuchia-Miao Autonomous Prefecture," Vol. 27, No. 7, p. 35.

Council for International Economic Cooperation and Development, 1972, *Manpower Development in Republic of China.* Taipei Manpower Development Committee.

Cressey, George B., 1955, *Land of the 500 Million, A Geography of China.* New York: McGraw-Hill.

Crook, Frederick, 1975, "The Commune System in the People's Republic of China, 1963–74." In Joint Economic Committee, *China: A Reassessment of the Economy.* Washington, D.C.: U.S. Government Printing Office, pp. 346–410.

Davidson, James W., 1903, *The Island of Formosa, Historical View from 1430–1900.* New York: Macmillan.

DeGlopper, Donald R., 1972, "Doing Business in Lukang." In W. E. Willmott (ed.), *Economic Organization in Chinese Society.* Stanford: Stanford University Press, pp. 297–326.

Dili zhishi, 1976, "Meilide Sandu Shuizu zizhixian" (The Beautiful Sandu Shui Nationality Autonomous County), No. 12, p. 14.

_______, 1976, "Miaoling Jubican" (Great Changes in the Miao Hills), No. 6, p. 1.

_______, 1977, "Yulong xueshanxia de Naxizu" (The Naxi Nationality of the Snowy Yulong Mountains), No. 10, p. 10.

Ding, Chen, 1980, "The Economic Development of China." *Scientific American*, Vol. 243, No. 3, pp. 152–165.

Donnithorne, Audrey, 1974, "Recent Economic Developments." *The China Quarterly*, Vol. 60, pp. 772–774.

Drake, Fred W., 1975, *China Charts the World: Hsu Chi-Yu and His Geography of 1848.* Cambridge: Harvard University, East Asian Research Center.

Dreyer, June T., 1976, *China's Forty Million.* Cambridge, Mass.: Harvard University Press.

Duan Wanti, Pu Qingyu and Wu Xihao, 1980, "Climatic Variations in China During the Quarternary." *Geojournal*, Vol. 4, No. 6, pp. 515–524.

Eckstein, Alexander, 1973, "Economic Growth and Change in China: A Twenty-Year Perspective." *The China Quarterly*, Vol. 54, pp. 211–241.

_______, 1977, *China's Economic Revolution.* Cambridge: Cambridge University Press.

_______, editor, 1980, *Quantitative Measures of China's Economic Output.* Ann Arbor: University of Michigan Press.

(Editorial Staff), 1977, Hsiang kexueh jinjun pandong dilixueh gaofen (Toward Advancing Science, To Climb the Highest Peaks of Geographic Study). *Dili zhishi* (*Geographical Knowledge*), No. 12, pp. 1–2.

Elvin, Mark, 1973, *The Pattern of the Chinese Past.* Stanford: Stanford University Press.

Evans, L. T., 1980, "The Natural History of a Crop Yield." *American Scientist*, Vol. 64, No. 8, pp. 388–397.

Fairbank, John K., Reischauer, Edwin O., and Craig, Albert M., 1973, *East Asia: Tradition and Transformation.* Boston: Houghton Mifflin.

FAO Fisheries Mission to China, 1977, *Freshwater Fisheries and Aquaculture in China.* Rome: Food and Agriculture Organization of the United Nations, FAO Fisheries Technical Paper No. 168.

FAO/UNDP Study Tour to the People's Republic of China, 1977, *China: Recycling of Organic Wastes in Agriculture.* Rome: Food and Agriculture Organization of the United Nations, FAO Soils Bulletin No. 40.

Fisher, Jack, 1962, "Planning the City of Socialist Man." *Journal of the American Institute of Planners*, Vol. 28, No. 4, 251–265.

Fountain, Kevin, 1980, "The Development of China's Offshore Oil." *The China Business Review*, Vol. 7, No. 1, pp. 22–36.

Fung, K., 1981, "Satellite Town Development in the Shanghai City Region." *Town Planning Review*, Vol. 52, pp. 26–46.

Gallin, Bernard, 1966, *Hsin Hsing, Taiwan: A Chinese Village in Change.* Berkeley: University of California Press.

Gallin, Bernard and Gallin, Rita, 1971, "The Integration of Village Migrants in Taipei." In Mark Elvin and G. William Skinner (eds.), *The Chinese City Between Two Worlds.* Stanford: Stanford University Press, pp. 331–358.

Gentelle, Pierre, 1965, "Recherche et enseignement géographiques en Republique populaire de Chine." *Annales De Géographie*, Vol. 74, No. 402, pp. 354–359.

Ginsburg, Norton, 1958, *The Pattern of Asia.* Englewood Cliffs, N.J.: Prentice-Hall.

_______, 1961, *Atlas of Economic Development.* Chicago, Ill.: University of Chicago Press.

_______, 1980, "Urbanization and Development: Processes, Policies and Contributions." In C. K. Leung and Norton Ginsburg (eds.), *China, Urbanization and National Development.* Chicago: University of Chicago, Department of Geography, Research Paper No. 196, pp. 259–280.

Greer, Charles, 1979, *Water Management in the Yellow River Basin of China.* Austin: University of Texas Press.

Groen, Henry J. and Kilpatrick, James A., 1978, "Chinese Agricultural Production."

In Joint Economic Committee of the U.S. Congress, *Chinese Economy Post-Mao*, Vol. 1. Washington, D.C.: U.S. Government Printing Office, pp. 607–652.

Grubov, V. I., 1969, "Flora and Vegetation." In Institute of Geography, USSR Academy of Sciences, *The Physical Geography of China*, Vol. I. New York: Frederick A. Praeger, pp. 265–364.

Hanson, Jaydee, 1980, "China's Fisheries: Scaling up Production." *The China Business Review*, Vol. 7, No. 3, pp. 25–30.

Harris, C. and Ullman, E., 1945, "The Nature of Cities." *Annals of the American Association of Political and Social Sciences*, No. 242, pp. 7–17.

Harrison, Selig A., 1977, *China, Oil, and Asia: Conflict Ahead?* New York: Columbia University Press.

Harvey, David, 1973, *Social Justice and the City*. Baltimore: Johns Hopkins University Press.

Heaton, Bill, 1971, "Red Sun in Sinkiang." *Far Eastern Economic Review*, Vol. 71, No. 3 (Jan. 16), p. 46.

Herman, Theodore, editor, 1967, *The Geography of China: A Selected and Annotated Bibliography*. New York: University of the State of New York.

Hinton, William, 1966, *Fanshen, A Documentary of Revolution in a Chinese Village*. New York: Vintage Books.

Ho, Ping-ti, 1959, *Studies on the Population of China, 1368–1953*. Cambridge, Mass.: Harvard University Press.

_______, 1969, "The Loess and the Origin of Chinese Agriculture." *American Historical Review*, Vol. 75, No. 1, pp. 1–36.

_______, 1975, *The Cradle of the East*, An Inquiry into the Indigenous Origins of Techniques and Ideas of Neolithic and Early Historic China, 5000–1000 B.C. Hong Kong: The Chinese University of Hong Kong Press.

Ho, Samuel P. S., 1978, *Economic Development of Taiwan*. New Haven: Yale University Press.

Howe, Christopher, 1970, *Urban Employment and Economic Growth in Communist China, 1943–1957*. Cambridge: Cambridge University Press.

Hsiao, Kung-chuan, 1960, *Rural China, Imperial Control in the Nineteenth Century*. Seattle: University of Washington Press.

Hsieh, Chiao-min, 1958, "Hsia-ke Hsu-Pioneer of Modern Geography in China." *Annals of the Association of American Geographers*, Vol. 48, pp. 73–82.

_______, 1959, "The Status of Geography in Communist China." *Annals of the Association of American Geographers*, Vol. 49, pp. 535–551.

_______, 1964, *Taiwan-Ilha Formosa, A Geography in Perspective*. Woburn, Mass.: Butterworth.

_______, 1973, *Atlas of China*. New York: McGraw-Hill.

Hsu, Mei-ling, 1969, "Taiwan Population Distribution, 1965," Map Supplement No. 19. *Annals of the Association of American Geographers*, Vol. 59, pp. 611–617.

Hsu, Shin-yi, 1981, "The Ecology of Chinese Neolithic Cultural Expansion." *The China Geographer*, No. 11, pp. 1–26.

Hsu, Yi-rong Ann, Pannell, Clifton W., and Wheeler, James O., 1980, "The Development and Structure of Transportation Networks in Taiwan." In Ronald Knapp (ed.), *China's Island Frontier*, pp. 167–202.

Hu, Huon-yon, 1936, "The Agricultural Regions of China." *Journal of the Geographical Society of China*, Vol. 3, No. 1, pp. 1–17 (in Chinese).

Huang, Philip C. C., 1980, *The Development of Underdevelopment in China*. White Plains, N.Y.: M. E. Sharpe.

Husayin, Abayduila, 1966, "The New Sinkiang." *China Reconstructs*, Vol. 15, No. 1 (Jan.), p. 26.

Joint Economic Committee, Congress of the U.S., 1975, *China: A Reassessment of the Economy*. Washington, D.C.: U.S. Government Printing Office.

Kamm, John, 1980, "Importing Some of Hong Kong . . . Exporting Some of China." *The China Business Review*, Vol. 7, No. 2 (March–April), pp. 28–35.

Kao, Hsia, 1978, "Yangtze Waters Diverted to North China." *Peking Review*, No. 38 (Sept. 22), pp. 6–9.

Kikolski, Bohdan, 1964, "Contemporary Research in Physical Geography in the Chinese People's Republic." *Annals of the Association of American Geographers*, Vol. 54, No. 12, pp. 181–189.

King, Frank H., 1926, *Farmers of Forty Centuries*. London: Jonathan Cape Ltd.

Kirkby, Richard, 1977, "Geography and Planning at Nanking University." *The China Geographer*, No. 7, pp. 51–58.

Klatt, W., 1977, "Cost of Food Basket in Urban Areas of The People's Republic of China." *The China Quarterly*, June, No. 70, p. 407.

Knapp, Ronald, 1978, "The Geographer and Taiwan." *The China Quarterly*, No. 74, pp. 356–368.

_______, editor, 1980, *China's Island Frontier*. Honolulu: University of Hawaii Press.

Kono, Michihiro, 1966, "Scholars Learn from the Masses–Impressions of the People's Republic of China." *Chiri* (*Geography*), Vol. 11, p. 48.

Kramer, G. P. and Wu, George, 1970, *An Introduction to Taiwanese Folk Religions*. Taipei: Published by authors.

Kung, P., 1975, "Farm Crops of China." *World Crops*, May/June, pp. 122–132.

Kuo, Leslie T. C., 1972, *The Technical Transformation of Chinese Agriculture*. New York: Praeger.

Kuo, Ting-yee, 1973, "Early Stages in the Sinicization of Taiwan, 230-1683." pp. 21–57 and "The Internal Development and Modernization of Taiwan, 1863–1891," pp. 171–240. In Paul K. T. Sih (ed.), *Taiwan in Modern Times*. New York: St. Johns University Press.

Lai, Chuen-yan, 1970, "Chinese Written Language and Geographical Names." *Canadian Geographical Journal*, Vol. 80, pp. 20–25.

Lal, Amrit, 1970, "Signification of Ethnic Minorities in China." *Current Scene*, Vol. 8, No. 4, p. 16.

Lardy, Nicholas R., 1975, "Economic Planning in The People's Republic of China: Central Provincial Fiscal Relations." In *China: A Reassessment of the Economy*. Washington, D.C.: Joint Economic Committee, U.S. Government Printing Office, pp. 94–115.

_______, editor, 1977, *Chinese Economic Planning* (translation from Chi-hua Ching-chi). White Plains, N.Y.: M. E. Sharpe.

_______, 1978, Recent Chinese Economic Performance and Prospect for the Ten Year Plan. In U.S. Congress, Joint Economic Committee, *Chinese Economy Post Mao*. Washington, D.C.: U.S. Government Printing Office, pp. 48–62.

Lattimore, Owen, 1962, *Studies in Frontier History*. London: Oxford University Press.

Lee, J. S., 1939, *The Geology of China*. London: Thomas Murby.

Lee, Teng-hui, 1971, *Intersectoral Capital Flows in the Economic Development of Taiwan, 1895–1960*. Ithaca, N.Y.: Cornell University Press.

Leeming, Frank, 1979, "Progress Toward Triple Cropping in China." *Asian Survey*, Vol. 19, pp. 450–467.

Leszczycki, S., 1953, "The Development of Geography in The People's Republic of China." *Geography*, Vol. 48, pp. 139–154.

Leung, C. K., 1979, "Transportation and Spatial Integration." In Lee Ngok and Leung Chi-Keung (eds.), *China: Development and Challenge*, Proceedings of the Fifth Leverhulme Conference, Vol. II, "*Political Economy and Spatial Pattern and Process.*" Hong Kong: University of Hong Kong, Centre of Asian Studies, pp. 323–342.

_______ and Chiu, T. N., 1974, "Some Geographical Implications of the Revolution in Education in China." *Pacific Viewpoint*, Vol. 15, pp. 51–60.

Li, Choh-ming, 1962, *The Statistical System of Communist China.* Berkeley and Los Angeles: University of California Press.

Li, Tingdong, 1980, "The Development of Geological Structures in China." *Geojournal*, Vol. 4, No. 6, pp. 487–497.

Li, Victor H., 1980, *The Future of Taiwan.* White Plains, N.Y.: M. E. Sharpe.

Lin, Ching-yuan, 1973, *Industrialization in Taiwan, 1946–72.* New York: Praeger.

Lippit, Victor, 1966, "Development of Transportation in Communist China." *The China Quarterly*, No. 27, 101–119.

Liu, Ta-Chung and Yen, Kung-chia, 1963, *The Economy of the Chinese Mainland: National Income and Economic Development, 1933–1959.* Santa Monica, Calif.: The Rand Corporation.

Lo, C. P., 1977, "Landsat Images as a Tool in Regional Analysis: The Examples of Chu Chiang (Pearl River) Delta in South China." *Geoforum*, Vol. 8, pp. 79–87.

_______, 1979, "Spatial Form and Land Use Patterns of Modern Chinese Cities: An Exploratory Model." In Lee Ngok and Leung Chi-Keung (eds.), *China: Development and Challenge*, Proceedings of the Fifth Leverhulme Conference. Hong Kong: Centre of Asian Studies University of Hong Kong, pp. 233–272.

Lo, Chor-pang, Pannell, Clifton W., and Welch, Roy A., 1977, "Land Use Changes and City Planning in Shenyang and Canton." *Geographical Review*, Vol. 67, No. 3, pp. 268–283.

Ludlow, Nicholas, 1980, "Gezhouba on the Yangzi." *The China Business Review*, Vol. 7, No. 3, pp. 11–15.

_______, 1980, "Harnessing the Yangzi." *The China Business Review*, Vol. 7, No. 3, pp. 16–21.

Luo, Fu, 1980, "City Dwellers and the Neighborhood Committee." *Beijing Review*, No. 44 (Nov. 3), pp. 19–25.

Ma, Hsueh-liang, 1962, "New Scripts for China's Minorities." *China Reconstructs* (Aug.), pp. 24–25.

Ma, Laurence J. C., 1969, "Serial Publications for Geographical Research on Communist China from Hong Kong." *Professional Geographer*, Vol. 21, pp. 38–39.

_______, 1971, *Commercial Development and Urban Change in Sung China 960–1279.* Ann Arbor: University of Michigan, Department of Geography, Publication No. 6, 1971.

_______, 1977, "Counterurbanization and Rural Development: The Strategy of Hsia-Hsiang." *Current Scene*, Vol. 15, Nos. 8 and 9, pp. 1–12.

_______, 1977, "Rural Industrial Development in China." *The China Geographer*, No. 7, pp. 1–16.

_______, 1978, "Economic Aspects of Hsin-Hua People's Commune, Hau Hsien, Kuangtung." *The China Geographer*, No. 9, pp. 33–42.

_______, 1979, "The Chinese Approach to City Planning: Policy, Administration and Action." *Asian Survey*, Vol. 19, pp. 838–855.

_______, 1979, Field notes, Urumqi, Xinjiang Province (Aug. 16).

_______ and Hanten, Edward, editors, 1981, *Urban Development in Modern China.* Boulder, Colorado: Westview Press.

_______ and Noble, Allen, 1979, "Recent Developments in Chinese Geographic Research." *Geographical Review*, Vol. 69, pp. 63–78.

MacDougall, Colina, 1977, "The Chinese Economy in 1976." *The China Quarterly*, No. 70, p. 355.

March, Andrew L., 1974, *The Idea of China, Myth and Theory in Geographic Thought.* New York: Praeger.

Matley, Ian, 1966, "The Marxist Approach to the Geographical Environment." *Annals of the Association of American Geographers*, Vol. 56, No. 1, pp. 97–111.

McMillen, Donald H., 1979, *Chinese Communist Power and Policy in Xinjiang, 1949–1977.* Boulder, Colo.: Westview Press.

Moseley, George V. H., 1973, *The Consolidation of the South China Frontier.* Berkeley and Los Angeles: University of California Press.

Movius, Hallam L., 1944, *Early Man and Pleistocene Stratigraphy in Southern and Eastern Asia.* Papers of the Peabody Museum, No. 19, Harvard University.

Murzayev, E. A. and Chou, Li-san, 1959, *Natural Conditions in the Sinkiang Uighur Autonomous Region* (JPRS 18689, 15 April 1963).

Myers, Ramon H., 1980, *The Chinese Economy, Past and Present.* Belmont, Calif.: Wadsworth.

_______ and Ching, Adrienne, 1964, "Agricultural Development in Taiwan Under Japanese Colonial Rule." *Journal of Asian Studies*, Vol. 23, pp. 555–570.

Murphey, Rhoads, 1954, *Shanghai, Key to Modern China.* Cambridge, Mass.: Harvard University Press.

_______, 1973, "Geographic Study of China." In Marvin W. Mikesell (ed.), *Geographers Abroad*. Chicago: University of Chicago, Department of Geography, Research Paper No. 152, pp. 94–109.

_______, 1974, "The Treaty Ports and China's Modernization." In M. Elvin and G. W. Skinner (eds.), *The Chinese City Between Two Worlds.* Stanford, Calif.: Stanford University Press, pp. 17–72.

_______, 1980, *The Fading of the Maoist Vision, City and Country in China's Development.* New York: Metheun.

Nanjing Institute of Pedology, 1978, *Zhongguo Turang* (China's Soils). Beijing: Science Press.

National Foreign Assessment Center, 1978, *China: Economic Indicators.* Washington, D.C.: Central Intelligence Agency (ER 78-10750, Dec.).

_______, 1978, *China: International Trade, 1977–78.* Washington, D.C.: Central Intelligence Agency (ER 78-10721).

_______, 1980, *Electric Power for China's Modernization: The Hydroelectric Option.* Washington, D.C.: Central Intelligence Agency (ER-80-10089U, May).

Nuttonson, M. Y., 1968, *Agricultural Climates of China.* Washington, D.C.: American Institute of Crop Ecology.

Oksenberg, Michel, editor, 1973, *China's Developmental Experience.* New York: Praeger.

Orleans, Leo A., 1959, "The Recent Growth of China's Urban Population." *Geographical Review*, Vol. 49, pp. 43–57.

_______, 1972, *Every Fifth Child, The Population of China.* Stanford, Calif.: Stanford University Press.

_______, 1977, *China's Birth Rate, Death Rate, and Population Growth: Another Perspective.* A report prepared for the Committee on International Relations, U.S. House of Representatives, 95th Congress, 1st Session. Washington, D.C.: U.S. Government Printing Office.

_______, 1980, *Science in Contemporary China.* Stanford, Calif.: Stanford University Press.

Pannell, Clifton W., 1973, "Recent Change and Stagnation in the Pescadores Islands, Taiwan." *Philippine Geographical Journal*, Vol. 7, No. 2, pp. 31–45.

_______, 1974, "Development and the Middle City in Taiwan." *Growth and Change*, Vol. 5, No. 3, pp. 21–29.

_______, 1977, "Past and Present City Structure in China." *Town Planning Review*, Vol. 48, No. 2, pp. 157–172.

_______, 1980, "Geography." In Leo Orleans (ed.), *Science in Contemporary China.* Stanford: Stanford University Press, pp. 167–187.

_______, 1981, "Recent Growth and Change in China's Urban System." In Laurence J. C. Ma and Edward Hanten (eds.), *Urban Development in Modern China.* Boulder, Colo.: Westview Press, pp. 91–113.

_______, 1982 (forthcoming), "China's Shrinking Cropland." *Geographical Magazine*, Vol. 53.

_______ and Welch, R., 1980, "Recent Growth and Structural Change in Chinese Cities." *Urban Geography*, Vol. 1, No. 1, pp. 68–80.

Parish, William L and Whyte, Martin King, 1978, *Village and Family in Contemporary China.* Chicago: University of Chicago Press.

Pasternak, Burton, 1972, *Kinship and Community in Two Chinese Villages.* Stanford: Stanford University Press.

Peking Review, 1974, "Rapid Growth in China's Minority Population," No. 49 (Oct. 4), pp. 30–31, 40.

_______, 1975, "Books in Minority Languages," No. 50 (Dec. 12), p. 30.

Perkins, Dwight, 1966, *Market Control and Planning in Communist China.* Cambridge, Mass.: Harvard University Press.

_______, 1969, *Agricultural Development in China, 1368–1968.* Chicago: Aldine.

Perrolle, Pierre M., 1980, *Science and Socialist Construction in China.* White Plains, N.Y.: M. E. Sharpe.

Population Reference Bureau, 1980, *1980 World Population Data Sheet.* Washington, D.C.: Population Reference Bureau, Inc.

Posner, A. and de Keijzer, A., 1976, *China: A Resource and Curriculum Guide.* Chicago: The University of Chicago Press.

Qi, Ya, 1979, "Visiting the Ewenkis." *Beijing Review*, Vol. 22, No. 6, p. 25.

Raper, Arthur, 1953, *Urban Taiwan, Crowded and Resourceful.* Taipei: Joint Commission on Rural Reconstruction.

Rawski, Thomas G., 1980, *China's Transition to Industrialism.* Ann Arbor: The University of Michigan Press.

Ren, Beie, Yang Renzhang, and Bao Haoshen, 1979, *Zhongguo dzran dili gang yao* (*Physical Geography of China*). Beijing: Commercial Press.

1965 Renmin shouce, 1965 (*1965 People's Handbook*). Beijing: Xinhua shudian.

Richardson, S. R., 1966, *Forestry in Communist China.* Baltimore: Johns Hopkins Press.

Rodgers, Allan, 1975, "Some Observations on the Current Status of Geography in The People's Republic of China." *The China Geographer*, No. 1, (Spring), pp. 13–24.

Ross, Lester, 1981, "Forestry in the PRC: Estimating the Gains and Losses." *China Geographer*, No. 11, pp. 113–127.

Rozman, Gilbert, 1973, *Urban Networks in Ch'ing China and Tokugawa Japan.* Princeton: Princeton University Press.

Saifudin, 1975, "Zai Maozhuxi geming luxian zhiyin xia shengli qiangjin," (March Forward Victoriously Under the Revolutionary Line of Chairman Mao). *Hongqi* (*Red Flag*), No. 19, pp. 23–24.

Salter, Christoper L., 1972, "Hsia-Fang: The Use of Migration by the Chinese in Their Quest for a Classless Society." *Proceedings of the Association of American Geographers*, Vol. 4, pp. 96–99.

_______, 1976, "Chinese Experiments in Urban Space: The Quest for an Agrapolitan China." *Habitat*, Vol. 1, No. 1, pp. 19–35.

_______, 1977, "Ta-chai beyond Ta-chai: Some Unsuspected Lessons for the USA from a Chinese Campaign." *China Geographer*, No. 7, pp. 59–66.

Samuels, Marwyn S., 1977, "Geography in China: Trends in Research and Training." *Pacific Affairs*, Vol. 50, No. 3, pp. 406–425.

Schurmann, Franz, 1966, *Ideology and Organization in Communist China.* Berkeley and Los Angeles: University of California Press.

Selya, Roger, 1981, "Food for the Cities of Taiwan." *The China Geographer*, No. 11, pp. 73–87.

Schwarz, Henry G., 1971, *Chinese Policies Towards Minorities*, Western Washington State University, Program in East Asian Studies, Occasional Paper #2.

Shabad, Theodore, 1972, *China's Changing Map: National and Regional Development 1949–71*, (rev. ed.). New York: Praeger.

_______, 1976, "Hydroelectric Progress in The People's Republic of China." *The China Geographer*, No. 3, pp. 1–20.

Shen, T. H., 1951, *Agricultural Resources of China.* Ithaca: Cornell University Press.

Shen, Yuchang, et al., 1978, "Woguo dilixue de fangshang yu renwu ruogan wenti de shangtan" (The Orientation and Task of Geography in China–A Discussion of Some Problems). *Dili Xuebao* (*Acta Geographica Sinica*), Vol. 35, No. 2, pp. 108–115.

Shou Jinghua, 1979, "Interview with a Specialist on Population." *Beijing Review*, Vol. 22, No. 46, pp. 20–21.

Sigurdson, Jon, 1977, *Rural Industrialization in China.* Cambridge, Mass.: Harvard University Press.

Skinner, G. William, 1964–65, "Marketing and Social Structure in Rural China." *Journal of Asian Studies*, 24, pp. 3–44, 195–228, 363–400.

_______, editor, 1977, *The City in Late Imperial China.* Stanford, Calif.: Stanford University Press.

_______, 1977, "Regional Urbanization in Nineteenth-Century China." In G. William Skinner (ed.), *The City in Late Imperial China.* Stanford, Calif.: Stanford University Press, pp. 211–249.

_______, 1978, "Vegetable Supply and Marketing in Chinese Cities." *The China Quarterly*, Vol. 76, pp. 733–793.

Smil, Vaclav, 1976, *China's Energy.* New York: Praeger.

_______, 1976, "Energy in China: Achievements and Prospects." *China Quarterly*, No. 67, pp. 54–81.

Sowers, Victor, 1979, *World Facts and Figures.* New York: John Wiley & Sons.

Speare, Alden Jr., 1972, *The Determinants of Migration to a Major City in a*

Developing Country: Taichung, Taiwan. Taipei: Institute of Economics, Academia Sinica, Population Papers.

Spencer, J. E., 1978, "A China Geographer's Bookshelf." *The China Geographer*, No. 10, pp. 63–71.

_______ and Thomas, William L., 1971, *Asia, East by South: A Cultural Geography.* New York: John Wiley & Sons.

Sprague, G. F., 1975, "Agriculture in China." *Science*, Vol. 188, No. 4188, May, pp. 549–556.

State Statistical Bureau, People's Republic of China, 1960, *Ten Great Years.* Peking: Foreign Language Publishing House.

Stoddart, D. R., 1978, "Geomorphology in China." *Progress in Physical Geography*, Vol. 2, No. 2, pp. 187–236.

Sun Ching-chih, editor, 1959, *Economic Geography of South China.* Peking: K'o-hsüeh ch'u-pan-she. Washington, D.C.: U.S. Joint Publications Research Service.

_______ et al., editors, 1958, *Economic Geography of Central China.* Peking: K'o-hsüeh ch'u-pan-she. Washington, D.C.: U.S. Joint Publications Research Service, 10 Feb., 1960, p. 522.

_______, 1959, *Economic Geography of Northeast China.* Peking; K'o-hsüeh ch'u-pan-she. Washington, D.C.: U.S. Joint Publications Research Service, p. 211.

_______, 1959, *Economic Geography of the East China Region.* Peking; K'o-hsüeh ch'u-pan-she. Washington, D.C.: U.S. Joint Publications Research Service.

_______, 1960, *Economic Geography of Southwest China.* Peking; K'o-hsüeh ch'u-pan-she. Washington, D.C.: U.S. Joint Publications Research Service.

Sun, Dianqing, Chen Qingxuan, and Gao Qinghua, 1980, "Geomechanics and Their Application in Petroleum Geology." *Geojournal*, Vol. 4, No. 6, pp. 499–505.

Swamy, Subramanian, 1973, "Economic Growth in China and India, 1952–1970: A Comparative Appraisal." *Economic Development and Cultural Change*, Vol. 21, No. 4, Pt. 2, pp. 1–83.

_______, 1977, "The Economic Distance Between China and India, 1955–73." *The China Quarterly*, No. 70, p. 371.

Sweeting, M. M. et al., 1978, "British Geographers in China 1977." *The Geographical Journal*, Vol. 144, Pt. 2, pp. 187–207.

Taiwan Provincial Government, 1980, *Taiwan Statistical Abstract* (various numbers). Taipei: Bureau of Accounting and Statistics.

Tawney, R. H., 1962, *Land and Labour in China* (reprinted). New York: Harcourt Brace.

Teilhard de Chardin, Pierre, 1941, *Early Man in China.* Peking: Institut De Geo-Bilogie.

Thorpe, James, 1939, *Geography of the Soils of China.* Peking: National Geological Survey of China.

Tien, H. Yuan, 1973, *China's Population Struggle, Demographic Decision of the People's Republic, 1949–1969.* Columbus: Ohio State University Press.

_______, 1980, *Population Theory in China.* White Plains, N.Y.: M. E. Sharpe.

Ting, W. S., 1954, *Zhongguo dixing xue* (The Geomorphology of China), Vols. 1 and 2, Taibei.

Towers, Graham, 1973, "City Planning in China." *Journal of the Royal Town Planning Institute*, Vol. 59, pp. 125–127.

Travers, Lawrence, 1980, "Railroad Travel-Time Distances in China." Paper presented at the 76th Annual Meeting of the Association of American Geographers, Louisville, Ky., April 13–16.

Tregear, T. R., 1970, *An Economic geography of China.* New York: American Elsevier.

_______, 1980, *China, A Geographical Survey.* New York: John Wiley & Sons.

Trewartha, Glenn T., 1951, "Chinese Cities: Numbers and Distribution." *Annals of the Association of American Geographers*, Vol. 41, pp. 331–347.

Tuan, Yi-Fu, 1969, *China.* Chicago: Aldine.

Ullman, Morris B., 1961, *Cities of Mainland China: 1953 and 1958.* Washington, D.C.: Bureau of the Census, International Population Reports, Series p. 95, No. 59.

U.S. Bureau of Economic Analysis, 1976, *The Provinces of The People's Republic of China: A Political and Economic Bibliography.* International Population Statistics Reports, Series P-90, No. 25. Washington, D.C.: U.S. Government Printing Office.

U.S. Department of Agriculture, 1976, *The Agricultural Situation in The People's Republic of China.* Washington, D.C.: U.S.D.A. Economic Research Service, ERS-Foreign 362.

_______, 1977, *People's Republic of China Agricultural Situation*, Foreign Agricultural Economic Report, No. 137. Washington, D.C.: USDA.

_______, 1980, *Agricultural Situation, People's Republic of China.* Washington, D.C.: USDA, Economics, Statistics and Cooperative Service.

U.S. Department of State, 1980, *Review of Relations with Taiwan.* Washington, D.C.: Bureau of Public Affairs, Current Policy No. 190 (June 11).

VanderMeer, Paul, 1975, "Pacifying Space in Chinese Villages." *The China Geographer*, No. 2, pp. 27–39.

Wang, I-shou, 1977, "The Recent Patterns of Internal Migration in Taiwan." *The China Geographer*, No. 6, pp. 37–47.

Wang, K. P., 1977, *Far East and South Asia in MP-1 Mineral Perspective.* Washington, D.C.: U.S. Department of the Interior, Bureau of Mines.

_______, 1977, *Mineral Resources and Basic Industries in The People's Republic of China.* Boulder, Colo.: Westview Press.

_______, 1978, "China's Mineral Economy." In Joint Economic Committee, *Chinese Economy Post Mao.* Washington, D.C.: U.S. Government Printing Office, pp. 374–407.

Wang, William S-Y, 1973, "The Chinese Language." *The Scientific American*, Vol. 228, No. 2, pp. 50–60.

Welch, R. A., Lo, H. C., and Pannell, C. W., 1979, "Mapping China's New Agricultural Land." *Photogrammetric Engineering and Remote Sensing*, Vol. 45, pp. 1211–1228.

Welch, R., Pannell, C. W., and Lo, C. P., 1975, "Land Use in Northeast China, 1973–A View from Landsat-1." *Annals of the Association of American Geographers*, Vol. 65, Map Supplement, pp. 595–596.

Wheatley, Paul, 1971, *The Pivot of the Four Quarters, A Preliminary Enquiry into the Origins and Character of the Ancient Chinese City.* Chicago: Aldine.

Whitaker, Donald P. et al., 1972, *Area Handbook for The People's Republic of China.* Washington, D.C.: U.S. Government Printing Office.

Whitney, Joseph B. R., 1970, *China: Area Administration and Nation Building.* Chicago: University of Chicago, Department of Geography Research Papers, No. 123.

_______, 1973, "Ecology and Environmental Control." In Michel Oksenberg (ed.), *China's Developmental Experience.* New York: Praeger, pp. 95–109.

_______, 1979, "Temporal and Spatial Change in the Productivity of Chinese Farming Ecosystems." In Lee Ngok and Leung Chi-keung, *China's Development and Challenge*, Vol. II, Proceedings of the Fifth Leverhulme Conference. Hong Kong: University of Hong Kong, Centre of Asian Studies, pp. 183–215.

Whitton, Carolyn L., 1976, In *The Agricultural Situation in The People's Republic of China and Other Communist Asian Countries.* Washington, D.C.: U.S.D.A., Foreign Agricultural Economic Report No. 124, pp. 18–24.

Wiens, Herold J., 1958, "China, Agriculture and Food Supply." In Norton Ginsburg (ed.), *The Pattern of Asia.* Englewood Cliffs, N.J.: Prentice-Hall, pp. 168–189.

_______, 1961, "Development of Geographic Science, 1949–1960." In S. H. Gould (ed.), *Sciences in Communist China.* Baltimore: American Association for the Advancement of Science, pp. 411–481.

_______, 1967, *Han Chinese Expansion in South China.* Hamden, Conn.: Shoe String Press.

Wiens, T., 1980, "Agricultural Statistics in The People's Republic of China." In Alexander Eckstein (ed.), *Quantitative Measures of China's Economic Output.* Ann Arbor: University of Michigan Press, pp. 44–107.

_______, 1981, "Agriculture in the Four Modernizations." *China Geographer*, No. 11, pp. 57–72.

Williams, Jack F., 1974, *China in Maps, 1890–1960: A Selective and Annotated Cartobibliography.* East Lansing: East Asian Studies Center, Michigan State University.

_______, 1978, "Two Observations on the State of Geography in The People's Republic of China." *China Geographer*, No. 9, pp. 17–31.

_______, 1981, "The Use of Slopeland in Taiwan's Agricultural Development." *The China Geographer*, No. 11, pp. 89–111.

_______ and Yung Teng Chia-yee, 1970, *Readings in Chinese Geography.* Honolulu: University of Hawaii.

Willmott, W. E., editor, 1972, *Economic Organization in Chinese Society.* Stanford: Stanford University Press.

Wolf, Arthur, 1974, *Religion and Ritual in Chinese Society.* Stanford: Stanford University Press.

Wortman, S., 1975, "Agriculture in China." *Scientific American*, Vol. 232, pp. 13–21.

Wu, Ch'uan-chun, 1958, "The Geographical Organization and New Trends of Development in Geography in the USSR." *Ti-li hsueh-pao* (*Acta Geographica Sinica*), Vol. 24(4), pp. 438–456.

_______, 1981, "Agricultural Regionalization in China." *China Geographer*, No. 11, pp. 27–39.

_______, 1981, "The Transformation of Agricultural Landscapes in China." In Laurence J. C. Ma and Allen Noble (eds.), *Chinese and American Perspectives on the Environment.* New York: Metheun.

Wu, Yuan-li, 1967, *The Spatial Economy of Communist China.* New York: Praeger.

Yang, C. K., 1965, *Chinese Communist Society: The Family and the Village.* Cambridge, Mass.: The MIT Press.

Yang, Martin C., 1945, *A Chinese Village, Taitou, Shantung Province.* New York: Columbia University Press.

Yao, Shihmou, Shen Daoji and Cheng Fubao, 1981, "The Development of Small Cities and Towns in New China." In Laurence J. C. Ma and Allen Noble (eds.), *Chinese and American Perspectives on the Environment.* New York: Metheun.

Yu, Y. C., 1979, "The Population Policy of China." *Population Studies*, Vol. 33, No. 1, pp. 125–142.

Yu, Youhai, 1980, "U.S. $1,000 by the Year 2000." *Beijing Review*, Vol. 23, No. 43 (Oct. 27), pp. 16–18.

Zhang, Delin, 1979, "People of the Qiang Nationality." *China Pictorial*, No. 5, p. 25.

Zhang, Zhigan, 1980, "Karst Types in China." *Geojournal*, Vol. 4, No. 6, pp. 541–570.

Zhang, Zunghu, 1980, "Loess in China." *Geojournal*, Vol. 4, No. 6, pp. 525–540.

Zhi, Exiang, 1980, "The Tinous: China's Newest Nationality." *China Reconstructs*, Vol. 29, No. 2, p. 55.

Zhongguo Dituce, 1978, *China Map Folio*. Shanghai: Atlas Publishers.

Zhonghua renmin gongheguo fensheng dituji (Provincial Atlas of The People's Republic of China), 1974. Beijing: Ditu Chubanshe.

Index